Frederick James Furnivall, Clement Mansfield Ingleby, Lucy Toulmin Smith

Allusions to Shakspere

A.D. 1592-1693

Frederick James Furnivall, Clement Mansfield Ingleby, Lucy Toulmin Smith

Allusions to Shakspere
A.D. 1592-1693

ISBN/EAN: 9783337058418

Printed in Europe, USA, Canada, Australia, Japan

Cover: Foto ©ninafisch / pixelio.de

More available books at **www.hansebooks.com**

Allusions to Shakspere,

A.D. 1592—1693.

THE

TWO VOLUMES OF THE NEW SHAKSPERE SOCIETY,

'*SHAKESPEARE'S CENTURIE OF PRAYSE,*'
(SECOND ED., 1879,)

AND

'*SOME 300 FRESH ALLUSIONS TO SHAKSPERE,*'
FROM 1594 TO 1694 (1886),

BOUND TOGETHER.

PUBLISHT FOR

𝕿𝖍𝖊 𝕹𝖊𝖜 𝕾𝖍𝖆𝖐𝖘𝖕𝖊𝖗𝖊 𝕾𝖔𝖈𝖎𝖊𝖙𝖞

BY N. TRÜBNER & CO., 57, 59, LUDGATE HILL,

LONDON, E.C., 1879 & 1886.

CONTENTS.

	PAGE
CHRONOLOGICAL LIST OF THE ALLUSIONS TO SHAKSPERE IN THE 'CENTURIE OF PRAYSE' AND THE '300 FRESH ALLUSIONS'	vt

'THE Centurie of Prayse'
(for its 'Contents' see its p. vii).

Fresh Allusions.

CHRONOLOGICAL LIST OF THE ALLUSIONS TO SHAKSPERE IN THE 'CENTURIE OF PRAYSE' AND THIS VOLUME	ix
FOREWORDS	xvii
LIST OF QUARTO EDITIONS OF SHAKSPERE'S PLAYS ...	xxi
LIST OF SHAKSPERE ENTRIES IN THE STATIONERS' REGISTERS, 1593—1640	xxvii
MORE ALLUSIONS IN BOOK CATALOGS	xxxvii
FRESH ALLUSIONS TO SHAKSPERE	1
PERIOD I. 1592—1616. Pages 1—82	
PERIOD II. 1617—1641. „ 83—149	
PERIOD III. 1642—1659. „ 150—184	
PERIOD IV. 1660—1693. „ 185—357	
NOTES	358
GENERAL INDEX	359
INDEX TO SHAKSPERE'S WORKS REFERD TO IN QUOTATIONS	370
TABLE OF THE POPULARITY OF SHAKSPERE'S SEVERAL WORKS IN THE YEARS 1592-1693	372

CHRONOLOGICAL LIST OF THE
ALLUSIONS TO SHAKSPERE 1592-1693

IN THE '*CENTURIE OF PRAYSE*,' ED. 2. (N. SH. SOC. 1879), AND THE
'*FRESH ALLUSIONS*,' 1886.

(*Those in the 'Centurie' are inset; those in the 'Fresh Allusions' project.*)
(*Doubtful Allusions have a star (*) before them.*)

First Period. 1592—1616.

1591-4.	*Edmund Spenser. *Cent.*1	1599.	Henry Porter. *Fr. Al.* 9
1592.	Robert Greene. *Cent.* 2	,,	Ben Jonson. *Cent.* 31
,,	Henry Chettle. *Cent.* 4	1599-1636.	Thos. Dekker. *Fr. Al.* 10
,,	*Thomas Nash. *Cent.* 5	1600.	John Bodenham. *Fr. Al.* 13
1594.	Henry Helmes. *Fr. Al.* 1	,,	A Munday, &c. *Fr. Al.* 15
,,	In 'Willobie his Avisa.'	,,	*Chr. Middleton. *Fr. Al.* 19
	Cent. 6	,,	*Sam. Nicholson. *Fr. Al.* 20
,,	*Hy. Willobie. *Cent.* 7	,,	Sam. Nicholson. *Cent.* 33
,,	Sir Wm. Harbert. *Cent.* 12	,,	*John Lane. *Cent.* 32
,,	*Michael Drayton. *Cent.* 13	,, ?	Charles Percy. *Cent.* 38
		,,	Sir Wm. Cornwallis. *Cent.* 41
1595.	Robert Southwell. *Cent.* 14	,,	In 'England's Parnassus'. *Cent.* 430
,,	William Clarke. *Cent.* 15	,,	N. Breton. *Cent.* 457
,,	John Weever. *Cent.* 16	,,	'Returne from Pernassus', Part I. *Fr. Al.* 12*
,,	Thomas Edwardes. *Cent.* 17	1600-10.	Two letters. *Cent.* 40
1596.	In 'Wily Beguilde.' *Cent.* 19	1600-12.	*J. M. *Cent.* 98
,,	Richard Carew [prob. 1605]. *Cent.* 20	1601.	*Ben Johnson. *Fr. Al.* 22
		,,	William Lambard. *Cent.* 449
1597-1603.	In a MS. of Bacon's 'Tribute'. *Fr. Al.* 2	,,	'Essex Rebellion.' *Cent.* 35
1597-1616.	Nicholas Breton. *Cent.* 457	,,	John Weever. *Cent.* 42
		,,	Robert Chester. *Cent.* 43, 44
1598.	I. M. *Fr. Al.* 4	,,	John Manningham. *Cent.* 45
,,	*R. S. *Fr. Al.* 8	,,	W. J. *Cent.* 47
,,	Francis Meres. *Cent.* 21, 24	1601-2.	'Returne from Pernassus', Part II. *Cent.* 48
,,	Robert Tofte. *Cent.* 25	1602.	*John Marston. *Fr. Al.* 23
,,	Richard Barnfield. *Cent.* 26	,,	*Thomas Dekker. *Fr. Al.* 22
,,	John Marston. *Cent.* 27, 29	,,	Thomas Decker. *Cent.* 50
,,	Gabriel Harvey (prob. after 1600). *Cent.* 30	,,	*Thomas Middleton. *Cent.* 51
		,,	Thomas Acherley. *Cent.* 52
		1602-23.	John Webster. *Fr. Al.* 24
		1603.	Father Parsons. *Fr. Al.* 29
		,,	*Michael Drayton. *Cent.* 53
		,,	*Henry Chettle. *Cent.* 55

CHRONOLOGICAL LIST OF ALLUSIONS TO SHAKSPERE.

1603. 'Elizabeth's Losse.' *Cent.* 56
,, *J. C. *Cent.* 57
,, John Davies. *Cent.* 58
,, William Camden. *Cent.* 59
,, N. Breton. *Cent.* 457
1604. John Marston. *Fr. Al.* 30
,, John Marston. *Cent.* 66
,, Anthony Scoloker. *Fr. Al.* 33
,, Anthony Scoloker. *Cent.* 64
,, *T. M. *Cent.* 60
,, 'Meeting of Gallants.' *Cent.* 65
,, N. Breton. *Cent.* 457
1604-19. Thomas Middleton. *Fr. Al.* 35
1605. Peter Woodhouse. *Fr. Al.* 39
,, *Thomas Heywood. *Fr. Al.* 40
,, *John Marston. *Fr. Al.* 40*
,, Geo. Chapman, &c. *Fr. Al.* 41, 42
,, Geo. Chapman. *Cent.* 69
,, Sir Thomas Smith. *Cent.* 453
,, 'Ratsei's Ghost'. *Cent.* 67
1606. Barnabe Barnes. *Fr. Al.* 45
,, *Wm. Warner. *Fr. Al.* 43
,, Thos. Heywood. *Fr. Al.* 46*
,, William Drummond. *Cent.* 71
,, John Raynolds. *Cent.* 451
1607. Thomas Heywood. *Fr. Al.* 47
,, George Chapman. *Fr. Al.* 49
,, Edward Sharpham. *Fr. Al.* 50, 51
,, T. Dekker and J. Webster. *Fr. Al.* 52, 53
,, Thos. Decker. *Cent.* 74
,, John Fletcher. *Cent.* 72
,, 'Merry Divel'. *Cent.* 73
,, George Peele. *Cent.* 75
,, William Barkstead. *Cent.* 76
,, John Marston. *Cent.* 77
,, W. S. ('Puritaine'). *Cent.* 78
,, Captain Keelinge. *Cent.* 79
,, Thomas Heywood. *Cent.* 80
1608. T. Dekker. *Fr. Al.* 55
,, Thos. Middleton. *Fr. Al.* 56
,, *Robt. Armin. *Fr. Al.* 57, 59
,, J. Markham. L. Machin. *Cent.* 81
,, *John Day. *Cent.* 82

1608-25. Beaumont (d. 1616) and Fletcher. *Fr. Al.* 61
1609. Robt. Armin. *Fr. Al.* 59
,, John Davies. *Cent.* 84
,, Samuel Rowlands. *Cent.* 85
,, Thomas Decker. *Cent.* 453
,, Thomas Thorpe. *Cent.* 86
,, 'Troilus Forewords.' *Cent.* 87
,, 'Pimlyco'. *Cent.* 89
,, Ben Jonson. *Cent.* 90
1610. Roger Sharpe. *Fr. Al.* 69
,, 'Copy of Sh.'s 8th Sonnet.' *Fr. Al.* 70
,, Beaumont and Fletcher. *Fr. Al.* 61
,, Edmund Bolton. *Cent.* 91
,, J. Wurmsser. *Cent.* 93
,, John Davies. *Cent.* 94
,, *Lodovic Barry. *Cent.* 95
,, W. Drummond. *Cent.* 71
1611. Cyril Tourneur. *Fr. Al.* 71
,, John Speed. *Fr. Al.* 75
,, *Lod. Barrey. *Fr. Al.* 73
,, Beaumont and Fletcher. *Fr. Al.* 61, 62
,, Beaumont and Fletcher. *Cent.* 117
,, John Davies. *Cent.* 96
,, Simon Forman. *Cent.* 97
1612. *Sir John Hayward. *Fr. Al.* 77
,, *Thos. Heywood. *Fr. Al.* 78
,, Thomas Heywood. *Cent.* 99
,, *J. M. *Cent.* 98
,, John Webster. *Cent.* 100
1613. Beaumont and Fletcher. *Fr. Al.* 62
,, John Marston. *Fr. Al.* 78*
,, Beaumont and Fletcher. *Cent.* 117
,, Joseph Fletcher. *Cent.* 101
,, Thomas Lorkins. *Cent.* 102
,, 'Globe Sonnet'. *Cent.* 455
,, Lord Treasurer Stanhope. *Cent.* 103
1614. *John Cooke. *Fr. Al.* 79
,, *Barnabe Rich. *Fr. Al.* 79
,, Ben Jonson. *Cent.* 105
,, Thomas Freeman. *Cent.* 106
,, Robert Tailor. *Cent.* 107
,, Edmund Howes. *Cent.* 108
,, Chr. Brooke. *Cent.* 109
,, Sir Wm. Drummond. *Cent.* 111
1615. Alex. Niccholes. *Fr. Al.* 80
,, Richard Brathwaite. *Cent.* 112, 113

CHRONOLOGICAL LIST OF ALLUSIONS TO SHAKSPERE. viit

1615. 'Characters'. *Cent.* 114
1616. *W. Drummond. *Fr. Al.* 82
,, W. Drummond. *Cent.* 116
,, Robert Anton. *Cent.* 115
,, Beaumont and Fletcher. *Cent.* 117
,, Ben Jonson. *Cent.* 118

1616. 'Sh.'s Grave-Tablet'. *Cent.* 121
,, N. Breton. *Cent.* 457-8
1616-18. Beaumont and Fletcher. *Fr. Al.* 63
[Shakspere died on April 23, 1616.]

Second Period. 1617—1641.

1617-22. 'Sh.'s Tablet-Inscription'. *Cent.* 125
1617. John Taylor, the Water-Poet. *Cent.* 126
1618. Beaumont and Fletcher. *Fr. Al.* 63
,, Geffray Mynshul. *Cent.* 456
,, Nathaniel Field. *Cent.* 127
1618-21. Richard Corbet. *Cent.* 128
1618-19. 'Elegy on Richard Burbage'. *Cent.* 131
1619. Sir Gerrard Herbert. *Fr. Al.* 83
,, Ben Jonson. *Cent.* 129
1620. 'Hæc Vir'. *Fr. Al.* 85
,, Sam. Rowlands. *Cent.* 454
,, John Taylor, the Water-Poet. *Cent.* 133
1620-56. 'Choyce Drollery'. *Cent.* 134
1621. Robert Burton. *Fr. Al.* 85
,, John Fletcher. *Cent.* 135
1622. John Taylor. *Fr. Al.* 86
,, Thomas Walkley. *Fr. Al.* 87
,, John Fletcher. *Fr. Al.* 88*, 98
,, Ph. Massinger. *Fr. Al.* 89-94
,, William Basse. *Cent.* 136
,, Thomas Robinson. *Cent.* 140
1623. Ben Jonson. *Cent.* 141, 147-150
,, Heminge and Condell. *Cent.* 143, 145
,, Hugh Holland. *Cent.* 153
,, Leonard Digges. *Cent.* 154
,, J. M. *Cent.* 155
1623-36. Sir Hy. Herbert. *Cent.* 157
1624. Ph. Massinger. *Fr. Al.* 90, 94, 95
,, Robert Burton. *Fr. Al.* 98*
,, E. S. (B. of D). *Cent.* 159
,, John Gee. *Cent.* 160
,, Robert Burton. *Cent.* 161
1625. Fletcher, &c. *Fr. Al.* 64-8
,, Fletcher, &c. *Cent.* 166, 167

1625. Ben Jonson. *Cent.* 163
,, Richard James. *Cent.* 164
1626. Ben Jonson. *Fr. Al.* 99
,, Ph. Massinger. *Fr. Al.* 95
1627. Ph. Massinger. *Fr. Al.* 91, 95
,, *John Milton. *Cent.* 460
,, Michael Drayton. *Cent.* 168
1628. 'Prince Hal's Speech'. *Fr. Al.* 100
,, 'A Newsletter'. *Fr. Al.* 101
,, (?) 'The Wandering Jew'. *Fr. Al.* 142
,, Robert Gell. *Cent.* 169
1628-31. Abraham Cowley. *Cent.* 170
1629. Ph. Massinger. *Fr. Al.* 92
,, *Philip Massinger. *Cent.* 171
,, Sir Hy. Herbert. *Cent.* 173
1629-30. Ben Jonson. *Cent.* 172
1630-7. ,, ,, 174
1630. John Milton. *Cent.* 176.
,, John Taylor, the Water-Poet. *Cent.* 178, 179
,, Owen Feltham. *Cent.* 180
,, 'Banquet of Jeasts'. *Cent.* 181
1631. Ph. Massinger. *Fr. Al.* 93, 95-6
,, Wye Saltonstall. *Fr. Al.* 102
,, Richard Brathwait. *Fr. Al.* 104
,, Peter Heylyn. *Fr. Al.* 104*
,, 'Funeral Monument'. *Fr. Al.* 105
,, *James Shirley. *Fr. Al.* 106
,, *John Spencer. *Cent.* 182
,, Sir Hy. Herbert. *Cent.* 173
1632. Philip Massinger. *Fr. Al.* 97, 107
,, Philip Massinger. *Cent.* 185
,, G. Chapman and J. Shirley *Cent.* 186
,, *Thomas Randolph. *Cent.* 187
,, 'Second Folio of Sh.'s Works'. *Cent.* 189

viii† CHRONOLOGICAL LIST OF ALLUSIONS TO SHAKSPERE.

1632. J. M. S. *Cent.* 190
,, Wm. Prynne. *Cent.* 195
,, Sir Aston Cokaine. *Cent.* 196
b. 1633. John Hales. *Cent.* 198
1633. Ph. Massinger. *Fr. Al.* 97
,, Jas. Shirley. *Fr. Al.* 108
,, Thomas Nabbes. *Fr. Al.* 109
,, Th. Bancroft. *Fr. Al.* 110
,, John Ford. *Fr. Al.* 116-118
,, *Wm. Rowley. *Cent.* 197
1633-4. Sir Jn. Suckling. *Fr. Al.* 111-115
1634. Ph. Massinger. *Fr. Al.* 93
,, Tho. Randolph. *Fr. Al.* 120
,, Wm. Habington. *Cent.* 200
,, James Shirley. *Cent.* 201
1635. 'The Lady Mother'. *Fr. Al.* 120
,, Sir. H. Mildmay. *Fr. Al.* 121
,, James Shirley. *Fr. Al.* 150
,, Thomas Heywood. *Fr. Al.* 122
,, Thomas Heywood. *Cent.* 202
,, Thomas Cranley. *Cent.* 204
,, John Swan. *Cent.* 459
1636. Ph. Massinger. *Fr. Al.* 93, 97
,, William Sampson. *Fr. Al.* 124
,, John Trussell. *Fr. Al.* 125
,, 'Book of Bulls'. *Fr. Al.* 127
1636-41. Sir John Suckling. *Cent.* 205-211
1637. Tho. Heywood. *Fr. Al.* 128
,, *Shakerley Marmion. *Fr. Al.* 130
,, Jasper Mayne. *Cent.* 212
,, Owen Feltham. *Cent.* 213
,, Richard West. *Cent.* 214
,, H. Ramsay. *Cent.* 215
,, Sir W. Davenant. *Cent.* 216
,, T. Terrent. *Cent.* 218
,, Abraham Wright. *Cent.* 219

1637. 'Elegy on Shakspere'. *Cent.* 220
b. 1638. Thomas Carew. *Fr. Al.* 131
1638. 'Songs from *The Tempest*'. *Fr. Al.* 132
,, John Ford. *Fr. Al.* 118
,, Henry Adamson. *Fr. Al.* 134
,, James Mervyn. *Cent.* 222
,, Wm. Chillingworth. *Cent.* 223
,, Thomas Randolph (?). *Cent.* 224
,, Richard Brome. *Cent.* 225
1639. John Clarke. *Fr. Al.* 135
,, G. Rivers. *Fr. Al.* 139
,, 'Conceits, Clinches &c.' *Fr. Al.* 141
,, Robert Chamberlain. *Cent.* 226
,, Thomas Bancroft. *Cent.* 227
,, 'Witts Recreations'. *Cent.* 228
1640. 'The Wandering Jew'. *Fr. Al.* 142
,, *Jas. Shirley. *Fr. Al.* 144, 144* (*Cent.* 236)
,, 'A Helpe to Discourse'. *Fr. Al.* 144
,, Rich. Goodridge. *Fr. Al.* 145
,, Geo. Lynn. *Fr. Al.* 146
,, John Benson. *Cent.* 229
,, Lewis Sharpe. *Cent.* 230
,, Leonard Digges. *Cent.* 231
,, John Warren. *Cent.* 235
,, James Shirley. *Cent.* 236
1641. Rich. Brathwaite *Fr. Al.* 147
,, *Shakerly Marmion. *Fr. Al.* 148
,, Abraham Cowley. *Fr. Al* 149
,, John Johnson. *Cent.* 238
,, Martine Parker. *Cent.* 239

Third Period. 1642—1659.

1642. James Shirley. *Fr. Al.* 150
,, John Milton. *Fr. Al.* 151
,, Sir Thomas Browne. *Fr. Al.* 153
,, Charles Butler. *Cent.* 243
,, 'Rump Songs'. *Cent.* 244

1643. Sir Richard Baker. *Cent.* 250
1643-62. Thomas Fuller. *Cent.* 246, 249
1644. John Cleveland. *Fr. Al.* 154
,, John Cleveland. *Cent.* 254

CHRONOLOGICAL LIST OF ALLUSIONS TO SHAKSPERE. ix+

1644. 'London Post'. *Cent.* 251
,, 'Mercurius Britanicus'. *Cent.* 252
,, Thomas Prujean. *Cent.* 255
,, 'Vindex Anglicus'. *Cent.* 256
1645. Sir Richard Baker. *Fr. Al.* 155
,, 'A Comedy'. *Fr. Al.* 156
,, Paul Aylward. *Cent.* 257
,, Daniell Breedy. *Cent.* 257
,, George Withers. *Cent.* 258
1646. R. Wilde (?). *Fr. Al.* 158*
,, Samuel Sheppard. *Cent.* 261
1647. *Sam. Sheppard. *Fr. Al.* 159
,, 'Epistle of ten Players'. *Cent.* 262
,, Sir John Denham. *Cent.* 263
,, James Howell. *Cent.* 264
,, George Daniel. *Cent.* 265, 266
,, William Cartwright. *Cent.* 270
,, J. Berkenhead. *Cent.* 271
,, George Buck. *Cent.* 272
,, T. Palmer. *Cent.* 272
1648. J. S. *Fr. Al.* 159, 160
,, 'Perfect Occurrences'. *Cent.* 273
1648-54. Henry Tubbe. *Fr. Al.* 161
1649. 'Trinarchodia'. *Fr. Al.* 163
,, John Milton. *Cent.* 274
,, J. Cook. *Cent.* 276
1650. 'Ashmole MS.' *Cent.* 277
,, Robert Baron. *Cent.* 279
,, Anthony Davenport. *Cent.* 281
,, Sir N. L'Estrange. *Cent.* 282
1651. John Milton. *Fr. Al.* 164
,, Richard Whitlock. *Fr. Al.* 165
,, Samuel Sheppard. *Cent.* 283-7
,, William Bell. *Cent.* 288
,, Jasper Mayne. *Cent.* 289

1651. 'Hermeticall Banquet'. *Cent.* 290
,, J. S. *Cent.* 291
,, Thos. Randolph. *Cent.* 293
1652. Francis Kirkman. *Fr. Al.* 166
,, R. Loveday. *Fr. Al.* 167
,, Jo. Tatham. *Cent.* 295
1653. Nathaniel Hooke. *Fr. Al.* 168
,, Richard Flecknoe. *Fr. Al.* 169
,, Alexander Brome. *Cent.* 296
,, Sir Aston Cokaine. *Cent.* 297
,, Sir Wm. Dugdale. *Cent.* 298
1654. Edmund Gayton. *Fr. Al.* 170
,, Edmund Gayton. *Cent.* 299
,, Richard Flecknoe. *Fr. Al.* 169
,, Alex. Brome. *Fr. Al.* 172
1655. J. Quarles. *Fr. Al.* 174
,, 'The Hectors'. *Cent.* 301
1656. Richard Flecknoe. *Fr. Al.* 169
,, Samuel Holland. *Fr. Al.* 171
,, T. Goff. *Fr. Al.* 175
,, Edward Archer. *Fr. Al.* 176
,, (?) *Fr. Al.* 179
,, 'Parnassus Biceps'. *Fr. Al.* 180
,, Samuel Holland. *Cent.* 302
,, Abraham Cowley. *Cent.* 303
1657. Richard Ligon. *Cent.* 304
1658. 'Naps upon Parnassus'. *Fr. Al.* 181
,, Gilbert Swinhoe. *Fr. Al.* 183
,, 'Isham MS.' *Fr. Al.* 184
,, 'London Chanticleres'. *Fr. Al.* 184
,, W. London. *Fr. Al.* 183*
,, Sir Aston Cokain. *Cent.* 305-7
,, In 'Brome's Plays'. *Cent.* 308
,, Samuel Austin. *Cent.* 309
[1659. *No Allusion yet found.*]

Fourth Period. 1660—1693.

1660. 'Stationers Register'. *Fr. Al.* 169
,, 'Friend'. *Fr. Al.* 185
,, 'A Poetical Revenge'. *Fr. Al.* 185
,, Lady Dolly Long. *Fr. Al.* 185

1660. 'Elegy on Rich. Lovelace'. *Cent.* 313
,, Richard Flecknoe. *Cent.* 314
,, Sir Richard Baker. *Cent.* 315
,, Samuel Pepys. *Cent.* 316

xt   CHRONOLOGICAL LIST OF ALLUSIONS TO SHAKSPERE.

1660-4. Thomas Jordan. *Cent.* 330
1661. 'Prolog. to Rich. III'. *Fr. Al.* 186
,, 'Merry Humors of Bottom'. *Fr. Al.* 188
,, Francis Kirkman. *Fr. Al.* 190, &c., and 343
,, Robert Davenport. *Fr. Al.* 196
,, Thomas Fuller. *Fr. Al.* 197
,, Samuel Pepys. *Cent.* 316
,, 'A Catch'. *Cent.* 325
,, John Evelyn. *Cent.* 326
1661-3. John Ward. *Cent.* 327
b. 1662. Wm. Hemings. *Fr. Al.* 200
1662. Theatro-Philos. *Fr. Al.* 198
,, Edmund Gayton. *Fr. Al.* 199
,, T. S. *Fr. Al.* 202
,, Samuel Pepys. *Cent.* 317
1663. J. Kelynge. *Fr. Al.* 204
,, Thos. Jordan. *Fr. Al.* 205
,, Samuel Pepys. *Cent.* 317
,, 'Hudibras'. *Cent.* 329
1653-93. John Downes. *Fr. Al.* 348-357
1664. Henry Bold. *Fr. Al.* 206
,, Samuel Pepys. *Cent.* 318
,, Thomas Jordan. *Cent.* 330
,, Margaret Cavendish. *Cent.* 332
1665. Charles Cotton. *Cent.* 336
1666. 'The Dutch Gazette'. *Fr. Al.* 207
,, Samuel Pepys. *Cent.* 319
,, ,, ,, 319-21
,, 'Prolog to Shirley's Love-Tricks'. *Cent.* 337
,, John Dryden. *Cent.* 338
b. 1668. Sir W. Davenant. *Fr. Al.* 208
1668. Tho. Shadwell. *Fr. Al.* 209
,, Sir W. Davenant. *Fr. Al.* 210-15[1]
,, John Dryden. *Fr. Al.* 216-221
,, John Dryden. *Cent.* 341
,, Samuel Pepys. *Cent.* 321
,, Robert Wild. *Cent.* 340
,, Sir John Denham. *Cent.* 343
1669. John Dryden. *Fr. Al.* 221, 222
,, Samuel Pepys. *Cent.* 322
,, Edward Phillips. *Cent.* 344
1670. Watson. *Fr. Al.* 230
,, Richard Flecknoe. *Cent.* 345

1671. Francis Kirkman. *Fr. Al.* 191, 194
,, John Dryden. *Fr. Al.* 223
,, George Villiers. *Cent.* 346
1672. John Dryden. *Fr. Al.* 224
,, John Dryden. *Cent.* 348, 350-2
,, W. Ramesey. *Fr. Al.* 231
,, 'Covent Garden Drollery'. *Fr. Al.* 231*
,, Thomas Fuller. *Fr. Al.* 202
,, Andrew Marvel. *Cent.* 347
1673. John Dryden. *Fr. Al.* 225
,, 'The Transproser Rehearst'. *Fr. Al.* 232
,, Sir W. Davenant. *Fr. Al.* 233
,, Mr. Arrowsmith. *Fr. Al.* 234
,, 'The Censure of the Rota'. *Fr. Al.* 235
,, Richard Ward. *Fr. Al.* 236
,, Francis Kirkman. *Fr. Al.* 237
,, Francis Kirkman. *Cent.* 354
,, * 'Of Education'. *Cent.* 353
,, Thomas Isham. *Cent.* 355
1674. 'Love's Garland'. *Fr. Al.* 239
,, Thomas Duffett. *Fr. Al.* 240
,, John Dryden. *Cent.* 357
,, Samuel Speed. *Cent.* 358
1675. Thomas Duffett. *Fr. Al.* 242
,, W. Wycherley. *Fr. Al.* 246
,, Sir Francis Fane, junr. *Fr. Al.* 247
,, Matthew Lock. *Fr. Al.* 249
,, R. Bentley. *Fr. Al.* 250
,, 'The New-Married Couple'. *Fr. Al.* 251
,, Richard Head. *Fr. Al.* 252
,, Edward Phillips. *Cent.* 259
1676. Scarron's Englisher. *Fr. Al.* 253*
,, John Dryden. *Cent.* 362
1676-7. Duke of Newcastle. *Fr. Al.* 253
1677. John Dryden. *Fr. Al.* 225
,, Octavian Pulleyn. *Fr. Al.* 254
1677-8. Sir Carr Scrope. *Cent.* 363
1678. Tho. Shadwell. *Fr. Al.* 255
,, Tho. Shadwell. *Cent.* 365
,, Thos. Otway. *Fr. Al.* 256
,, John Oldham. *Fr. Al.* 257
,, 'Booksale Catalog'. *Fr. Al.* 335-6
,, Thomas Rymer. *Cent.* 366
,, John Dryden. *Cent.* 368
1678-83. Elias Travers. *Fr. Al.* 258
1679. Tho. Shadwell. *Fr. Al.* 259

---

[1] Tho' I now hold that Shakspere didn't write any of the *Two Noble Kinsmen*, yet Davenant must have thought he did.

CHRONOLOGICAL LIST OF ALLUSIONS TO SHAKSPERE. xit

1679. 'Ballad of Bothwel-Bridge'. *Fr. Al.* 261
,, John Dryden. *Cent.* 369-375, 376
,, John Martyn, &c. *Cent.* 377
,, Earl of Rochester. *Cent.* 378
1680. John Crowne. *Fr. Al.* 262
,, Thomas Durfey. *Fr. Al.* 263
,, Nahum Tate. *Cent.* 379
,, Thomas Otway. *Cent.* 381
1680-5. Nathaniel Lee. *Fr. Al.* 264
1680-90. Sir Wm. Temple. *Cent.* 382
ab. 1680. John Aubrey. *Cent.* 383
1681. John Crowne. *Fr. Al.* 265
,, Nahum Tate. *Fr. Al.* 267-9, 270
,, Nahum Tate. *Cent.* 380
,, Thomas Otway. *Fr. Al.* 271
,, 'Essay on Dramatick Poetry'. *Cent.* 386
,, 'Ballad on the Duke of Monmouth'. *Cent.* 387
,, 'Heraclitus Ridens'. *Cent.* 388
,, J. Crown. *Cent.* 389
,, Nahum Tate. *Cent.* 390-1
,, ,, ,, ,, 392
1682. Tho. Durfey. *Fr. Al.* 273
,, 'Poeta de Tristibus'. *Fr. Al.* 277
,, Nahum Tate. *Fr. Al.* 278
,, Sir George Raynsford. *Cent.* 392
,, Alexander Radcliffe. *Cent.* 393
,, Earl of Mulgrave. *Cent.* 394
,, John Banks. *Cent.* 395
,, Saint Evremond. *Cent.* 396
,, D. G. Morhoff. *Cent.* 342
1683. Jo. Harris. *Fr. Al.* 279
,, John Dryden. *Fr. Al.* 225
1684. 'Thomas Southerne. *Fr. Al.* 280
,, 'Booksale Catalog'. *Fr. Al.* 336-7
,, John Dryden. *Cent.* 398
,, Knightly Chetwood. *Cent.* 399
,, Lord Chief-Justice Jefferies. *Cent.* 296
,, William Winstanley. *Cent.* 400
b. 1685. Henry Bold. *Fr. Al.* 281
1685. Nahum Tate. *Fr. Al.* 283

1685. John Dryden. *Fr. Al.* 226
,, Book-Catalog. *Fr. Al.* 337-8
,, Thomas Otway. *Fr. Al.* 272
,, 'Prolog to Valentinian'. *Cent.* 403
1686. Nahum Tate. *Fr. Al.* 284
,, Tho. Jevon. *Fr. Al.* 286
,, Aphra Behn. *Fr. Al.* 287
,, 'Booksale Catalog'. *Fr. Al.* 339
,, Edward Ravenscroft. *Cent.* 404
1687. Aphra Behn. *Fr. Al.* 289
,, Martin Clifford. *Fr. Al.* 291
,, 'Booksale Catalog'. *Fr. Al.* 340-1
1688. Gerard Langbaine. *Fr. Al.* 294
,, 'List of Plays'. *Fr. Al.* 297
,, 'Booksale Catalog'. *Fr. Al.* 341
,, W. Fulman and R. Davies. *Cent.* 405
,, Thomas Browne. *Cent.* 406
1689. John Evelyn. *Cent.* 407
1690. T. Betterton. *Fr. Al.* 298
,, T. D'Urfey. *Fr. Al.* 300
,, Wm. Mountfort. *Fr. Al.* 301
1691. ,, ,, ,, 302-3
,, Tho. Shadwell. *Fr. Al.* 304
,, Elkanah Settle. *Fr. Al.* 305
,, Gerard Langbaine. *Fr. Al.* 306-332
,, Gerard Langbaine. *Cent.* 408. (Correct the headings 409, 410.)
,, J. N. *Fr. Al.* 333
,, 'Booksale Catalog'. *Fr. Al.* 341
,, 'The Athenian Mercury'. *Fr. Al.* 345
,, John Dryden. *Cent.* 411
,, William Walsh. *Cent.* 412
1692. Athenian Society. *Fr. Al.* 346
,, 'The Fairy-Queen'. *Fr. Al.* 347
1692-3. Peter Ant. Motteux. *Cent.* 415
1693. John Dryden. *Fr. Al.* 227-8
,, John Dryden. *Cent.* 413, 414
,, W. Dowdall. *Cent.* 417
,, Sir Charles Sedley. *Cent.* 413
(?) 'Ye merry Wives of Windsor'. *Cent.* 419
1663-93. John Downes. *Fr. Al.* 348-57
(1694. John Dryden. *Fr. Al.* 229, and *Cent.* 349.)

xii†

ERRATA TO THE *CENTURIE OF PRAYSE*.
2nd Edition, Series IV, No. 2.

Forespeech, p. xi. l. 21: dele 'Lodge (1596)'; ? add 'others'.
pp. of text—
pp. 5 and 113: prefix * to the names of Nash and Brathwaite, the allusions being doubtful, as shown in the notes.
p. 45, ll. 12, 16, 18, 24: for 'gaene' read 'grue'; for 'Burbedge' read 'Burbidge'; and for 'Shakespere' read 'Shakespeare'.
p. 68, l. 3: for 'Studiofo' read 'Studioso'.
p. 171, l. 8: dele full-stop.
[p. 186: title at head should be in Roman capitals (not Italics).
[p. 313: the like; and title should only be 'ANONYMOUS'.
p. 260, l. 4 from foot: for 'Oxoniensis' read 'Oxonienses'.
[p. 272: dele 'Sir'. This 'George Buck', says Mr. A. H. Bullen, was quite a different person from *Sir* George Buck, the Master of the Revels, who was in his grave many years before lines were written.—F.]
p. 276, l. 5 from foot: for 'you' read 'to'.
p. 402, note, l. 9: for 'Quarternion' read 'Quaternion'.
p. 409: add headline 'Gerard Langbaine, 1691'.
p. 410: dele headline, and substitute 'Gerard Langbaine, 1691', and add ? to end of note, l. 3 from foot.
p. 424, l. 22: for 'labours' read 'savours'.
p. 451: add 'Primerose, Dolarnys, 451'.
p. 462: add 'Valentinian, 403' to 'Anonymous'.
p. 466: add 'Newcastle, Duchess of, 332'. See 'Southampton' as an instance in justification of this addition.—C. M. I.

'Makes a vertue of necessity' (*Centurie of Sh.'s Prayse*, N. S. S. ed. p. 112) is not a quotation from Sh.; the proverb being much older. It is used by St. Jerome. In making this correction, blame me for the mistake, if you like.—W. G. STONE.

Many of the extracts in the *Centurie* had been given before by other writers: thus, that on p. 65 is in the *Variorum* Shakspere (1821), xvi. 412 (tho I did not know this when I sent it in from the Percy Soc. reprint); the quotation on p. 459 was printed by Joseph Hunter in his *New Illustrations of Shakspere*, ii. 123; the 'Scoloker' on p. 64 was quoted by Douce; the Marston and Webster bits on p. 65 were used by Steevens, and so on.

[The Allusions or extracts below, on p. 144*, James Shirley, 1640, and on p. 156, 'A Comedy 1645,' are the same, though the latter is fuller. It was sent from the MS.; and when the former came from the printed book, its identity with the other was overlookt.]

SOME 300
FRESH ALLUSIONS TO SHAKSPERE.

SOME 300

Fresh Allusions to Shakspere

FROM 1594 TO 1694 A.D.

GATHERD BY

MEMBERS OF THE NEW SHAKSPERE SOCIETY

AS A SUPPLEMENT TO

'Shakespeare's Centurie of Prayse,' ed. 2, 1879,

AND EDITED BY

FREDK. J. FURNIVALL,

M.A. CAMB.; HON. DR. PHIL., BERLIN;

FOUNDER AND DIRECTOR OF 'THE NEW SHAKSPERE SOCIETY.'

PUBLISHT FOR

The New Shakspere Society
BY N. TRÜBNER & CO., 57, 59, LUDGATE HILL,
LONDON, E.C. 1886.

DEDICATED

TO MY SON

Percy Furniball,

OF ST. BARTHOLOMEW'S HOSPITAL, LONDON,

(Born April 5, 1867,)

One-Mile Tricycle Champion, 1885 and 1886;

One-Mile and Five-Mile Bicycle Champion, 1886;

Champion of the English Team in America, 1885 (11 races, 11 prizes; 7 firsts, 3 seconds, 1 third);

Champion of the Berretta Club, 1884-6, and of the Racing Cyclists' Club, 1886;

Winner of the International Challenge Shield, and City Challenge Cup, Kildare Challenge Cup, Surrey Challenge Cup and Trophy, &c., 1886;

Rider of One Mile in 2 min. 30 sec., Aug. 1886;

18 Firsts, 3 Seconds (thro illness), in his 21 Races, 1886;

Captain of the Berretta Club;

Captain of the North-Road Cyclists' Boxing-Club.

CONTENTS.

	PAGE
CHRONOLOGICAL LIST OF THE ALLUSIONS TO SHAKSPERE, 1592-1693, IN *THE CENTURIE OF PRAYSE*, ED. 2, 1879, AND THIS VOLUME	ix
FOREWORDS	xvii
TABLE OF SHAKSPERE QUARTOS 1593—1685	xxi
LIST OF ENTRIES AND ASSIGNMENTS OF SHAKSPERE QUARTOS AND FOLIOS IN THE *STATIONERS' REGISTERS* TO 1640	xxvii
MORE ALLUSIONS IN BOOK-CATALOGS	xxxvii
𝕾𝖔𝖒𝖊 300 𝕱𝖗𝖊𝖘𝖍 𝕬𝖑𝖑𝖚𝖘𝖎𝖔𝖓𝖘 𝖙𝖔 𝕾𝖍𝖆𝖐𝖘𝖕𝖊𝖗𝖊	1—358
FIRST PERIOD, 1592-1616, From Greene's first Allusion to Shakspere's Death	1—82
SECOND PERIOD, 1617-1641, From Shakspere's Death to the Civil War	83—149
THIRD PERIOD, 1642-1659, From the Closing of the Theatres to the Stuart Restoration	150—184
FOURTH PERIOD, 1660-1693, From Charles II's accession to Dryden	185—357
NOTES	358
GENERAL INDEX TO *THE CENTURIE OF PRAYSE*, ED. 2, 1879, AND THIS VOLUME	359
INDEX OF REFERENCES TO SHAKSPERE'S WORKS (taking FALSTAFF as one of them) IN *THE CENTURIE OF PRAYSE*, ED. 2, 1879, AND THIS VOLUME	370
ORDER OF MENTION OF SHAKSPERE'S WORKS IN ALL THE 'ALLUSIONS': (FALSTAFF, 1, HAMLET, 2; ETC.) ...	372

CHRONOLOGICAL LIST OF THE
ALLUSIONS TO SHAKSPERE 1592-1693
IN THE '*CENTURIE OF PRAYSE*,' ED. 2. (N. SH. SOC. 1879), AND THE
'*FRESH ALLUSIONS*,' 1886.

(*Those in the 'Centurie' are inset; those in the 'Fresh Allusions' project.*)
(*Doubtful Allusions have a star (*) before them.*)

First Period. 1592—1616.

1591-4. *Edmund Spenser. *Cent.* 1
1592. Robert Greene. *Cent.* 2
,, Henry Chettle. *Cent.* 4
,, *Thomas Nash. *Cent.* 5
1594. Henry Helmes. *Fr. Al.* 1
,, In 'Willobie his Avisa.' *Cent.* 6
,, *Hy. Willobie. *Cent.* 7
,, Sir Wm. Harbert. *Cent.* 12
,, *Michael Drayton. *Cent.* 13
1595. Robert Southwell. *Cent.* 14
,, William Clarke. *Cent.* 15
,, John Weever. *Cent.* 16
,, Thomas Edwardes. *Cent.* 17
1596. In 'Wily Beguilde.' *Cent.* 19
,, Richard Carew [prob. 1605]. *Cent.* 20
1597-1603. In a MS. of Bacon's 'Tribute'. *Fr. Al.* 2
1597-1616. Nicholas Breton. *Cent.* 457
1598. I. M. *Fr. Al.* 4
,, *R. S. *Fr. Al.* 8
,, Francis Meres. *Cent.* 21, 24
,, Robert Tofte. *Cent.* 25
,, Richard Barnfield. *Cent.* 26
,, John Marston. *Cent.* 27, 29
,, Gabriel Harvey (prob. after 1600). *Cent.* 30

1599. Henry Porter. *Fr. Al.* 9
,, Ben Jonson. *Cent.* 31
1599-1636. Thos. Dekker. *Fr. Al.* 10
1600. John Bodenham. *Fr. Al.* 13
,, A Munday, &c. *Fr. Al.* 15
,, *Chr. Middleton. *Fr. Al.* 19
,, *Sam. Nicholson. *Fr. Al.* 20
,, Sam. Nicholson. *Cent.* 33
,, *John Lane. *Cent.* 32
,, ? Charles Percy. *Cent.* 38
,, Sir Wm. Cornwallis. *Cent.* 41
,, In 'England's Parnassus'. *Cent.* 430
,, N. Breton. *Cent.* 457
,, 'Returne from Pernassus', Part I. *Fr. Al.* 12*
1600-10. Two letters. *Cent.* 40
1600-12. *J. M. *Cent.* 98
1601. *Ben Johnson. *Fr. Al.* 22
,, William Lambard. *Cent.* 449
,, 'Essex Rebellion.' *Cent.* 35
,, John Weever. *Cent.* 42
,, Robert Chester. *Cent.* 43, 44
,, John Manningham. *Cent.* 45
,, W. J. *Cent.* 47
1601-2. 'Returne from Pernassus', Part II. *Cent.* 48
1602. *John Marston. *Fr. Al.* 23
,, *Thomas Dekker. *Fr. Al.* 22
,, Thomas Decker. *Cent.* 50
,, *Thomas Middleton. *Cent.* 51
,, Thomas Acherley. *Cent.* 52
1602-23. John Webster. *Fr. Al.* 24
1603. Father Parsons. *Fr. Al.* 29
,, *Michael Drayton. *Cent.* 53
,, *Henry Chettle. *Cent.* 55

x   CHRONOLOGICAL LIST OF ALLUSIONS TO SHAKSPERE.

1603. 'Elizabeth's Losse.' *Cent.* 56
,, *J. C. *Cent.* 57
,, John Davies. *Cent.* 58
,, William Camden. *Cent.* 59
,, N. Breton. *Cent.* 457
1604. John Marston. *Fr. Al.* 30
,, John Marston. *Cent.* 66
,, Anthony Scoloker. *Fr. Al.* 33
,, Anthony Scoloker. *Cent.* 64
,, *T. M. *Cent.* 60
,, 'Meeting of Gallants.' *Cent.* 65
,, N. Breton. *Cent.* 457
1604-19. Thomas Middleton. *Fr. Al.* 35
1605. Peter Woodhouse. *Fr. Al.* 39
,, *Thomas Heywood. *Fr. Al.* 40
,, *John Marston. *Fr. Al.* 40*
,, Geo. Chapman, &c. *Fr. Al.* 41, 42
,, Geo. Chapman. *Cent.* 69
,, Sir Thomas Smith. *Cent.* 453
,, 'Ratsei's Ghost'. *Cent.* 67
1606. Barnabe Barnes. *Fr. Al.* 45
,, *Wm. Warner. *Fr. Al.* 43
,, Thos. Heywood. *Fr. Al.* 46*
,, William Drummond. *Cent.* 71
,, John Raynolds. *Cent.* 451
1607. Thomas Heywood. *Fr. Al.* 47
,, George Chapman. *Fr. Al.* 49
,, Edward Sharpham. *Fr. Al.* 50, 51
,, T. Dekker and J. Webster. *Fr. Al.* 52, 53
,, Thos. Decker. *Cent.* 74
,, John Fletcher. *Cent.* 72
,, 'Merry Divel'. *Cent.* 73
,, George Peele. *Cent.* 75
,, William Barkstead. *Cent.* 76
,, John Marston. *Cent.* 77
,, W. S. ('Puritaine'). *Cent.* 78
,, Captain Keelinge. *Cent.* 79
,, Thomas Heywood. *Cent.* 80
1608. T. Dekker. *Fr. Al.* 55
,, Thos. Middleton. *Fr. Al.* 56
,, *Robt. Armin. *Fr. Al.* 57, 59
,, J. Markham. L. Machin. *Cent.* 81
,, *John Day. *Cent.* 82

1608-25. Beaumont (d. 1616) and Fletcher. *Fr. Al.* 61
1609. Robt. Armin. *Fr. Al.* 59
,, John Davies. *Cent.* 84
,, Samuel Rowlands. *Cent.* 85
,, Thomas Decker. *Cent.* 453
,, Thomas Thorpe. *Cent.* 86
,, 'Troilus Forewords.' *Cent.* 87
,, 'Pimlyco'. *Cent.* 89
,, Ben Jonson. *Cent.* 90
1610. Roger Sharpe. *Fr. Al.* 69
,, 'Copy of Sh.'s 8th Sonnet.' *Fr. Al.* 70
,, Beaumont and Fletcher. *Fr. Al.* 61
,, Edmund Bolton. *Cent.* 91
,, J. Wurmsser. *Cent.* 93
,, John Davies. *Cent.* 94
,, *Lodovic Barry. *Cent.* 95
,, W. Drummond. *Cent.* 71
1611. Cyril Tourneur. *Fr. Al.* 71
,, John Speed. *Fr. Al.* 75
,, *Lod. Barrey. *Fr. Al.* 73
,, Beaumont and Fletcher. *Fr. Al.* 61, 62
,, Beaumont and Fletcher. *Cent.* 117
,, John Davies. *Cent.* 96
,, Simon Forman. *Cent.* 97
1612. *Sir John Hayward. *Fr. Al.* 77
,, *Thos. Heywood. *Fr. Al.* 78
,, Thomas Heywood. *Cent.* 99
,, *J. M. *Cent.* 98
,, John Webster. *Cent.* 100
1613. Beaumont and Fletcher. *Fr. Al.* 62
,, John Marston. *Fr. Al.* 78*
,, Beaumont and Fletcher. *Cent.* 117
,, Joseph Fletcher. *Cent.* 101
,, Thomas Lorkins. *Cent.* 102
,, 'Globe Sonnet'. *Cent.* 455
,, Lord Treasurer Stanhope. *Cent.* 103
1614. *John Cooke. *Fr. Al.* 79
,, *Barnabe Rich. *Fr. Al.* 79
,, Ben Jonson. *Cent.* 105
,, Thomas Freeman. *Cent.* 106
,, Robert Tailor. *Cent.* 107
,, Edmund Howes. *Cent.* 108
,, Chr. Brooke. *Cent.* 109
,, Sir Wm. Drummond. *Cent.* 111
1615. Alex. Niccholes. *Fr. Al.* 80
,, Richard Brathwaite. *Cent.* 112, 113

CHRONOLOGICAL LIST OF ALLUSIONS TO SHAKSPERE. xi

1615. 'Characters'. *Cent.* 114
1616. *W. Drummond. *Fr. Al.* 82
,, W. Drummond. *Cent.* 116
,, Robert Anton. *Cent.* 115
,, Beaumont and Fletcher. *Cent.* 117
,, Ben Jonson. *Cent.* 118

1616. 'Sh.'s Grave-Tablet'. *Cent.* 121
,, N. Breton. *Cent.* 457-8
1616-18. Beaumont and Fletcher. *Fr. Al.* 63
[Shakspere died on April 23, 1616.]

Second Period. 1617—1641.

1617-22. 'Sh.'s Tablet-Inscription'. *Cent.* 125
1617. John Taylor, the Water-Poet. *Cent.* 126
1618. Beaumont and Fletcher. *Fr. Al.* 63
,, Geffray Mynshul. *Cent.* 456
,, Nathaniel Field. *Cent.* 127
1618-21. Richard Corbet. *Cent.* 128
1618-19. 'Elegy on Richard Burbage'. *Cent.* 131
1619. Sir Gerrard Herbert. *Fr. Al.* 83
,, Ben Jonson. *Cent.* 129
1620. 'Hæc Vir'. *Fr. Al.* 85
,, Sam. Rowlands. *Cent.* 454
,, John Taylor, the Water-Poet. *Cent.* 133
1620-56. 'Choyce Drollery'. *Cent.* 134
1621. Robert Burton. *Fr. Al.* 85
,, John Fletcher. *Cent.* 135
1622. John Taylor. *Fr. Al.* 86
,, Thomas Walkley. *Fr. Al.* 87
,, John Fletcher. *Fr. Al.* 88*, 98
,, Ph. Massinger. *Fr. Al.* 89-94
,, William Basse. *Cent.* 136
,, Thomas Robinson. *Cent.* 140
1623. Ben Jonson. *Cent.* 141, 147-150
,, Heminge and Condell. *Cent.* 143, 145
,, Hugh Holland. *Cent.* 153
,, Leonard Digges. *Cent.* 154
,, J. M. *Cent.* 155
1623-36. Sir Hy. Herbert. *Cent.* 157
1624. Ph. Massinger. *Fr. Al.* 90, 94, 95
,, Robert Burton. *Fr. Al.* 98*
,, E. S. (B. of D). *Cent.* 159
,, John Gee. *Cent.* 160
,, Robert Burton. *Cent.* 161
1625. Fletcher, &c. *Fr. Al.* 64-8
,, Fletcher, &c. *Cent.* 166, 167

1625. Ben Jonson. *Cent.* 163
,, Richard James. *Cent.* 164
1626. Ben Jonson. *Fr. Al.* 99
,, Ph. Massinger. *Fr. Al.* 95
1627. Ph. Massinger. *Fr. Al.* 91, 95
,, *John Milton. *Cent.* 460
,, Michael Drayton. *Cent.* 168
1628. 'Prince Hal's Speech'. *Fr. Al.* 100
,, 'A Newsletter'. *Fr. Al.* 101
,, (?) 'The Wandering Jew'. *Fr. Al.* 142
,, Robert Gell. *Cent.* 169
1628-31. Abraham Cowley. *Cent.* 170
1629. Ph. Massinger. *Fr. Al.* 92
,, *Philip Massinger. *Cent.* 171
,, Sir Hy. Herbert. *Cent.* 173
1629-30. Ben Jonson. *Cent.* 172
1630-7. ,, ,, 174
1630. John Milton. *Cent.* 176
,, John Taylor, the Water-Poet. *Cent.* 178, 179
,, Owen Feltham. *Fr. Al.* 180
,, 'Banquet of Jeasts'. *Cent.* 181
1631. Ph. Massinger. *Fr. Al.* 93, 95-6
,, Wye Saltonstall. *Fr. Al.* 102
,, Richard Brathwait. *Fr. Al.* 104
,, Peter Heylyn. *Fr. Al.* 104*
,, 'Funeral Monument'. *Fr. Al.* 105
,, *James Shirley. *Fr. Al.* 106
,, *John Spencer. *Cent.* 182
,, Sir Hy. Herbert. *Cent.* 173
1632. Philip Massinger. *Fr. Al.* 97, 107
,, Philip Massinger. *Cent.* 185
,, G. Chapman and J. Shirley. *Cent.* 186
,, *Thomas Randolph. *Cent.* 187
,, 'Second Folio of Sh.'s Works'. *Cent.* 189

xii CHRONOLOGICAL LIST OF ALLUSIONS TO SHAKSPERE.

1632. J. M. S. *Cent.* 190
,, Wm. Prynne. *Cent.* 195
,, Sir Aston Cokaine. *Cent.* 196
b. 1633. John Hales. *Cent.* 198
1633. Ph. Massinger. *Fr. Al.* 97
,, Jas. Shirley. *Fr. Al.* 108
,, Thomas Nabbes. *Fr. Al.* 109
,, Th. Bancroft. *Fr. Al.* 110
,, John Ford. *Fr. Al.* 116-118
,, *Wm. Rowley. *Cent.* 197
1633-4. Sir Jn. Suckling. *Fr. Al.* 111-115
1634. Ph. Massinger. *Fr. Al.* 93
,, Tho. Randolph. *Fr. Al.* 120
,, Wm. Habington. *Cent.* 200
,, James Shirley. *Cent.* 201
1635. 'The Lady Mother'. *Fr. Al.* 120
,, Sir. H. Mildmay. *Fr. Al.* 121
,, James Shirley. *Fr. Al.* 150
,, Thomas Heywood. *Fr. Al.* 122
,, Thomas Heywood. *Cent.* 202
,, Thomas Cranley. *Cent.* 204
,, John Swan. *Cent.* 459
1636. Ph. Massinger. *Fr. Al.* 93, 97
,, William Sampson. *Fr. Al.* 124
,, John Trussell. *Fr. Al.* 125
,, 'Book of Bulls'. *Fr. Al.* 127
1636-41. Sir John Suckling. *Cent.* 205-211
1637. Tho. Heywood. *Fr. Al.* 128
,, *Shakerley Marmion. *Fr. Al.* 130
,, Jasper Mayne. *Cent.* 212
,, Owen Feltham. *Cent.* 213
,, Richard West. *Cent.* 214
,, H. Ramsay. *Cent.* 215
,, Sir W. Davenant. *Cent.* 216
,, T. Terrent. *Cent.* 218
,, Abraham Wright. *Cent.* 219

1637. 'Elegy on Shakspere'. *Cent.* 220
b. 1638. Thomas Carew. *Fr. Al.* 131
1638. 'Songs from *The Tempest*'. *Fr. Al.* 132
,, John Ford. *Fr. Al.* 118
,, Henry Adamson. *Fr. Al.* 134
,, James Mervyn. *Cent.* 222
,, Wm. Chillingworth. *Cent.* 223
,, Thomas Randolph (?). *Cent.* 224
,, Richard Brome. *Cent.* 225
1639. John Clarke. *Fr. Al.* 135
,, G. Rivers. *Fr. Al.* 139
,, 'Conceits, Clinches &c.' *Fr. Al.* 141
,, Robert Chamberlain. *Cent.* 226
,, Thomas Bancroft. *Cent.* 227
,, 'Witts Recreations'. *Cent.* 228
1640. 'The Wandering Jew'. *Fr. Al.* 142
,, *Jas. Shirley. *Fr. Al.* 144, 144* (*Cent.* 236)
,, 'A Helpe to Discourse'. *Fr. Al.* 144
,, Rich. Goodridge. *Fr. Al.* 145
,, Geo. Lynn. *Fr. Al.* 146
,, John Benson. *Cent.* 229
,, Lewis Sharpe. *Cent.* 230
,, Leonard Digges. *Cent.* 231
,, John Warren. *Cent.* 235
,, James Shirley. *Cent.* 236
1641. Rich. Brathwaite *Fr. Al.* 147
,, *Shakerly Marmion. *Fr. Al.* 148
,, Abraham Cowley. *Fr. Al.* 149
,, John Johnson. *Cent.* 238
,, Martine Parker. *Cent.* 239

Third Period. 1642—1659.

1642. James Shirley. *Fr. Al.* 150
,, John Milton. *Fr. Al.* 151
,, Sir Thomas Browne. *Fr. Al.* 153
,, Charles Butler. *Cent.* 243
,, 'Rump Songs'. *Cent.* 244

1643. Sir Richard Baker. *Cent.* 250
1643-62. Thomas Fuller. *Cent.* 246, 249
1644. John Cleveland. *Fr. Al.* 154
,, John Cleveland. *Cent.* 254

CHRONOLOGICAL LIST OF ALLUSIONS TO SHAKSPERE.   xiii

1644.   'London Post'. *Cent.* 251
  ,,   'Mercurius   Britanicus'.
        Cent. 252
  ,,   Thomas Prujean. *Cent.* 255
  ,,   'Vindex Anglicus'. *Cent.*
        256
1645.   Sir Richard Baker. *Fr. Al.*
        155
  ,,   'A Comedy'. *Fr. Al.* 156
  ,,   Paul Aylward. *Cent.* 257
  ,,   Daniell Breedy. *Cent.* 257
  ,,   George Withers. *Cent.* 258
1646.   R. Wilde (?). *Fr. Al.* 158*
  ,,   Samuel Sheppard. *Cent.* 261
1647. *Sam. Sheppard. *Fr. Al.* 159
  ,,   'Epistle of ten Players'.
        Cent. 262
  ,,   Sir John Denham. *Cent.*
        263
  ,,   James Howell. *Cent.* 264
  ,,   George Daniel. *Cent.* 265,
        266
  ,,   William Cartwright. *Cent.*
        270
  ,,   J. Berkenhead. *Cent.* 271
  ,,   George Buck. *Cent.* 272
  ,,   T. Palmer. *Cent.* 272
1648.   J. S. *Fr. Al.* 159, 160
  ,,   'Perfect Occurrences'. *Cent.*
        273
1648-54. Henry Tubbe. *Fr. Al.* 161
1649. 'Trinarchodia'. *Fr. Al.* 163
  ,,   John Milton. *Cent.* 274
  ,,   J. Cook. *Cent.* 276
1650.   'Ashmole MS.' *Cent.* 277
  ,,   Robert Baron. *Cent.* 279
  ,,   Anthony Davenport. *Cent.*
        281
  ,,   Sir N. L'Estrange. *Cent.*
        282
1651.   John Milton. *Fr. Al.* 164
  ,,   Richard Whitlock. *Fr. Al.* 165
  ,,   Samuel Sheppard. *Cent.*
        283-7
  ,,   William Bell. *Cent.* 288
  ,,   Jasper Mayne. *Cent.* 289

1651.   'Hermeticall   Banquet'.
        Cent. 290
  ,,   J. S. *Cent.* 291
  ,,   Thos. Randolph. *Cent.* 293
1652.   Francis Kirkman. *Fr. Al.* 166
  ,,   R. Loveday. *Fr. Al.* 167
  ,,   Jo. Tatham. *Cent.* 295
1653.   Nathaniel Hooke. *Fr. Al.* 168
  ,,   Richard Flecknoe. *Fr. Al.* 169
  ,,   Alexander Brome. *Cent.*
        296
  ,,   Sir Aston Cokaine. *Cent.*
        297
  ,,   Sir Wm. Dugdale. *Cent.*
        298
1654.   Edmund Gayton. *Fr. Al.* 170
  ,,   Edmund Gayton. *Cent.* 299
  ,,   Richard Flecknoe. *Fr. Al.* 169
  ,,   Alex. Brome. *Fr. Al.* 172
1655.   J. Quarles. *Fr. Al.* 174
  ,,   'The Hectors'. *Cent.* 301
1656.   Richard Flecknoe. *Fr. Al.*
        169
  ,,   Samuel Holland. *Fr. Al.* 171
  ,,   T. Goff. *Fr. Al.* 175
  ,,   Edward Archer. *Fr. Al.* 176
  ,,   (?)   *Fr. Al.* 179
  ,,   'Parnassus Biceps'. *Fr. Al.*
        180
  ,,   Samuel Holland. *Cent.* 302
  ,,   Abraham Cowley. *Cent.*
        303
1657.   Richard Ligon. *Cent.* 304
1658. 'Naps upon Parnassus'. *Fr.*
        Al. 181
  ,,   Gilbert Swinhoe. *Fr. Al.* 183
  ,,   'Isham MS.' *Fr. Al.* 184
  ,,   'London Chanticleres'. *Fr.*
        Al. 184
  ,,   W. London. *Fr. Al.* 183*
  ,,   Sir Aston Cokain. *Cent.*
        305-7
  ,,   In 'Brome's Plays'. *Cent.*
        308
  ,,   Samuel Austin. *Cent.* 309
[1659. *No Allusion yet found.*]

Fourth Period. 1660—1693.

1660. 'Stationers Register'. *Fr. Al.*
        169
  ,,   'Friend'. *Fr. Al.* 185
  ,,   'A Poetical Revenge'. *Fr. Al.*
        185
  ,,   Lady Dolly Long. *Fr. Al.*
        185

1660.   'Elegy on Rich. Lovelace'.
        Cent. 313
  ,,   Richard Flecknoe. *Cent.*
        314
  ,,   Sir Richard Baker. *Cent.*
        315
  ,,   Samuel Pepys. *Cent.* 316

1660-4. Thomas Jordan. *Cent.* 330
1661. ' Prolog. to Rich. III '. *Fr.
Al.* 186
" 'Merry Humors of Bottom '.
Fr. Al. 188
" Francis Kirkman. *Fr. Al.*
190, &c., and 343
" Robert Davenport. *Fr. Al.* 196
" Thomas Fuller. *Fr. Al.* 197
" Samuel Pepys. *Cent.* 316
" 'A Catch '. *Cent.* 325
" John Evelyn. *Cent.* 326
1661-3. John Ward. *Cent.* 327
b. 1662. Wm. Hemings. *Fr. Al.* 200
1662. Theatro-Philos. *Fr. Al.* 198
" Edmund Gayton. *Fr. Al.* 199
" T. S. *Fr. Al.* 202
" Samuel Pepys. *Cent.* 317
1663. J. Kelynge. *Fr. Al.* 204
" Thos. Jordan. *Fr. Al.* 205
" Samuel Pepys. *Cent.* 317
" 'Hudibras '. *Cent.* 329
1653-93. John Downes. *Fr. Al.* 348-357
1664. Henry Bold. *Fr. Al.* 206
" Samuel Pepys. *Cent.* 318
" Thomas Jordan. *Cent.* 330
" Margaret Cavendish. *Cent.*
332
1665. Charles Cotton. *Cent.* 336
1666. 'The Dutch Gazette '. *Fr.
Al.* 207
" Samuel Pepys. *Cent.* 319
" " " " 319-21
" ' Prolog to Shirley's Love-
Tricks '. *Cent.* 337
" John Dryden. *Cent.* 338
b. 1668. Sir W. Davenant. *Fr. Al.* 208
1668. Tho. Shadwell. *Fr. Al.* 209
" Sir W. Davenant. *Fr. Al.*
210-15[1]
" John Dryden. *Fr. Al.* 216-221
" John Dryden. *Cent.* 341
" Samuel Pepys. *Cent.* 321
" Robert Wild. *Cent.* 340
" Sir John Denham. *Cent.* 343
1669. John Dryden. *Fr. Al.* 221, 222
" Samuel Pepys. *Cent.* 322
" Edward Phillips. *Cent.* 344
1670. Watson. *Fr. Al.* 230
" Richard Flecknoe. *Cent.*
345

1671. Francis Kirkman. *Fr. Al.*
191, 194
" John Dryden. *Fr. Al.* 223
" George Villiers. *Cent.* 346
1672. John Dryden. *Fr. Al.* 224
" John Dryden. *Cent.* 348,
350-2
" W. Ramesey. *Fr. Al.* 231
" ' Covent Garden Drollery '.
Fr. Al. 231*
" Thomas Fuller. *Fr. Al.* 202
" Andrew Marvel. *Cent.* 347
1673. John Dryden. *Fr. Al.* 225
" ' The Transproser Rehearst '.
Fr. Al. 232
" Sir W. Davenant. *Fr. Al.* 233
" Mr. Arrowsmith. *Fr. Al.* 234
" ' The Censure of the Rota '.
Fr. Al. 235
" Richard Ward. *Fr. Al.* 236
" Francis Kirkman. *Fr. Al.* 237
" * ' Of Education '. *Cent.* 353
" Thomas Isham. *Cent.* 355
1674. ' Love's Garland '. *Fr. Al.* 239
" Thomas Duffett. *Fr. Al.* 240
" John Dryden. *Cent.* 357
" Samuel Speed. *Cent.* 358
1675. Thomas Duffett. *Fr. Al.* 242
" W. Wycherley. *Fr. Al.* 246
" Sir Francis Fane, junr. *Fr.
Al.* 247
" Matthew Lock. *Fr. Al.* 249
" R. Bentley. *Fr. Al.* 250
" 'The New-Married Couple '.
Fr. Al. 251
" Richard Head. *Fr. Al.* 252
" Edward Phillips. *Cent.* 259
1676. Scarron's Englisher. *Fr. Al.*
253*
" John Dryden. *Cent.* 362
1676-7. Duke of Newcastle. *Fr. Al.*
253
1677. John Dryden. *Fr. Al.* 225
" Octavian Pulleyn. *Fr. Al.* 251
1677-8. Sir Carr Scrope. *Cent.* 363
1678. Tho. Shadwell. *Fr. Al.* 255
" Tho. Shadwell. *Cent.* 365
" Thos. Otway. *Fr. Al.* 256
" John Oldham. *Fr. Al.* 257
" ' Booksale Catalog '. *Fr. Al.*
335-6
" Thomas Rymer. *Cent.* 366
" John Dryden. *Cent.* 368
1678-83. Elias Travers. *Fr. Al.* 258
1679. Tho. Shadwell. *Fr. Al.* 259

---

[1] Tho' I now hold that Shakspere didn't write any of the *Two Noble Kinsmen*, yet Davenant must have thought he did.

1679. 'Ballad of Bothwel-Bridge'.
          Fr. Al. 201
    "   John Dryden. *Cent.* 369-
          375, 376
    "   John Martyn, &c. *Cent.* 377
    "   Earl of Rochester. *Cent.* 378
1680. John Crowne. *Fr. Al.* 262
    "   Thomas Durfey. *Fr. Al.* 263
    "   Nahum Tate. *Cent.* 379
    "   Thomas Otway. *Cent.* 381
1680-5. Nathaniel Lee. *Fr. Al.* 264
1680-90. Sir Wm. Temple. *Cent.* 382
ab.1680. John Aubrey. *Cent.* 383
1681. John Crowne. *Fr. Al.* 265
    "   Nahum Tate. *Fr. Al.* 267-9,
          270
    "   Nahum Tate. *Cent.* 380
    "   Thomas Otway. *Fr. Al.* 271
    "   'Essay on Dramatick Poetry'.
          Cent. 386
    "   'Ballad on the Duke of Monmouth'. *Cent.* 387
    "   'Heraclitus Ridens'. *Cent.*
          388
    "   J. Crown. *Cent.* 389
    "   Nahum Tate. *Cent.* 390-1
    "   "   "   " 392
1682. Tho. Durfey. *Fr. Al.* 273
    "   'Poeta de Tristibus'. *Fr. Al.* 277
    "   Nahum Tate. *Fr. Al.* 278
    "   Sir George Raynsford. *Cent.*
          392
    "   Alexander Radcliffe. *Cent.*
          393
    "   Earl of Mulgrave. *Cent.*
          394
    "   John Banks. *Cent.* 395
    "   Saint Evremond. *Cent.* 396
    "   D. G. Morhoff. *Cent.* 342
1683. Jo. Harris. *Fr. Al.* 279
    "   John Dryden. *Fr. Al.* 225
1684. *Thomas Southerne. *Fr. Al.*
          280
    "   'Booksale Catalog'. *Fr. Al.*
          336-7
    "   John Dryden. *Cent.* 398
    "   Knightly Chetwood. *Cent.*
          399
    "   Lord Chief-Justice Jefferies.
          Cent. 296
    "   William Winstanley. *Cent.*
          400
b. 1685. Henry Bold. *Fr. Al.* 281
1685. Nahum Tate. *Fr. Al.* 283

1685. John Dryden. *Fr. Al.* 226
    "   Book-Catalog. *Fr. Al.* 337-8
    "   Thomas Otway. *Fr. Al.* 272
    "   'Prolog to Valentinian'.
          Cent. 403
1686. Nahum Tate. *Fr. Al.* 284
    "   Tho. Jevon. *Fr. Al.* 286
    "   Aphra Behn. *Fr. Al.* 287
    "   'Booksale Catalog'. *Fr. Al.* 339
    "   Edward Ravenscroft. *Cent.*
          404
1687. Aphra Behn. *Fr. Al.* 289
    "   Martin Clifford. *Fr. Al.* 291
    "   'Booksale Catalog'. *Fr. Al.*
          340-1
1688. Gerard Langbaine. *Fr. Al.* 294
    "   'List of Plays'. *Fr. Al.* 297
    "   'Booksale Catalog'. *Fr. Al.* 341
    "   W. Fulman and R. Davies.
          Cent. 405
    "   Thomas Browne. *Cent.* 406
1689. John Evelyn. *Cent.* 407
1690. T. Betterton. *Fr. Al.* 298
    "   T. D'Urfey. *Fr. Al.* 300
    "   Wm. Mountfort. *Fr. Al.* 301
1691. "   "   " 302-3
    "   Tho. Shadwell. *Fr. Al.* 304
    "   Elkanah Settle. *Fr. Al.* 305
    "   Gerard Langbaine. *Fr. Al.*
          306-332
    "   Gerard Langbaine. *Cent.*
          408. (Correct the headings 409, 410.)
    "   J. N. *Fr. Al.* 333
    "   'Booksale Catalog'. *Fr. Al.* 341
    "   'The Athenian Mercury'. *Fr.
          Al.* 345
    "   John Dryden. *Cent.* 411
    "   William Walsh. *Cent.* 412
1692. Athenian Society. *Fr. Al.* 316
    "   'The Fairy-Queen'. *Fr. Al.*
          347
1692-3. Peter Ant. Motteux. *Cent.*
          415
1693. John Dryden. *Fr. Al.* 227-8
    "   John Dryden. *Cent.* 413,414
    "   W. Dowdall. *Cent.* 417
    "   Sir Charles Sedley. *Cent.*
          413
(?)   'Ye merry Wives of Windsor'. *Cent.* 419
1663-93. John Downes. *Fr. Al.* 348-57
(1694. John Dryden. *Fr. Al.* 22),
          and *Cent.* 349.)

ERRATA TO THE *CENTURIE OF PRAYSE*.

2nd Edition, Series IV, No. 2.

Forespeech, p. xi. l. 211 dele 'Lodge (1596)'; ? add 'others'.
pp. of text—
pp. 5 and 113: prefix * to the names of Nash and Brathwaite, the allusions being doubtful, as shown in the notes.
p. 45, ll. 12, 16, 18, 24: for 'gaene' read 'grue'; for 'Burbedge' read 'Burbidge'; and for 'Shakespere' read 'Shakespeare'.
p. 68, l. 3: for 'Studiofo' read 'Studioso'.
p. 171, l. 8; dele full-stop.
{ p. 186: title at head should be in Roman capitals (not Italics).
{ p. 313: the like; and title should only be 'ANONYMOUS'.
p. 260, l. 4 from foot: for 'Oxoniensis' read 'Oxonienses'.
[p. 272: dele 'Sir'. This 'George Buck'; says Mr. A. H. Bullen, was quite a different person from *Sir* George Buck, the Master of the Revels, who was in his grave many years before lines were written.—F.]
p. 276, l. 5 from foot: for 'you' read 'to'.
p. 402, note, l. 9: for 'Quarternion' read 'Quaternion'.
p. 409: add headline 'Gerard Langbaine, 1691'.
p. 410: dele headline, and substitute 'Gerard Langbaine, 1691', and add ? to end of note, l. 3 from foot.
p. 424, l. 22: for 'labours' read 'savours'.
p. 451: add 'Primerose, Dolarnys, 451'.
p. 462: add 'Valentinian, 403' to 'Anonymous'.
p. 466: add 'Newcastle, Duchess of, 332'. See 'Southampton' as an instance in justification of this addition.—C. M. I.

'Makes a vertue of necessity' (*Centurie of Sh.'s Prayse*, N. S. S. ed. p. 112) is not a quotation from Sh.; the proverb being much older. It is used by St. Jerome. In making this correction, blame me for the mistake, if you like.—W. G. STONE.

Many of the extracts in the *Centurie* had been given before by other writers: thus, that on p. 65 is in the *Variorum* Shakspere (1821), xvi. 412 (tho I did not know this when I sent it in from the Percy Soc. reprint); the quotation on p. 459 was printed by Joseph Hunter in his *New Illustrations of Shakspere*, ii. 123; the 'Scoloker' on p. 64 was quoted by Douce; the Marston and Webster bits on p. 66 were used by Steevens, and so on.

[The Allusions or extracts below, on p. 144*, James Shirley, 1640, and on p. 156, 'A Comedy 1645,' are the same, though the latter is fuller. It was sent from the MS.; and when the former came from the printed book, its identity with the other was overlookt.]

vii

FOREWORDS.

WHEN our second edition of *Shakespeare's Centurie of Prayse* came out in 1879, I felt sure that the 128 quotations added in it [1] to the original 228 collected by the late Dr. Ingleby and his correspondents might have another couple of hundred added to them, with a moderate amount of search. Several likely sources had evidently not been tapt, and others which had been were (like Dryden, for instance) clearly not exhausted. So one day I took my copy of the *Centurie* to the Museum to test how the work had been done, and unluckily soon chanst on Shadwell's *Timon* of 1678. I turnd out the quotation from the 'Epistle Dedicatory' on p. 365, *Centurie;* and then naturally lookt at the Prolog: there I found another Shakspere-Allusion (p. 255 below); then, as naturally, I turnd to the Epilog; and there found two more Shakspere Allusions (p. 256 below). So, out of four Allusions in the places where every one would first look for them, our *Centurie* had only got one. I felt rather savage, wrote in the margin of my book, "1 out of 4 taken. Nothing like care!" and went on.[2] Soon came Nahum Tate (the 'Nahum' always attracted me: it's almost as comforting as 'Mesopotamia'), and having identified the *Centurie* quotation (p. 391) from the Prolog to the worthy Nahum's *King Lear*, I of course lookt at the Epilog, and there—of course too, one may fairly say— found another Shakspere Allusion not in the *Centurie.* Then I uttered 'a big, big D,'[3] set to work to look at the Prologs and Epilogs of all the plays I could get hold of; prowld about in likely

[1] Dr. Ingleby sent over 30, I sent 10, others different numbers, and the editress added the rest.
[2] So 1 only out of 6 was taken from T. Heywood's *Fayre Mayde of the Exchange.* See p. 47-8, below, and p. 78.
[3] This profanity did not prevent the acknowledgment that there was a lot of solid and sound work in the *Centurie,* in both editions 1 and 2.

FRESH ALLUSIONS. *b*

xviii FOREWORDS.

spots, and askt my friends to do so too. I had no time to carry out the searching thoroughly, but just skimd the surface of the material. Gradually a fair lot of Fresh Allusions was gatherd together by the hands of our Members and other friends and myself; and then I put the heap by, in the hope of being able to read at least Marston, Massinger, Fletcher, for echoes of Shakspere. But as years went on, new things sprang up: Browning Society, Wyclif Society, Sculling Fours, Kangaroo Bicycle, boat-races, Shelley Society, Sculling-Eights and Fours,[1] a bit of lawn-tennis, &c., while the 'Old Spelling Shakspere,' 'Shakspere Quarto Facsimiles,' and the like had to be carried on. This year 1886, a book of some kind had to be produced for the Society; and as time for further work at Fresh Allusions had no chance of forthcoming, I have just turnd the old set out as they stood,[2] though knowing that if any fresh searcher follows me carefully, and reads through a play of which I've only lookt at the Prolog and Epilog, he may find—as I did with Miss Smith—that I've only got one Allusion out of four in the volume. If this comes about, no one'll be gladder than I, if I'm alive to witness it. I specially want an Allusion to Sha' spere in the year 1639. At present it's the only year in his *Century of Praise* without its tribute.

As the publication of a Quarto, and its entry and transfer in the Stationers' Registers, are an 'allusion' to Shakspere as we have defined the term, I have printed at the end of these Forewords Mr. Fleay's Table of the Quartos from our *Transactions* 1874, with a few corrections by a friend, and have added a list of the *Stat. Reg.* entries, so far as I have noted them in occasional references to the book, but cutting out Mr. Arber's hateful insertions 'th[e h]andes' in 'thandes.'

To save future searchers the trouble of looking into two separate 'Contents' and Indexes, I have put the Allusions in both the *Centurie* and the present book into the one 'Chronological List' which follows the Dedication above; and I have also amalgamated the Index to the *Centurie* with that to these '*Fresh Allusions*.' To the *Centurie* list of Shakspere's Works referd to (p. 469-70) is added

[1] Oh the thick-headedness of boating-men in not taking em up at once!
[2] Want of time must also be my apology for the incompleteness of the Indexes.

the present book's; and the number-summary of it which I made for the *Centurie* in totals—afterwards interestingly split up by the year 1642—is repeated below, with our new additions,[1] just to show that *Hamlet* gets nearly level with Falstaff, and also that *Venus and Adonis* follows *Hamlet* in the list before 1642, and is (as before) so strikingly lessend after it, whereas Falstaff, no. 4 before 1642, becomes no. 1 after it. The later humourous folk were more in number than the earlier amourous ones, at least in Shakspere saws, as is witnest by Trinculo bringing *The Tempest* so far up in the list.

Granting that we have now, in our two Society books, over 600 Allusions to Shakspere ('Allusions' including imitations) in the hundred years since Greene first sneerd at him in 1592, few students will doubt that the number will be largely increast, if not doubled, when the century's plays and other literature are carefully read for the purpose. Many of the plays are not edifying, as occasional dips into the middles of em have shown me. But if one wants nuggets, one mustn't be afraid of a little dirt. In the worst days of the drama, however, the playwrights' minds seem to have been too degraded to have ever read Shakspere. How could they import him into their folly and beastliness?

Two men made me very angry during the course of my work: 'the bog Duffett' (p. 242, 245) for his burlesque of *The Tempest*, and Mr. J. O. Halliwell-Phillipps (Hall-P.—I think all the 'Hells' are alterd; but the best abbreviation for his name is 'Johp') for his veild system of reference,—calling a play by its second title 'Good Luck at Last' (p. 263), instead of its first and better known name, referring vaguely to authorities (see p. 164 below) which ought to have been plainly stated, so that any enquirer might verify the quotation. I rated this sinner soundly to his face for this evil practise; and he answerd, that there was a great art in the giving of references : your object should be, to give enough to inspire confidence in the reader, and yet not enough to enable him to follow you up, and quote any passage from its original, and not from you.[2]

[1] I could not spare the time to be able to guarantee the correctness of my figures; but they are not far off the mark.
[2] See p. 142 below, Johp's omission of Reed.

xx   FOREWORDS.

So in Johp's first 'Life of Shakspere,' no whereabouts of any document printed is given. (But some are stated in the last edition I have seen, that of 1886.) The practise seems to me (as I said to its user) unworthy of him who has done so much good work at Shakspere's personal history. One cannot fancy Dr. Aldis Wright or Mr. P. A. Daniel being guilty of it. Power of verification should be put into every reader's hands, so far as full references are concernd. But to the said Johp, and many other Shakspere students, friends and foes alike, this book is greatly indebted, as the names under the several extracts testify. I haven't wittingly left out the name of any helper. To all of them I return thanks, and specially to Mr. Macray for his fresh *Parnassus* Allusions of 1600; and to Mr. P. A. Daniel for supplying omissions in my entries from the Stationers' Registers. If any extracts are unsigned, they are (I believe) due to me.

I hope the present volume may stimulate other readers of seventeenth-century literature to continue their search for Shakspere Allusions; and wherever they may first print their finds, I trust that they will send them to me, or to our Hon. Sec., in order that these new extracts may find place in another Supplement to the *Centurie* some years hence.

British Museum, 17 *Nov.* 1886, 7.30 *p. m.*

In the *Chronological List* of Allusions I have not included the publications of the Quartos, and the Book-Catalog and Sale entries which immediately follow these Forewords.

TABLE OF
SHAKSPERE QUARTOS
1593—1685

From the New Shakspere Society's Transactions 1874, Pt. I, pp. 43—45.

COMPILED

BY F. G. FLEAY,

FROM THE CAMBRIDGE EDITION;

WITH CORRECTIONS AND ADDITIONS.

EXPLANATION.

A star, *, prefixt to Q (for 'Quarto') means, an edition without Shakspere's name on the title page: a dagger, †, the edition from which, in the opinion of the Cambridge editors, the Folio was printed.

xxii   GROUP I. POEMS.   GROUP II. GENUINE EDITIONS.

Date of Publication.	Name of Work.	EDITION.	PRINTER.	PUBLISHER.	Name of Play.	EDITION.	PRINTER.	PUBLISHER.
1593	Ven. & Ad.	*Quarto 1	R. Field	see Note				
1594	do.	*Q2 from Q1	do.	do.				
,,	Lucrece	*Q1	do.	J. Harrison				
1595								
1596	Ven. & Ad.	*Q3 from Q2	do.	do.				
1597					Richard II.	*Quarto 1	V. Simmes	A. Wise
,,					Richard III.	*Q1	do.	do.
1598	Lucrece	*Q2 from Q1	P. S[hort]	do.	1 Henry IV.	*Q1	P. S[hort]	do.
,,					Richard II.	Q2 from Q1	V. Simmes	do.
,,					Richard III.	Q2 from Q1	T. Creede	do.
1599	Pass. Pilg.	Q1	for W. Jaggard	W. Leake	1 Henry IV.	Q2 from Q1	S. S.	do.
,,	Ven. & Ad.	*Q4 from Q3		do.				
1600	Ven. & Ad.	*Q5 from Q4	J. H[arrison]	J. Harrison	2 Henry IV.	Q1	V. Simmes	A. Wise and W. Aspley
,,	Lucrece	*Q3 from Q2	do.	do.				
,,					Much Ado	†Q1	do.	do.
1602	Ven. & Ad.	*Q6 *Q7 fr. Q5		W. Leake	Richard III.	Q3 from Q2	T. Creede	A. Wise
1603								
1604					1 Henry IV.	Q3 from Q2	V. Simmes	M. Law
1605					Richard III.	Q4 from Q3	T. Creede	do.
1607	Lucrece	*Q4 from Q3	N. O.	J. Harrison				
1608					1 Henry IV.	Q4 from Q3		do.
,,					Richard II.	Q3 from Q2	W. W[aterson]	do.
1609	Sonnets		G. Eld	T. T[horpe] Sold by J. Wright and W. Aspley				
,,					Tr. & Cr.(bis)	Q1	G. Eld	R. Bonian and H. Whalley
1611								
1612	Pass. Pilg.	Q2		W. Jaggard	Richard III.	Q5 from Q3	T. Creede	M. Law
1613					1 Henry IV.	†Q5 from Q4	W. W[aterson]	do.
1615					Richard II.	†Q4 from Q3		do.
1616	Lucrece	Q5	T. S.	R. Jackson				
1617	Ven. & Ad.	*Q8		W. B[arret]				
1619								
1620	do.	*Q9		J. P[arker]				
1622								
,,					Richard III.	Q6 from Q5	T. Purfoot	do.
,,					1 Henry IV.	Q6 from Q5	do.	do.
1624	Lucrece	Q6 from Q5	J. B[enson]	R. Jackson				
1627	Ven. & Ad.	*Q10	J. Wreittoun					
1629					Richard III.	Q7 from Q6	J. Norton	do.
1630	do.	*Q11 ?	do.					
,,	do.	*Q12	J. H.	F. Coules				

GROUP III. MIXED EDITIONS.   GROUP IV. SPURIOUS EDITIONS.   xxiii

Name of Play.	EDITION.	PRINTER.	PUBLISHER.	Name of Play.	EDITION.	PRINTER.	PUBLISHER.	Date of Publication
				† Tit. And.	not extant	J. Danter		1593
				1st Cont.	*Quarto 1	T. Creede	T. Millington	1594
								"
				True Trag.	*Q1	P. S[hort]	do.	1595
								1596
Rom. & Jul.	*Q1 imperf.	J. Danter						1597
								"
Loves Lab. L.	†Q1	W. W[aterson]	C. Burbie					1598
								"
								"
Rom. & Jul.	*Q2	T. Creede	do.					1599
								"
Mids. N. D.	†Q2		J. Roberts	1st Cont.	*Q2 from Q1	V. Simmes	do.	1600
do.	Q1		T. Fisher	True Trag.	*Q2 from Q1	W. W[aterson]	do.	"
Mer. of Ven.	†Q2	J. Roberts	L. Heyes	Henry V.	*Q1 imperf.	T. Creede	T. Millington and T. Busbie	"
do.	Q1	do.		Tit. And.	*Q1	J. R[oberts]	E. White	"
Merry Wives	Q1 imperf.	T. C[reede]	A. Johnson.	Henry V.	*Q2 from Q1	T. Creede	T. Pavier	1602
Hamlet	Q1		N. L[ing] and J. Trundell					1603
do.	Q2	J. R[oberts]	N. L[ing]					1604
do.	Q3 from Q2	do.	do.					1605
								1607
Lear	Q1 Q2		N. Butter	Henry V.	*Q3 from Q1		T. P[avier]	1608
								"
Rom. & Jul.	†*Q3 from Q2		J. Smethwicke	Pericles	Q1 Q2		H. Gosson	1609
†do.	Q4 from Q3		do.					"
Hamlet	Q4 from Q3		do.	do.	Q3 from Q2	S. S.		1611
				Tit. And.	†*Q2 from Q1		E. White	"
								1612
								1613
								1615
								1616
								1617
Merry Wives	Q2 from Q1		A. Johnson	Whole Cont. and Pericles	Q3 from Q2 Q4 from Q3		T. P[avier]	1619
								1620
Othello	Q1	N. O.	T. Walkley					1622
								"
								1624
								1627
								1629
do.	Q2	A. M.	R. Hawkins	Pericles	Q5 (incorrect)	J. N[orton]	R. B[ird]	1630
Merry Wives	Q3 from F1	T. H.	R. Meighen					"

xxiv   GROUP I. POEMS.   GROUP II. GENUINE EDITIONS.

Date of Publication	Name of Work.	EDITION.	PRINTER.	PUBLISHER.	Name of Play.	EDITION.	PRINTER.	PUBLISHER.
1631								
?								
1631								
1637					1 Henry IV.	Q7 from Q6	J. Norton	W. Sheares
1634					Richard II.	Q5 from F2	do.	
"					Richard III.	Q8 from Q7	do.	
1635								
1636	Ven. and Ad.	*Q13	J. H.	F. Coules				
1637								
"								
"								
1639					1 Henry IV.	Q8 from Q7	do.	H. Perry
1640	Poems.		T. Cotes	I. Benson				
1652								
1655								
"								
1676								
1683								
1685								

GROUP III. MIXED EDITIONS.   GROUP IV. SPURIOUS EDITIONS.

Name of Play.	EDITION.	PRINTER.	PUBLISHER.	Name of Play.	EDITION.	PRINTER.	PUBLISHER.	Date of Publication
Loves Lab.L.	Q1 from F1	W. S.	J. Smethwicke					1631
Hamlet	Q5 from Q4	do.	do.					?
Tam. Shrew	Q1 from F1	do.	do.					1631
								1634
								1634
				Pericles	†Q6	T. Cotes		"
								1635
								1636
Hamlet	Q6 from Q5	R. Young	do.					1637
Rom. & Jul.	Q5 from Q4	do.	do.					"
Mer. of Ven.	Q3 from Q2	M. P.	L. Hayes					"
								1639
								1640
do.	Q4 from Q3		W. Leake					1652
Lear	Q3 from Q2	Jane Bell						1655
Othello	Q3 from Q2		do					"
Hamlet								,676
do.	{ Players'							1683
do.	{ Quartos							1685

xxvii

ENTRIES OF SHAKSPERE'S WORKS

IN

THE STATIONERS' REGISTERS 1593—1640

(ED. ARBER).

	[1593] xviij° Aprilis.	(*Arber*, ii. 630)

Richard Feild Assigned ouer to master Harrison senior 25 Junij 1594 |
Entred for his copie vnder thandes of the Archbisshop of Canterbury and master warden Stirrop, a booke intituled / Venus and Adonis. / vj^d ˢ /

[1594] vj^{to} die Februarij. /. (*Arber*, ii. 644)

John Danter./.
Entred for his Copye vnder thandes of bothe the wardens a booke intituled a Noble Roman Historye of Tytus Andronicus • vj^d

[1594] 9 maij. (*Arber*, ii. 648)

Master harrison Senior
Entred for his copie vnder thand of master Cawood Warden, a booke intituled the Ravyshement of Lucrece vj^d C

[1594] 25 Iunij (*Arber*, ii. 655)

Master Harrison Senior
Assigned ouer vnto him from Richard Field in open Court holden this Day a book called Venus and Adonis vj^d
The which was before entred to Richard Field. 18. Aprilis / 1593/

[1596] 25 Iunij (*Arber*, iii. 65)

William leeke
Assigned ouer vnto him for his copie from master harrison thelder, in full Court holden this day. by the said master harrisons consent. A booke called. Venus and Adonis vj^d

* As I hold that Shakspere had no hand in the *Contention* of 1594, I put its entry in a note :

[1594] xij° marcij [*Arber*, ii. 646]

Thomas myilington /
Entred for his copie vnder the handes of bothe the wardens / a booke intituled, the firs'e parte of the Contention of the tw o famous houses of York and Lancaster with the deathe of the good Duke Humfrey and the banishement and Deathe of the Duke of Suffolk and the tragicall ende of the prowd Cardinall of Winchester / with the notable rebellion of Jack Cade and the Duke of Yorkes Firste clayme vnto the Crowne vj^d

'The *Tayminge of a Shrowe*' and 'the famous victories of Henrye the Fyſt' are on ii. 648. A *Rich. III.*, with Shore's wife, on ii. 654.

xxviii   ENTRIES OF SHAKSPERE'S WORKS IN

    [1597] 29 ° Augusti (*Arber*, iii. 89)
Andrew Entred for his Copie by appoyntment from master Warden
Wise./. man / The Tragedye of Richard the Second vj^d

    [1597] 20 Octobris (*Arber*, iii. 93)
Andrew Entred for his copie vnder thandes of master Barlowe, and
wise / master warden man./ The tragedie of kinge Richard the
  Third with the death of the Duke of Clarence vj^d

    [1598] xxv^{to} die Februarij (*Arber*, iii. 105)
Andrew Entred for his Copie vnder thhandes of Master Dix: and
Wyse./. master Warden man a booke intituled The historye of Henry
  the iiijth with his battaile of Shrewsburye against Henry Hott-
  spurre of the Northe with. the conceipted mirthe of Sir John
  Falstoff vj^d./.

    [1598] xvij° Iulij (*Arber*, iii. 122)
James Entred for his copie vnder the handes of bothe the wardens, a
Robertes./ booke of the Marchaunt of Venyce or otherwise called the
  Iewe of Venyce / Prouided that yt bee not prynted by the said
  Iames Robertes or anye other whatsoeuer without lycence first
  had from the Right honorable the lord Chamberlen vj^d

    [1600] 4. Augusti (*Arber*, iii. 37)
  As you like yt / a booke
  Henry the Fift / a booke . . . . . } to be
  The commedie of much A doo about nothing a booke / staied.

    [1600] 14. Augusti (*Arber*, iii. 169)
Thomas Entred for his Copyes by Direction of master white warden
Pavyer vnder his hand wrytinge. These Copyes followinge beinge
  thinges formerlye printed and sett over to the sayd Thomas
  Pavyer
    viz. . . .
  The historye of Henry the Vth with the battell of Agen-
  court vj^d

    [1600] 23 Augusti (*Arber*, iii. 170)
Andrewe Entred for their copies vnder the handes of the wardens Two
Wyse bookes, the one called Muche a Doo about nothinge. Thother
William the second parte of the history of kinge Henry the iiijth with
Aspley the humours of Sir Iohn Fallstaff: Wrytten by master
  Shakespere * xij^d

---

* This is the first time our great poet's name appears in these Registers.
—E. Arber.

	[1600] 28 Octobris (*Arber*, iii. 175)
Thomas haies	Entred for his copie under the handes of the Wardens and by Consent of master Robertes. A booke called the booke of the merchant of Venyce vj^d

	[1602] 18 Ianuarij (*Arber*, iii. 199)
John Busby	Entred for his copie vnder the hand of master Seton / A booke called An excellent and pleasant conceited commedie * of Sir Iohn Faulstof and the merry wyves of Windesor } vj^d Conceited Commedie
Arthure Johnson	Entred for his Copye by assignement from Iohn Busbye, A booke Called an excellent and pleasant conceyted Comedie of Sir Iohn Faulstaff and the merye wyves of Windsor † vj^d

	[1602] 19 aprilis (*Arber*, iii. 204)
Thomas pavier	Entred for his copies by assignement from Thomas millington these bookes following, Saluo Iure cuiuscunque
	viz. . . .
	The first and Second parte of Henry the vj^t ij bookes xij^d
	A booke called Titus and Andronicus vj^d
	Entred by warrant vnder master Setons hand

	[1602] xxvj^{to} Julij (*Arber*, iii. 212)
James Robertes	Entred for his Copie vnder the handes of master Pasfeild and master waterson warden A booke called the Revenge of Hamlett Prince [of] Denmarke as yt was latelie Acted by the Lord Chamberleyne his servantes vj^d

	[1603] 7 februarij (*Arber*, iii. 226)
master Robertes	Entred for his copie in full Court holden this day to print when he hath gotten sufficient authority for yt, The booke of Troilus and Crefseda as yt is acted by my lord Chamberlens Men vj^d

---

* The word *conceited* not being very clearly written in the text, it is repeated at the side as here printed.—E. Arber.

† It is quite clear [that is, there is no reason whatever for supposing] that the *Merry Wives of Windsor* was printed by J. Busby before this date, but not entered in the Registers until he came to assign it [his copyright in the MS play] to A. Johnson. See the similar case of *King Lear* [*Leir* and his Three Daughters; not Shakspere's] at p. 289.—E. Arber.

xxx ENTRIES OF SHAKSPERE'S WORKS IN

[1603]   25 Junij   (*Arber*, iii. 239)
Mathew   Entred for his copies in full courte Holden this Day. These
Lawe   Fyve copies followinge   ij vj^d
                                viz.
          iij enterludes or playes
              The First is of Richard the .3.
              The second of Richard the .2.
              The Third of Henry the .4 the firste part. all kinges
          . . . .
          all whiche by consent of the Company are sett ouer to him from
          Andrew Wyse.*

[1607]   22. Januarij   (*Arber*, iii. 337)
Master   Entred for his copies by direccon of A Court and with con-
Linge   sent of Master Burby vnder his handwrytinge These .iij copies
                                viz.
              Romeo and Iuliett
              Loues Labour Loste
              [The taminge of A Shrewe]   xviij^d R

[1607]   19. Novembris   (*Arber*, iii. 365)
John   Entred for his copies vnder thandes of the wardens. these
Smythick bookes followinge Whiche dyd belonge to Nicholas Lynge
                                viz. . . . . .
              6   A booke called Hamlett   vj^d
              10 Romeo and Iulett   vj^d
              11 Loues Labour Lost   vj^d

[1607]   26 Nouembris   (*Arber*, iii. 366)
Nathanael Entred for their copie vnder thandes of Sir George Buck
Butter   knight and Th wardens A booke called. Master William
John   Shakspeare his historye of Kinge Lear as yt was played
Busby   before the kinges maiestie at Whitehall vppon Sainct Stephens
          night † at Christmas Last by his maiesties servantes playinge
          vsually at the Globe on the Banksyde   vj^d

---

* On 12° Februarij, 1605 (*Arber*, iii. 283), is this entry:

Nathanaell yf he gett good alowance for the enterlude of King Henry the
Butter   8th before he begyn to print it. And then procure the
           wardens handes to yt for the entrance of yt, He is to haue the
           same for his copy

But I do not suppose that this is the spurious play by Fletcher and some
other man which is printed in Shakspere's works. (See Note, p. xxxv,
below.)   † 26 December, 1606.

THE 'STATIONERS' REGISTERS,' 1593--1640.   xxxi

	[1608] 2do die maij (*Arber*, iii. 377.)
Master Pavyer.	Entered for his Copie vnder the handes of master Wilson and master Warden Seton A booke Called A Yorkshire Tragedy written by Wylliam Shakespere vj^d

	[1608] 20 maij. (*Arber*, iii. 378)
Edward Blount	Entred for his copie vnder thandes of Sir George Buck knight and Master Warden Seton A booke called. The booke of Pericles prynce of Tyre vj^d
Edward Blunt	Entred also for his copie by the lyke Aucthoritie. A booke Called, Anthony. and Cleopatra.* vj^d

	[1609] 28^{uo} Januarii / (*Arber*, iii. 400)
Richard Bonion Henry Walleys	Entred for their Copy vnder thandes of Master Segar deputye to Sir George Bucke and master warden Lownes a booke called the history of Troylus and Cressida vj^d /

	[1614] primo Martij. 1613. (*Arber*, iii. 542)
Roger Jackson	Entred for his Coppies by consent of Master John Harrison the eldest and by order of a Court, these 4 bookes followinge ij^s
	vizt . . . . Lucrece †

	8° Julij 1619 (*Arber*, iii. 651)
Lawrence Hayes	Entred for his Copies by Consent of a full Court theis two Copies following which were the Copies of Thomas Haies his fathers
	viz. A play Called The Marchant of Venice xij^d

. . . .

	6° Octobris 1621 (*Arber*, iv. 59)
Thomas Walkley	Entred for his copie vnder the handes of Sir George Buck, and Master Swinhowe warden, The Tragedie of Othello, the moore of Venice. vj^d

* A Romane tragedie called 'The Rape of Lucrece', enterd on June 3 1608, *Arber*, iii. 380, is not the 1607 edition of Shakspere's poem of the same name.

† Harrison brought out the first four editions of *Lucrece* in 1594, 1598, 1600, and 1607. He sold the book to Roger Jackson in 1614 ; and Jackson publisht the 5th edition in 1616, and the 6th in 1624.

xxxii ENTRIES OF SHAKSPERE'S WORKS IN

      8° Nouembris 1623 (*Arber*, iv. 107)

Master Blounte Isaak Jaggard Entred for their Copie vnder the hands of Master Doctor Worrall and Master Cole warden Master William Shakspeer's Comedyes Histories, and Tragedyes soe manie of the said Copies as are not formerly entred to other men. vizt vij^s

Comedyes
- The Tempest
- The two gentlemen of Verona
- Measure for Measure
- The Comedy of Errors
- As you like it
- All's well that ends well
- Twelfe night
- The winters tale

Histories
- The thirde parte of Henry ye sixt
- Henry the eight

Tragedies
- Coriolanus
- Timon of Athens
- Julius Cæsar
- Mackbeth
- Anthonie and Cleopatra
- Cymbeline

  [1626] 16°· Januarij 1625 (*Arber*, iv. 149)

Francis Williams Assigned ouer vnto him by mistris Jackson wife of Roger Jackson Deceased, and by order of a full Court holden this Day. all her estate in the Copies here after mencioned xiiij^s

 . . . .

23 Lucrece by Shackspeare

      7° Maij 1626 (*Arber*, iv. 160)

John Haviland John Wright Assigned ouer vnto them by master Parker and by Consent of master Islip warden A booke called Venus and Adonis vj^d

      4° Augusti 1626 (*Arber*, iv. 164-5)

Edward Brewster Robert Birde Assigned ouer vnto them by Mistris Pavier and Consent of a full Court of Afsistantes all the estate right title and Interest which Master Thomas Pavier her late husband had in the Copies here after mencioned xxviij^s

More to Edward Brewster
- The history of Henry the fift and the play of the same . . .
- Master Paviers right in Shakesperes plaies or any of them . .
- Tytus and Andronicus . . . .
- Historye of Hamblett

THE 'STATIONERS' REGISTERS,' 1593-1640. xxxiii

                [? 19 June 1627]   (*Arber*, iv. 182)

Thomas Cotes
Richard Cotes
    Assigned ouer vnto him by Dorathye Jaggard widowe and Consent of a full Court holden this Day, All the estate right title and Interest which Isaacke Jaggard her late husband had in the Copies following   xjˢ vjᵈ
                vizᵗ /....
her parte in Shackspheere playes./

      [1628]   jᵐᵒ Martij 1627   (*Arber*, iv. 194)

Master Richard Hawkins
    Assigned ouer vnto him by Thomas Walkeley, and Consent of a Court holden this Day all the estate right title and Interest which he hath in these Copies following   xviijᵈ
                vizᵗ /...
Othello the more of Venice.

      [1630]   29 Januarij 1629.   (*Arber*, iv. 227)

Master Meighen
    Assigned ouer vnto him by master Johnson and Consent of Master Purfoote Warden, All the said master Johnsons estate in the 4 Copies hereafter menconed   vizᵗ /   ijˢ
. . . .
The merry Wives of Winsor

             29 Junij 1630   (*Arber*, iv. 237)

Master Harison
    Assigned ouer vnto him by master Francis Williams and order of a full Court all his estate right title and Interest in the Copies hereafter menconed   xijˢ vjᵈ /
                viz.ᵗ ....
Lucrece

         8° Nouembris 1630 /   (*Arber*, iv. 242)

Richard Cotes
    Assigned ouer vnto him by master Bird and Consent of a full Court holden this day All his estate right and interest in the Copies hereafter menconed   iiijˢ
    Henrye the fift . . .
    Titus and Andronicus . . . .
    Persiles [or rather Pericles ; III. 378—*Arber*]
    Hamblet
    [Yorkeshire Tragedie]

         16 November 1630   (*Arber*, iii. 242-3)

Master Allott
    Memorandum master Blount assigned ouer vnto him all his estate and right in the Copies hereafter menconed as appeareth by a note vnder master Blountes hand, Dated the 26 of June 1630 in the time of master Warden Purfoote, his [or rather whose—*Arber*] hand is subscribed therevnto /   vijˢ

FRESH ALLUSIONS.   c

xxxiv ENTRIES OF SHAKSPERE'S WORKS IN

    The Tempest
    Two gentlemen of Verona
    Measure for measure
    Comedie of Errors
    As you like it
    All^s well that endes well
    Twelfe night
    Winters tale *
    3 part of Henry .6^t
    Henry : the 8^t
. Coriolanus

    Timon of Athens
. Julius Cæsar.
    Mackbeth.
    Antony and Cleopatra.
    Cymbolyne.

    [1634]   8° Aprilis   (*Arber*, iv. 316)

Master John Waterson — Entred for his Copy vnder the hands of Sir Henry Herbert and master Aspley warden a TragiComedy called the two noble kinsmen by John Fletcher and William Shakespeare   vj^d

    19° Augusti 1635.   (*Arber*, iv. 346)

Master John Waterson — Entred for his Copies by order of a full Court and by vertue of a Noate vnder the hand and seale of Master Simon Waterson and subscribed by both the wardens All the copies and parts of Copies which did belong vnto the said Master Simon waterson and are hereafter expressed   viij^s

    (vizt) . . . .
    The Tragedy of Cleopatra

    1° Julij 1637.   (*Arber*, iv. 387-8)

Master Legatt and Andrew Crooke — Entred for their Copies by Consent of Mistris Allott and by order of a full Court holden the Seauenth day of Nouember last [1636] All the Estate Right Title and Interest which the said Master Allott hath in these Copies and parts of Copies hereafter following which were Master Roberte Allotts deceased saluo Jure cuiuscunque   xxx^s· vj^d·

    . . . .
    37. Shakespeares workes their Part.

---

* *A Wynters nightes pastime*, enterd on May 22, 1594 (*Transcript*, ii. 650), is referd to by Prof. Arber. It may possibly have been a source of Shakspere's play, if he ever saw it.

THE 'STATIONERS' REGISTERS,' 1593—1640.   xxxv

      29⁰· Maij 1638 (*Arber*, iv. 420)

Master
Mead
and
Mister
Meredith

Entred for their Copies by order of a full Court held the fifth day of June Last [1637] according to the request of vrsula Hawkins widdow (laste wife of Richard Hawkins deceased) then present in Court all these Copies and parts of Copies following which did belong vnto her said husband as followeth. xijˢ vjᵈ

 · · · · · · · · ·

Orthello the More of Venice a play.

      4⁰. die Septembris 1638 (*Arber*, iv. 431)

Master
John
Haviland
and
John
Wright
senior

Entred for their Copies according to a note vnder the hand and Seale of the said Master Haviland and subscribed by Master Mead warden these Copies and parts of Copies following Saluo Jure cuiuscunque the same being the proper Copies and parts of Copies of the said Master Haviland xvˢ

 · · · · · · · · ·

Venus and Adonis.

    1639. 25ᵗʰ. of Januarij 1638 (*Arber*, iv. 452-3).

Master
William
Leake

Assigned ouer vnto him by vertue of a warrant vnder the hands and seales of Master Mead and Master Meredith and with the Consent of a full Court of Assistants holden this day. All the Estate Right Title and Interest which the said Master Mead and Master Meredith haue in these Copies and partes of Copies following which were Entred vnto them from Mistris Hawkins the 29ᵗʰ of May last [1638] xijˢ vjᵈ·

 · · · · · · · · ·

Orthello the More of Venice a Play.

      21⁰. Maij 1639 (*Arber*, iv. 456)

Master
Flesher

Assigned ouer vnto him by vertue of a note vnder the hand and seale of Master Butter, subscribed by both the wardens and alsoe by order of a full Court hol len the Eleaventh day of May last [1639]. All the Estate right title and interest which the said Master Butter hath in these Copies and parts of Copies following (vizᵗ) saluo iure cuiuscunque xijs. vjᵈ.

The history of King Lear. by William Shakspeare*

* 'The Roman Tragedy called the Rape of Lucrece' is the next entry. See p. xxxi, note*, abov. An entry before Lear is

   'The Interlude of King Henry the Eight.'

This is, says Mr. Daniel, "Rowley's *Where you see me you know me. Or the famous Chronile History of King Henry the eight*, etc. Printed for N. Butter 1605. There can be no doubt it's the same play, entered to Butter 12 Feby, 1605, [*Arber*, iii. 283] and now transferred by him to Flesher. There were editions of it 1605, 1613, 1621, 1632, all published by Butter. Butter gave up work in 1640. From the above entry, 21 May, 1639, it is clear he was now disposing of his old stock."

1639

4°. Nouembris 1639 . . . . eodem die (*Arber*, iv. 487)

John Benson. Entred for his Copie vnder the hands of doctor Wykes and Master Fetherston warden An Addicion of some excellent Poems to Shakespeares Poems by other gentlemen.[1] vizt. His mistris·drawne. and her mind by Beniamin : Johnson. An Epistle to Beniamin Johnson by Francis Beaumont./ His Mistris shade. by R : Herrick. &c. . . . .   vj^d

These are "An Addition of some Excellent Poems, to those precedent, of Renowmed Shakespeare, By other Gentlemen,"[2] as the head-title (sign. I 2] of the 1640 edition of Shakspere's Poems[3] says. They occupy the last eleven pages of that edition. The head-title ought to have been given on p. 229 of *The Centurie*, or to have followd the Commendatory Verses, &c. on p. 231-5. It might well have been in the present volume under 1640 too.

---

[1] As Shakspere's own Poems had been enterd on the Registers before, only the Additions had to be enterd in 1639.

[2] Some of these poems are copied from Thomas Heywood's General History of Women.—Bohn's *Lowndes*, p. 2307, col. 2.

[3] Prefixed to this edition, principally consisting of translations which never proceeded from Shakspere's pen, is a portrait of Shakspere, W. M(arshall) sculpsit.—Bohn's *Lowndes*, p. 2307, col. 2.

BOOK-CATALOGS.

[1660-]1680. R. CLAVELL.

The Names of fuch Playes as have been printed fince 1660.
Antony and *Cleopatra*[1], T[2] . . . . .
Henry the Fifth, T[3] . . . . .
Hamlet Prince of *Denmark*, T[4] . . . . .
Macbeth, T.[5] . . . . .
Tempeſt, C.[6] . . . . .
Troylus and *Creſſyda*, T.[7] . . .

> The / General Catalogue / of / Books, / Printed in / England / Since the Dreadful Fire of London / MDCLXVI. To the End of *Trinity*-/ *Term* MDCLXXX. / Together with the Texts of Single Sermons, / With the Authors Names: Playes Acted at both the / Theaters: And an Abstract of the General Bills of / Mortality since 1660. With an Account of the / Titles of all the Books of *Law*, *Navi-/ gation*, *Musick*, &c./ And a Catalogue of / School Books./ To which is now added a Catalogue of Latin Books / Printed in Foreign Parts and in *England* / since the Year MDCLXX./ Collected by *R. Clavell*. / *London*, / Printed by *S. Roycroft* for *Robert Clavell* at the / *Peacock* in St. *Paul's Church-Yard*. / 1680./

The edition of 1699 has these entries :

Poetry (p. 107).

Shakespear's Venus and Adonis. J. Wright

[1] ? By Sir C. Sedley, 1677, 4to.   [2] Tragedy. 'C.' is Comedy.
[3] By the Earle of Orrery, 1672, fol.
[4] Publ. by Andrew Clark, 1676, 4to.
[5] With Sir Wm. Davenant's alterations, &c., 1673, 1674, 4to.
[6] ? By Dryden and Davenant, 1669, 1670, 1674, 1676, 4to.
[7] ? By Dryden, 1679, 4to.

(p. 108). **Plays Printed or Reprinted since 1660.**

A
Antony and Cleopatra. T. . . .

H
Henry the V. T.
Hamlet Prince of *Denmark.* T.
History of King *Lear.*
History of King Richard II
Henry the 6th in two Parts.

I
Julius Cæsar. T.

M.
Macbeth. T.

O.
Othello Moor *Venice.* T.

T
Tempest. C.
Titus Andronicus. T.
Timon of Athens . . . .
Shakespear's Plays. Reprinted.

1673.

Numb. 13.

A CATALOGUE of BOOKS Continued, Printed and Publifhed in *London,* in *Eafter Term,* 1673.

Licenfed *May* 6. 1673. *Roger L'Eftrange.*

Poetry and Plays.

Mackbeth. A Tragedy[1] acted at the Dukes Theatre. In quarto, price ftitcht 1*s.* Printed for *W. Cadman* at the Popes Head in the *New Exchange.* (sign. Q bk, col. 2)

[1] With all the alterations, amendments, additions, and New Songs, by Sir William Davenant. Also in 1674.

1674.
                                    Numb. 18.
A CATALOGUE of BOOKS Continued, Printed and Publifhed
in *London* in *Trinity Term*, 1674.

Licenfed *July* 6. 1674.   *Roger L'Eſtrange.*

Poetry and Plays.

Macbeth, a Tragedy ; with all the Alterations, Amendments, Additions, and new Songs[1] : As it is now Acted at the Dukes Theatre : In quarto : price flicht 1s.   (sign. C c 2, col. 2)

1675.
                                    Numb. 1.
A CATALOGUE of BOOKS Continued, Printed and Publifhed
at *London* in *Michaelmas Term*, 1674 [1675]

Licenfed *Novemb.* 25. 1674. *Roger L'Eſtrange.*

Poetry and Plays . . . .

The Tempeſt or the Inchanted Iſland[2] : A Comedy as it is now acted at his Royal Highneſs the Duke of *York*'s Theatre[3] ; in quarto ; price 1s. . . . printed for *Harry Herringman* in the *New Exchange*.   (sign. A2, bk. col. 2)

[1] By Sir William Davenant.
[2] By John Dryden and Sir Wm. Davenant.
[3] Duffett's *Mock-Tempest* (p. 242, *Fresh Allusions*) is enterd in Number 2 (Hilary Term, 1674-5), sign C. back, col. 2.

1676.
Numb. 6.

A CATALOGUE of Books Continued, Printed, and Publiſhed at *London* in *Hilary-Term*, 1675[-6].

Licenſed *Feb.* 10. 1675[-6]. *Roger L'Eſtrange.*

Poetry and Plays. [p. 2, col. 1] sign. I, bk.
The Tragedy of *Hamlet*, Prince of *Denmark*, as it is now acted at his Highneſs the Duke of *Yorks* Theatre. By *Will. Shakeſpear*, in *quarto*, price ſtitcht 1s. printed for *J. Martyn*, and *H. Herringman*, at the Bell in St. *Pauls* Churchyard, and the Blew-Anchor in the *New-Exchange.*

Books Reprinted.
Venus and *Adonis*, a Poem. By *Will Shakeſpear*, price 6d. Printed for *F. Coles, T. Vere, J. Wright,* and *J. Clark.* [sign. I2 bk. col. 2]

1680 (?)
English in Quarto.

6 { Volume of 4 Plays. Tyrannick Love, Tempeſt,[1] Villain, Tartuffe. And a defence of an Eſſay of Dramatique Poeſie. [sold for "0—4—1".] ....

11 { —— Of 16 Old Plays, by *Beaumont* and *Fletcher* (viz.) *Thierry* and *Theodoret, Cupids* Revenge, King and no King, Monſieur *Tho.* Faithful Shepherdeſs, *Philaſter,* Two Noble Kinſmen[2], Maids Tragedie ....

[The above entries are on p. 66 of the *Bibliotheca Biſſeana:* the Catalog of the books of Sir Edward Byſhe, Clarencieux King of Arms (who died Dec. 15, 1679[3]) to be ſold by Auction at the Woolſack in Ivy Lane near Pater-Noſter-Row, on Nov. 15, (? 1680,) tho' the Catalog implies his being alive.]

[1] Dryden's recast.
[2] I suppose this had Shakspere's name on the Title-page, as in the original Quarto.
[3] See his Life by Thomson Cooper in *Dict. National Biography.*

BOOK-CATALOGS.

1681.   **Numb.** 5.

A CATALOGUE of Books Continued, Printed and Publiſhed at *LONDON*, In *Michaelmas* Term. 1681.

Reprinted . . .

Othello, the Moor of *Venice*. A Tragedy, as it hath been divers times acted at the Globe, and at the *Black-Fryers*, and now at the Theatre Royal, by his Majeſties Servants. Written by *William Shakeſpear*.[1] quarto: price 1s.

1683, 1684.   **Numb.** 13.

A CATALOGUE of Books Continued, Printed, and Publiſhed at *LONDON*, in *Michaelmas*-Term, 1683.

Reprinted.

[22. The Rehearſal . . . . .]

23. The Tragedy of *Hamlet* Prince of *Denmark*, as it is now acted[2] at his Highneſs the Duke of *York*'s Theatre, by *William Shakeſpeare*, both printed for *R. Bently*, in Ruſſel ſtreet in Covent Garden.   (sign. Kk 2, col. 1)

[1684]   **Numb.** 14.

A CATALOGUE of Books Continued, Printed and Publiſhed at LONDON in *Hillary*-Term, 1683/4.

Reprinted.

8. *Julius Cæsar*, a Tragedy, as it is acted at the Theatre Royal; Written by *W. Shakeſpear*, quarto, price 1s. Sold by *R. Bentley* in *Ruſſel-ſtreet* in *Covent*-garden, *J. Knight* and *F. Saunders* on the New Exchange.

[1] Alterd by Dryden. Other editions in 1670, 1674, 1687.
[2] Hamlet, by Betterton. 'In this edition . . . Hamlet's instructions to the players are marked for omission.'—Bohn's *Lowndes*, 2277, col. 2.

1686.

Catalogi / Variorum / In Quavis / Lingua & Facultate / Insigniam / Tam Antiquorum quam Recentium / Librorum / Richardi Davis Bibliopolæ. Pars Secunda./ Quorum Auctio (in gratiam & commodum Eruditorum) Oxoniæ habenda eſt è regione / Ecclefiæ D. Michaelis, Octobris 4, 1686. . . . .
(p. 114) 457 Shakefpear's (Will.) Comedies Hiſtories and Tragidies [so] Lond. 1685.[1]

1687.

[2] A / Catalogue / of the Libraries / of / Mr. *Jn. Copping*, late of *Sion Colledge*, Gent. / and / *Anfcel Beaumont*, late of the *Middle Temple*, Esq ; / With others / . . which are / to be expofed to Sale by way of *Auction* at / *Jonathan's* Coffee-Houfe, in *Exchange-Alley* in *Cornhil*, / London, on *Monday* the 21ſt Day of March 168$\frac{6}{7}$

p. 2. Divinity, Hiſtory, &c, in Folio.
62 Shakefpears Plays.

[1] In the Catalog 'Bibliothecæ Nobilissimæ' to be sold at 'Roll's Auction-House in Petty-Canon Hall in Petty-Canon Alley,' in St. Paul's Churchyard, Feb. 169$\frac{4}{5}$, No. 597 is '*Shakespear's* Plays, 1664'.

[2] This *Richard III* in a Booksale Catalog of 1681, is not Shakspere's: see Bohn's *Lowndes*, p. 2085, col. 2:
"Catalogus Librorum . . Gvlielmi Ovtrami . . Nec non . . D. Thomæ . Gatakeri . . . . Quorum Auctio habebitur Londini, ex Adverso Areæ Warwicensis, in Vico vulgo dicto 𝔚𝔞𝔯𝔴𝔦𝔠𝔥-𝔍𝔲𝔫𝔱, 12 Decembris 1681. Per *Gulielmum Cooper* Bibliopolam. p. 61. Volumes of Tracts in Quarto. 12 . . . King Richard the third reviv'd, *London* 1657."
At the sale of the books of Stephen Watkins, Dr. Thomas Sherley and another, held at the sign of the Golden Lion, opposite the Queen's Head in Pater-Noster-Row, on June 2 [print '*Maii*' corrected] 1679, among the 'Manuscripts in Folio,' p. 30, No. "322 *Richardus Tertius*, 2 parts ; a sort of Play in Latine Verse," was sold for 6*d*.—"0—0—6."— Brit. Mus. 821. i. 1, art. 10.

1687.
                                    Numb. 25.
A Catalogue of Books Continued, Printed and Publiſhed at *London* in *Hillary*-Term, 168$\frac{6}{7}$

Poems, Plays.

3. *Titus Andronicus,* or the Rape of *Lavinia*, acted at the Theatre Royal, a Tragedy altered from Mr. *Shakeſpear's* Works, by Mr. *Ed. Ravenſcroft*, quarto. Printed for *J. Hindmarſh* at the Golden Ball in *Cornhill.*   (sign. M m m, bk. col. 2.)

1690.
                                    Numb. 37.
A Catalogue of Books Continued, Printed and Publiſhed at *London*, in *Trinity*-Term, 1690 . . . .

Reprinted.

· 10. The Tempeſt, or the Enchanted Iſland,[1] a Comedy, as it is now acted at Their Majesty's Theatre, 4to. Theſe three[2] printed for *R. Bentley* at the *Poſt-houſe* in *Ruſſel-ſtreet, Covent-Garden.* (sign. Q q q q, col. 2)

1691.
                                    Numb. 42.
A Catalogue of Books Continued, Printed / and Publiſhed in *London* in *Michaelmas*=Term, 1691.

Reprinted. .

30. *Julius Cæſar:* a Tragedy, as it is now acted at their Majesties Theatre-Royal, written by *William Shakeſpear:* 4to. price 12d.[3]

[1] By Dryden and Davenant.
[2] '8. The Kind Keeper, or Mr. *Limberham*'; & 9. The 'Rival Queens, or the death of *Alexander* the Great,' are the other two.
[3] Earlier editions: 'Lond. *n. d.* (1680) 4to. On the reverse of the title is a List of the Actors, in which Betterton is set down for acting Brutus.— Lond. 1684, 4to.'—Bohn's *Lowndes*, 2283, col. 1.

BOOK-SALE-CATALOG.

35. The Tempeſt, or the Enchanted Iſland,[1] a Comedy: As it is now aƈted at their Majeſties Theatre in *Dorſet-garden*, 4to. price 12d.

29 NOVEMBER, 1687.

On Tueſday *the* 29th. *of this Inſtant* November, 1687. *at the* Black-Swan *in St.* Pauls-Church-Yard, *amongſt the Woollen-Drapers; will be Sold by Auƈtion the Engliſh part of the Library, of the (Rev. Mr. W.* Sill *late Prebend of* Weſtminſter, *Deceaſed*) *conſiſting of Divinity, Hiſtory, Philology, &c. in all Volumes Curiouſly Bound* . . . . . .
  (p. 91) Engliſh Miſcellanies in Folio.
  (p. 93) 98. W. Shakeſpear's *Comedies,* Hiſtories and Tragedies [2]
. . Lond. 1632.

[1] This edition of 1691 isn't noted in Bohn's *Lowndes,* 2299, col. 1.
[2] (No.) 156. *Stubbs* his Anatomy of Abuses. Both Parts—1584 (p. 101).

FRESH ALLUSIONS TO SHAKSPERE

FIRST PERIOD.

1592—1616.

(*From Greene's first Allusion, to Shakspere's Death.*)

HENRY HELMES, 1594.

In regard whereof. . . it was thought good not to offer any thing of Account, saving Dancing and Revelling with Gentlewomen; and after such Sports, a Comedy of Errors (like to Plautus his *Menechmus*) was played by the Players. So that Night was begun, and continued to the end, in nothing but Confusion and Errors; whereupon, it was ever afterwards called *The Night of Errors*.

Gesta Grayorum,[1] p. 22, ed. 1688. (Nichols's *Progresses of Queen Elizabeth*, iii. 279 (2nd ed. 1823).

This *Comedy of Errors* was, without doubt, Shakspere's. It was playd in Gray's Inn Hall on the night of Innocents' Day, Dec. 28, 1594, and most probably Shakspere and Bacon were both at the performance. See Spedding's *Letters and Life of Bacon*, i. 326. There was such a row and such crowding by Gentlewomen and others on the Stage, that the Temple visitors to Gray's Inn went away disgusted, and so the Gray's-men had only dancing and Shakspere's play.—F. J. F.

---

[1] The full title of the book—printing its red letters in italics—is :—*Gesta Grayorum :* / Or, the / History / Of the High and mighty Prince, / *Henry* / Prince of *Purpoole*, Arch-Duke of *Stapulia* and / *Bernardia*, Duke of *High* and *Nether Holborn*, / Marquis of St. *Giles* and *Tottenham*, Count / Palatine of *Bloomsbury* and *Clerkenwell*, Great / Lord of the Cantons of *Islington*, *Kentish-/Town*, *Paddington* and *Knights-bridge*, / Knight of the most Heroical Order of the / *Helmet*, and Sovereign of the *Same* ; / Who Reigned and Died, A.D. 1594. / Together with / *A Masque*, as it was presented (by *His Highness's* Command) for the Entertainment of *Q. Elizabeth* ; / who, with the *Nobles* of both *Courts*, was present / thereat. / *London*, Printed for *W. Canning*, at his Shop in / the *Temple-Cloysters*, / MDCLXXXVIII. / Price, one Shilling. / It's a jocose account of the Gray's-Inn men's entertainment to their brethren of the Temple, the Queen, &c. *Stapulia* and *Bernardia* are Staples Inn and Barnards Inn. It includes only the first Part of Helmes's MS. Nichols printed the second Part in the 1st ed. of his *Progresses of Q. Eliz.*

1597—1603.

William Shakefpeare

Rychard the fecond   Shakefpeare

Rychard the third

hakfpeare reuealing
day through
euery Crany   by Thomas Nafhe & inferior places [1]
peepes and
fee your

William Shakefpeare
              Sh
Shak   h   Sh   Shake   hakefpeare
Sh   h Shak your

william Shakefpeare
william Shakefpeare

Willi   Shakfpeare
william
Shakefpe
will Shak

Title-page of the Duke of Northumberland's MS. of Lord Bacon's " Of Tribute, or giving what is dew," facsimiled in the late James Spedding's edition of " A Conference of Pleasure, composed for some Festive Occasion about the year 1592 by Francis Bacon," p. xxxiii. (Longmans, 1870).

The MS., now incomplete, containd several Essays, Speeches and Tracts by Bacon. After the list of these on the title, follows, among other words and scribbles, the names of Shakspere's two plays and himself, and (as Dr. Ingleby notes) line 1086 and part of 1087 of the *Rape of Lucrece*, with one word wrong, *peepes* (? caught by error of memory from 'peeping,'

---

[1] ? for 'plaiers.'

l. 1089) for *spies*. If the scribbler meant to put Shakspere's name to his *Lucrece* bit, this is the earliest quotation from S. with his name to it. Mr. Spedding says, *Introduction*, p. xxii :—

"That 'Richard the second' and 'Richard the third' are meant for the titles of *Shakespeare's* plays so named, I infer from the fact—of which the evidence may be seen in the *facsimile*—that, the list of contents being now complete, the writer (or more probably another into whose possession the volume passed) has amused himself with writing down promiscuously the names and phrases that most ran in his head ; and that among these the name of *William Shakespeare* was the most prominent, being written eight or nine times over for no other reason than can be discerned [1] . . (p. xxiii) . . the date of the writing . . I fear cannot be determined with any approach to exactness. All I can say is, that I find nothing in these later scribblings, or in what remains of the book itself, to indicate a date later than the reign of Elizabeth [2] ; and if so, it is probably one of the earliest evidences of the growth of Shakespeare's *personal* fame as a dramatic author ; the beginning of which cannot be dated much earlier than 1598. It was not until 1597 that any of his plays appeared in print ; and though the earliest editions of Richard II, Richard III, and Romeo and Juliet, all bear that date, his name is not on the title-page of any of them. They were set forth as plays which had been 'lately,' or 'publicly,' or 'often with great applause' acted by the Lord Chamberlain's servants. Their title to favour was their popularity as acting plays at the Globe [3] ; and it was not till they came to be read as books that it occurred to people unconnected with the theatre to ask who wrote them. It seems, however, that curiosity was speedily and effectually excited by the publication ; for in the very next year a second edition of both the Richards appeared with the name of William Shakespeare on the title-page ; and the practice was almost invariably followed by all publishers on like occasions afterwards. We may conclude, therefore, that it was about 1597 that play-goers and readers of plays began to talk about him, and that his name would naturally present itself to an idle penman in want of something to use his pen upon."—F. J. F.

---

[1] It does not seem to have been written at the same time with the titles, or by the same hand.

[2] I agree.—F.

[3] That is, the "*Theatre*" : the *Globe* or transferrd and rebuilt "*Theatre*" was not built till 1598-9.

I. M. 1598.

I verily beleeue his preferment fhould be rather a Remuneration then a Guerdon, if he get any in this Leaden and laft age. But what is the difference betwixt the Remuneration and the Guerdon, may fome fay, we would faine know: otherwife we can not tell how you meane this well qualited Seruingmans defartes fhould be rewarded. Your queftion is reafonable, and therefore I will diftinguifh them as their difference was tolde me not long fince by a friende of mine.

There was, fayth he, a man (but of what eftate, degree, or calling, I will not name, leaft thereby I might incurre difpleafure of any) that comming to his friendes houfe, who was a Gentleman of good reckoning, and being there kindly entertayned, and well vfed, as well of his friende the Gentleman, as of his Seruantes: one of the fayd Seruantes doing him fome extraordinarie pleafure during his abode there; at his departure he comes vnto the fayd Seruant, and faith vnto him, Holde thee, heere is a remuneration for thy paynes, which the Seruant receyuing, gave him vtterly for it (befides his paynes) thankes, for it was but a Three-farthinges peece: and I holde thankes for the fame a fmall price, howfoeuer the market goes. Now an other comming to the faid Gentlemans houfe, it was the forefayd Seruants good hap to be neare him at his going away, who calling the Seruant vnto him, fayd, Holde thee, heere is a Guerdon for thy defartes: Now the Seruant

I. M. 1598.

payde no deerer for the Guerdon then he did for the Remuneration, though the Guerdon was xi. d. farthing better, for it was a Shilling, and the other but a Three-farthinges.

> A | *Health to the* | *Gentlemanly pro-* | *fession of Seruing men : or, The Seruingmans* | *Comfort :* | *With other thinges not impertinent* | *to the Premisses, as well pleasant* | *as profitable to the cour-* | *teous Reader.* | *Felix qui socij nauim perijsse procellis* | *cum vidit, in tutum flectit sua carbasa portum.* | *Imprinted at London by W. W.* | 1598. *Sig. I.* (*Roxburghe Library Reprint*, p. 159.)

Steevens quoted this passage as the original of Costard's remarks (*L. L. Lost*, III. i.), giving the date 1578. Farmer afterwards stated that this date was incorrect. The true date is 1598 ; and perhaps some of the wording and the rather elaborate introduction of the story, in the first paragraph, seem to point to I. M.'s "friend" having been Costard himself, who was introduced to the reading public by the first Quarto of *L. L. L.* in 1598, and no doubt played long before he " was presented before her Highness this last Christmas," at Whitehall,[1] 1597.—B. Nicholson.

In his *Mem. on L. L. L.*, &c., 1879, Mr. Hall.-Phillipps says on p. 65— " In MS. Addit. 14,047 in the British Museum is preserved a copy of a play called Love's Hospital dated in 1636. On the flyleaf of this manuscript is written,—

Loues Hospitall.
Leues Labores Lost.

a circumstance which would appear to show that about that period there was in existence a manuscript transcript of Shakespeare's comedy originally bound up with the other play."

This is a mere mare'snest. I have examind the Addit. MS. It is one originally of 3 plays by George Wilde, LL.B., Fellow of St. John's, Oxford ; and contains these 3 plays by him, written in this order in the MS. : "*Loves Hospitall* as it was acted before the Kinge & Queens Majestyes by the students of S^t Jo. Baptists Coll. in Oxon : Augustij 29º. 1636," " *The converted Robber* A Pastorall Acted by s^t Johns College. 1637 " (lf 44 bk), and a Latin comedy "*Eumorphus* sive *Cupido Adultus*. Comœdia Acta

---

[1] to Richard Brakenburie, for altering and making readie of soundrie chambers at Whitehall against Christmas, and for the plaies, and for making ready in the hall for her Majestie, and for altering and hanging of the chambers after Christmas daie, by the space of three daies, mense Decembris, 1597, viij.*li.* xiij.*s.* iiij*d.*—Hll.-P.'s *Memoranda*, p. 59.—F.

6   MARESNESTS ABOUT *LOVES LABOUR'S LOST.*

A Joan*n*ensib*us.* Oxon. Feb. 5°. 1634." On the blank leaves are written poems by later hands; and on the first flyleaf are some lines, names, and scribblings, in three or four hands. Among the names, in one of the later hands, is, under an older "Loves Hospitall,"

"Loues Hospitall,
Loues Labores Lost"

The entry therefore no more implies the existence then of a MS. of Shakspere's play, than it does that all later readers of the entry should be reasonable beings. Wilde's 'Loves Hospitall' is followd by his 'Converted Robber,' and there is no possibility of 'Loues Labores Lost' having followd the former play, or the *Eumorphus,* in the MS.

Another suggestion by Mr. Hall.-P. with regard to *L. L. L.* must also be set down as worthless. He says (*Mem. on L. L. L.,* &c., p. 70)[1]—

"I have a memorandum that the name of the comedy was perhaps suggested by lines in the Handful of Pleasant Delights, 1584, "ye loving wormes," &c., sig. C 6, but I have no convenient means just now of referring to that work."

The little *Handful,* by Clement Robinson and others, is known to Shakspere students from Ophelia's supposd allusion to a line of its first poem—
"A Nosegaie alwaies / sweet, for Louers to send for Tokens, / of loue, at Newyeres tide, or for fairings, / as they in their minds shall be disposed to write,"—namely·

"¶ *Rosemarie* is for remembrance,
    betweene vs daie and night :
    Wishing that I might alwaies haue,
    you present in my sight."

· The "labour lost" passage on C 6 comes thus :—

"¶ *A warning for Wooers, that they be not ouer hastie, nor deceiued with womens beautie. To, Salisburie Plaine.*

YE louing wormes come learne of me
The plagues to leaue [*for* loue] that linked be :
The grudge, the grief, the gret anoy,
The fickle faith, the fading ioy :
in time, take heed,

---

[1] Before accepting the copy of a possibly correct copy of the possibly genuine audit accounts of 1605 as "authentic" (*ib.* p. 62) evidence of the playing of *L. L. Lost* on New Years Day and Twelfth Day 1605 before James I, I must see the original accounts.

In fruitlesse soile sow not thy seed :
   buie not, with cost,
   the thing that yeelds but labour lost.
      *   *   *
        Flie baits, shun hookes,
Be thou not snarde with louely lookes
  *   *   *   *   *
        But hie or lowe,
Ye may be sure she is a shrow.
¶ But sirs, I vse to tell no tales,
Ech fish that swims doth not beare scales,
In euerie hedge I finde not thornes :
Nor euerie beast doth carie hornes :
   I saie not so,
That euerie woman causeth wo :
   That were too broad,
Who loueth not venom must shun the toade. . . ."

    The object of the poem has nothing to do with that of Shakspere's play. He sets up women as the teachers of men, wiser and truer far than they, and shows the treasure of their love, only to be bought at the cost of self-control and humanizing work.—F. J. F.

* R. S. 1598.

[Flora] . . Who on a welthy Palfrey vaunted . . . .
Young and in dainty ſhape dygeſted,
  His Lookes with Pride, not Rage inueſted :
  His Mayne thin haird, his Neck high creſted,
  Small Eare, ſhort Head, and burly Breſted.
His brode Backe ſtoopt to this Clerks-loued,
  which with hir preſſure nought was moued :
  Strait Legd, large Thighd, & hollow Houed,
  All Natures ſkill in him was proued.

> *Phillis and Flora.| The ſweete and | ciuill contention of |
> two amorous Ladyes.| Translated out of Latine : by |
> R. S. Esquire. Aut Marti vel Mercurio.| Imprinted
> at London by* W. W.*| for* Richarde Iohnes.*| 1598.|
> sign. C. 2, back, 3.*

It has been suggested (*Centurie*, p. 427 : from elsewhere ?) that this is more or less imitated from Shakspere's description of the horse in *Venus and Adonis* (1593), st. 50, l. 295-300 :

> Round-*hoof'd*, short-jointed, fetlocks shag and long,
> Broad *breast*, full eye, small *head*, and nostril wide,
> *High crest*, short ears, *straight legs*, and passing strong,
>   *Thin mane*, thick tail, broad buttock, tender hide :
> Look what a horse should have, he did not lack,
> Save a proud rider on so proud a back.

But as no one *could* describe a horse without noting most of the points in him that Shakspere does, one need not suppose that R. S. referrd in any way to his predecessor.—F. J. F.

9

HENRY PORTER, 1599.

Mrs. Bar[nes]. How fir your wife ? wouldſt thou my daughter
haue ?
He rather haue her married to her graue.

> *The | Pleasant | Historie of | the two angrie women | of*
> Abington. / *With the humourous mirthe of* Dick Coomes /
> *and* Nicholas Prouerbes, *two | Seruingmen | . . .* By
> Henry Porter *Gent. . . London . . .* 1599, *sign.* G 2, *back.*

'A recollection perhaps of Shakespeare's " Romeo and Juliet," act iii.
sc. 5 —
    " I would the fool were married to her grave." '
                    A. Dyce, in Hazlitt's *Dodsley*, vii. 329.

Falstaff's "good manhood¹" is usd by Coomes in this play, *ib.* vii. 318 :
"I am sorry for it ; I shall never see good manhood again, if it [sword-
and-buckler fight] be once gone ; this poking fight of rapier and dagger will
come up then."
                                                F. J. F.

---

¹ Go thy ways, old Jack ; die when thou wilt ; if manhood, good man
hood, be not forgot upon the face of the earth, then am I a shotten herring.
1 *Henry IV.* II. iv. 139-142.

The reference in the *Variorum* Shakspere, 1821, xxi. 393, and Collier's
Memoirs of E. Alleyn (1841), p. 122, to a play of 1599 in which Rich. III.
appears—see sc. 2, and sc. 5 : " K. Rich. Catesb. Lovell, Norf. Northumb.
Percye," is no doubt, as Mr. P. A. Daniel says, to 'The Second Part of
Henry Richmond, by Robert Wilson,' Nov. 1599, named in the *Variorum*,
iii. 323, and in Henslowe's Diary, p. 159.

"The playe of John a gante," by "Mr. hathwaye," also in *Var.* xxi. 393,
Mr. Daniel identifies with "the conqueste of spayne by John a Gant," on
which Henslowe made three advances of money to "Mr. Hathwaye and
Mr. Rankens" in the spring of 1600-1. The date 1601 is on *Var.* xxi. 391.

THOS. DEKKER, 1599—1636.

Enter Rofe alone making a garland.
" *Rofe.* Here fit thou downe vpon this flowry bank
And make a garland for thy *Lacies* head.
Thefe pinkes, thefe rofes, and thefe violets,
Thefe blufhing gilliflowers, thefe marigoldes,
The faire embrodery of his coronet,
Carry not halfe fuch beauty in their cheekes,
As the fweete countnaunce of my *Lacy* doth."
The | Shomakers | Holiday.| or | the Gentle Craft.] . . .
1600. *Works,* 1873, i. 16, 17.

["*Come, sit thee down upon this flowery bed,*
While I thy amiable cheeks do coy,
And stick musk roses in thy sleek smooth head."
Mid.'s Night's Dream, IV. i.—H. C. HART.]

" *Cypr[us].* The Ruby-coloured portals of her fpeech
Were clofde by mercy."
The | Pleasant Comedie of | Old Fortunatus. . . 1600.
Works, 1873, i. 132.

["Once more the ruby coloured portal opened,
Which to his speech did honey passage yield."
1593. *Venus and Adonis,* l. 451, 2.—H. C. HART.]

" Genius.
I am the places Genius, *whence now fprings
A Vine, whofe yongeft Braunch fhall produce Kings :
This little world of men ; this precious Stone,
That fets out* Europe: . . . . . .

"This Iewell of the Land : Englands right Eye :
Altar of Loue and Spheare of Maieſtie."
1604. *The King's Entertainment through the City of
London*, 15. *of March* 1603. *Works*, 1873, i. 274.

[Evidently borrowed from Gaunt's speech in *Richard II*. Act II. sc. i.—II.]

"*Hip*[*olito*]. Oh, you ha kild her by your cruelty.
Du[*ke*]. Admit I had, thou kill'ſt her now againe ;
And art more ſavage then a barbarous Moor."
1604. *The Honest Whore*. *Works*, 1873, ii. 4.

[Conjecturally an allusion to Aaron in *Titus Andronicus*, who is twice called the "barbarous Moor" in that play; II. iii. 78, "Accompanied but with a barbarous Moor " ; V. iii. 4, "Good uncle, take you in this barbarous Moor."—II. C. HART.]

What's here ?
Perhaps this ſhrewd pate was mine enemies :
Las ! ſay it were : I need not feare him now :
For all his braves, his contumelious breath,
His frownes (tho' dagger-pointed) all his plot,
(Tho ne're ſo miſchievous) his *Italian* pilles,
His quarrels, and (that common fence) his law.
 * * * * * *
And muſt all come to this ; fooles, wife, all hither,
Muſt all heads thus at laſt be laid together :
 * * * * * *
But here's a fellow ; that which he layes on,
Till domes day alters not complexion :
Death's the beſt Painter then :
1604. *The Honest Whore*. *Part I*. *Works*, 1873, ii. 56.

[Though no passages are exactly similar, yet the whole idea of moralizing thus upon a skull (especially as it would show upon a stage) seems to me unmistakably taken from *Hamlet's* gravedigger's scene, and therefore worthy of insertion as Shakespeare's Prayse.—II. C. HART.]

THOS. DEKKER, 1599—1636.

Wife. Sure, I fhould thinke twere the leaft of fin,
To miftake the Mafter, and to let him in.
Geo[*rge*]. Twere a good Comedy of Errors that ifaith.
The Honest Whore, ib. ii. 62.

["An allusion probably to Shakespeare's play of that name."—Note in Dekker's *Works*, 1873, ii. 372. See the same phrase, p. 35, below.]

(Has the jealous husband Candido's saying in this play, ii. 40·1, about his wife's brother Fustigo's kissing her—"when I touch her lip, I shall not feele his kisses"—anything to do with Othello's "I found not Cassio's kisses on her lips"? III. iii. 341. *Othello* dates in 1604?—F.)

May[*bury*]. Of what ranck was fhe I befeech you.
Leth[*erftone*]. Vpon your promife of fecrefie.
Bel[*lamont*]. You fhall clofe it vp like treafure of your owne, and your felfe fhall keepe the key of it.

North-VVard | Hoe.| Sundry times Acted by the children */* of Paules./ *By Thomas Decker, and | John Webster.|* . . 1607. *Works*, 1873, iii. 5.

["From Shakespeare :—
'Tis in my memory lock'd
And you yourself shall keep the key of it.'—*Hamlet*, act. i. sc. 3."—Note in Dekker's *Works*, iii. 361.]

Iasp[*ero*]. I never heard 'mongft all your *Romane* fpirits,
That any held fo bravely up his head,
In fuch a fea of troubles (that come rouling
One on anothers necke) as *Lotti* doth.

The Wonder | of | A Kingdome.| . . . 1636. *Works*, 1873, iv. 230.

["*In such a sea of troubles.* In all probability borrowed from *Hamlet's* famous soliloquy." Note in Dekker's *Works*, 1873, iv. 438.]

Flo[*rence*]. . . . . . nay, nay, pray rife,
I know your heart is up, tho' your knees down. *Ib.* iv. 285.

[" So Shakespeare in *Richard II.* :—
'Up, cousin, up; your heart is up, I know,
Thus high at least, although your knee be low.'"
Note, ib. p. 440].—F. J. F.

RETURNE FROM PERNASSUS, PART I. 1600.

Gull. Pardon, faire lady, thoughe ficke-thoughted Gullio maks amaine unto thee, and like a bould-faced futore 'gins to woo thee[1].   1008

Ingen. (We fhall have nothinge but pure Shakfpeare and fhreds of poetrie that he hath gathered at the theators!)

Gull. Pardon mee, moy mittreffa, aft[2] am a gentleman, the moone, in comparifon of thy bright hue[3] a meere flutt, Anthonio's Cleopatra a blacke browde milkmaide, Hellen a dowdie.   1013

Ingen. (Marke, Romeo and Juliet! O monftrous theft[4]! I thinke he will runn throughe a whole booke of Samuell Daniell's!)

Gull. Thrife fairer than myfelfe (—thus I began—)
The gods faire riches, fweete above compare,
Staine to all nimphes, [m]ore lovely the[n] a man.
More white and red than doves and rofes are!   1020
Nature that made thee with herfelfe had[5] ftrife,
Saith that the worlde hath ending with thy life[6].

Ingen. Sweete Mr. Shakfpeare!

Act III. sc. i. pp. 56, 7.

---

[1] 'Sick-thoughted Venus makes amain unto him,
'And like a bold-faced suitor 'gins to woo him.'
                                              Venus and Adonis, st. 1.
[2] *for* as I.   [3] *for* hue's.   [4] Cf. *Romeo and Juliet*, ii. 4.
[5] *sic : for* at.   [6] *Venus and Adonis*, st. 2.

THE RETURNE FROM PERNASSUS.

Ingen. My pen is youre bounden vaſſall to commande. But what vayne woulde it pleaſe you to have them in? 1049

Gull. Not in a vaine veine (prettie, i'faith!): make mee them in two or three divers vayns, in Chaucer's, Gower's and Spencer's and Mr. Shakſpeare's. Marry, I thinke I ſhall entertaine thoſe verſes which run like theſe:

>Even as the ſunn with purple coloured face
>Had tane his laſte leave on[1] the weeping morne, &c. 1055

O ſweet Mr. Shakſpeare! I'le have his picture in my ſtudy at the courte.

Act III. sc. i. p. 58.

Gull.—Let mee heare Mr. Shakſpear's veyne. 1212

Ingen. Faire Venus, queene of beutie and of love,
>Thy red doth ſtayne the bluſhinge of the morne,
>Thy ſnowie necke ſhameth the milkwhite dove,
>Thy preſence doth this naked worlde adorne;
>Gazinge on thee all other nymphes I ſcorne.
>When ere thou dyeſt flowe ſhine that Satterday,
>Beutie and grace muſte ſleepe with thee for aye! 1219

Gull. Noe more! I am one that can judge accordinge to the proverbe, *bovem ex unguibus.* Ey marry, Sir, theſe have ſome life in them! Let this duncified worlde eſteeme of Spencer and Chaucer, I'le worſhipp ſweet Mr. Shakſpeare, and to honoure him will lay his Venus and Adonis under my pillowe, as wee reade of one (I doe not well remember his name, but I am ſure he was a kinge) ſlept with Homer under his bed's heade.

Act III. sc. i. p. 63.

---

[1] 'of': *Venus and Adonis,* l. 2.

Ing. Our *Theater* hath loſt, *Pluto* hath got,
A Tragick penman for a driery plot   295
    Beniamin Iohnſon[1].
Iud. The wittieſt fellow of a Bricklayer in England.
Ing. A meere Empyrick, one that getts what he hath by
obſeruation, and makes onely nature priuy to what he indites,
ſo ſlow an Inuentor that he were better betake himſelfe to his
old trade of Bricklaying, a bould whorſon, as confident now in
making a [2] booke, as he was in times paſt in laying of a brick.
    William Shakeſpeare[3].
Iud. Who loues [not *Adons* loue, or *Lucrece* rape?[4]]   304
His ſweeter verſe contaynes hart [throbbing line[5]],
Could but a grauer ſubiect him content,
Without loues fooliſh lazy[6] languiſhment.

Act IV. sc. ii. p. 87.

The Pilgrimage to Parnassus, with the Two Parts of the Returne from Parnassus. Three Comedies performed in St. John's College, Cambridge, A.D. MDXVII—MDCI. Edited from MSS. by the Rev. W. D. Macray, F.S.A. Oxford, Clarendon Press. 1886.

The Rev. W. D. Macray of the Bodleian lately found among Thomas Hearne's volumes of miscellaneous collections in the Bodleian, the long missing couple of Plays which preceded *The Returne from Pernassus* [Part II.] so long known to us. The first play is 'The Pilgrimage to Pernassus', and the second is the first part of 'The Returne' from it. It is the most interesting dramatic find for very many years, as it sets Shakspere at the head of English Poets—above Chaucer and Spenser—so early as A.D. 1600.

---

[1] 'B.I.,' B.   [2] 'of a,' MS.   [3] Mis-spelt 'Shatespeare' in A.
[4] 'Who loves Adonis love or Lucres' rape,' edits.
[5] 'robbing life,' edits.   [6] 'lazy' omitted in B.

JOHN BODENHAM, 1600.

To the Reader:

IT ſhall be needleſſe (gentle Reader) to make any Apologie for the defence of this labour, becauſe the ſame being collected from ſo many ſingular mens workes; and the worth of them all hauing been ſo eſpecially approued, and paſt with no meane applauſe the cenſure of all in generall, doth both diſburden me of that paines, and ſets the better approbation on this excellent booke. . . . A 3.

[A 4] Now that euery one may be fully ſatiſfied concerning this Garden, that no one man doth aſſume to him-ſelfe the praiſe thereof, or can arrogate to his owne deſeruing thoſe things which haue been deriued from ſo many rare and ingenious ſpirits; I haue ſet down both how, whence, and where theſe flowres had their firſt ſpringing, till thus they were drawne togither into the *Muſes Garden,* that euery ground may challenge his owne, each plant his particular, and no one be iniuried in the iuſtice of his merit

. . . out of. . .
    [A 5] *Edmund Spencer.*
           Henry Conſtable Eſquier. . . .
  [A 5, bk] *Iohn Marſtone.*
           Chriſtopher Marlow.
           Beniamin Iohnſon.
           VVilliam Shakſpeare. . . .

Theſe being Moderne and extant Poets, that haue liu'd

togither; from many of their extant workes, and fome kept in
priuat.
ib. p. 30.
Loue goes toward loue like fchoole-boyes from their bookes:
But loue from loue, to fchoole with heauie lookes.

> Bel-vedére | or | The Garden of | The Mvses.| . . .
> Imprinted at London by F. K. for Hugh Astley,
> dwelling at | Saint Magnus corner. 1600.|

The two 'Loue' lines are from the first Quarto, 1597, of *Romeo and Juliet*, II. ii. 160-1, p. 58, Daniel's *Parallel-Text*. N. Sh. Soc. 1874 :—

> *Ro.* Loue goes toward loue like schoole boyes from their bookes,
> But loue from loue, to schoole with heauie lookes.

Quarto 2, 1599, has *as* for *like* in l. 160, and *toward* for *to* in l. 161.
There are many other passages in Bodenham's volume which look like recollections of other poets, if not quotations from them, as:

> The fairest blossome, deaths sterne winter nips.—p. 230.

> To die, is all as common, as to liue.—p. 231.

> Louers best like to see themselues alone,
> Or with their loues, if needs they must haue one.—p. 32.

> No hell can be compard to iealousie.—p. 45.

Was the first of these suggested by *Rom. & Jul.* (Qo. 2, 159)) IV. 5, 30-1?

> Death lies on her like an vntimely frost
> Vpon the sweetest flower of all the field.

The author's name, 'M. Iohn Bodenham,' is given by A. M.[1] in the title of his verses on sign. A 7. The occurrence of Shakspere's name as above is noted in *Centurie*, p. 4, 8.

The mere fact of there being a *Rom. & Jul.* quotation in Bodenham, was stated by Mr. Hll.-P. in his *Outlines*, p. 115.—F. J. F.

---

[1] Anthony Munday?

A. MUNDAY, &c., 1600.

Pri[*eſt*]. Sirra, no more ado; come, come, giue me the money you haue. Diſpatch, I cannot ſtand all day.

Kin[*g Hen. V.*] Well, if thou wilt needs haue it, there it is[1]: iuſt the Prouerbe, one theefe robs another. Where the diuel are all my old theeues[2]? Falſtaffe that[3] villaine is ſo fat, hee cannot get on's horſe, but me thinkes Poines and Peto ſhould bee ſtirring hereabouts.[4]

* * * * * *

[5] *Pri.* Me thinkes the King ſhould be good to theeues becauſe he has bin a theefe himſelfe, though I thinke now hee be turned true man.

Kin. Faith I haue heard indeede h'as[6] had an ill name that way in's[7] youth; but how canſt thou tell that he[8] has beene a Theefe?

Prieſt. How? becauſe he once robb'd me before I fell to the

[1] there tis—V. S. ed.†
[2] theeues that were wont to keepe this walke?—V. S.
[3] the—V. S.   [4] here abouts.
[5] For *Pri.* read *Sir John* throughout, *i. e.* Sir John Butler, parson of Wrotham (Sig. B).
[6] he has—V. S.   [7] in his—V. S.
[8] till he—V. S. (Smaller differences of spelling and punctuation are not noted.—F.)

---

† The first part / Of the true and honor/able historie, of the life of Sir / *John Old-castle, the good* / Lord Cobham./ As it hath been lately acted by the right / honorable the Earle of Notingham / Lord high Admirall of England his / seruants./ LONDON / Printed by V. S. for Thomas Pauier, and are to be solde at / his Shop at the Signe of the Catte and Parrots / neere the Exchange./ 1600. 4to. sign. F2.

trade my felfe, when that foule villanous guts, that led him to all that Roguery, was in's company there, that Falſtaffe.

King aſide. Well, if he did rob thee then, thou art but euen with him now, Ile be fworne: Thou knoweſt not the King nowe I thinke, if thou faweſt him!

> The firſt part / of the true and hono-/rable history of the Life of / Sir John Old-castle, the good / *Lord-Cobham.*/ As it hath bene lately acted by the Right / honorable the Earle of Notingham / Lord High Admirall of Eng-land,/ his Seruants./ Written by William Shakespeare./ London printed for T. P. 1600. 4to. sign. F 2.

The edition "Printed by V. S. for Thomas Pauier, and are to be solde at his shop at the signe of the Catte and Parrots neere the Exchange, 1600," differs somewhat from this edition, and seems the better one, tho I have only collated it. A longer extract from this scene is given by Mr. Halliwell in his 'Character of Sir John Falstaff,' 1841, p. 31-4. The earlier scene at the Inn with Doll, (the Priest's or Wrotham Parson's wench,) old Harpoole, 'a most sweet old man,' the kissing, &c. (sign. C. 4)

"*harp. Imbracing her.* Doll canst thou loue me? a mad merie Lasse, would to God I had neuer seene thee.

Doll. I warrant you you will not out of my thoughts this tweluemonth, truely you are as full of favour, as a man may be. Ah these sweet gray lockes, by my troth, they are most louely."—

and the quarrel following, are evidently from Falstaff's tavern-scene with his Doll, 2 *Henry IV*, II. iv.

In Henslowe's Diary, p. 158, are the following entries:

" This 16 of october [15]99

Receved by me, Thomas Downton, of phillip Henslow, to pay Mr. Monday, Mr. Drayton, and Mr. Wilson and Hathway, for the first parte of the lyfe of Sr Jhon Ouldcasstell, and in earnest of the second parte, for the use of the compayny, ten pownd, I say receved . . . . 10ˡˡ.

[On or after Nov. 1, and before Nov. 8] Receved of Mr. Hinchloe, for Mr. Mundaye and the Reste of the poets, at the playnge of Sr John Old-castell, the ferste time. As a geſte . . . . xˢ.

[p. 162. Between Dec. 19 and 26, 1599] Receved of Mr. Henchlow, for the use of the company, to pay Mr. Drayton for the second parte of S Jhon Ouldcasell, foure pownd: I say receved . . . . iiijˡˡ.

[p. 166] Dd unto the litell tayller, at the apoyntment of Robart Shawe, the 12 of marche 1599[-1600] to macke thinges for the 2 parte of owld castell, some of xxxˢ."

Before this last date I thought that Shakspere might probably have acted in the play, which might have been lent, before its publication, to the Lord Chamberlain's Company, by the Lord Admiral's Company:[1] see the following:—

"*Baynards* Castell, *this Saturday*, 8 of *March*, 1599" [·1600]. "Rowland Whyte, *Esq.;* to *Sir* Robert Sydney" . . . "All this Weeke the Lords haue bene in *London*, and past away the Tyme in Feasting and Plaies; for *Vereiken* dined vpon *Wednesday*, with my Lord Treasurer, who made hym a Roiall Dinner; vpon *Thursday* my Lord Chamberlain feasted hym, and made hym very great, and a delicate Dinner, and there in the After Noone his Plaiers acted, before *Vereiken*, Sir *John Old Castell*, to his great Contentment." *Letters and Memorials of State*, ed. Arthur Collins, 1746, ii. 175, 176, 4, 17 (noted in the Variorum).

But Mr. P. A. Daniel suggests "that the Admiral lent his Company to the Chamberlain on this occasion. It seems altogether improbable that Shakspere and his company should have taken the places of the Admiral's Company for one single performance only."

Both Parts of the play were enterd to Thos. Pavier in the Stationers' Register on Aug. 11, 1600.—Arber's *Transcript*, iii. 63—

"*The firste parte of the history of the life of Sir* JOHN OLCASTELL *lord* COBHAM.

Item the second and last parte of the history of Sir JOHN OLDCASTELL *lord* COBHAM *with his martyrdom*"

The second Part of the Play is not now known.

By Aug. 17, 1602, "my Lorde of Worsters players" (afterwards Queen Anne's—James I.'s wife) had evidently become entitled to *Sir John Old-*

---

[1] They had both acted together or alternately at Henslowe's Newington Theatre for 2 years and 6 days in 1594-6. Collier's Pref. to Henslowe's Diary, p. xviii. The names of the Admiral's Company in 1600 (eleven sharers in profits) are given in Henslowe, p. 172—

J. Singger.
Thomas Downton.
Humfry Jeffes.
Anthony Jeffes.
Charles Massye.
Samuell Rowlye.

Robt. Shaa.
Thomas Towne.
W. Birde.
Richard Jones.
Edward Jubye.

castle, and Henslowe lent them 40s. " to paye unto Thomas Deckers, for new adicyons in Owldcaselle " (*Diary*, p. 236), and 10s. more on Sept. 7, 1602 (p. 239).

On the attributing of spurious plays to Shakspere, note this by Baker:
" THE THREE BROTHERS. Trag. by Wentworth Smith. Acted by the Lord Admiral's servants, 1602. Not printed.—This author wrote, or assisted in, several other plays ; and by only using the initials of his name, it is supposed that many of them were obtruded on the public as the products of Shakspeare's pen." 1812.—Baker's *Biogr. Dram*. iii. 333.

F. J. F.

If the following passage had been written after *Macbeth* instead of 4 years before it, should we not all have said that the writers had recollected Shakspere's
"Come, seeling night,
Scarf up the tender eye of pitiful day " (III. ii. 46-7)?

And if so, ought we not in like wise to hold that in *Macbeth* Shakspere recollected his predecessors' work ?—E. PHIPSON.

War[*man*]. The man is blinde. Muffle the eye of day,
Ye gloomie clouds (and darker than my deedes,
That darker be than pitchie sable night)
Muster together on these high topt trees,
That not a sparke of light thorough their sprayes,
May hinder what I meane to execute.

[A. Munday & H. Chettle] *The | Downfal | of Robert, | Earle of Huntington, | afterward Called | Robin Hood of merrie Sherwodde: |* with his loue to chaste Matilda, the *| Lord* Fitzwaters *daughter, afterwardes |* his faire Maide Marian.*| . . . Imprinted at London, for* William Leake, 1601, sign. I4, back.

* CHR. MIDDLETON, 1600.

[The following uses of "famine, sword and fire," and "Soul-killing witches," should perhaps be quoted rather as illustrations than recollections of Shakspere's like words in the Prologue to *Henry V*, line 7,[1] and *Comedy of Errors*, I. ii. 100.[2]—H. C. HART.]

(5)
What time this land difquieted with broyles,
Wearied with wars and fpent for want of reft,
Sawe her adioyning neighbours free from th' fpoyles,
Wherewith her felfe had difpofeft
Of peace and plenty, which men moft defire,
And in their fteeds brought famine, fword and fire.

(89)
They charge her that fhe did maintaine and feede,
Soul-killing witches, and conuers'd with deuils,
Had conference with fprits, who fhould fucceede
The King.

> The / Legend / Of Hvmphrey / *Dvke of Glo-/cester.* / By *Chr: Middleton.* / London / Printed by *E. A.* for *Nicholas Ling*, and are / to be solde at his shop at the west doore of / S. Paules Church. 1600./

---

[1] and at his heels
Leasht in like hounds, should *famine, sword and fire*
Crouch for employment. [A.D. 1599.]
[2] Soul-killing witches that deform the body. [? A.D. 1591.]

* SAM. NICHOLSON. 1600.

Dr. Grosart has given in his Memorial Introduction to his reprint of Sam. Nicholson's *Acolastus, his After-witte*, many instances of that writer's borrowings from Shakspere's *Venus and Adonis, Lucrece*, &c. Of these the most certain are quoted in the *Centurie of Prayse*.
Mr. Hll.-Phillipps adds one possibly fresh taking:

> We of all people once that were the pelfe
> Thruft in a frozen corner of the North.
> Sign. B. l. 44, p. 7, reprint.

This he compares with "the frozen bosome of the North," in *Romeo and Juliet*:

> Which is as thin of substance as the ayre,
> And more inconstant then the wind, who wooes
> Euen now the frozen bosome of the North.
> 1599. *Rom. & Jul.* Qo. 2, I. v. 93.

1597. Qo. 1.
> Which is as thinne a substance as the aire,
> And more inconstant than the winde
> Which wooes euen now the frosen bowels of the north.
> F. J. F.

* 1601. BEN JONSON.

MINO. Sir, your oathes cannot ferue you, you know I haue forborne you long.

CRIS. I am confcious of it, fir. Nay, I befeech you, gentlemen, doe not exhale me thus;

> Poëtaster, / Or / His Arraignement./ *A Comicall Satyre./* Acted, in the yeere 1601. By the then / Children of Queene Elizabeths / Chappel./ The Author B. I./ Mart./ *Et mihi de nullo fama rubore placet.*/ London,/ Printed by William Stansby, / for *Matthew Lownes.*/ M.DC.XVI./ Act. III. Scene III. B. J.'s *Workes*, 1616, p. 301.

On the word *exhale*, Gifford says "i.e. drag me out." This is the language of ancient Pistol, and corroborates the conjecture of Malone on the meaning of the expression in *Henry V*, act ii. sc. 1.—Jonson's Works, 2-col. ed. Cunningham, i. 228, note 2.

> *Pist.* O Braggard vile, and damned furious wight,
> The Graue doth gape, and doting death is neere,
> Therefore exhale,—*Henry V.* II. i. 58.

F. J. F.

THOMAS DEKKER. 1602.

All the men. Faire Cælestine!
Ladies. The Bride!
Ter. She that was faire,
   Whom I cal'd faire and Cælestine.
Omnes. Dead!
Sic quia. Dead, sh's deathes Bride, he hath her maidenhead.

> Satiro-mastix. / Or / *The vntrussing of the Humo-/rous Poet. / As it hath bin presented publiquely,* / by the Right Honorable, the Lord Cham-/berlaine his Seruants; and priuately, by the / Children of Poules./ By *Thomas Dekker* . / . . . . London, / Printed for *Edward White,* and are to bee / solde at his shop, neere the little North doore of Paules / Church, at the signe of the Gun. 1602./ sign. K. 3, back.

(Sent to Dr. Ingleby from a later edition, by J. O. IIll.-P.)

In this Play, and another of 1602,[1] a 'somniferous potion' is given to a woman who seemingly dies from its effects, and is buried, but revives again. Mr. Daniel hesitates with me to consider this as necessarily borrow'd from Shakspere's *Romeo and Juliet.* Sh. didn't invent the incident; and his contemporaries may have taken it from the same source as he did. In the second play named below, the fool-husband thinks he has poizond his true wife with the potion. He at once marries the strumpet he is in love with. She turns-out a shrew and adulteress. And when he mourns for the loss of his first loving wife, she has revived, to release him from his suppozed second marriage.

---

[1] A Pleasant conceited Comedie, Wherein is showed how a man may chuse a good Wife from a bad. As it hath been Sundry times Acted by the Earle of Worcesters Seruants. London. Printed for Matthew Lawe, and are to be solde at his shop in Paules Churchyard, neare vnto S. Augustines gate, at the signe of the Foxe. 1602. (By Joshua Cooke.)

*JOHN MARSTON, 1602.

And[*rugio*]. Andrugio lives, and a faire caufe of armes,—
Why that's an armie all invincible !
He who hath that, hath a battalion
Royal, armour of proofe, huge troups of barbed fteeds,
Maine fquares of pikes, millions of harguebufh,
O, a faire caufe ftands firme, and will abide.
Legions of Angels fight upon her fide.

     1602. JOHN MARSTON. *Antonio and Mellida*. Marston's Works, 1856, i. 33. (Works, 1633, vol. i. sign. C 6, back.)

 Seeing how often the author of *What you will* copied Shakspere, we can hardly be wrong in saying that the passage above is an expansion of Henry VI.'s

> " What stronger breastplate than a heart untainted ?
> Thrice is he armed that hath his quarrel just."
>   *2 Hen. VI*, III. ii. 233-4.

 The following are illustrations of Coriolanus's " beast with many heads " (IV. i. 1-2) in 1607 (?), and Brutus's ' tide in the affairs of men ' (*Jul. Cæs.* IV. iii. 218) :—

> ' I' faith, my lord, that beast with many heads,
> The staggering multitude recoiles apace,
> Though thorow great men's envy, most men's malice,
> Their much intemperate heat hath banisht you ;
> Yet now they find envie and mallice neere
> Produce fainte reformation.'
> 1604. Marston. *The Malcontent*, III. iii. Works, 1856, ii. 248.

> ' There is an hour in each man's life appointed
> To make his happiness, if then he seize it.'
>   Beaumont & Fletcher. *The Custom of the Country.*

> ' There is a nick in Fortune's restless wheel
> For each man's good.'
>   Chapman. *Bussy d'Ambois.* See 1 *Notes & Queries,* vol. i. p. 330.
>   E. PHIPSON.

The following bits from Joshua Cooke, 1602, may serve as illustrations of the description of Pinch in *The Comedy of Errors*, V. i. 237-241, and Rosalind's account of a Lover with 'hose ungartered . . bonnet unbanded,' &c. in *As you like it*, III. iii. 377-8. Cooke's making his good wife take a sleeping potion, be buried, and then wake up when her strumpet-successor turn'd out 'a Bad Wife' is a parallel rather than an imitation of *Romeo and Juliet*.

"When didst thou see the starueling Schoole-maister? That Rat, that shrimp, that spindleshanck, that Wren, that sheep-biter, that leane chittiface, that famine, that leane Enuy, that all bones, that bare Anatomy, that Iack a Lent, that ghost, that shadow, that Moone in the waine."

    A / Pleasant / conceited Comœdie,˙/ Wherein is shewed / how a man may chuse a good / Wife from a bad./ [Written By Ioshua Cooke *in later MS.*] *As it hath bene sundry times acted by the Earle of* / Worcesters *Seruants* / London / Printed for Mathew Lawe, and are to be solde at his / shop in Paules Church-yard, neare vnto S. Au-/gustines gate, at the signe of the Foxe. / 1602./ sign. E. back.

B 3 back.
 I was once like thee,
 A sigher, melancholy, humorist,
 Crosser of armes, a goer without garters,
 A hatband-hater, and a busk-point wearer,
 One that did vse much bracelets made of haire,
 Rings on my fingers, Iewels in mine eares,
 And now and then a wenches Carkanet,
 That had two letters for her name in Pearle :
 Skarfes, garters, bands, wrought wastcoats, gold, stitcht caps,
 A thousand of those female fooleries.
 But when I lookt into the glasse of Reason, strait I beganne
 To loath that femall brauery, and henceforth
 Studie to cry *peccaui* to the world.

JOHN WEBSTER, 1602-7, 1612, 1616, 1623.

> *Guildford.* Peace rest his soul!
> His sins be buried in his grave,
> And not remember'd in his epitaph.
> *The Famous History of Sir Thomas Wyatt.* Works, ed.
> Dyce, 1871, p. 195, col. 2.

From Shakespeare, says Dyce,

> "Thy ignomy sleep with thee in the grave,
> But not remember'd in thy epitaph.
> *First Part of Henry IV*, act V. sc. iv."

This play was first printed, as "Written by Thomas Dickers and John Webster," in 1607, but, says Dyce, *Webster's Works*, 1871, p. 182, "There can be no doubt that *The Famous History of Sir Thomas Wyatt* consists merely of fragments of two plays,—or rather, a play in Two Parts,—called *Lady Jane*, concerning which we find the following entries [1] in *The Diary of Henslowe* . . . Pp. 242-3, *ed. Shakespeare Soc.* (old) :

"Whether the present abridgment of *Lady Jane* was made by Dekker and Webster (see its title page [Written by D. and W.]), or by some other playwright, cannot be determined; that it has suffered cruelly from the hands of the transcriber or printer, is certain."

---

[1] "Lent unto John Thare, the 15 of october 1602, to geve unto harey chettell, Thomas Deckers, Thomas Hewode, and Mr Smyth, and *Mr Webster*, in earneste of a playe called Ladey Jane, the some of . . . . l^s

"Lent unto Thomas Hewode, the 21 of octobr 1602, to paye unto Mr. Dickers, chettell, Smythe, *Webester*, and Hewode, in fulle payment of ther playe of ladye Jane, the some of . . . v^{ll} x^s

"Lent unto John Ducke, the 27 of octobr 1602, to geve unto Thomas Deckers, in earneste of the 2 part of Ladye Jane, the some of . v^s

JOHN WEBSTER, 1602-7, 1612, 1616, 1623.

(1) *Vit. Cor.* . . . You did name your duchess.
Brach. Whose death God pardon!
Vit. Cor. Whose death God revenge!

The White Devil; or, Vittoria Corombona, p. 31, col. 1, ed. Dyce, 1857.

"A recollection of Shakespeare;
'*Glo.* Poor Clarence did forsake his father, Warwick;
Ay, and forswore himself,—which Jesu pardon!
Q. Mar. Which God revenge!'—RICHARD III., act i. sc. 3" [l. 135-7].[1]
A. Dyce.

In this *Vittoria Corombona*, p. 45, ed. Dyce, the madness of Cornelia, her singing—with prose remarks intersperst—and her flowers, seem suggested by Ophelia's—according to Steevens's reference to *Hamlet*, IV. v, in Dyce—

"*Cor.* O reach mee the flowers.
Moo. Her Ladiships foolish.   *Wom.* Alas! her grief
Hath turn'd her child againe.   *Cor.* You're very wellcome.
There's rosemarie for you and rue for you,
Hearts-ease for you. (Quarto, sign. L.)"[2]

Dyce also says that Reed calls Cornelia's
    "here's a white hand:
    Can blood so soon be wash'd out?" p. 45, col. 2,

---

[1] Reed, as cited by Dyce, compares the following lines in *The White Devil*, p. 39, col. 1—
    Cor. Fetch a looking-glass; see if his breath will not stain it: or pull some feathers from my pillow, and lay them to his lips. Will you lose him for a little pains-taking?
with "Shakespeare in *King Lear*, A. 5. sc. 3—
    'Lend me a *looking-glass*;
    If that her breath will *mist* or *stain* the stone,
    Why, then she lives. . . . .
    This feather stirs; she lives!'. . ."

[2] "He [a Gardener] cannot endure a great frost, for that kils his Rosemary, and makes him rue for it . . . . . the chiefe flower in his Garden is heartease, because tis very scarce in the world.' 1635. Wye Saltonstall. *Picturæ Loquentes* (2nd ed), sigr. F 11, back.

27   JOHN WEBSTER, 1602-7, 1612, 1616, 1623.

"an imitation of Lady Macbeth's sleeping soliloquy;" and that Reed charges Webster with imitating part of the following dirge from the well-known passage in Shakspere's *Cymbeline*, IV. ii. 224, "The ruddock would With charitable bill," &c. :—
> " Call for the robin red-breast and the wren,
> Since o'er shady groves they hover,
> And with leaves and flowers do cover
> The friendless bodies of unburied men," &c.

The Duchess of Malfi, ab. 1616.

The *Duchess of Malfi*, "first produced about 1616," and printed 1623, has many echoes of Shakspere. Dyce compares Puck's "I'll put a girdle round about the earth," *M. N. Dr.*, II. ii, with Webster's
> "He that can compass me, and know my drifts,
> May say he hath put a girdle 'bout the world,
> And sounded all her quick-sands." (III. i.)—*Works*, p. 75, col. 1.

Webster's "He could not abide to see a pig's head gaping" (III. ii. p. 78, col. 2) with Shylock's "Why he cannot abide a gaping pig" (*Merchant*, IV. i.); Webster's
> "O, the secret of my prince,
> Which I will wear on the inside of my heart" (IV. ii. p. 80, col. 1),

with Hamlet's "I will wear him In my heart's core," III. ii. On the following lines, IV. ii. p. 89, col. 2—
> "Yet stay ; heaven-gates are not so highly arch'd
> As princes' palaces ; they that enter there
> Must go upon their knees—"

Dyce remarks, "When Webster wrote this passage, the following charming lines of Shakespeare were in his mind :—
> 'Stoop, boys : this gate
> Instructs you how to adore the heavens, and bows you
> To a morning's holy office : the gates of monarchs
> Are arch'd so high, that giants may jet through
> And keep their impious turbans on, without
> Good morrow to the sun.' *Cymbeline*, Act III. sc. 3."

On the end of Act IV. sc. ii.,—when Bosola has, at her brother Ferdinand's bidding, had the Duchess and her children strangled, and Ferdinand has refused his reward and bidden him

"Get thee into some unknown part o' the world,
That I may never see," p. 91, col. 1,

like King John to Hubert, after Arthur's supposed murder, "Out of my sight, and never see me more," IV. ii. 242,—Dyce says: "In composing this scene, Webster seems to have had an eye to that between King John and Hubert in Shakespeare's *King John*, Act IV. sc. 2." And just after, when the strangled Duchess revives, to utter "Antonio" and "Mercy!" (p. 91, col. 2), Dyce remarks, "The idea of making the Duchess speak after she had been strangled, was doubtless taken from the death of Desdemona in Shakespeare's *Othello*, Act V. last scene." The latter is due to Desdemona's having been beaten nearly to death with a stocking full of sand, in the foundation story of the play, and not smother'd (once and for all, as it ought to be,) as Shakspere makes her.

In Act V. sc. ii. of the *Duchess of Malfi*, p. 93, col. 2, Ferdinand says, "What I have done, I have done: I'll confess nothing"; and Dyce notes "Like Iago's

'Demand me nothing: what you know, you know;
From this time forth I never will speak word.'
Othello, Act V. last scene."[1]

Again, on the Cardinal's speech to Julia, in the *Duchess*, V. ii. p. 96, col. 1—

"Satisfy thy longing,—
The only way to make thee keep my counsel
Is, not to tell thee."

Dyce comments: "So Shakespeare, whom our author so frequently imitates:

'and for secrecy,
No lady closer; for I well believe
Thou wilt not utter what thou dost not know.'
First Part of *Henry IV.*, Act II. sc. 3."

Lastly, Malatesti's "Thou wretched thing of blood," V. v. p. 101, col. 1, is compar'd by Dyce with Shakspere's "from face to face He was a thing of blood." *Coriolanus*, Act II. sc. 2.

---

[1] On the Cardinal's speech to the Doctor, a little lower down, "How now! put off your gown!" Dyce remarks, "A piece of buffoonery similar to that with which the Grave-digger in *Hamlet* still amuses the galleries, used to be practised here; for in the 4to. of 1708, the Doctor, according to the stage-direction, '*puts off his four cloaks, one after another.*' What precedes was written in 1830: since that time, the managers have properly restricted the Grave-digger to a single waistcoat." A later note of this kind is in Mr. Hall.-Phillipps's *Mem. on Hamlet*, p. 68-9.

JOHN WEBSTER, 1602-7, 1612, 1616, 1623.

In the *Devil's Law-Case*, 1623, Dyce says, on Webster's "O young quat," II. i, p. 115, col. 2, "Quat means originally a pimple. Compare Shakespeare, 'I have rubb'd this *young quat* almost to the sense,' *Othello*, Act V. sc. i."

In Webster's *Appius and Virginia*, date unknown, but printed in 1654, occurs the passage,

"The apparel and the jewels that she were,
More worth than all her tribe," IV. i. ; *Works*, p. 171, col. 2;

and Dyce notes that this "Reads like a recollection of Shakespeare ;

'Whose hand,
Like the base Indian, threw a pearl away,
Richer than all his tribe.' *Othello*, Act V. sc. ii."

Again, in *Ap. and Vir.*, V. iii. p. 179, col. 1, Virginius's line "This sight hath stiffen'd all my operant powers" is compard by Dyce with Hamlet's father's " *My operant powers* their functions leave to do," *Hamlet*, III. ii. In *Westward Ho*, V. iv., Tenterhook's "Let these husbands play mad Hamlet, and cry Revenge," p. 241, col. 2, has been separately noted, p. 52. Several other uses in common of phrases by Webster and Shakspere occur.

In *Northward Ho*, 1607, IV. i. p. 268, col. 1—by Dekker and Webster—Dyce compares the Servingman's "Here's a swaggering fellow, sir, that speaks not like a man of God's making," with the Princess's "He speaks not like a man of God's making" in *Love's Labour's Lost*, Act V. sc. ii.; and Bellamont's words to Doll (p. 269, col. 2), "Would I were a young man for thy sake," with Shallow's "Would I were young for your sake, Mistress Anne!" *Merry Wives*, I. i.

Mr. Hall.-Phillipps (*Mem. on Hamlet*, p. 62-3) thinks that "there is another allusion to Shakespeare's tragedy [of *Hamlet*] in the following lines in Fletcher's *Scornful Ladie*,[1] 1616,"—

"Sa[uill, *the Steward*]. Now must I hang my selfe, my friends will looke for 't.
Eating and sleeping, I doe despise you both now ;
I will runne mad first, and if that get not pitty,
Ile drowne my selfe to a most dismall ditty " (*Finis Actus tertij. sign. G*).

But, tho' he quotes from Q1 the Stage-direction 'Enter Ofelia playing on a lute, and her haire downe singing,' ed. 1603, I doubt the allusion to her. —F. J. F.

---

[1] A Comedie./ As it was Acted / with great applause / by / *the Children of Her Maiesties* / Reuals in the Blacke / Fryers./

[From *The Academy*, Aug. 23, 1879, p. 142.]

1603.

FATHER PARSONS, FALSTAFF, AND SHAKSPERE.

Ilkley: Aug. 18, 1879.

Since my letter upon this subject (ACADEMY, March 8, 1879), I have ascertained that some copies of the third volume of Parsons' *Three Conversions* have a division headed "Of th' Examen of the First Six Monthes," in which occurs the following passage :—

"The second moneth of *February* is more fertile of rubricate Martyrs, then *January*, for that yt hath eight in number, two Wickliffians, *Syr John Oldcastle*, a Ruffian-Knight as all England knoweth, and commonly brought in by comediants on their ftages : he was put to death for robberyes and rebellion under the forefaid K. Henry the Fifth, and *Sir Roger Onely*, Prieft-martyr," &c.

The dedication of the third volume is dated 1603. I doubt whether this is the passage to which allusion is made by Speed in his *History of Great Britaine*. Except in the number of the page it does not correspond with his reference, and the language appears too indefinite to account for Speed's scornful invective against "his [Parsons'] poet."

It is suggestive to note the gradual development of Oldcastle's turpitude in Parsons' book. He is introduced in the first volume as a sectary who made his peace with the Church by recanting his errors. In the second volume he is a traitor, and his life is "dissolute ;" while in the third he has blossomed into the notoriety whom "all England knoweth."

We can readily understand the indignation of Speed and the Puritans at this quoting of the authority of "comediants," and their desire to pay him back in his own coin. It was a favourite contention of Parsons (as in the *Warn-Word to Sir F. Hastings*) that among the Protestants all sorts of books were allowed to be "read promiscuously of all men and women, even the Turks' *Alcaron* itself, *Machevile* and *Boden* tending to atheisme, and bawdy *Boccace*, with the most *pestilent English Pallace of Pleasure* [1] (all forbidden among us Catholyks)."

Another point about Oldcastle wants clearing up. What were his personal relations to Henry V. ? Speed says of him that "he was a man strong and valorous, and in especiall favour with his Prince" (*History of Great Britaine*, 1627, p. 637), and again calls him *par excellence* "his [the King's] knight."

C. ELLIOT BROWNE.

---

[1] Is there any evidence that Painter's *Palace of Pleasure* was officially forbidden to English Catholics ? It was of course mainly a compilation from authors who were upon the *Index*.

JN. MARSTON, 1604.

Men[*doza* (*fpeaking of the Duchefs, and after much other praife, fays*)]. . . . in body how delicate, in foule how wittie, in difcourfe how pregnant, in life how warie, in favours how iuditious, in day how fociable, and in night how? O pleafure unutterable!

> *The* / Malcontent./ Augmented by *Marston*./ With the Additions played by the Kings / Maiesties servants./ Written by *Ihon Webster*./ 1604./ At London / Printed by V. S. for William Aspley, and / are to be sold at his shop in Paules / Church-yard./ Actus Primus. Scena Quinta. sign. C, back. (Act I. sc. i., end. Webster's *Works*, ed. Dyce, 1871, p. 333, col. 2.)

Dyce notes, "The author had here an eye to the well-known passage of Shakespeare;—'What a piece of work is man! How noble in reason, how infinite in faculties! in form, and moving, how express and admirable! in action, how like an angel! in apprehension, how like a god! the beauty of the world! the paragon of animals!' *Hamlet*, Act II. sc. ii."

And in an earlier part of this scene, p. 330, col. 2, Malevole uses the phrase "Pompey the Huge," which Dyce notes is Shakspere's in *Love's Labour's Lost*, Act V. sc. ii., 'Greater than Great, great, great, great Pompey ! *Pompey the Huge !*' In Act III. sc. ii. p. 345, on Malevole's "Entic'd by that great bawd, opportunity," Dyce quotes from Shakspere's *Lucrece*,—as he does for Ford's like lines, p. 118, below,—

> "O *Opportunity*, thy guilt is great! . . . . .
> Thou foul abettor ! thou notorious *bawd !*"

Steevens's identification of Oseric's "No, in good faith, for mine ease," in Webster's (?) Induction to *The Malcontent*, and of Mendoza's "Illo, ho, ho ho! art there old truepenny?" III. ii, p. 346, col. 1, are in the *Centurie*, p. 66, and should have Steevens's name to them. Malone too had (I find, *Variorum Shaksp.*, 1821, xvi. 412) spotted the Oldcastle allusion in *Centurie*, p. 65, before I saw it in the Percy Soc. reprint and sent it to Dr. Ingleby.

I think that we may likewise fairly see echoes of Shakspere in at least the following 'Damnation' and 'traps to catch polecats' bits from this *Malcontent* of Marston's:

Aur. ... looke where the base wretch comes.
   ib. Scena Sexta. sign. C. back.
Men. God night; to-morrow morne.
   [*Exit Mendozo.*
Mal. I, I wil come, friendly Damnation,[1] I will come.
   Actus Secundus, Scena Quinta. sign. D. 4 back.
Maq. On his troth la beleeue him not . . . promise of matrimony by a yong gallant, to bring a virgin Lady into a fooles paradise . . . of his troth la, beleeue him not, traps to catch polecats.
   Actus Quintus, Scena Quarta. sign. H. 4 back.

Quee. But looke where sadly the poore wretch comes reading.
   Hamlet, Q 2. II. ii. 168.

Ju. Aunciient damnation, ô most wicked fiend.
   Rom. & Jul. III. v. 245.

Pol. Doe you believe his tenders, as you call them? . . .   103
Marry I will teach you, thinke your selfe a babie
That you have tane these tenders for true pay
Which are not sterling . . .   107
Doe not believe his vowes, for they are brokers   127
I, spring[e]s to catch Woodcockes   115
   Hamlet, I. iii. Quarto 2.

---

[1] "make her a great woman and then cast her off: tis as common, as naturall to a Courtier, as jelosie to a Citizen . . pride to a Tayler, or an empty handbasket to one of these sixpenny damnations."
   ib. sign. H 4 back.

ANTHONY SCOLOKER, 1604.

(1) *Fortune,* Oh be fo good to let me finde
A Ladie liuing, of this conftant minde.

Oh, I would weare her in my hearts heart-gore,
And place her on the continent of ftarres :
Sig. E, st. 3, 4.

* * * * * * * *

(2) As a black vaile vpon the wings of morne,
Brings forth a day as cleere as *Venus* face,
Or, a faire Iewell by an *Ethiope* worne,
It richeth much the eye, which it doth grace,
Such is her beautie, if it well be told,
Plac'ft in a Iettie Chariot fet with gold.
Sig. B4, st. 4.

Daiphantus, or The Passions of Loue, by An[thony] Sc[o-loker] Gentleman. 1604. 4to. Sigs. E and B 4.

---

1. For *gore* read of course *core.* Mr. Hl.-Phillipps in his *Memoranda on Hamlet,* p. 54,[1] says—"the corresponding passage in Shakespeare [III. ii. 79 —9] being found in the edition of 1604, not in that of 1603." The character of the lady he desires, should be, it may be remarked, as constant in love as Hamlet says that Horatio is in his whole character.

2. As also line 3 resembles that in *Rom. and Jul.* (I. 5), so also the general thought and wording are similar, and Scoloker in his Dedication says— " Also if he [Scoloker] haue caught vp half a Line of any others, It was out of his *Memorie,* not of any ignorance."

He (*Mem. on Hamlet,* p. 54) quotes both stanzas in full, and prints *Will learne them action,* in italics.— P. A. LYONS.

I am inclined also to increase the quotation, No. 2 on p. 64 of the *Centurie*, by one line—

"Calls Players fooles, the foole he iudgeth wisest,
Will learne them Action out of *Chaucer's* Pander."

I would do this because there appears to me to be here a remembrance of Hamlet's speech to the players. I the more think so, because there are other bits, besides the run of the story, which show remembrances of the play of *Hamlet*. See, for instance, st. 4, ll. 1—4, Sig. F; and st. 4, Sig. E 4, back.

Dr. A. B. Grosart would print a much longer extract from *Daiphantus* than that already given (*Cent.*, p. 64), but though interesting to the Shakspere student in other ways—as is indeed the piece generally—the two stanzas and these two bits give all that the object of the *Centurie* requires.

When also Dr. Grosart quotes the "in his shirt" as proof determinative that Hamlet was then considered mad, I would note that it does not do so; for whether Hamlet's madness were real or assumed, he would dress in character, indeed the more so if the madness were assumed.—B. N.

[There are two Revenge passages in Scoloker's book, but they can hardly allude to *Hamlet*:—

"Then like a spirit of pure Innocence,
Ile be all white and yet behold Ile cry
Reuenge, Oh Louers this my sufferance,
Or else for Loue, for Loue, a soule must die."
Sig. F., st. 4, ll. 1—4.

"Who calls me forth from my distracted thought?
Oh Serberus, If thou, I prethy speke?
Reuenge if thou? I was thy Riuall ought,
In purple gores Ile make the ghosts to reake:
Vitullia, oh *Vitullia*, be thou still,
Ile haue reuenge, or harrow vp my will.'
Sig. E4, back, st. 4. P. A. l.]

THOMAS MIDDLETON, 1604—1619.

1604: *The Honest Whore*, Part I. (Works, ed. Dyce, iii. 1—122).

    Candido. No matter, let 'em : when I touch her lip
I shall not feel his kisses,[1] no, nor miss
Any of her lip.

    Hippolito. . . . I was, on meditation's spotless wings,
Upon my journey hither.[2]—ib. IV. i. p. 79.

    George. 'Twere a good Comedy of Errors,[3] that, i' faith.
                              ib. Act IV. sc. iii. p. 85.

        1607-8. *The Family of Love.*

Believe .t, we saw Sampson bear the town-gates on his neck from the lower to the upper stage, with that life and admirable accord, that it shall never be equalled, unless the whole new livery of porters set [to] their shoulders.[4]

    The Family of Love (licenst 12 Oct. 1607, publisht 1608), Act I. sc. iii. Middleton's Works, ed. Dyce, 1840, ii. 125.

---

[1] "Imitated by Shakspeare in *Othello*, Act III. sc. iii.
    'I slept the next night well, was free and merry ;
    I found not Cassio's kisses on her lips.' "—REED.
If there be any imitation in the case, I believe it to be on the part of Dekker or Middleton [to whom Henslowe assigns this play, p. 3].—Dyce : ed. Middleton's Works, iii. 56.

[2] So in *Hamlet*, Act I. sc. i.—
    "Haste, let me know it ; that I, with *wings* as swift
      As *meditation*," &c.—Reed : Dyce's *Middleton*, iii. 79.

[3] An allusion, probably, to Shakespeare's play of that name.—Dyce. See too p. 314-15, note, ib. ; and p. 12 above.

[4] Middleton seems to have had in his recollection a passage of Shakespeare's *Love's Labour's Lost*, . . "Sampson, master, he was a man of good carriage, great carriage ; for he carried the town-gates on his back, like a porter." Act I. sc. ii. [l. 73-5].—Dyce.

(ib. Act V. sc. iii. p. 203.) .. *Mistriss Purge.* Husband, I see you are hoodwinked in the right use of feeling and knowledge— as if I knew you not [1] then as well as the child knows his own father.

A Mad World, my Masters.

(Act I. sc. i.) *Follywit.* Hang you, you have bewitched me among you! I was as well given [2] till I fell to be wicked! my grandsire had hope of me: I went all in black; swore but a' Sundays; never came home drunk but upon fasting-nights to cleanse my stomach. 'Slid, now I'm quite altered! blown into light colours; let out oaths by th' minute; sit up late till it be early; drink drunk till I am sober; sink down dead in a tavern, and rise in a tobacco-shop: here's a transformation! (&c., &c.)

(Act IV. sc. i. p. 386.) Shield me [3] you ministers of faith and grace!

ab. 1619 (pr. 1662). *Any thing for a quiet Life.*

Lord Beaufort. And whither is your way, sir?
Water-Camlet. E'en to seek out a quiet life, my lord:

---

[1] Imitated from Falstaff's "I knew ye, as well as he that made ye."— Shakespeare's *Henry IV, Part I*, Act II. sc. iv.—Dyce.
With Goldstone's "Yes, at your book so hard?" Middleton's *Your Five Gallants*, Works, iii. 274, Dyce compares in 3 *Henry VI*, Act V. sc. vi, Gloster's "what, at your book so hard;" and with Pursenet's "he'd away like a chrisom," ib. 276, Mrs. Quickly's "'a made a finer end, and went away an it had been any christom child," *Henry V*, Act II. sc. iii.

[2] Imitated from Shakespeare's *First Part of K. Henry IV*, Act III. sc. iii, where Falstaff says, "I was as virtuously given as a gentleman need to be; virtuous enough: swore little, diced not above seven times a-week; went to a bawdy-house not above once in a quarter of an hour; paid money that I borrowed, three or four times; lived well, and in good compass: and now I live out of all order, out of all compass." Reed.—Dyce's *Middleton*, ii. 331, n.

[3] See *Hamlet* ["Angels and ministers of grace defend us!" Act I. sc. iv].—Steevens, *ib.*

To hear of a fine peaceable island.
L. Beau. Why 'tis the same you live in.
W. Cam. No; 'tis so fam'd,
But we th' inhabitants find it not so:
The place I speak of [1] has been kept with thunder.

I do not look on the words "Alas, poor ghost ! " in *The Old Law*—printed in 1656, and stated on its title to be "by Phil. Massinger, Tho. Middleton. William Rowley"—as borrowd from *Hamlet*, I. v. 4. The young courtier Simonides is telling the old husband Lysander, that he, Simonides, has come to Lysander's house "to beg the reversion of his wife," a loose young woman, after his death : "thou are but a dead man, therefore what should a man do talking with thee?"
"*Lysander.* Impious blood-hounds !
Simonides. Let the ghost talk, ne'er mind him !
Lys. Shames of nature !
Sim. Alas, poor ghost ! consider what the man is ! "
Massinger's Works, ed. Cunningham, p. 571, col. 2.

Nor do I think anything of Mr. Hall.-Phillipps's suggestion, that if this "play was really written in the year 1599, as would seem from an allusion in it, those three words may have been taken from the earlier tragedy of *Hamlet*" (*Mem.*, p. 55). The Clerk is telling Gnotho that his (Gnotho's) wife Agatha, the daughter of Pollux, was "born *in an.* 1540, and now 'tis 99." III. i : Massinger's *Works*, p. 573, col. 1. From this, the theory was started, that *The Old Law* was first written in 1599, and then re-cast by Massinger before his death in 1640. The internal evidence of the play seems to me against the 1599 date. Middleton died in 1626. The year of Rowley's death is not known.—F. J. F.

The following, considering Gifford's authority, may be worth noting:—

? THOS. MIDDLETON, BEF. 1626.

"*Cook.* That Nell was Helen of Greece too.
Gnotho. As long as she tarried with her husband, she was Ellen ; but after she came to Troy, she was Nell of Troy, or Bonny Nell, whether you will or no.
Tailor. Why, did she grow shor[t]er when she came to Troy?
Gnotho. She grew longer,* if you mark the story. When she grew to be

---

[1] Evidently 'the Bermothes,' p. 450.
* "This miserable trash, which is quite silly enough to be original, has

an ell, she was deeper than any yard of Troy could reach by a quarter;
there was. Cupid was Troy weight, and Nell was avoirdupois; † she held
more, by four ounces, than Cressida."

The Old Law, or *A New Way to please you*, 1656.

---

yet the merit of being copied from Shakespeare."—Gifford. This is on the
supposition that the play, which was not printed till 1656, was not acted in
1599, as has been suggested. Dyce gives the title, p. 1, " *The Excellent
Comedy*, called *The Old Law, or A new way to please you. By Phil. Massinger. Tho. Middleton. William Rowley* . . . . 1656," and says, " Steevens
(Malone's *Shakespeare*, by Boswell (*Variorum* of 1821), ii. 425) remarks, that
this drama was acted in 1599, founding the statement most probably on a
passage in Act iii. Sc. 1, where the Clerk, having read from the Church-
book, ' *Agatha, the daughter of Pollux—born in an.* 1540,' adds, ' and *now
'tis* 99 ' . . . Gifford (*Introd.* to Massinger, p. lv, 2nd ed.) inclines to
believe that *The Old Law* was really first acted in 1599, and that Massinger (who was then only in the fifteenth year of his age) was employed, at a
subsequent period, to alter or to add a few scenes to the play. What portion of it was written by Middleton cannot be determined . . . Gifford . .
published *The Old Law* in the ivth vol. of his Massinger."

† Old ed. " haberdepoyse."—DYCE.

PETER WOODHOUSE, 1605.

Extoll that with admiration, which but a little before thou didſt rayle at, as moſt carterly. And when thou ſitteſt to conſult about any weighty matter, let either Iuſtice *Shallowe*, or his Couſen, Mr. *Weathercocke*, be foreman of the Iurie.

Epiſtle Dedicatorie, sign. A 2 back.

The / Flea : / *Sic parua componere magnis.* / *London* / Printed for *Iohn Smethwick* and *are to be* solde at his Shop / in Saint *Dunstanes* Churchyard *in Fleet-street*, vnder / the Diall. 1605./

I but true valour neuer danger ſought,
Raſhnes, it ſelfe doth into perill thruſt :
Thats onely valour where the quarrel's iuſt. sign. D.

A Shadowe of a ſhadow thus you ſee,
Alas what ſubſtance in it then can bee ?
If anything herein amiſſe doe ſeeme :
Conſider, 'twas a dreame, dreamt of a dreame.

FINIS

In 1877 Dr. Grosart reprinted this Poem from the unique copy in Lord Spencer's library at Althorpe, and in his Introduction, p. vii, cald attention to the above three bits, comparing the second with Shakspere's 2 *Henry VI*, III. ii. :

"Thrice is he arm'd that hath his quarrel just,"

and the third with *Hamlet*, II. ii. :

"*Guil.* What dreams indeed are ambition, for the very substance of the ambitious is merely the shadow of a dream.

Ham. A dream itself is but a shadow.

Ros. Truly, and I hold ambition of so airy and light a quality that it is but a shadow's shadow."

Prof. Dowden sent me the first Allusion, and later, Mr. Hll.-P. quoted the latter part of it.

The phrase "*bombast out a blank verse*" of Greene's *Groatsworth* occurs again in ' *Vertues Common-wealth: or The Highway to Honoor,*' by Henry Crosse, 1603 :

"Hee that can but bombast out a blancke verse, and make both the endes iumpe together in a ryme, is forthwith a poet laureat, challenging the garland of baies " (Grosart's reprint, p. 109).—E. DOWDEN.

• THOMAS HEYWOOD, 1605.

Glo. Let me awake my sleeping wits awhile :
Ha, the marke thou aimst at *Richard* is a Crowne,
And many stand betwixt thee and the same,
What of all that? Doctor play thou thy part,
Ile climbe by degrees through many a heart.

> *The First and Second Parts of King Edward the Fourth* . . .
> *As it hath diuerse times been publickly Acted. The fourth*
> *Impression.*[1] *London, Printed by* Humfrey Lownes.
> Anno 1626. sign. Q 2. (Heywood's *Works*, 1874, i. 135.)

[1] The 1st edition of 1605 is in the Douce Collection at South Kensington.

Heywood may have had in his mind Gloucester's lines in 3 *Henry VI*,
III. ii. 168-181 :

> " I'll make my heav'n to dream upon the crown,
> And, whiles I live, to account this world but hell,
> Until my mis-shaped trunk that bears this head
> Be round impaled with a glorious crown.   171
> And yet I know not how to get the crown,
> For *many lives stand between me and home.*
> And I . . .
> Torment myself to catch the English crown :
> And from that torment I will free myself,   180
> Or hew my way out with a bloody axe."

E. PHIPSON.

JOHN MARSTON, 1605.

Tis. Then thus, and thus, fo Hymen fhould begin :—
Sometimes a falling out proves falling in.

> *The Dutch Courtesan*, as it was playd in the Blacke Friars by the Children of her Maiesties Reuels. Act IV. sc. i. Vol. ii. p. 164, ed. Halliwell, 1856.

Probably from Shakspere's *Troilus*, III. i. 112—

Pand. Hee? no? sheele none of him : they two are twaine.
Hel. Falling in after falling out may make them three.

Teena Rochfort Smith.

G. CHAPMAN, &C., 1605.

Gyr[*tred*]. *His head as white as milke, All flaxen was his haire: But now he is dead, And laid in his Bed, And neuer will come againe.* God be at your labour.

    Eastward / Hoe./ As / It was playd in the / *Black-friers*./ *By* The Children of her Maiesties Reuels./ *Made by* / Geo: Chapman. Ben : Ionson. Ioh : Marston. / At London / Printed for *William Aspley*./ 1605./ Actus tertii. Scena Secunda. Sign. D2.

[This is from Ophelia's *No, no he is dead,*
       Go to thy death-bed;
       He never will come again.
       His beard as white as snow,
       All flaxen was his poll: . . . . .
. . . I pray God. God be wi' you.
       Hamlet, IV. vi. 189—197.
           H. C. HART.]

GEO. CHAPMAN, &c., 1605.

Enter Quickſiluer vnlaid, a towell about his necke, in his flat Cap, drunke.

Quick. Eaſtward Hoe; *Holla ye pampered Iades of* Aſia ....
Goul[*ding*]. Fie fellow *Quickſiluer,* what a pickle are you in?
Quick. Pickle? pickle in thy throat; zounes pickle ...
Lend me ſome monye
Gould. .... Ile not lend thee three pence.
Quick. Sfoote lend me ſome money, *haſt thou not Hyren here?*

> Eastward / Hoe. / As / It was playd in the / *Black-friers.* /
> *By* / The Children of her Maiesties Reuels. / *Made by* /
> Geo: Chapman, Ben: Ionson, Ioh: Marston. / At London /
> Printed for *William Aspley.* / 1605. / Actus secundi.
> Scena Prima. sign. B 3.

As we have "*Hamlet;* are you madde?" in this play, sign. D.—see *Centurie,* p. 69—and as Quicksiluer's language, says Gifford, "like Pistol's, is made up of scraps from old plays" (B. Jonson's *Works,* ed. Cunningham, 2-col., i. 233, col. 2 *n.*), the authors of *Eastward Hoe* no doubt allude, in the passage abuv, to Pistol's speeches in 2 *Henry IV,* II. iv.:
"downe Dogges, downe Fates: haue wee not *Hiren* here? ... Shall Pack-horses, and hollow-pamper'd Iades of Asia, which cannot goe but thirtie miles a day, compare with *Cæsar,* and with Caniballs, and Troian Greekes? ... Haue we not *Hiren* here?"

* WM. WARNER, 1606.

ONe *Makebeth*, who had traitrouſly his ſometimes Souereigne ſlaine,
And like a Monſter not a Man vſurpt in *Scotland* raigne,
Whoſe guiltie Conſcience did it ſelfe ſo feelingly accuſe,
As nothing not applide by him, againſt himſelfe he vewes;
No whiſpring but of him, gainſt him all weapons feares he borne,
All Beings iointly to reuenge his Murthres thinks he ſworne,
Wherefore (for ſuch are euer ſuch in ſelfe-tormenting mind)
But to proceed in bloud, he thought no ſafetie to find.
All Greatneſſe therefore, ſaue his owne, his driftings did inſeſt * * * *
One *Banquho*, powrefulſt of the Peers, in popular affection
And proweſſe great, was murthred by his tyrannous direction.
Fleance therefore this *Banquhos* ſonne fled thence to Wales for feare,
Whome *Gruffyth* kindly did receiue, and cheriſht nobly there.

   Booke 15. Chap. 94 of *A Continuance of Albions England*, 1606. By William Warner, being Books 14—16 of his *Albions England*, ed. 1612,* p. 375-6.

As the date of Shakspere's *Macbeth* must be late in 1605 or early in 1606, Warner may well hav been led to deal with King Macbeth by the popularity of Shakspere's play. And though he in no way follows Shakspere's lines, but instead, the chronicler's history of Fleance's amour with Griffith's

---

* There is no copy of the 1606 edition in the British Museum, unless the titleless *Continuance* of the 1612 copy is in fact the 1606 book. (Jan. 11, 1881.)

daughter and his death for it,* I yet believe that his introductory lines abuv, and specially the 'bloud' one, refer to Shakspere's play, and his lines—

"I am in blood
Stept in so far, that, should I wade no more,
Returning were as tedious as go o'er."
Macbeth, III. iv. 136-8.

The editions of Warner's *Albion's England* run thus:—

1586	Part I.	4 Books,	22 Chaps.	with Prose Addn. for Bk. 2.
1589	Parts I. and II.	6 ,,	33 ,,	,,
1592	,, (enlarged)	9 [1] ,,	44 ,,	,,
†1596	,,	12 [2] ,,	77 ,,	,,
1597	(*reprint of* 1596)	12 [2] ,,	77 ,,	,,
1602	(enlarged)	13 ,,	79 ,,	And a prose Epitome of the whole Historie of England.

† 1606 *A Continuance.* Books 14—16, ch. 80 - 107.
1612 (The Whole Work) 16 Books, 107 Chaps. ,,

The late Prof. G. L. Craik (died June, 1866) pointed out the Warner passage to Mr. S. Neil, who printed a few lines of it in his edition of *Macbeth* (1876), p. 9, note (Collins's School and College Classics). Mr. Joseph Knight noted the allusion independently, and I quoted the lines from his *Warner* of 1612 in the *Academy*, Jan. 1, 1881, p. 8, col. 1. In the next *Academy*, Jan. 8, Mr. Neil claimd his priority.—F. J. F.

---

* His son Walter afterwards goes back to Scotland, and there founds the royal strain from which James I. descended.
† Not in the British Museum, Jan. 11, 1880.
[1] But Bk. 9, ch. 44, has only 8 lines.
[2] Bk. 9 really for the first time. It incorporates the 8 lines of ed. 1592.

1606. BARNABE BARNES.

I will not omit that which is yet freſh in our late Chronicles; and hath been many times repreſented vnto the vulgar vpon our Engliſh Theaters, of *Richard Plantaginet*, third ſonne to *Richard* Duke of *Yorke*, who (being eldeſt brother next ſuruiuing to King *Edward* the fourth), after hee had vnnaturally made away his elder brother, *George* Duke of *Clarence* (whom he thought a grieuous eye-ſore betwixt him and the marke at which he leuelled), did vpon death of the King his brother, take vpon him protection of this Realme, vnder his two Nephewes left in his butcherly tuition: both which he cauſed at once to be ſmothered together, within a keepe of his Maieſties Tower, at *London*: which ominous bad lodging in memoriall thereof, is to this day knowne, and called by name of *the bloodly Tower*. Hereupon, this odious Vncle vſurped the crowne; but within little more then two yeares was depoſed, & confounded in the Battell at *Boſworth* in *Leyceſterſhire:* 1485. by King *Henry* the ſeuenth, ſent by God to make reſtitution of the peoples liberties; and after ſo long and horrible a ſhowre of ciuill blood, to ſend a golden ſun-ſhine of peace, cloſed vp in the princely leaues of that ſweet, & modeſt Roſe of *Lancaſter;* which being worne in the beautifull boſome of Lady *Elizabeth* the daughter of King *Edward*, (late mentioned of the Family of *Yorke*) diſperſed thoſe ſeditious cloudes of warre which had a long time obſcured our firmament of peace, baniſhing that ſulphurous ſmoke of the newly deuiſed Cannon, with the diuine odour of that bleſſed inoculation of Roſes: yeelding by their ſacred vnion the Lady *Margaret*, the firſt flower of that coniunction; and great Grandmother (as I declared) to our Soueraignes Maieſtie, in theſe happy bodyes raigning ouer vs: whoſe bleſſed raigne, I beſeech God to lengthen as the dayes of heauen.

> *Foure Bookes | of Offices: | Enabling Privat | persons for the speciall seruice of | all good Princes and Policies.| Made and deuised by Barnabe Barnes. | London | Printed at the charges of* George Bishop, | T. Adams, *and* C. Burbie. | 1606./ p. 113.

46*

THOMAS HEYWOOD, 1606.

Leic. But, madam, ere that day come,
There will be many a bloody nofe, ay, and crack'd crown:
We fhall make work for furgeons.

    1606. Heywood's *If You Know Not Me, You Know Nobody*, 2nd Part, Old Sh. Soc. ed., p. 157.

This may refer to
  'We must have bloody noses and crack'd crowns,
  And pass them current too.'
          1 *Hen. IV.*, II. iii. 96.
Or it may be a common phrase.—W. G. Stone.

THOMAS HEYWOOD, 1607.

Crip[*ple*]. What Mafter *Bowdler*, have you let her paffe unconquer'd?
Bow[*dler*]. Why what could I doe more? I look'd upon her with judgement, the ftrings of my tongue were well in tune, my embraces were in good meafure, my palme of a good conftitution, onely the phrafe was not moving; as for example, *Venus* her felfe with all her fkill could not winne *Adonis*, with the fame words; O heavens? was I fo fond then to think that I could conquer *Mall Berry*? O the naturall influence of my owne wit had beene farre better.

> *The* / Fayre Mayde of the / Exchange : With / the pleafaunt Humours of the / *Cripple* of *Fanchurch.* / Very delectable, and full of mirth. / London . . . 1607. Thos. Heywood's *Dramatic Works*, 1874, ii. 56.

This passage ought of course to have been quoted in *The Centurie*, p. 80, after the *Venus and Adonis* extract there.
The *Fayre Mayde* is full of echoes of Shakspere. Berry and the forfeit of Barnard's bond for a loan for 3 months, *Works*, ii. 23, 28, are from Shylock ; Franke Golding's soliloquy on himself, the scorner, falling in love, p. 20, is from Berowne's in *L. L. Lost*, III. i. 175-207, and Benedick's in *Much Ado*, II. iii. 27-30 ; Fiddle's "'tis most tolerable and not to be endured," p. 57, is Dogberry's ; Fiddle's leave-taking, " you, Cripple, to your shop," &c., is Jaques's in *As you like it*, V. iv. 192-8 ; and the plot of Flower and his wife each promising their daughter to a different man, while a third gets her, is more or less from the *Merry Wives*. The play or full passages should be read. I quote only a few lines :

THOMAS HEYWOOD, 1607.

HEYWOOD.

I could not indure the carreir of her wit for a million . . . .

I tell thee Cripple, I had rather encounter *Hercules* with blowes, than *Mall Berry* with words: And yet by this light I am horribly in love with her. Vol. ii. p. 54.

but the name of Russetting to Master *Fiddle* . . . 'tis most tolerable, and not to be endured. *Works*, ii. 57.

and so gentlemen I commit you all: you *Cripple* to your shop; you sir, to a turn-up and dish of capers; and lastly you, M. *Bernard*, to the tuition of the Counter-keeper: *Works*, ii. 58.

SHAKSPERE.

I cannot endure my Ladie Tongue. *M. Adoe*, II. i. 284.

I will go on the slightest arrand now to the Antypodes . . . rather than holde three words conference with this harpy. II. i. 273-9.
I will be horribly in loue with her. *Much Adoe*, II. iii. 245.

you shall also make no noise in the streetes: for, for the watch to babble and to talke, is most tollerable, and not to be indured. *Much Adoe* (Qo 1), III. iii. 37.

you to your former Honor I bequeath . . .
you to a loue that your true faith doth merit . .
you to your land, and loue, and great allies . . .
And you to wrangling . .
As you like it, V. iv. 192-5. Fo p. 207, col. 2.—F. J. F.

GEO. CHAPMAN, 1607.

..... great Seamen, uſing all their wealth
And ſkills in *Neptunes* deepe inviſible pathes,
In tall ſhips richly built and ribd with braſſe,
To put a Girdle round about the world.

> Buſſy D'Ambois. A Tragedie: As it hath been often preſented at Paules. London. Printed for *William Aſpley*, 1607 (ed. 1657, sign. A3), I. i. 20-3. *Works*, ed. Shepherd, 1874, p. 140, col. 2.

Pucke. Ile put a girdle about the earth, in forty minutes.—*A Midſomer nights Dreame.* Folio, p. 149, col. 2; II. i. 175.

Was not Chapman considering the fate of Duncan's horses in *Macbeth*, II. iv, when he wrote the following in his *Byrons Tragedie*, 1608, *Works*, 1874, p. 256, col. 1:—

> "And to make this no less than an ostent,
> Another that hath fortun'd since, confirms it:
> Your goodly horse Pastrana, which the Archduke,
> Gave you at Brussels, in the very hour
> You left your strength, fell mad, and kill'd himself;
> The like chanced to the horse the great Duke sent you;
> And, with both these, the horse the duke of Lorraine,
> Sent you at Vimie made a third presage ...
> Who like the other, pined away and died.
> . . . .
> The matchless Earl of Essex, whom some make ...
> A parallel with me in life and fortune,
> Had one horse likewise, that the very hour
> He suffer'd death, (being well the night before,)
> Died in his pasture."—H. C. HART.

EDWARD SHARPHAM, 1607.

Old Lord. And hee is welcome, what suddaine guft (my Sonne) in haft hath blowne thee hither, & made thee leaue the Court, where fo many earth-treading ftarres adornes the sky of ftate?

> 1607. Edward Sharpham. *Cupids Whirligig* / As it hath bene sundry times Acted / by the Children of the Kings Majesties / Reuels./ Sign. B 1, back.

Compare *Romeo & Juliet*, Act I. sc. ii. l. 25 :—
 "At my poor house look to behold this night
 Earth-treading stars that make dark heaven light."

and y faith he was a neate lad too, for his beard was newly cut bare; marry it fhowed fomething like a Medow newly mowed: ftubble, ftubble.

> 1607. E. Sharpham. *The Fleire.*/ As it hath beene often played in the / *Blacke-Fryers* by the Children of / the Reuells./ Sign. B 3, back, at foot.

Compare 1 *Hen. IV*, Act I. sc. iii, on the fop's beard :
 "and his chin new reap'd
 Show'd like a stubble-land at harvest-home."

(The following passage illustrates one of Shakspere's words :

 "I can no longer hold my patience
 Impudent villaine, & lascivious Girles,
 I have ore-heard your vild convertions ;
 You scorne Philosophy : You'le be no *Nunne*,
 You must needs kisse the Purse, because he sent it,
 And you forsooth you *flurgill*, minion
 You'le have your will forsooth."
> 1578. Wm. Haughton. *A Woman Will Have Her Will*, ed. 1631.

Compare the Nurse in *Romeo & Juliet*, II. iv. 162 : "Scurvy knave ! I am none of his *flirt-gills* ; I am none of his skains-mates.")

E. DOWDEN.

EDWARD SHARPHAM, 1607.

Kni[ght]. And how liues he with am.
Fle[ire]. Faith like *Thifbe* in the play, a has almoft kil'd himfelfe with the fcabberd :

> The | Fleire. | As it hath beene often played in the | Blacke-Fryers by the Children of | the Reuells. | Written by Edward Sharpham of the Middle Temple, Gentleman. At London. | Printed and are to be solde by F. B. in Paules Church|yard, at the signe of the Flower de Luce and the | Crowne, 1607. Actus Secundus. Sign. E, back.

This bit of business,—to which Mr. Halliwell-Phillipps calld attention in his *Memoranda, M. N. Dr.*, 1879, p. 35, and which must have been due to one of Shakspere's fellows, if not to Shakspere himself,—became a tradition on the Stage, and was followd by the actor who playd Flute with Charles Kean between 1850 and 1860 (?). But Mr. Righton, the last actor who playd Flute to Phelps's Bottom at the Gaiety in 1875,[1] tells Mr. E. Rose that he didn't follow the custom : he stabd himself with the sword hilt, his own thumb, or anything that came handiest.

I doubt whether the following mention of Pyramus and Thisbe, cited by Mr. Hll.-P., p. 10, is a reference to Shakspere's *M. N. Dr.*, tho the lines occur in the next poem to one containing an allusion to the old play of *Hamlet* :—

> I note the places of polluted sinne
> Where your kind wenches and their bawds put in.
> I know the houses where base cheaters vse,
> And note what Gulls (to worke vpon) they chuse :
> I take a notice what your youth are doing,
> When you are fast a sleepe, how they are woing,
> And steale together by some secret call,
> Like *Piramus* and *Thisby* through the wall.
> I see your prentises what pranks they play,
> And things you neuer dreame on can bewray :

(† 1620. Sam. Rowlands.) *The Night | Raven.* | *By S. R.* | *London.* | Printed by *G : Eld* for *Iohn Deane and Thomas Baily*. 1620. 4to. sign. D 2, back ; p. 28, Hunterian Soc. reprint, 1872.—F. J. F.

---

[1] It was produced on Febr. 15, 1875.—E. Rose.

† It was popular, and having been first published, as far as we know, in 1618, it was reprinted in 1620 and 1634, each time with a wood-cut of a raven on the title-page. (Bibliographical Index to the Works of Samuel Rowlands (Hunt. Soc.), p. 37.)—P. A. L.

• T. DECKER AND J. WEBSTER, 1607.

Par. . . . when women are proclaymed to bee light, they ſtriue to be more light, for who dare diſproue a Proclamation. *Tent.* I but when light Wiues make heauy huſbands, let theſe huſbands play mad *Hamlet*; and crie reuenge, come, and weele do ſo.

> *West-ward | Hoe.| As it hath beene diuers times Acted | by the Children of Poules.| Written by Tho: Decker, and Iohn Webster.| Printed at London, and to be sold by Iohn Hodgets | dwelling in Paules Churchyard.|* 1607 / 4to., sign. H 3.

Tho it is very doubtful whether the above refers to Shakspere's *Hamlet*, yet as the three Hamlet allusions excluded by Dr. Ingleby from his first edition of the *Centurie* have been let into the second, pp. 453-4, this *West-ward Hoe* one may keep them company. Dr. Ingleby tells me that he gave it to Miss Smith for the 2nd edition, but it was inadvertently overlookt, and returnd to him.—F. J. F.

* FR. BEAUMONT AND JN. FLETCHER, 1607.

That pleasing piece of frailty that we call woman.
The Woman-hater, III. i.

Possibly from Hamlet's "Frailty, thy name is woman," *Hamlet*, I. ii. 146, Q2.—E. H. HICKEY.

THOS. DEKKER & JN. WEBSTER, 1607.

(1) The Fox is futtle, and his head once in,
The flender body eafily will follow.
    sign. D1, back.

(2) *Guil*[ford]. Peace reft his foule, his finnes be buried in his graue,
And not remembred in his Epitaph:
    sign. D3.

(3) *Iane*. Is greefe fo fhort? twas wont to be full of wordes,
    sign. D3, back.[1]

> The / Famovs / History of Sir Tho-/mas Wyat, / *With The Coronation of Queen Mary*, / and the coming in of King / Philip. / As it was plaied by the Queens Maiesties / Seruants. / Written by *Thomas Dickers*, / and *Iohn Webster*. / 'London / Printed by E. A. for *Thomas Archer*, and are to be / solde at his shop in the Popes-head Pallace, nere the Royall Exchange. / 1607. /

(1) is a recollection of Shakspere in 3 *Henry VI*, IV. vii.
"*Gloucester* [*Aside*] But when the fox hath once got in his nose,
He'll soon find means to make the body follow."

(2) is from Prince Hal's speech over Douglas's corpse, 1 *Henry IV*, V. iv. 99—101 :—
"Adieu, and take thy praise with thee to heaven !
Thy ignominy sleep with thee in the grave,
But not remembred in thy epitaph !"

---

[1] Perhaps Guilford's
" We are led with pomp to prison,
O propheticke soule," (sign. A4)
may be a recollection of *Hamlet*.—F. J. F.

(3) is perhaps a recollection of the Duchess of York and Queen Elizabeth's talk in *Richard III*, IV. iv. 124—131 :—

" *Q. Eliz.* My words are dull ; O, quicken them with thine. . . .
Duch. Why should calamity be full of words ?
Q. Eliz. Windy attorneys to their client woes,
Airy succeeders of intestate joys,
Poor breathing orators of miseries !
Let them have scope ! though what they do impart,
Help not at all, yet do they ease the heart."—EMMA PHIPSON.

T. DEKKER, 1608.

Their faces therefore do they turne vpon *Barnwell* (neere *Cambridge*) for ther was it[1] to be acted: thither comes this counterfet mad man running: his fellow Iugler following aloofe, crying ftoppe the mad-man, take heed of the man, hees madde with the plague. Sometimes would he ouertake him, and lay hands vppon him (like a Catch-pole) as if he had arretted him, but furious *Hamlet* woulde prefently eyther breake loofe like a Beare from the ftake, or elfe fo fet his pawes on this dog that thus bayted him, that with tugging and tearing one anothers frockes off, they both looked like mad *Tom* of Bedlam . . . At length he came to the houfe where the deade man had bin lodged: from this dore would not this olde *Ieronimo* be driuen, that was his Inne, there he woulde lie, that was his Bedlam, and there or no where muft his mad tricks be plaid.

> The / Dead Tearme./ or,/ *Westminsters Complaint for long
> Va/cations and short Termes./ Written in manner of
> a Dialogue betweene / the two Cityes London and
> Westminster./ . . . London./ *Printed and are to be
> sold by John Hodgets at his house in Pauls / Churchyard.*
> 1608./ Sign. G 3./

Part quoted in Mr. Hall.-P.'s *Mem. on Hamlet*, p. 20.—F. J. F.

---

[1] The Comedy or trick of 2 London Porters, of whom one shammd mad, getting the goods out of the bedroom of a young London tradesman, who had died suddenly at Stourbridge Fair, Barnwell, and whose corpse the two porters had carried to the grave.

THOS. MIDDLETON, 1608.

Harebrain. . . . . .
" I have conveyed away all her wanton pamphlets ; as *Hero and Leander, Venus and Adonis ;* O, two luscious marrow-bone pies for a young married wife ! "

A Mad World, my Masters. Middleton's Works, ed. Dyce, 1840, ii. 340.

The jealous Harebrain is speaking of his newly-married wife.—H. C. HART.

Mr. Hll.-Phillipps, in his *Discursive Notes on Rom. and Jul.*, p. 115, says that there is a quotation from *R. & J.* in John Day's *Humour out of Breath,* 1608. Not being up in his Ovid, he no doubt alludes to this passage :

" *Oct.* Tut, louers othes, like toyes writ down in sands   [F 2.
Are soone blowne ore, contracts are common wiles,
T' intangle fooles, *Ioue* himselfe sits and smiles
At louers periuries,"

Humour out of breath./ *A Comedie* / Diuers times latelie acted, / *By the Children* / Of / *The Kings Reuells.*/ Written / *By* / Iohn Day./ Printed at London for *Iohn Helmes,* and are to be sold / at his shop in Saint Dunstans Church-yard / in Fleet-street. 1608./ *Actus Quartus,* sign. F 2, and back (p. 55, ed. A. H. Bullen, 1881).

But, as Mr. Bullen notes in his Introduction, p. 95, this is one of the many allusions to Ovid's lines, *Ars Am.* l. 633-4 :

"Juppiter ex alto perjuria ridet amantum,
Et jubet Aeolios irrita ferre notos."

'Shakespeare, as everybody knows, has alluded to this passage of Ovid in *Rom. and Jul.* ii. 2.' [95.]
" At Louers periuries they say Ioue smiles." Q 1. ' laughes,' Q 2.

*ROBERT ARMIN, 1608.

Ther are, as Hamlet faies, things cald whips in ftore.

A / Nest of Ninnies[1] / *Simply of themselues without* / *Compound* / Stultorum plena sunt omnia./ *By Robert Armin.*/ London :/ *Printed by T. E. for Iohn Deane.* 1608./ *Repr. Old Shakespeare Soc.* 1842, *ed. J. P. Collier*, p. 55, l. 8.

Mr. Collier's note, p. 67, is : "No such passage is to be found in Shakespeare's *Hamlet*, as it has come down to us, either in the editions of 1603, 1604, or in any later impression. Possibly Armin may refer to the old *Hamlet* which preceded Shakespeare's tragedy ; but this seems unlikely, as he was an actor in the same theatre as that for which Shakespeare wrote.[2]"

Mr. Hall.-P. says that the sentence above seems to have been well-known and popular, for it is partially cited in the *Spanish Tragedie*, 1592, and in the First Part of the *Contention*, 1594 (*Mem. on Hamlet*, 1879, p. 19).

On looking up the latter of these vague references, the reader will find that the passage is :—

"*Hum.*[*phrey*]. My Maisters of saint Albones,
Haue you not Beadles in your Towne,
And things called whippes ?"[3]

(ed. Halliwell, Old Shakespeare Soc. 1843, p. 23), with a note on p. 87, quoting Mr. Collier's comment, and making the following suggestion, doubtless long since repented of: "It is not impossible that Armin may have confused the two plays together, and wrote incorrectly 'as Hamlet saies,' instead of 'as Gloster saies.'"

---

[1] The *Nest of Ninnies* is but "a reprint of Armin's *Foole vpon Foole*, 1605 (Mr. Huth, unique), with certain alterations," according to Mr. Hazlitt. *Handbook*, p. 12.

[2] Armin belonged to Lord Chandos's Players : see Collier's *Lives of Actors*, p. 196, &c.—B. N.

[3] Collier, *Shakespeare's Library*, Vol. V. p. 445. Second Part of *K. Hen. VI*, II. i.

ROBERT ARMIN, 1608.

The first reference is not, I assume, to Isabella's speech in *Span. Trag.* Act IV, ed. 1594, Sign. F4, back (Hazlitt's *Dodsley*, v. 94-5)—

Isa[bell]. "Why, did I not giue you gowne and goodly things,
Bought you a whistle and a whipstalke too ;
To be reuenged on their villanies."

—though that is the only one I see in the (?)1592 play,—but to two later lines (*ib.* p. 105) of Hieronimo's in Ben Jonson's 'Additions' of 1601 (see note there, p. 103) :—

"Well, heauen is heauen still,
And there is *Nemesis* and Furies,
And things called whippes.
And they do sometimes meete with murderers,
They doe not alwayes scape, that's some comfort." [1]
      So 1623, 4º. G2, back, G3, and 1633 ed., ibid.—P. A. L.

May not this phrase, as well as the 'trout with four legs,' from Jn. Clarke's *Paræmiologia*, 1639, p. 135, below, be part of some actor's gag—not Burbage's, I hope.—[F. J. F.]

---

[1] The Spanish Tragedy, 1610 (G4). Actus Tertius. Hieronimo.

ROBERT ARMIN, 1608, 1609.

(1) Likewife moſt affable Lady, kinde and debonere, the ſecond of the firſt which I fawcily falute, pardon I pray you the boldnes of a Begger, who hath been writ downe for an Aſſe in his time, & pleades under *forma pauperis* in it ſtill, not-withſtanding his Conſtableſhip and Office :

(2) *I haue ſeene the ſtars at midnight in your ſocieties, and might have Commenſt like an Aſſe as I was, but I lackt liberty in that, yet I was admitted in Oxford to be of Chriſts Church, while they of Al-ſoules gaue ayme : ſuch as knew me remember my meaning.*†

(3) tho not fo quaint
As courtly dames or earths bright treading ſtarres,
They are maids of More-clacke, homely milke-bob things,
Such as I loue, and faine would marry well.

(4) Scarlet is fcarlet, and her fin blood red,
Wil not be waſht hence with a fea of water,

    (1) Dedication of *The Italian Taylor, and his Boy*, 1609.
    (2) *Epiſtle-dedicatory* before *A Neſt of Ninnies*, 1608.
    (3) *The Hiſtorie of the two Maids of More-clacke* (Sig. C, bk.).
    (4) Ibid. (Sig. E 2).

Mr. J. P. Collier firſt noticed (1) as proof that R. A. had played Dogberry.[1] I would add (2) as a ſecond evidence, becauſe like the firſt it is brought as it were by head and ſhoulders into the context. (3) is a remembrance of *Rom. & Jul.*, I. ii. l. 25,[2] and (4) of Macbeth, II. ii. 60-3

---

† The old Shakespeare Soc. reprint, 1842, p. 3, reads 'meaſures,' not 'meaning.'
   [1] O that I had been writ down an ass !—*Much Ado*, V. ii. 89-90.
    [2] At my poor houſe, look to behold this night,
      Earth-treading ſtars that make dark heaven light.

> Will all great Neptune's ocean wash this blood
> Clean from my hand? No, this my hand will rather
> The multitudinous seas incarnadine,
> Making the green one red.

There are other expressions in Armin which recal Shakespeare, notably
> The divell has scripture for his damned ill.—*Two Maids.*

and
> What is thy haste in leathe steept.—*Ibid.*

which may be paralleled by *The Mer. of Ven.*, I. iii. 89,[1] *Twelfth Night*, IV. i. 66,[2] and *An. and Cleop.*, II. vii. 114,[3] but these, like others, may have been ordinary phrases of the day.—B. N.

---

[1] Mark you this, Bassanio,
The devil can cite Scripture for his purpose.
[2] Let Fancy still my sense in Lethe steep.
[3] Till that the conquering wine hath steep'd our sens
In soft and delicate Lethe.

BEAUMONT (*died* 1616) AND FLETCHER (*died* 1625), 1608-25.

[The quotations are from Dyce's edition, in eleven volumes, 8vo, Moxon, 1843-6. In the left-hand column are B. and F.'s words; in the right, the parallel passages, from Dyce's notes. I have left out a few which seem to me straind beyond bearing.—F. J. F.]

—But how can I
Look to be heard of gods that must be just,
Praying upon the ground I hold by wrong?
? 1608-10 (printed 1620). *Philaster*, II. iv. Works, i. 242.

'In this sentiment our authors seem to be copying Shakespeare, in a noble passage of his Hamlet:
—"Forgive me my foul murder!
That cannot be; since I am possess'd
Of those effects for which I did the murder.
My crown, mine own ambition, and my queen.
May one be pardon'd, and retain the offence?" &c.—Theobald.

But there is
Divinity about you, that strikes dead
My rising passions: as you are my king,
I fall before you.
? 1610 (printed 1619). *The Maid's Tragedy*, Act III. sc. i. Works, i. 369.

'So Shakespeare said, before our poets, in his *Hamlet*:
"Let him go, Gertrude; do not fear our person:
There's such divinity doth hedge a king,
That treason can but peep to what it would,
Acts little of his will."—Theobald.'

Arane [the penitent Queen-mother of King *Arbaces*, kneels to him]
As low as this I bow to you; and would
As low as to my grave, to shew a mind
Thankful for all your mercies.

"There is a fine passage, upon a similar occasion, in Shakespeare's *Coriolanus*, to which our authors might possibly have an eye:—
'*Volumnia.* Oh, stand up bless'd
Whilst with no softer cushion than the flint

BEAUMONT (d. 1616) AND FLETCHER (d. 1625), 1608-25. 62

Arbaces Oh, stand up, And let me kneel! the light will be asham'd To see obseivance done to me by you. *Arane.* You are my king. *Arbaces.* You are my mother: rise 1611 (printed 1619). *A King and no King*, III. i. Works, ii. 275.	I kneel before thee; and unproperly Show duty, as mistaken all the while Between the child and parent. *Coriolanus.* What is this? Your knees to me? to your corrected son.' [act v. sc. 3]. Theobald."
Arb. If there were no such instruments as thou, We kings could never act such wicked deeds. *ib.* III. iii, end. Works, ii. 297.	'The Editors of 1778 cite the passage in Shakspere's *King John*, IV. ii.: It is the curse of kings to be attended By slaves that take their humours for a warrant To break within the bloody house of life; &c.'
tell me of a fellow That can mend noses? and complain, so tall A soldier should want teeth to his stomach? And how it was great pity, that it was, That he that made my body was so busied He could not stay to make my legs too. . . . 1613. Fletcher's *Captain* (printed in 1st Folio, 1647), II. i. Works, iii. 246.	'Weber says, "Perhaps the poet had the following line of Hotspur's speech in *King Henry IV*, Part I, in his mind: And that it was great pity, so it was," &c.'
"Base is the slave commanded:" come to me *The little French Lawyer*, IV. vi. Works, iii. 541.	'A parody on Pistol's exclamation "Base is the slave that pays!" Shakespeare's *Henry V*, act ii, sc. 1.' —Dyce.
Look up, brave friend. I have no means to rescue thee: "My kingdom for a sword!" *ib.*, iii. 542.	'Another parody on Shakespeare; "My kingdom for a horse!"— Richard III, act v. sc. 4.'

63 BEAUMONT (*d.* 1616) AND FLETCHER (*d.* 1625), 1608-25.

Zanthia. Then know,
It was not poison, but a sleeping
potion,
Which she receiv'd ; yet of sufficient
strength
So to bind up her senses, that no sign
Of life appear'd in her ; and thus
thought dead,
In her best habit, as the custom is,
You know, in Malta, with all cere-
monies
She's buried in her family monu-
ment,
In the Temple of St. John : I'll
bring you thither,
Thus, as you are disguis'd. Some
six hours hence,
The potion will leave working.
    before March 1618-19 (printed
    1647). Fletcher. *The Knight
    of Malta*, IV. i, end. Works,
    v. 177.

'This speech bears an obvious
similitude to one of Friar Laurence
in Shakespeare's *Romeo and Juliet*
[act iv. sc. 5.¹ D.]. *Ed.* 1778.'
  ¹ See too IV. i. 92—115.

[Then gave I her, so tutor'd by my
  art,
A sleeping potion ; which so took
  effect
As I intended, for it wrought on her
The form of death. V. iii. 242-5]
[and, as the custom is,
In all her best array bear her her to
  church. IV. v. 80-1.]
  [meantime I writ to Romeo,
That he should thither come as this
  dire night,
To help to take her from her borrow'd grave,
Being the time the potion's force
  should cease. V. iii. 245-9]

Belisa. . . . . . . by my life,
The parting kiss you took before
  your travel
Is yet a virgin on my lips, preserv'd
With as much care as I would do
  my fame,
To entertain your wish'd return.
    1616-18 (printed 1647). *The
    Queen of Corinth*, I. ii ;
    Works, v. 403.

' The writer was thinking here of a
passage in Shakespeare's *Coriolanus ;*
"Now by the jealous queen of
  heaven, that kiss
I carried from thee, dear ; and my
  true lip
Hath virgin'd it e'er since." Act v.
  sc. 3.'

I yet remember when the Volga curl'd,
The agèd Volga, when he heav'd his
  head up,
And rais'd his waters high, to see
  the ruins,
The ruins our swords made, the
  bloody ruins :
    1618 (printed 1647). Fletcher.
    The Loyal Subject, I. iii.
    Works, vi. 16.

' Here, as Reed notices, Fletcher
seems to have had an eye to a passage in Shakespeare's *Henry IV.*
(First Part) act i. sc. 3 ;
"Three times they breath'd, and
  three times did they drink,
Upon agreement, of swift Severn's
  flood ;
Who then, affrighted with their
  bloody looks,

"Ran fearfully among the trembling
    reeds,
And hid his crisp head in the hollow
    bank,
Blood-stained with these valiant
    combatants."

       sure, to tell
of Cæsar's amorous heats : and how
  he fell
In the Capitol *,[1] can never be the   * An allusion to Shakespeare's
  same   *Julius Cæsar* [wherein he is made to
To the judicious : nor will such   die in the Capitol, instead of in the
  blame   *Curia Pompeii*, where the Senate
Those that penn'd this for barrenness,   met, in the Campus Martius.]
  when they find
Young Cleopatra here . . . .
We treat not of what boldness she
  did die,†   † An allusion to Shakespeare's
Nor of her fatal love to Antony . . .   *Antony and Cleopatra*. [?—F.]
  (printed 1647) *The False One.*
  Prologue. *Works*, vi. 217.

[1] "So in Fletcher and (?) Shirley's *Noble Gentleman*, (licenst—after Fletcher's death in 1625—on Feb. 3, 1625-6, pr. 1647,) V. i. Works, 1846, x. 186—
      "So Cæsar fell, when in the Capitol
      They gave his body two-and-thirty wounds."
'Here we have two blunders,' says Sympson ; 'the first with respect to the place where Cæsar fell, which was not in the *Capitol*, but in *Curiâ Pompeii* ; the other as to the number of wounds he fell by : as to the first, it was a blunder peculiar to the playwrights of that time ; Shakespeare began it in *Hamlet*, act iii. sc. 2 . . . .
  "*Polonius.* I did enact Julius Cæsar : I was killed i' the *Capitol.*"
'Our authors, treading in their master's steps, took up the same mistake here ; and after them Shakerley Marmion, in his *Antiquary*, inadvertently continued the same error, making Veterano say,
  "And this was Julius Cæsar's hat when he was killed in the *Capitol.*"
'As for the second fault, 'twas made no where but at the press, for the number (I suppose) in the original MS. was wrote in figures, thus, 23, which, by an easy [mistake,] shifting place, was altered to 32, and thus we have nine wounds more than Cæsar ever received.'—SYMPSON. 'The notion that Julius Cæsar was killed in the Capitol is as old as Chaucer's time : see Malone's note on the above-cited passage of *Hamlet*.' "—Dyce.

65 BEAUMONT (d. 1616) AND FLETCHER (d. 1625), 1608-25.

Celia. . . . . . How does he?
Governess. Oh, God, my head!
Celia. Prithee be well, and tell me, Did he speak of me since he came?
(printed 1647). Fletcher. *The Humorous Lieutenant,* III. ii. Works, vi. 467 [see the whole scene.]

'A recollection of Shakespeare's *Romeo and Juliet,* act ii. sc. 5—
Nurse. Lord, how my head aches, &c.'

Petronius. Thou fond man Hast thou forgot the ballad, *Crabbed Age?*
Can May and January match together,
And never a storm between 'em?
(pr. 1647). Fletcher. *The Woman's Prize, or The Tamer Tamed* ["avowedly intended to form the Second Part" of Shakspere's *Shrew*], IV. i. Works, vii. 172.

'The well-known lines by Shakespeare, contained in his *Passionate Pilgrim.*' [And though this collection was by no means all Shakspere's (see *Introd. to Leopold Shaksp.,* p. xxxv, and *Centurie,* p. 99), yet I incline to think that *Crabbed Age* may be his.—F.]

Rowland. Swear to all these . . .
Tra. I will . . . .
. . . . . Let's remove our places.*
Swear it again.
ib. V. iii. Works, vii. 206.

Petruchio. Come: something I'll do; but what it is, I know not.
Woman's Prize, II. iv, end. Works, vii. 142.

* "This is plainly a sneer at the scene in *Hamlet* [i. 5] where (on account of the Ghost calling under the stage) the prince and his friends two or three times remove their situations. Again, in this play, p. 142, Petruchio's saying [opposite] seems to be meant as a ridicule on Lear's passionate exclamation [act ii. sc. 4],
——I will do such things—
What they are, yet I know not."
J. N. Ed. 1778.
'Nonsense: there is more of compliment than "sneer" in these recollections of Shakespeare.'— Dyce.
'And so say all of us.'—F.

Mirabel. Well; I do take thee upon mere compassion;
And I do think I shall love thee.
1621 (pr. 1679). Fletcher. *The Wild-Goose Chase,* V. vi. Works, 1845, viii. 205.

'Here our poet was thinking of what Benedick says to Beatrice at the conclusion of Shakespeare's *Much Ado about Nothing;*
"Come, I will have thee; but by this light, I take thee for pity."'

BEAUMONT (d. 1616) AND FLETCHER (d. 1625), 1608-25. 66

[For the " Farewell, pride and pomp ! " &c. from Fletcher's *Prophetess*, licenst May 14, 1622, pr. 1647, see p. 60, set before Dyce's edition was referrd to.]

Higgen. Then bear up bravely
with your Brute,† my lads!
Higgen hath prigg'd the prancers in
his days,
And sold good penny-worths: we
will have a course ;
The spirit of Bottom is grown bottomless
(pr. 1647). Fletcher. *Beggars'
Bush*,‡ V. ii. Works, ix. 103.

† . . . [on the last line opposite,] says Steevens, "there seems to be a sneer at this character of Bottom [in *M. N. Dr.*] ; but I do not very clearly perceive its drift. . ."—Note on *M. N. Dr.* act v. sc. 1.

Chatillion. Sir, you shall know
My love's true title, mine by marriage.
[He then sets it forth,¹ more

'This seems a flirt on the English king's title to France, in *Henry the Fifth*.' — Theobald. 'Not a flirt,

---

‡ I put in a note the following lines from this play, *Beggar's Bush*, II. i. *Works*, viii. 29,

"under him,
Each man shall eat his own stoln eggs and butter,
In his own shade or sun-shine, and enjoy
His own dear dell, doxy, or mort, at night,
In his own straw, with his own shirt or sheet
That he hath filch'd that day."

as I'm certain that Fletcher is here only parodying his own lines in that *Henry VIII* which he completed from Shakspere's unfinisht leaves. Dyce does not give Shakspere the lines, but calls them "the words of Cranmer concerning Q. Elizabeth in Shakespeare's *Henry the Eighth*, act v. sc. 4 ;

"In her days every man shall eat in safety,
Under his own vine, what he plants, and sing
The merry songs of peace to all his neighbours."

¹ Setting aside the first race of French kings,
Which will not here concern us, as Pharamond,
With Clodion, Meroveus, and Chilparic,

And to come down unto the second race,
Which we will likewise slip . . . .
. . . . of Martel Charles
The father of king Pepin, who was sire

67 BEAUMONT (*d.* 1616) AND FLETCHER (*d.* 1625), 1608-25.

shortly than, tho after the manner of, the Archbishop in Shakspere's *Henry V.* I. ii.]

 1626 (pr. 1647). ? Shirley & Fletcher. *The Noble Gentleman*, III. iv. B. & F.'s *Works*, x. 160.

certainly, but an innocent parody.' Weber.

Take, oh, take those lips away,
 That so sweetly were forsworn,
And those eyes, like break of day,
 Lights that do mislead the morn!
But my kisses bring again,
Seals of love, though seal'd in vain.
Hide, oh, hide those hills of snow,
 Which thy frozen bosom bears,
  &c., &c.
  (pr. 1639) Fletcher & Rowley (?). *The Bloody Brother, or, Rollo Duke of Normandy*, V. ii. *Works*, x. 459.

"The first stanza of this song (with two very trifling variations) occurs in Shakespeare's *Measure for Measure*, act iv. sc. 1, and both stanzas are found in the spurious edition of his poems, 1640. In a long note to which I refer the reader (Malone's Shakespeare, xx. 417 [Variorum, 1821]), Boswell urges the probability that the song was composed neither by Shakespeare nor Fletcher, but by a third unknown writer: I am inclined, however, to believe that it was from the pen of the great dramatist."—Dyce. It is now generally given to 'Kit Marlowe,' on Isaac Walton's authority.

Clarangè. Myself and (as I then deliver'd to you)
A gentleman of noble hope, one Lydian,
Both brought up from our infancy together,
One company, one friendship, and one exercise
Ever affecting, one bed holding us,

'In this description of the friendship of Clarangè and Lydian, our author seems to have intended an imitation of the excellent account of female friendship in Shakespeare's *M. N. Dream*, iii. 2.'—REED.
 O! is all forgot?
All school-days' friendship, childhood innocence?

To Charles, the great and famous Charlemagne;	Hugh Capet was the first;
And to come to the third race of French kings,	Next his son Robert, Henry then, and Philip,
Which will not be greatly pertinent in this cause	With Louis, and his son, a Louis too,
Betwixt the king and me, of which you know	And of that name the seventh: but all this
	Springs from a female, as it shall appear.

One grief, and one joy parted still
  between us,
More than companions, twins in all
  our actions,
We grew up till we were men, held
  one heart still.
Time call'd us on to arms; we were
  one soldier . . .
When arms had made us fit, we were
  one lover,
We lov'd one woman
    (pr. 1647) Fletcher & (?) Mas-
    singer. *The Lovers' Pro-
    gress*, II. i. Works, xi. 46.

We, Hermia, like two artificial gods,
Have with our needles created both
  one flower,
Both on one sampler, sitting on one
  cushion,
Both warbling of one song, both in
  one key,
As if our hands, our sides, voices,
  and minds,
Had been incorporate. So we grew
  together,
Like to a double cherry, seeming
  parted,
But yet an union in partition;
Two lovely berries moulded on one
  stem;
So, with two seeming bodies, but
  one heart;
Two of the first, like coats in her-
  aldry.
Due but to one, and crowned with
  one crest.

Diego. . . . instinct, signior,
Is a great matter in an host.
    (pr. 1647) Fletcher & Mas-
    singer; *Love's Pilgrimage*,
    I. ii. *Works*, xi. 247.

'Steevens has observed, that this is the same phrase used by Falstaff . . . "but beware *instinct*; the lion will not touch the true prince. *Instinct is a great matter*." [1 *Hen. IV.* II. iv. 299-300.] The passage in the text seems to have been suggested by the one quoted from Shakespeare.' Weber.

See p. 71 on a passage from Fletcher's *Fair Maid of the Inn*.—F. J. F.

ROGER SHARPE, 1610.

In Virofum.

How *Falſtaf* like, doth fweld *Viroſus* looke,
As though his paunch did fofter euery finne;
And fweares he is iniured by this booke,
His worth is taxt he hath abufed byn:
Swell ftill *Viroſus*, burft with emulation,
I neither taxe thy vice nor reputation.

> *MORE FOOLES yet.* Written by *R. S.* [*Small Plate.*] At *LONDON*, *Printed for* Thomas Caſtleton, *and are to be sold at his shop without Cripple-gate.* An. 1610. *Bodleian (Malone* 299) 4*to. sign.* E 3. "*To the Reader*" *is signed* "*Roger Sharpe.*"

Quoted (and partly modernizd) in Mr. Halliwell's *Character of Sir John Falstaff*, 1841, p. 41. The quotation there on p. 42, from the document printed by Mr. Collier, was evidently made in that innocence of incapacity to distinguish between a genuine and a forgd MS. which Mr. Halliwell, oddly enough, often showd in former days. I quote the bit[1] only to show what sham old-spelling is like : A character is to be dressed " ' *Like* a Sr Jon Falsstaff : in a roabe of russet, quite low, with a great belley, like a swolen man, long moustacheos, the sheows shorte, and out of them great toes like naked feete : buskins to sheaw a great swolen leg.' "—New Facts regarding the Life of Shakespeare in a letter to Thomas Amyot, &c., from J. Payne Collier, London, 1835, 8vo. p. 39.[2] See further extracts on Falstaff, under Anon. 1640 ; John Speed, 1611 ; Anon. 1600.—F. J. F.

---

[1] From Collier, and not with Halliwell's mistakes in reprinting from Collier's *New Facts.*—P. A. L.

[2] Ingleby's *Complete View* (of the Shakspere Forgeries), p. 310-11 ; N. E. S. A. Hamilton's Inquiry, p. 84 ; Collier, 1860 ; *New Facts*, p. 38-9. 1835.

? About 1610. A MS. copy of Shakspere's 8th Sonnet.

"IN LAUDEM MUSICE ET OPPRODRIUM
CONTEMPTORIJ EIUSDEM.

1.

Muficke to heare, why heareft thou Muficke fadly
Sweete w.th fweetes warre not, Joy delights in Joy
Why loueft y.^u that wch thou receaueft not gladly
or els receaueft w.th pleafure thine annoy

2.

If the true Concord of well tuned Soundes
By Vnions maried doe offend thy eare
They doe but fweetlie chide thee, whoe confoundes
In finglenes a parte, w.^{ch 1} thou fhouldft beare

3.

Marke howe one ftringe, fweet hufband to another
Strikes each on [2] each, by mutuall orderinge
Refemblinge Childe, & Syer,[3] and happy Mother
w.^{ch 4} all in one, this fingle note dothe [5] finge
whofe fpeechles fonge beeinge many feeming one
Sings this to thee, Thou fingle, fhalt [6] proue none.
W: SHAKSPEARE."

(*Readings of the Quarto*, 1609.)

[1] the parts that.   [2] in.   [3] sier, and child.
[4] who.   [5] one pleasing note do. [6] will.

This occurs in a little miscellany of Poems, &c., the Addit. MS. 15,226 in the British Museum. It is in a hand of the earlier part of James I's reign, and has some worthless various readings. As I'd not seen a print of it before, and it wasn't notist in the Cambridge Shakspere, I copied it and sent it to the *Academy*, and then found it in Halliwell's Folio Shakspere.— F. J. F.

CYRIL TOURNEUR, 1611 (?).

Soqu(ette). But we want place and opportunity.
Snu(ffe). We haue both. This is the backe fide of the Houfe which the fuperftitious call Saint Winifred's Church, and is verily a conuenient unfrequented place. Where vnder the close Curtaines of the Night;
Soq. You purpofe i' the darke to make me light.

[1] The Atheist's Tragedie, IV. iii. Sign. H4. (*Tourneur's Plays and Poems. Ed. Churton Collins*, 1878. *Vol.* 1, *p.* 109.)

The "close Curtaines of the Night" is an unmistakeable allusion to *Rom. and Jul.* III. ii. 5, or rather a plagiarism from it. Langenhean Snuffe is the hypocritical stage Puritan of the time—
The following speech seems to have been modelled on that of Portia in the *Merchant of Venice*:—

Enter D'AMVILLE and CASTABELLA.

D'Am. Daughter, you doe not well to vrge me. I
   Ha' done no more than Iustice. *Charlemont*
   Shall die and rot in prison ; and 'tis iust.
Casta. O Father ! Mercie is an attribute
   As high as Iustice ; an essentiall part

---

[1] *The | Atheist's | Tragedie : |or, | The Honest Man's Reuenge.|* As in diuers places it hath often beene Acted */ Written / By /* Cyril Tourneur./ *At London, |Printed for* John Stepneth *and* Richard Redmer, */ and are to be sold at their Shops at | the West End of Paules. /* 1611. 4to.
The play is entered in the Stationers' Books on September 11th of the same year, but was probably written earlier. The dates of Tourneur's plays are very uncertain, but it seems probable that he wrote nothing before 1600. Nothing of his is quoted in "England's *Parnassus*" (1602), and he is not named by Henslowe.

CYRIL TOURNEUR, 1611 (?).

> Of his vnbounded goodnesse, whose diuine
> Impression, forme, and image man should beare.
> And (me thinks) Man should loue to imitate
> His Mercie ; since the onely countenance
> Of Iustice, were destruction ; if the sweet
> And louing fauour of his mercie did
> Not mediate betweene it and our weakenesse.
>> The Atheist's Tragedie, III. iv. Sign. G4. (*Tourneur's
>> Plays and Poems, ed. Churton Collins*, vol. i. p. 93.)

What follows is suggestive of the words of Proteus:

> Say that vpon the altar of her beauty
> Yow sacrifice your tears, your sighs, your heart.
>> *Two Gentlemen of Verona*, III. ii. 73-4.

> *Casta*[bella] . . . . . be not displeas'd, if on
> The altar of his Tombe, I sacrifice
> My teares. They are the iewels of my loue
> Dissolued into griefe : and fall vpon
> His blasted Spring ; as Aprill dewe, vpon
> A sweet young blossome shak'd before the time.
>> The Atheist's Tragedie, III. i. (1878, vol. i. p. 79).
>> Sign. F4, back.

The whole of the churchyard scene in IV. iii. is suggestive of the churchyard scene in *Hamlet*, and the speech of Charlemont (see p. 5) seems an echo of Hamlet's meditations :

Charl[emont]. "This graue,—Perhappes th' inhabitant was in his life time the possessour of his owne desires. Yet in the midd'st of all his greatnesse and his wealth ; he was lesse rich and lesse contented, then in this poore piece of earth, lower and lesser then a Cottage. For heere he neither wants, nor cares. Now that his body sauours of corruption ; Hee enjoyes a sweeter rest than e'er hee did amongst the sweetest pleasures of this life. For heere, there's nothing troubles him.—And there.—In that graue lies another. He (perhaps) was in his life as full of miserie as this of happinesse. And here's an end of both. Now both their states are equall." Sig. H3, back, H4 (ed. 1878, vol. i. p. 106-7).—J. N. HETHERINGTON.

* LOD. BARREY, 1611.

[Sir Oliuer Smaleſhanke, to his ſon Thomas Smaleſhanke]
I am right harty glad, to heare thy brother
Hath got ſo great an heire: [= *has carried off an heireſs*]...
A, ſirra, has a borne the wench away.
My ſonne ifaith, my very ſonne ifaith,
When I was yong and had an able back,
And wore the briſſell on my vpper lippe,
In good *Decorum* I had as good conuayance,
And could haue ferd, and ferkt y' away a wench,
As ſoone as eare a man aliue; tut boy
I had my winks, my becks, treads on the toe
Wrings by the fingers, ſmyles and other quirkes,
Noe Courtier like me, your Courtiers all are fooles
To that which I could doe, I could haue done it boy,
Euen to a hare, and that ſome Ladies know.

> *Ram-Alley: | Or | Merrie-Trickes.| A Comedy | Diuers times here-to-fore acted.| By | the Children | of | the Kings Reuels.| Written by* Lo: Barrey.| *At London | Printed by* G. Eld, *for* Robert Wilson, | *and are to be sold at his shop in Holborne,* | *at the new gate of Grayes Inne.*| 1611.| *sign.* C, *back.*

The "fer'd" in line 8 above is modernizd into "ferk'd" in Hazlitt's *Dodsley*, x. 292. The phrase—writes Dr. Ingleby, who referd me to Barrey —is probably from Pistol's play on "Mounsieur le Fer"'s name in *Henry V*, IV. iv. 29. "*M. Fer:* Ile fer him, and firke him, and ferret him:" *firk* occurs, in one sense or another, some dozen times in the play: thrice in two pages, Hazlitt's *Dodsley*, x. 328-9. See too p. 373.

LOD. BARREY, 1611.

In 'Actus 3. Scæna 1.' line 13, sign. D 3, back, is the phrase "will still be doing¹" of *Henry V*, III. vii. 107 (Hazlitt's *Dodsley*, x. 313):—

    I likewise haue a sonne,
A villanous Boy, his father vp and downe,
What should I say, these Veluet bearded boyes
will still be doing, say what we old men can . . . .
. . . the villaine boy . . . has got the wench

And a little further on, sign. E, occurs Pistol's "die men like dogs," 2 *Henry IV*, II. iv. 188, as is noted in Hazlitt's *Dodsley*, x. 319 :—²

"*IV. S.* Whats the matter Leiftenant. 2. *Gen.* Your Lieftenants an asse. *Bea*[rd]. How an asse ; die men like dogs. *IV. S.* hold gentlemen. *Bea.* An asse, an asse."

In *The Merry Devil of Edmonton*, licenst Oct. 22, 1607, printed 1608, and mentiond in T. M.'s *Blacke Booke*, 1604, there is a speech by the Host, with some phrases recalling Falstaff's, as in 2 *Henry IV*, II. i. 66— "I'll tickle your catastrophe :"—"I'll tickle his catastrophe for this . . . The villanous world is turned mangy . . . Have we comedies in hand, you whoreson villanous male London lecher?" Hazlitt's *Dodsley*, x. 259, 203.

And, as is noted on p. 225, *ib*, the phrase is used there too "a plague of this wind! O, it tickles our catastrophe!" No doubt there were plenty of Elizabethan wits able to call a man's hinder 'end' his catastrophe ; but I don't know the phrase earlier than Shakspere. Banks's 'Take me with you' in the *Merry Devil*, p. 224, is uzd by at least Peele, before Shakspere.

                                                      F. J. F.

---

[1] The use of *doing* in this sense is common of course : see Throate's speech in *Ram Alley*, D 4, back, Schmidt's *Shaksp. Lexicon*, &c.

[2] Die men like dogs ; give crowns like pins,
Have we not Hiren here ?

JOHN SPEED, 1611.

The reulew by N. D. pag. 31. That *N. D.*[1] author of the three conuerſions hath made *Ouldcaſtle* a Ruffian, a Robber, and a Rebell, and his authority taken from the *Stage-plaiers*, is more befitting the pen of his ſlanderous report, then the [2] Credit of the iudicious, being only grounded from this Papiſt and his Poet, of like conſcience for lies, the one euer faining, and the other euer falſifying the truth : . . I am not ignorant :

The | History | of | Great Britaine | Under the Conquests of y^e | Romans, Saxons, | Danes and | Normans. | . . . by Iohn Speed. . London. . . . 1611. *Book* 9, *chap.* 15, p. 637 (p. 788, ed. 1632), *col.* 1, *par.* (47).

That Shakspere was at first one of the dramatists who degraded Oldcastle into Falstaff is certain (*Centurie*, p. 269), though he afterwards declard that Oldcastle was 'not the man.' And that the actors of Shakspere's Falstaff were among the *Stage-plaiers* alluded to by Speed, admits of no reasonable doubt. The extract above is given by Ritson (*Var. Shaksp.* 1821, xvi, 411), and Mr. Elliot Browne, *Academy*, March 8, 1879, p. 217, col. 3.

Mr. Browne (*ib.* p. 218) says that "Henry Care, in the *Pacquet of Advice from Rome*, March 31, 1682, alludes to the aspersions upon Oldcastle's memory 'by Parsons the Jesuit and others.'" He quotes part of what follows : 'Having given this *Succinct* Relation of this Affair of Sir *John Old-Castle*,

---

[1] Nicholas Doleman, that is, Robert Parsons, the celebrated Jesuit, author of " A Treatise of three Conversions of England from Paganism to Christian Religion. . . Divided into three partes . . . (wherunto is annexed . . another . . treatise called ; A review of ten publike disputations, or Conferences, held in England about matters of religion, especially about the Sacrament . . . . of the Altar, *etc.*). By N. D., author of the Ward-word. . . . [St. Omers ?] 1603, 1604, 8°." B. Mus. Catal.

[2] ed. 1632 has *credit* with *c*.

JOHN SPEED, 1611.

I am not Ignorant what *rubbs* have been thrown in the way, and Scandals rais'd upon his Memory, by *Parsons* the Jesuit, and others, which are reducible unto Two sorts, *viz*. 1*st*. That he was a Traitor to his Soveraign. 2ly. That he was a Drunken Companion, or *Debauchee*.

' As to the First, being a very material and heinous Charge, we shall refer the confutation thereof to our next Placquet. But this last being as *groundless* as Trivial wee'l dispatch it at present.

' That Sir *John Old-Castle* was a Man of *Valour*, all Authentick (though prejudic'd) Histories agree, That he was a Gentleman, both of *good Sense*, sober Life, and sound Christian *Principles*, is no less apparent by his *Confession of Faith*, delivered under his own hand, (Extant in *Foxe*,) and his Answers to the *Prelates*. But being for his Opinions hated by the Clergy, and suffering such an Ignominious Death ; Nothing was more obliging to the then Domineering Ecclesiastick *Grandees*, then to have him [Oldcastle] represented as a *Lewd* fellow ; in compliance thereof to the *Clergy*, the *Wits* (such as they were) in the succeeding Ages brought him in, in their *Interludes*, as a *Royster*, *Bully* or *Hector* : And the *Painter*[s] borrowing the Fancy from their *Cozen Poets* have made his *Head* commonly an *Ale-house Sign* with a *Brimmer* in his hand ; and so foolishly it has been *Tradition'd* to Posterity.'

The Weekly Pacquet / of / Abbies from Rome. Vol. IV. p. 117. n°. 15. Friday 31. Mar. 1682.

"And he goes on to quote the remarks of Fuller in his *Church History*." (*Cent.* p. 249 *n*.)—F. J. F.

[I cannot verify either Speed's or Care's references (p. 31, 2nd part, p. 107). The Second Part begins at p. 173. and is paged continuously to p. 658. Sir John Oldcastle and Sir Roger Acton are spoken of in Part 2. chap. 9. par. 13 to 23, pages 490 to 498. Parsons says they were by act of parliament " condemned of open treason and confessed rebellion," p. 491.

P. A. LYONS.]

*SIR JOHN HAYWARD, 1612.

[*Harl. MS. 6021, leaf 69, back*] Excellent Queene! what doe my wordes, but wrong thy worth? what doe I but guild gold? what, but ſhew the Sunne with a candle in attempting to prayſe thee, whoſe honor doth fly ouer the whole world vppon the two winges of magnanimity, and juſtice, whoſe perfectione ſhall much dimme the Luſtre of all other, that ſhall be of thy Sexe.

The late Director of the Camden Society, John Bruce, when editing the copy of Hayward's MS. for his Society, "Annals of the first four Years of the Reign of Queen Elizabeth, By Sir John Hayward, Knt. D.C.L." 1840, put the following note to this "guild gold" passage, p. 8 :—

"We have here a proof that Shakspeare's King John was written before 1612, the date of the present composition. It does not appear to have been printed until included in the first folio edition of the plays in 1623. The words referred to—

'To gild refined gold . . . . .
. . . . . or with a taper light
To seek the beauteous eye of heaven to garnish'

(King John, Act IV. scene 2), are not to be found in 'The Troublesome Raigne of King John,' the play which Shakspeare used in the composition of his noble drama, and which some persons [the Lord forgive them!] have thought to be Shakspeare's first rough draft, as it were, of the play which we now possess."

Miss E. Phipson sends the extract from the printed book.

Mr. Hall.-Phillipps quotes Hayward's words, evidently from Mr. Bruce's edition, but without referring to it or its note.—F. J. F.

* THO. HEYWOOD, 1612.

To come to Rhetoricke, it not onely emboldens a scholler to speake, but instructs him to speake well, and with iudgement, to obserue his comma's, colons, & full poynts, his parenthesses, his breathing spaces, and distinctions, to keepe a decorum in his countenance, neither to frowne when he should smile, nor to make vnseemely and disguised faces in the deliuery of his words, not to stare with his eies, draw awry his mouth, confound his voice in the hollow of his throat, or teare his words hastily betwixt his teeth, neither to buffet his deske like a mad-man, nor stand in his place like a liuelesse Image, demurely plodding, & without any smooth & formal motion. It instructs him to fit his phrases to his action, and his action to his phrase, and his pronuntiation to them both.

> An / Apology / for Actors,/ Containing three briefe / Treatises./ 1 Their Antiquity./ 2 Their ancient Dignity./ 3 The true vse of their quality./ Written by Thomas Heywood./ / London, / Printed by Nicholas Okes./ 1612, sign. C 3, back, C 4.[1] (ed. 1658, p. 14, 15.)

The last lines (noted in Mr. Hall.-P.'s Mem. on Hamlet, p. 65) should have been quoted on p. 99 of Centurie. They are perhaps founded on Hamlet's "suit the action to the word, the word to the action," III. ii. 19, 20.— F. J. F.

[1] The Historical plays of Cæsar and Richard III. alluded to on F 3, back, F 4, back, are not Shakspere's. The 'Countesse of Salisbury' on G 1, back, is the heroine of Edw. III.

JOHN MARSTON, 1613.

Count Arſ[enu]. Sancta Maria, what thinkſt thou of
this change?
A Players paſſion Ile beleeue hereafter,
And in a Tragicke Sceane weepe for olde *Priam*,
When fell revenging *Pirrhus* with ſuppoſde
And artificiall wounds mangles his breaſt,
And thinke it a more worthy act to me,
Then truſt a female mourning ore her loue.

> The / Insatiate / Countesse / A / Tragedie : / Acted at
> White-Fryers./ Written / By Iohn Marston. / *London,*/
> Printed by *I. N.* for *Hugh Perrie,* and are to be / sould
> at his shop, at the signe of the *Harrow* in *Brittaines-
> burse.* 1631. sign. A. 3 back. Act I. ed. Halliwell,
> iii. 109. [First printed, 1613.]

Alluding to the Player's speech in *Hamlet,* II. ii. 494, &c., 577-8. Noted
by K. Elze, *Hamlet,* 1882, p. 168. On p. 249 is a note that the following,
alluding probably to "Flights of Angels," &c., *Hamlet,* V. ii. 371, was not
admitted into the *Centurie:*

"*Cardin[all].* An host of Angels be thy conuey hence."
Marston. *The Insatiate Countesse,* sign. I. 2, Act V.
(M.'s Works, ed. Halliwell, iii. 188.)

F. J. F.

There are heaps of echoes from *Hamlet* in this play; and one passage
very closely modelled on some lines in *Richard II,* Act I. sc. i.
A. H. BULLEN.

* JOHN COOKE, 1614.

"*Staines.* There is a devil has haunted me thefe three years in likenefs of an ufurer; a fellow that in all his life neuer eat three groat loaves out of his own purfe, nor ever warmed him but at other mens fires;" &c.
     Greene's *Tu Quoque,* Or, *The Cittie Gallant:* in *Anc. Brit. Drama,* II. 541.

"there is a devil haunts thee in the likenefs of an old fat man."
    I Henry IV, Act II. Sc. iv. l. 492-3.
           HY. C. HART.

Mr. Hll.-P. (*Cursory Memoranda on Macbeth,* 1880, p. 10) says that Barnabe Rich's *Hag of Hell* in the following lines probably alludes to the Witches of *Macbeth.* But this is very doubtful.—F.

"My lady holdeth on her way, perhaps to the tire-makers shop, where she shaketh out her crownes to bestowe upon some new-fashioned attire, upon such artificial deformed periwigs, that they were fitter to furnish a theatre, or for her that in a stage-play should represent some hag of hell, than to be used by a Christian woman." *Honestie of this Age,* 4to. Lond. 1615 [the 1st ed. is 1614].

ALEX. NICCHOLES, 1615.

(1) one thus writeth/.
Loue comforteth like funne-fhine after raine,
But Lufts effect is tempeft after funne.
Loue's golden fpring doth ever frefh remaine,
Lufts winter comes ere fummer halfe be done.
(p. 31-2, ed. 1620 : Harl. Misc. ii.)

(2) For me I vow, if death depriue my bed,
I neuer after will to Church be led
A fecond Bride, nor neuer that thought haue,
To adde more weight vnto my hufbands graue,
In fecond hufband let me be acurft,
None weds the fecond, but who kils the firft.
(p. 40, ed. 1620 : Harl. Misc. ii.)

> A / Discovrse, / of Marriage / And Wiving : / and / Of
> the greatest Mystery therein / contained : how to chuse a
> good / Wife from a bad./ . . . By Alex. Niccholes,
> Batchelour in the Art he / neuer yet put in practise./
> *He that stands by, and doth the game suruey,*
> *Sees more oft-times then those that at it play.*
> *Si voles disce, si vales doce :*
> *Si voles cape, si velles carpe.*
> London, / Printed by *G. Eld*, for Leonard Becket, and are
> to be sold / at his Shop in the Temple. 1620.

The first lines are taken from *Venus and Adonis*, ll. 799—802, with the words 'gentle' altered to 'golden,' and 'always' to 'ever.' (*Venus and Adonis* seems to have been known by heart to every poet and poetaster of the time.)

The second lines (in italic) are quoted from *Hamlet*, III. ii. 189-90, with the words 'weds' and 'kills' altered from 'wed' and 'kill'd.'—H. C. HART.

ALEX. NICCHOLES, 1615. (Illustr. for *Rom. & Jul.*) 81

[In the same work of Niccholes is a good illustration of the following passage in *Romeo and Juliet*, I. iii. B.

" *La. Cap. (to J.)* Well, think on marriage now; younger than
 you
Here in Verona, ladies of efteem,
Are made already mothers: by my count
I was your mother much upon these years
That you are now a maid

* • * * * •

So shall you share all that he [Paris] doth possess
By having him, making yourself no less
Nurse. No less! nay bigger; women grow by men."

Juliet's age is fourteen.

Compare with this, "*A Discourse of Marriage and Wiving*, &c., by Alex. Niccholes. 1615 (*Harleian Miscellany*, 1809, vol. ii. p. 164), quoted here (with my italics) from the edition of 1620*, that of 1615 not being in the Brit. Mus. Catalogue:—

CHAP. V.

" What yeares are moft conuenient for marriage./

" THe forward Virgins of our age are of opinion, that this commodity can neuer be taken vp too foone, and therefore howfoeuer they neglect in other things, they are fure to catch time by the forelock in this, if you afke them this queftion, they will refolue you *fourteene is the beft time* of their age, if thirteene bee not better then that, and they haue for the moft [part] *the example of their mothers before them*, to confirme and approue their ability, and this withall they hold for a certaine ground, that be they neuer so little they are fure thereby to become no lefle;"

E. DOWDEN.]

A Discovrse, / of Marriage / and Wiving : / London 1620.

*W. DRUMMOND, 1616.

MADRIGAL.

Dear night, the ease of care,
Untroubled seat of peace,
Time's eldest child, which oft the blind do see,
On this our hemisphere
What makes thee now so sadly dare to be?

> Poems : by William Drummond of *Hawthorne-Denne*.
> The Second Impression. Edinburgh : Printed by
> Andro Hart. 1616. Modernizd, in his Poetical
> Works, ed. W. B. Turnbull (J. R. Smith, 1856),
> p. 58.

The third line may allude to Shakspere's Sonnet 27, l. 8,
    And keep my drooping eyelids wide,
    Looking on darkness, which the blind do see.—E. PHIPSON.

FRESH ALLUSIONS TO SHAKSPERE.

SECOND PERIOD.
1617—1641.
(From Shakspere's Death to the Civil War.)

SIR GERRARD HERBERT, 24 May, 1619.

——" The Marquife Trenell [Tremouille], on thurfday laft tooke leane of the Kinge : that night was feafted at white hall, by the duke of Lenox in the Queenes greate chamber : where many great Lordes weare to keep them Company but no ladyes. the Sauoy Imbafladour was alfo there : The englifh Lordes, was the Marquife Buckingham my lord Pryuy feale, my lord of lenox, my lord of Oxford, my lord Chamberlayne, my l: Hamelton, my lord Arundell, my Lord of Leycefter : my lord Cary, my lord Diggby, m^r. Treafurer, m^r. Secretary Callvart : my lord Beaucham, and my Lord Generall, the reft Englifh Gallantes, and all mixed wth the french alonge the table : the Marquife Trenell fittinge alone at the tables ende : at the right hande, the Sauoy Imbaflador, by him the Marquife Buckingham, then a french Counte, &c. mixt : on his left hand my lord Priuy feale, the earle of Oxford, a french Marquife, my lord Chamberlayne, & fo forth mixed wth french & Englifh. The fupper was greate & the banquett curious, ferued in 24 greate Chynay worcke platters or voyders, full of glaffe fcales or bowles of fweete meates : in the middft of each voyder a greene tree of eyther, lemon, orenge, Cypers, or other refemblinge. After fupper they weare carried to the queenes pryuy chamber, where french finginge was by by the Queenes Mufitians : after in the Queenes bedd Chamber, they h.arde the Irifh harpp, a violl, & m^r Lanyer, excellently finginge & playinge on the lute. In the kinges greate Chamber they went to fee the play of Pirrocles,[1] Prince of Tyre. which lafted till 2 aclocke. after two actes, the players ceafed till the french all refrefhed them wth fweetmeates brought on Chinay voiders, & wyne & ale in bottells, after the players, begann anewe. The Imbaffadour parted next morninge for Fraunce at 8 aclocke, full well pleafed beynge feafted alfo at Tiballes & exceedinge gracioufly vfed of the kinge, who at taking leaue gaue him a very rich chayne of Diamondes, wth a wach donne aboute wth Diamondes & wherein the kinges effigie was very excellently donne."

..... " wth the remembraunce of my fervice to my Lady Carlton & yor Lo : I take leaue allwayes refting :

Yo^r Lo : affuredly to Comande :

Gerr : Herbert.

London, Munday 24 May. *veteri*.

From a Letter " To the right honorable Sir Dudley Carlton, knight : Lord Imbassadour for his M.^{ties} at ye Hage." State Papers. Domestic. James I. Vol. 109, No. 46. (p. 2 of MS.)

[W. D. SELBY. Part printed in Halliwell's *Folio Shaksp.*]

[1] Mr. Hall, wrongly prints ' Pirracles.'

1620.

Baker says, *Biogr. Dram.* ii. 289, of " 134. THE HEIR. Com. by Thomas May. Acted by the company of Revels, 1620. 4to. 1622 ; second impression, 4to. 1633. . . .

"The demand of the king that Leucothoë shall yield to his desires, as the sole condition upon which he would spare the life of her lover, appears to be borrowed from Shakspeare's *Measure for Measure ;* as the constable and watch who seize Eugenio seem to have had their language and manners from those in the same author's *Much Ado about Nothing ;* and the enmity of the two houses reminds us of *Romeo and Juliet.*"

ANON. 1620.

Goodneffe leave mee, if I have not heard a man court his miftris with the fame words that Venus did Adonis, or as neere as the booke could inftruct him.

Hæc Vir, or the Womanish-Man, 1620.

J. O. H.-P.

ROBERT BURTON, 1621 (?).

" Young Men will do it when they come to it."
Robert Burton's *Anatomy*, ed. 1651, p. 563.

This is a quotation from Ophelia's Valentine Song, *Hamlet*, IV. v.

R. ROBERTS.

JOHN TAYLOR, 1622.

And laſt he laughed in the Cambrian tongue, and beganne to declare in the Vtopian ſpeech, what I haue heere with moſt diligent negligence tranſlated into the Engliſh Language, in which if the Printer hath placed any line, letter or ſillable, whereby this large volume may be made guilty to bee vnderſtood by any man, I would haue the Reader not to impute the fault to the Author, for it was farre from his purpoſe to write to any purpoſe, ſo ending at the beginning, I ſay as it is applawsfully written and commended to poſterity in the Midſommer nights dreame. If we offend, it is with our good will, we came with no intent, but to offend, and ſhow our ſimple ſkill.

Rolihayton.

> Sir Gregory Nonsence. His Newes from no place. . . . for the vndestanding of Nobody. By Iohn Taylor. *Printed in* London, *and are to bee sold betweene* Charing-Crosse, *and* Algate. 1700. [*The real date is in the colophon:* Finis. *Printed at London by N. O.* 1622.] A 4, back.

In Mr. Hall.-P.'s. *Mem. on M. N. Dr.*, p. 35. The words meant to be quoted are those of Manager Quince, the Prologue, in *M. N. Dr.*, 1st Folio, p. 160, col. 1 :

> "*Pro.* If we offend, it is with oure good will.
> That you should thinke, we care not to offend,
> But with good will. To show our simple skilL"

The word 'intent' was recollected from the later lines—

> "We do not come, as minding to content you,
> Our true *intent* is. All for your delight.
> We are not heere."—F. J. F.

87

THOMAS WALKLEY, 1622.

The Stationer to the Reader

O set forth a booke without an Epistle, were like to the old English prouerbe, A blew coat without a badge, & the Author being dead, I thought good to take that piece of worke vpon mee: To commend it, I will not, for that which is good, I hope euery man will commend, without intreaty: and I am the bolder, because the Authors name is sufficient to vent his worke. Thus leauing euery one to the liberty of iudgement: I haue ventered to print this Play, and leaue it to the generall cenfure.

Yours,
Thomas VValkley.

The / Tragœdy of Othello, / The Moore of Venice. / As it hath beene diuerse times acted at the / Globe, and at the Black-Friers, by / his Maiesties Seruants./ Written by VVilliam Shakespeare./ London, / Printed by N. O. / for Thomas Walkley, and are to be sold at his / shop, at the Eagle and Child, in Britans Bursse./ 1622./ sign. A 2.

Mr. Herbert A. Evans calld my attention to Walkley's Foreword not being in the Centurie.
At the end of 'The Fourth Edition' of Othello, 1655, in its publisher's List of Books, "Printed or sold by William Leake, at the signe of the

Crown in Fleetstreet between the two Temple Gates: *These Bookes* following," are

"Playes.
"*Hen* the Fourth . . . . .
"The Merchant of *Venice*."

In the alterd version of *Othello* printed in 1687 'for Richard Bentley and S. Magnes in Russel-Street near Covent-Garden,' a Catalogue of some of their Plays is on the 2nd leaf, A2; and in it are

"*Henry* the 6th. with the Murder of the Duke of *Glocester*, in 2 parts . .
King Lear . . .
Othello, the Moor of *Venice*."

F. J. F.

JOHN FLETCHER, 1622.

Hig. Then beare up bravely with your Brute my lads
Higgen hath prig'd the prancers in his dayes,
And fold good peny-worthes; we will have a courfe,
The fpirit of *Bottom*, is growne bottomleffe.

> 1647. *Beggars Bush*, Actus Quintus, Scæna Secunda. p. 95, col. 2 of 'Comedies / and / Tragedies / Written by Francis Beaumont And Iohn Fletcher Gentlemen. Never printed before, / And now published by the Authours / Originall Copies. / *Si quid habent veri Vatum præsagia, vivam.* / *London,* / Printed for *Humphrey Robinson*, at the three *Pidgeons*, and for / *Humphrey Moseley* at the *Princes Armes in S^t. Pauls* / Church-yard. 1647./'

J. O. HILL.-P.

The date of the play is 1622, tho it was not printed till long after Fletcher's death in 1625. Beaumont died in 1616.—A. H. Bullen.

PHILIP MASSINGER, 1622-36.†

(Text)

for know, your son,
The ne'er-enough commended An-
toninus,
So well hath flesh'd his maiden sword.
1622. *The Virgin Martyr*,
∴ I. i. Massinger's Works,
Gifford's 2nd edn, 1813, i. 9.

(Gifford's Notes)

Massinger was a great reader and admirer of Shakspeare; he has here not only adopted his sentiment but his words:
'Come, brother John, full bravely hast thou *flesh'd* Thy *maiden sword.*'—[1 *Hen. IV,** V. iv. 133.]

. * Gifford adds: "But Shakspeare is in every one's head, or, at least, in every one's hand; and I should therefore be constantly anticipated in such remarks as these. I will take this opportunity to say, that it is not my intention to encumber the page with tracing every expression of Massinger to its imaginary source . . . "

In a word,
Thy plurisy of goodness is thy ill.
? 1621, pr. 1639. The *Unnatural Combat*, IV. i. Works, 1813, i. 197.

the thought is from Shakspeare:
'For goodness, growing to a *plurisy*, Dies in his own too much.'
[*Hamlet*, IV. vii. 118.]

Let his passion work, and, like a hot-rein'd horse,
'Twill quickly tire itself
ib. IV. ii. Works, i. 204.

This is from Shakspeare:
'—Anger is like
'A full hot horse, who being allow'd his way,
Self-mettle tires him.' [Henry VIII, I. i. 133.] Coxeter.

Marcella. For you, puppet—
Mariana. What of me, pine-tree?
. . . . O that I could reach y m !
The little one you scorn so, with her nails

Puppet and *maypole*, and many other terms of equal elegance, are bandied about in the quarrel between Hermia and Helena, in *Midsummer Nights Dream* [III. ii. 289—298].

---

† There are many more Sh. imitations in Massinger. The list of some made by Mr. D. B. Brightwell follows on pp. 94-97.

Would tear your painted face, and
    scratch those eyes out.
        1623 (pr. 1638). *The Duke
        of Milan*, II. i. Works,
        1813, i. 268-9.

which is here too closely imitated.
I forbear to quote the passages,
which are familiar to every reader of
Shakspeare.

                    Let me wear
Your colours, lady; and though
    youthful heats,
That look no further than your out-
    ward form
Are long since buried in me; while
    I live
I am a constant lover of your mind,
That does transcend all precedents.
        1624 (pr. 1638). *The Bond-
        man*, I. iii. Works, ii. 30.

This is evidently copied from that
much contested speech of Othello,
act I. sc. iii. :
"—I therefore beg it not
[To please the palate of my appetite;
Nor to comply with heat, the young
    affects
In me defunct, and proper satisfac-
    tion,] &c."
as is the following passage, in the
Fair Maid of the Inn [Fletcher's] :
'Shall we take our fortune? and
    while our cold fathers,
In whom long since their *youthful
    heats were dead*,
Talk much of Mars, serve under
    Venus' ensigns,
And seek a mistress.'

Cleora. I restore
This kiss, so help me goodness!
    which I borrow'd
When I last saw you.
        The Bondman, IV. iii. Works,
        ii. 86.

This is a modest imitation of Shak-
speare :
' Now by the jealous queen of heaven,
    that kiss
I carried from thee, dear; and my
    true lip
Hath virgin'd it e'er since.'
        Coriolanus [V. iii. 48].

Then, with a kind of state, I take my
    chair,
Command a sudden muster of my
    servants,
And, after two or three majestic hums,
It being known all is mine, peruse
    my writings,
Let out this manor, at an easy rate,
To such a friend, lend this ten thou-
    sand crowns,

This is imitated from the soliloquy
of Malvolio, in *Twelfth Night;* which
is itself an imitation [?] of the reverie
of Alnaschar, in the *Arabian Nights
Entertainment*.

For the redemption of his mortgaged
  land,
Give to each by-blow I know of mine,
  a farm.
  1624. *The Parliament of
    Love*, II. i. Works, ii. 253.

Lidia. O the difference of natures!
Giovanni,
A prince in expectation, when he
  lived here,
Stole courtesy from heaven, and
  would not, to
The meanest servant in my father's
  house,
Have kept such distance.
  1627 (pr. 1636). *The Great
    Duke of Florence*, II. iii.
    Works, 1813, ii. 468.

This is from Shakspeare, and the
plain meaning of the phrase is, that
the affability and sweetness of Giovanni
were of a *heavenly* kind, i. e.
more perfect than was usually found
among men ... the commentators on
our great poet have altogether mistaken
him:
"And then I *stole all courtesy from
  heaven,*
And dress'd myself in such humility,
That I did pluck allegiance from
  men's hearts."
    Hen. IV. Part I. Act III.
      sc. ii.

Sanazarro. I have seen a maid,
  sir;
But, if that I have judgment, no such
  wonder
As she was deliver'd to you.
  ib. III. i. Works, ii. 478.

.. an expression of Shakspeare might
not improbably have hung on Massinger's
mind:
Mir. —*No wonder*, sir;
But certainly a maid. *Tempest.*

Cozimo. So: come nearer;
This exercise hath put you into a
  sweat;
Take this and dry it.
  ib. III. i. Works, ii. 480.

This is from Shakspeare; if he
had been suffered to remain in quiet
possession of it, the reader would
have little to regret on the score of
delicacy:
—"He's fat, and scant of breath:
Here, Hamlet, *take my napkin, rub
  thy brow.*"

Ricardo. ... This military art,
I grant to be the noblest of professions;
And yet, I thank my stars for 't, I
  was never

In this passage .... Massinger,
as Coxeter observes, had Shakspeare
in his thoughts, and principally Falstaff's
humorous catechism.

Inclined to learn it; since this
bubble honour
(Which is indeed the nothing soldiers
fight for,)
With the loss of limbs or life, is, in
my judgment,
Too dear a purchase.
    1629 (pr. 1630). *The Picture*,
    I. ii. Works, 1813, iii. 126.

Theodosius. . . Can you think
This masterpiece of heaven, this pre-
  cious vellum,
Of such a purity and virgin white-
  ness,
Could be design'd to have perjury
  and whoredom,
In capital letters, writ upon 't?
    1631 (pr. 1632). *The Emperor
    of the East*, IV. v. Works,
    1813, iii. 328.

Was this fair paper, this most goodly
  book,
Made to write whore upon?
    Othello.
There are several other short passages in this scene copied or imitated
from the same play; which, as sufficiently obvious, I have forborn to
notice.[1]

Theodosius.   Wherefore pay you
This adoration to a sinful creature?
I am flesh and blood, as you are, sensible
Of heat and cold, as much a slave unto
The tyranny of my passions, as the meanest

---

[1] The scene between Theodosius and Eudocia about the apple he sent her, is modelld on that of Othello and Desdemona about his mother's hand-kerchief that he gave her:

Theo.—Did not Philanax
From me deliver you an apple?
    Eud.   Yes, sir;
Heaven! how you frown! pray
you, talk of something else.
    Theo.   How, a trifle!—
. . . . I prized it, lady,
At a higher rate than you believe;
  and would not
Have parted with it, but to one I
  did
Prefer before myself.

    Eud.   It was indeed,
The fairest that I ever saw.
    Theo.   It was;
And it had virtues in it, my Eu-
  docia,
Not visible to the eye . . .
What did you with it?—tell me
  punctually;
I look for a strict accompt.
  Eud. What shall I answer?
  Theo. Do you stagger? Ha!
  Eud. No, sir. I have eaten it:
  [*a lie.*]
    Works, iii. 326-7.

Of my poor subjects. The proud attributes,
By oil-tongued flattery imposed upon us,
As sacred, glorious, high, invincible,
The deputy of heaven, and in that
Omnipotent, with all false titles else,
Coin'd to abuse our frailty, though compounded,
And by the breath of sycophants applied,
Cure not the least fit of an ague in us.
We may give poor men riches, confer honours
On undeservers, raise, or ruin such
As are beneath us, and, with this puff'd up,
Ambition would persuade us to forget
That we are men : but He that sits above us,
And to whom, at our utmost rate, we are
But pageant properties, derides our weakness :
In me, to whom you kneel, 'tis most apparent.
Can I call back yesterday, with all their aids
That bow unto my sceptre ? or restore
My mind to that tranquillity and peace
It then enjoy'd ?—Can I make Eudocia chaste,
Or vile Paulinus honest ?

    1631. *The Emperor of the East*, V. ii. Works, 1813, iii. 339.

"In this fine speech Massinger has ventured to measure weapons with Shakspeare [in *Henry V*, IV. i. 250—301, *Macbeth*, and *Lear*], and if I may trust my judgment, not ungracefully. The feelings, indeed, are more interested by the latter, but that arises from the situation of his chief character."

Slave. I'll make them real, And you the Neptunes of the sea ; you shall No more be sea-rats.	"There be land-rats and *water-rats* (says Shylock,) I mean *pirates*." Hence, I suppose, the allusion.

    ? 1624-1634. *A very Woman*,
      V. i., Works, iv. 329.

Grave, sir, o'er-rule your passion, and defer The story of her fortune.	There are several incidental resemblances to Shakspeare in this scene, of which the reader must be well aware.[1]

    1636 (pr. 1655). *The Bashful Lover*, III. i. Works, iv. 401.

—F. J. F.

---

[1] Compare the following with Capulet's speech in *Rom. & Jul.*, III. v. 165-9, and Leonato's in *Much Ado*, IV. i. 129—131 :

    Octavio. My only child ; I murmur'd against heaven
    Because I had no more, but now I find
    This one too many. p. 401.

PHILIP MASSINGER, 1622-36.

MASSINGER.	SHAKSPERE.
Queen of fate, Imperious Fortune! mix some light disaster With my so many joys, to season them, &c. 1622. *Virgin Martyr*, Act I. sc. i. p. 4, col. 2, ed. Cunningham.	O love Be moderate; allay thy ecstasy; In measure rein thy joy; scant this excess; I feel too much thy blessing: make it less, For fear I surfeit. *M. of Ven.* III. ii. 111.
As the sun Thou didst rise gloriously, keptst a constant course In all thy journey: and now, in the evening When thou shouldst pass with honour to thy rest, Wilt thou fall like a meteor. 1622. *Virgin Martyr*, V. ii. p. 33, col. 2.	from that full meridian of my glory I haste now to my setting: I shall fail Like a bright exhalation in the evening And no man see me more. [Fletcher in] *Henry VIII*.
'tis said, And truly, Jupiter and Venus smile At lovers' perjuries. 1624. *Parliament of Love*, V. i. p. 192, col. 1.	At lovers' perjuries They say Jove laughs. [Ovid: see p. 56 above]. *Romeo and Juliet*, II. ii. (*Var. Sh.*, Vol. VI. p. 83.)
I will have thee Pictured as thou art now, and thy whole story Sung to some villainous tune in a lewd ballad. 1624. *Parliament of Love*, IV. v. p. 186, col. 1. So also the *Bondman*, V. iii., &c &c.	And I have not ballads made on you all, and sung to filthy tunes, &c. 1 *Henry IV*.

MASSINGER.	SHAKSPERE.
Look not on me As I am Cleremond : I have parted with The essence that was his, and entertained The soul of some fierce tigress, or a wolf New-hanged for human slaughter. 1624. *Parliament of Love*, p. 182, col. 2.	thy currish spirit Governed a wolf, who hanged for human slaughter Even from the gallows did his fell soul fleet And while thou layest in thy unhallowed dam Infused itself in thee. *Merchant of Venice*, IV. i.
Tremble to think how terrible the dream is After this sleep of death. 1626. *The Roman Actor*, III. ii. p. 208, col. 1.	in that sleep of death what dreams may come. *Hamlet.*
Are you on the stage, You talk so boldly? *Par.* The whole world being one This place is not exempted. 1626. *Roman Actor*, I. iii. p. 198, col. 1.	All the world's a stage. *As You Like It*, II. vii. (*Var. Sh.*, Vol. VI. p. 408.)
Pray you, believe, sir What you deliver to me shall be lock'd up In a strong cabinet of which you yourself Shall keep the key : for here I pawn my honour * * It shall not be discovered. 1627. *The Great Duke of Florence*, III. i. p. 235, col. 2.	'Tis in my memory lock'd And you yourself shall keep the key of it. *Hamlet*, I. iii. (*Var Sh.*, Vol. VII. p. 221. Decker, Webster.)
What is he? At his best, but a patrician of Rome His name Titus Flaminius; and speak mine Berecinthios, arch-flamen to Cybele It makes as great a sound. 1631. *Believe as You List*, I. ii. (p. 598, col. 1, Cunningham's Ed.)	What should be in that "Cæsar"? Why should that name be sounded more than yours? Write them together, yours is as fair a name : Sound them ; it doth become the mouth as well : &c. *Julius Cæsar*, I. ii. 142. (See *Var. Sh.*, 1821, Vol. XII. p. 17. Heywood.)

MASSINGER.	SHAKSPERE.
pomp and circumstance Of glory. 1631. *Believe as You List*, I. i. p. 596, col. 1.	Pride, pomp and circumstance of glorious war. *Othello*, III. iii. 354. (*Var. Sh.*, 1821, Vol. IX. p. 382. D'Avenant, Fletcher.)
Take heed, lord Philanax, that for your private spleen, Or any false conceived grudge against me . . . . you do not that My royal master must in justice punish. 1631. *The Emperor of the East*, V. i. p. 347, col. 2.	Take good heed You charge not in your spleen a noble person And spire your nobler soul. *Henry VIII.*, I. ii. 173.
Methinks I find Paulinus on her lips. 1631. *The Emperor of the East*, IV. iv. p. 345, col. 1.	I found not Cassio's kisses on her lips. *Othello*, III. iii. 341.
Putting a girdle round about the world. 1631-2. *Maid of Honour*, I. i. p. 256, col. 1.	I'll put a girdle round about the earth In forty minutes. *Mids. Night's Dream*, II i. (*Var.*, 1821, Vol. V. p. 228. Shirley, Chapman.)

Will it ever be, That to deserve too much is dangerous, And virtue, when too eminent, a crime?
1631-2. *Maid of Honour*, III. iii. p. 270, col. 2.
	Take note, take note, O world, To be direct and honest is not safe.
	  Othello, III. iii.
	for learn this, Silius, Better to leave undone, than by our deed Acquire too high a fame when him we serve's away . . .
	    ambition, The soldier's virtue, rather makes choice of loss, Than gain which darkens him.
	  Ant. and Cleop., III. i. 13-24.

PHILIP MASSINGER, 1622-36.

MASSINGER.

     I will help
Your memory, and tread you into
mortar;
?.1632. *New Way to Pay Old
Debts*, I. i. p. 389, col. 2.

SHAKSPERE.

I will tread this unbolted villain
into mortar.
    King Lear, II. ii. 70.
(Noted by Stevens, in *Var. Sh.*, 1821,
Vol. X. p. 91).

    Heaven be pleased
To qualify this excess of happiness
With some disaster, or I shall expire
With a surfeit of felicity.
1633. *The Guardian*, II. iii. p. 468,
col. 1.

O Helicanus, strike me, honoured
 sir;
Give me a gash, put me to present
 pain;
Lest this great sea of joys rushing
 upon me
O'erbear the shores of my mortality
And drown me with their sweetness.
    Pericles, V. i. 192.
(*Var. Sh.*, 1821, Vol. XXI. p. 205.)

My only child; I murmured against
 heaven
Because I had no more, but now I
 find
This one too many.
1636. *The Bashful Lover*, III. i.
p. 542, col. 1.

 Wife, we scarce thought us blest
That God had lent us but this only
 child;
But now I see this one is one too
 much.
  Rom. and Juliet, III. v. 165.
  Much Ado, IV. i. 129-132.

      D. B. BRIGHTWELL.

JOHN FLETCHER, 1622.

Let it fuffice,
I have touch'd the height of humane happineſſe,
and here I fix *Nil ultra*.[1] Hitherto
I have liv'd a fervant to ambitious thoughts,
and fading glories: what [1] remains of life,
I dedicate to Vertue; and to keep
my faith untainted, farewell Pride and Pomp,
and [1] circumftance of glorious Majeftie,
farewell for ever.

> The Prophetefſe, Actus Quartus, Scena Sexta, No. 18, in
> B. & F.'s *Comedies and Tragedies*, Folio, 1647, p. 42, col. 1.

Mr. Leslie Stephen sends the last two lines, saying that they are "obvious recollections of *Othello*" ("Farewell . . . Pride, Pomp, and Circumstance of glorious War." III. iii. 354).

The first seem also recollections of Fletcher's own Wolsey lines in *Henry VIII*, III. ii. 221, &c.

> "Nay then, farewell!
> I have touch'd the highest point of all my greatness;
> And, from that full meridian of my glory,
> I haste now to my setting."

—F. J F.

[1] A later edition, "The Prophetess . . . London, 1690," reads
p. 55,   "And fix here my *Non ultra*," and
p. 56,   "; my Remains of Life," and
p. 56,   " farewell Pride and Pomp,
           " All Circumstance of glorious Majesty,
           Farewel for ever."—P. A. LYONS.

98*

ROBERT BURTON, 1624 (?).

"Young Men will do it when they come to it."

Robert Burton's Anatomy, ed. 1651, p. 563.

This is a quotation from Ophelia's Valentine Song, *Hamlet*, IV. v.
R. ROBERTS.

BEN JONSON, 1626.

Enter SKOGAN, and SKELTON in like habits, as they liv'd.

1626. Ben Jonson. *The Fortunate Isles.* Masques Works, Vol. ii. p. 136, ed. 1640.

From 'in his habit as he liv'd.'—*Hamlet*, III. iv. 135.

F. J. F.

	1628.
The Prince of Walles his speech. 165 [I. ii. 199 —221.] [1 *Hen. IV.*]	I Know you all, and will¹ a while vphold, the vnyokt humor of youre idleneſſe yet herein will I immitate the ſunne who doth permit the baſe contagious clouds, to ſmother vp his beauty from the world that when hee pleaſe againe to be him ſelfe, being wanted; he may be more wondered at; ² of vapours that did ſeeme to ſtrangle him, If all the yeare were playing holy dayes, to ſport would be as tedious as to worke, But when thay ſeldum cum, that wiſht fro ³ cum and nothing pleaſeth but rare accidents. ſo when this looſe behauiour I throw off, and pay the debt I neuer promiſed by how much better than my word I am, by ſo much ſhall I fal[ſ]ifie mens hopes, and like bright mettell one a ſullen ground, My refromation⁴ glittering ouer my faulr, ſhall
Aprill 14	ſhow more goodly, and attract more eyes, than⁵ that wich hath no ⁶ foile to ſet it forth
Anno Domin 1628	Ile ſo offend to make offence a ſkill, redeming time, when men think leaſt I will,

Egerton MS. 2446, British Museum, leaf 13. [This leaf only from Shakspere. Catalog of Addit. MSS., 1882, p. 295.]—F. J. F.

¹ 'I' here, crost out.
² The copier has left a line out here:
    'By breaking through the foule and vgly mists.'
³ they wisht for.   ⁴ reformation.   ⁵ ? MS. when.
⁶ Q1 reads 'soile', F1 'soyle'. I think the MS. writer meant 'foile'.

A Newsletter, 1628.

Part of the passage quoted in the *Centurie*, p. 169, from Robert Gell's letter of Aug. 9, 1628, occurs, says Mr. George Bullen, Keeper of Printed Books in the British Museum, in an earlier newsletter from "Lond. August 1, 1628," among the MSS. of Sir Charles Isham, Bart., at Lamport Hall. It is followd by a second notice of the Duke of Buckingham having seen *Henry VIII*:—

"On Teufday his Grace was p'fent at ye acting of King Henry 8 at ye Globe, a play befpoken of purpofe by himfelfe, w'at he ftayed till ye Duke of Buckingham was beheaded & then departed.

"On Wenefday his Grace was alfo fpectator of ye Rape of Lucrece at ye Cocke-pitt. . . .

"Another Dicto. . . .

"This day fevennight his Grace was at Cheefwick to vifit ye Earles of Sōmerfett & Banbury, and on ye L^{ds} day aft'noon againe there wth ye Earle of Somerfett at bowles. At his going thith^r he fent for ye Earle of Holland being at the fermon to have come forth & rid wth him, but he came not forth. On munday they dined at Cheefwick wth ye Earle of Somerfett & aft^r bowled againe.

"On teufday was a play at ye Globe of ye downfall of ye great Duke of Buckingham, w'unto ye Savoian Ambaffadour, ye Duke, Earle of Hollande & oth^{rs} came, yet ftayed only ye difgracing not ye beheading of ye great Duke of Buck."

Athenæum, *Oct.* 18, 1879, *p.* 497, *col.* 2. *See also Mr. Bullen's letter in* The Athenæum *of Oct.* 25, *p.* 529. The Rape of Lucrece *was by Tho. Heywood.*—F. J. F.

WYE SALTONSTALL, 1631.

18. *A Chamberlaine.*

IS the firſt Squire that gives entertainement to errant ſtrangers. At your firſt alighting hee ſtraight offers you to ſee a Chamber, but has got the tricke of tradeſmen to ſhow you the worſt firſt. Hee's as nimble as *Hamlets* ghoſt heere and everywhere, and when he has many gueſts, ſtands moſt upon his pantofles, for hee's then a man of ſome calling.

> *Picturæ Loquentes.* / Or / Pictvres / Drawne forth in / *Characters*. / With a Poeme of a / *Maid.* / By Wye Saltonstall. / Ne Sutor ultra crepidam. / *London,* / Printed by *Tho. Cotes,* and are to be sold / by *Tho. Slater,* at his shop in the / *Blacke Fryars.* 1631. / sign. E 3, back, E 4.

Quoted (with *is* for *Hee's*) from the 2nd ed. of 1635 in Mr. Hall.-P.'s *Mem. on Hamlet*, p. 22. The first words of the text, B 5, "1. *The World* is a Stage, men the Actors," are too common to be taken as a reference to Shakspere's like saying.

In no. '21. A Petty Countrey Faire,' is a bit for Autolycus: "A Ballet-singer may be sooner heard heere than seene, for instead of the violl hee sings to the croud. If his Ballet bee of love, the countrey wenches buy it, to get by heart at home, and after sing it over their milkepayles. Gipsies flocke thither, who tell men of losses, and the next time they looke for their purses, they find their words true."—F. J. F.

RICHARD BRATHWAIT, 1631.

Thirdly, *Books* treating of light fubiects, are Nurferies of wantonneffe: they inftruct the loofe Reader to become naught; whereas before, touching naughtineffe, he knew naught. A ftory of the rape of *Ganimedes*, or of light *Lais* in *Eurypedes*, are their daily Lectures. *Plato's* Diuine Philofophy, or *Dicearchus* pious Precepts of Morality, muft vaile to *Alcæus*, or *Anacreons* wanton Poefie. *Venus* and *Adonis* are vnfitting Conforts for a Ladies bofome. Remoue them timely from you, if they euer had entertainment by you, left, like the *Snake* in the fable, they annoy you.

> *The English Gentlewoman* [Engraved Title, in 10 compartments] . . . *by Richard Brathwait* . . . London./ Printed for / Michaell Sparke / and are to be / Sould, at the / Blew Bible / in / Greene Arbor./ 1631./ p. 139.
>
> J. O. Hll.-P. (revized).

Loues enteruiew betwixt *Cleopatra* and *Marke Anthony*, promifed to it felfe as much fecure freedome as fading fancy could tender; yet the laft Scene clozed all thofe Comicke paffages with a Tragicke conclufion.—*ib.* p. 197.

PETER HEYLYN, 1631.

Sir *Iohn Faſtolfe* . . . (as certainly he was a wife and valiant Captaine, however[1] on the ſtage, they haue beene pleaſed to make merry with him).

> *The | Historie | Of | That most famous Saint and Souldier | of Christ Iesus ; | St. George | of Cappadocia ; | . . . . The Institution of the most Noble Order of | St. George, named the Garter. |* A Catalogue of all the Knights thereof untill *this present. | By P.t. Heylyn. | . . . . London. | Printed for Henry Seyle, and are to be sold at his | Shop, the signe of the* Tygers-*head in St.* Pauls | *Church-yard.* 1631. (4to.) p. 308.

Noted in B. Quaritch's General Catalogue, p. 2,235, no. 22,827.—F. J. F.

---

[1] The third edition of 1633, p. 344, reads 'though' for 'however', and begins the parenthesis with 'though'.

ANON. 1631.

One lately hauing taken view of the Sepulchres of fo many Kings, Nobles, and other eminent perfons interred in this Abbey of Weftminfter, made thefe rimes following, which he called

A *Memento* for Mortalitie.

* * * * * * *

Then bid the wanton Lady tread,
Amid thefe mazes of the dead.
And thefe truly vnderftood,
More fhall coole and quench the blood,
Then her many fports a day,
And her nightly wanton play.
Bid her paint till day of doome,
To this fauour fhe muft come.

Ancient Funerall Monuments . . . . composed by the Studie and Travels of John Weever. Lon lon, 1631, p. 492-3 (partly quoted in Mr. Hall.-P.'s *Memoranda on Hamlet*, 1879, p. 64).

The last two lines are from Hamlet's prose (V. i. 181-3, Camb.): "Now get you to my lady's chamber, and tell her, let her paint an inch thick, to this favour she must come."

Is it likely that the following stanza in an "Ode ad B: J:" (Ben Jonson), by "Jo: Earles," ab. 1630 A.D., MS. Addit. Brit. Mus. 15,227, lf. 44, bk, alludes to the *Pericles* of which Shakspere wrote part?

"Sat est, si anili tradita de colo
Fabella lusit murcida Periclem.
Jocos*que* semesos, et ipso
Dicta magis repetita mimo."

Mr. Hall.-Phillipps calld attention to it in *N. & Q.*, Oct. 30, 1880, p. 343, col. 2. —F. J. F.

*JAMES SHIRLEY, 1631.

The Schoole of Complement.

Actus quartus, Scena prima.

* * * * *

Bub[ulcus]. O that I were a flea vpon his lip,
There would I fucke for euer, and not skip.

> The / Schoole / of / Complement./ As It Was Acted / by her Maiesties Seruants at the / Priuate house in Drury Lane. / — *Hæc placuit semel.*/ By *J. S.* / London, / Printed by *E. A.* for *Francis Constable*, and are to be sold at / his shop in *Pauls* Church-yard, at the signe of the *Crane.* 1631. / (The play was afterwards cald *Love-Tricks.*)

Probably parodying *Romeo and Juliet*, II. ii. 23:
> O that I were a gloue vpon that hand,
> That I might touch that cheeke.

J. O. HIL-P.

PHILIP MASSINGER, 1632.

Ferdi[*nand*]. Would they [his heart-firings] would breake,
Breake altogether, how willingly like *Cato*
Could I teare out my bowells, rather then
Looke on the conquerors infulting face,
But that religion, and the horrid dreame
To be fuffer'd in the other world, denyes it.

> The Maid / of / Honovr. *As* / It Hath Beene / Often Presented / with good allowance at the *Phœnix* / in Drvrie-Lane, by the / Queenes Majesties / Servants./ Written by Philip Massinger./ *London,* / Printed by *I. B.* for *Robert Allot*, and are to be / sold at his Shop at the signe of the blacke Beare in / *Pauls* Church-yard, 1632./ Act II. Scene IIII. sign. E, 3 (ed. Hartley Coleridge, p. 197, col. 2).

Noted by Dr. Elze, in his edition of *Hamlet*, 1882, p. 256, as alluding to Hamlet's Soliloquy in Act III. sc. i. 65-7, 78-80.—F. J. F.

JAS. SHIRLEY, 1633.

There Gold and trafh was impudently inferr'd,
2[nd. *Courtier*]. And 'twas a tafke too infolent, in that point
   You'd willingly give a pound of your proud flefh
   To be releaft.
Roll[*iardo.*] I heard a pound of flefh, a Iewes demand once,
   Twas gravely now remembred of your Lordfhip—releaft?
   Fortune, and courtefie of opinion
   Gives many men Nobility of Birth,
   That never durft doe nobly, nor attempt
   Any defigne, but fell below their Honors.

>   The / Bird in a cage./ [II. i.] A Comedie. As it hath
>   beene Presented at the *Phœnix* in *Drury Lane.* The
>   *Author* Iames Shirley, / Servan to Her Majesty. . . . .
>   London / Printed by *B. Alsop,* and *T. Fawcet:* for
>   *William* Cooke, and are to be sold at his Shop neere
>   *Furnivals-Inne* Gate, in *Holborne.* 1633. 4to. sign. E. 2.

A reference to Shylock, no doubt.—MISS E. PHIPSON.

THOMAS NABBES, 1633.

Iam[*es*]. How fhall we fpend the day *Sam* ?
Sam. Let's home to our ftudies and put cafes.
Iam. Hang cafes and bookes that are fpoyl'd with them. Give me *Iohnfon* and *Shakefpeare* ; there's learning for a gentleman. I tell thee *Sam*, were it not for the dancing-fchoole and Play-houfes, I would not ftay at the Innes of Court for the hopes of a chiefe Iuftice-fhip.

> Tottenham / Covrt./ A Pleasant / Comedie : / Acted in the Yeare MDCXXXIII./ At the private House in *Salisbury-Court*./ *The Author* / Thomas Nabbes./ *At London,/* Printed by Richard Ovlton, for / Charles Greene ; and are to be sold / at the Signe of the *White Lyon*, in / Pavls *Church-yard*./ 1638./ *Act*. 3 Scœn. 1. p. 27.

In the list of "The Persons," James and Sam are thus described :
"IAMES. *A wild young gentleman of the Innes of Court.*
SAM. *A fine Gentleman of the Innes of Court, and Brother to* BELLAMIE."

PONSONBY A. LYONS.

TH. BANCROFT, 1633.

But the chaſt bay not euery ſongſter weares,
Nor of Appollo's ſonnes prooue all his heires;
'Tis not for all to reach at Shakeſpeares *height,*
Or think to grow to ſolid Iohnſons *weight,*
To bid ſo faire as Chapman *for a fame,*
Or match (your family) the Beaumonts *name,*

Th. Bancroft, before his Glutton's Feaver, 1633,
To the Nobly accompliſht Gentleman, Wolſtan Dixie, Esquire. (Roxb. Club reprint, 1817, sign. A2.)

B. N.

SIR JOHN SUCKLING, (?) 1633—41.

The Prince of darkneſſe is a Gentleman,
Mahu, Mohu *is his name,*
The Goblins, III. i. ed. 1646, p. 25.

The 1643 ed. has "Maha, mahu," p. 26; but the words are rightly "Mahu, Mohu" in *Fragmenta Aurea*, ed. 1658, p. 112:

("The Prince of darkness is a gentleman,
Modo he's called and Mahu."
Lear, III. 148-9.)

" *Pel[legrin]. I*'ſt ee'n ſo? Why then,
Farewell the plumed Troops, and the big Wars,
Which made ambition vertue."
The Goblins, IV. i. p. 43, ed. 1646.

(*Othello*, III. iii. 349-50, altering 'That make' to 'which made.')

" 1 *Th[ief.]* You ſhall Sir.
Let me ſee—the Author of *bold Beauchams*, and *Englands Joy*."
" *Po[et.]* The laſt was a well writ peice, I aſſure you,
A Brittane *I* take it; and *Shakeſpeares* very way:
I deſire to ſee the man,"
The Goblins, IV. i. p. 45, ed. 1646.

[Other likenesses occur in the play, as,]
" *Orsa.* The ſlave of Chaunce
One of Fortune's fooles;

A thing fhe kept alive on earth
To make her fport."
The Goblins, III. i. p. 33, ed. 1648.

("so we profess
Ourselves to be the slaves of chance."
Winter's Tale, IV. iv. 551.
"*Rom.* O, I am fortune's fool."
R. & J. III. i. 141.)

"And give out that *Anne* my wife is dead."
. . . .
"*Na*[*ffuras*]. Rare Rogue in Buckram,
let me bite thee,"
The Goblins, III. i. p. 26, ed. 1646; p. 27, ed. 1648.

(The 'Anne' quotation of Suckling's is meant for
"give out
That Anne my wife is fick and like to die."
Rich. III, IV. ii. 57-8.

The second phrase is from Falstaff's "two rogues in buckram suits."—
1 *Hen. IV*, II. iv. 213.)

"No, no, it muft be that
His anger, and the fearch declare it;
The secret of the prison-house fhall out I fweare."
The Goblins, V. i. p. 49, ed. 1646.

(Cp. *Hamlet*, I. v. 14:
"But that I am forbid
To tell the secrets of my prison-house.")

H. C. HART.

SIR JOHN SUCKLING, (?) 1633—41.

(*Died* May 7, 1641.)

[*King*]. . The queftion is, whether we fhall rely
Upon our Guards agen ?
" *Zir*[*iff*]. By no meanes Sir ?
Hope on his future fortunes, or their Love
Unto his perfon, has fo ficklied o're
Their refolutions, that we muft not truft them,
Befides, it were but needleffe here ; "
Aglaura, Act IV. sc. i. *Fragmenta Aurea*, 1648, p. 33.

(A reminiscence of Hamlet's (III. i. 84-5).
" And thus the native hue of resolution
Is sicklied o'er with the pale cast of thought."
—LESLIE STEPHEN ; later, HY. C. HART.)

(I also think that in the Epilogue to *Aglaura*,
" Plays are like Feafts, and every Act fhould bee
Another Courfe, and ftill varietie :
But in good faith, provifion of wit
Is growne of late fo difficult to get,
That do we what we can, we are not able,
Without cold meats to furnifh out the Table."
Fragmenta Aurea, 1646, p. 82.

Suckling, as such a perpetual plagiarist from Shakspere, may have had an eye, in the last line above, to—
" The funeral baked meats
Did coldly furnish out the marriage Tables."
Hamlet, I. ii. 180-1.)

Aglaura was published in 1638 (Poems, play, etc., of Sir John Suckling, ed. Hazlitt, 1874, I, p. xxxvi.).
H. C. HART.

SIR JOHN SUCKLING, (?) 1633—41.

" *G[rainevert]*. So pale and fpiritleffe a wretch,
Drew *Priam's* curtaine in the dead of night,
And told him halfe his Troy was burnt――"
Brennoralt, A Tragedy, II. i. p. 16 (in Fragmenta Aurea), ed. 1646.

(A plagiarism from 2 *Henry IV*, I. i. 70-3:
" Even such a man, so faint, so spiritless,
So dull, so dead in look, so woe-begone,
Drew Priam's curtain in the dead of night,
And would have told him half his Troy was burnt.")

" *Iph[igene]*. Will you not fend me neither,
Your picture when y' are gone?
That when my eye is famifht for a looke,
It may have where to feed,
And to the painted Feaft invite my heart."
The Tragedy of Brennoralt, V. i. ib. 1646, p. 44.

(" Betwixt mine eye and heart a league is took
And each doth now good turn unto the other
When that mine eye is famished for a look,
Or heart in love with sighs himself doth smother,
With my loves picture then mine eye doth feast
And to the painted banquet bids my heart."
Shakspere, Sonnet 47.)

Sir John Suckling, baptized Feb. 10, 1608-9, died 7 May, 1641 (Lysons, *Environs of London*, iii. 588-9).

Brennoralt is supposed to have been published in 1639 (Poems, &c. I. xi), and appears to have been written about the time of the Scotch rebellion in 1639. It was first printed among Suckling's works in 8vo 1646 (Halliwell, Dict. of Old Plays).

"*Iph.* . . . . Shee's gone :
 Shee's gone. Life like a Dials hand hath ftolne
 From me the faire figure, e're it was perceiv'd."
The Tragedy of Brennoralt, V. i. (*in Fragmenta Aurea*), ed. 1646, p. 48.

(" Ah ! yet doth beauty like a dial-hand
 Steal from his figure and no pace perceived."
Shakspere, Sonnet 104.)

H. C. HART.

JOHN FORD, 1633, 1638.

I am wise enough to tell you I can bourd where I see occasion; [17]

> *'Tis pity she's a Whore* (1633). Act II, sc. iv. Ford's Works, ed. Dyce, 1869, i. 144.

[17] *i. e.* jest . . The words in the text are borrowed from Nic. Bottom, confessedly a very facetious personage.—Gifford.

---

ib. Act V. sc. iv. p. 195-6, let my hot hare have law ere he be hunted to his death, that, if it be possible, he may post to hell in the very act of his damnation.[9]

[9] "This infernal sentiment has been copied from Shakespeare [*Hamlet*, act iii. sc. 3] by several writers who were nearly his contemporaries. *Reed.*"—ib.

Love's Sacrifice, printed 1633.

On p. 65 of Ford's Works, ed. Dyce, vol. ii, Gifford says in a note, "Ford has contrived, by several direct quotations from Shakespeare, to put the reader in mind of Iago, to whom, for his misfortune, D'Avolos bears about the same degree of resemblance that the poor Duke does to Othello." Parts of Act III, scenes ii. and iii. are evidently model'd on *Oth.* III. iii, and the Rev. W. Harrison has kindly noted the following touches in proof of Gifford's remark :—

Ford, *Love's Sacrifice*, Act III, Works, vol. ii.	Shakspere, *Othello*, III. iii.
D'Avolos. A shrewd ominous token ; I like not that neither.	*Iago.* Ha! I like not that. *Othello.* What dost thou say? 35 *Iago.* Nothing, my lord : or if—I know not what.
Duke. Again! What is't you like not ? III. ii. *Works*, ii. 63.	
Duke. I hear you, Sir ; what is't? Nothing, I protest to your highness. *ib.* p. 65.	

D'Av. Beshrew my heart, but
that's not so good.
Duke. Ha, what's that thou mis-
likest?
D'Av. Nothing, my lord :—but I
was hammering a conceit of
mine own.—*ib.* p. 62.

        I'll know 't, I vow I will.
Did not I note your dark abrupted
   ends
Of words half spoke? your " wells,
   if all were known "?
Your short " I like not that "? your
   girds and " buts "?
Yes, sir, I did; such broken language
   argues
More matter than your subtlety shall
   hide :
Tell me, what is't? by honour's self,
   I'll know.
      ib. III. iii. *Works,* ii. 67.
D.'Av. What would you know, my
   lord!
. . . I know nothing.
Duke. Thou liest, dissembler! on
   thy brow I read
Distracted horrors figur'd in thy
   looks. . . . .
Speak, on thy duty; we thy prince
   command.

D'Av. I trust your highness will
   pardon me . . .
Should I devise matter to feed your
   distrust, or suggest likelihoods
   without appearance.   p. 67

Duke. The icy current of my
   frozen blood
Is kindled up in agonies as hot
As flames of burning sulphur.

Oth. Why dost thou ask?
Iago. But for a satisfaction of my
   thought
No farther harm.

By heaven, he echoes me,
As if there were some monster in his
   thought
Too hideous to be shown. Thou
   dost mean something.
I heard thee say but now,—Thou
   likedst not that,
When Cassio left my wife; What
   didst not like?
And, when I told thee—he was of
   my counsel
In my whole course of wooing, thou
   criedst, *Indeed!*
And didst contract and purse thy
   brow together,
As if thou then hadst shut up in thy
   brain
Some horrible conceit : If thou dost
   love me,
Shew me thy thought.
Therefore these stops of thine fright
   me the more.

Iago. Good my lord, pardon
   me.   133
I am to pray you, not to strain my
   speech
To grosser issues, nor to larger reach
Than to suspicion.   220

Oth. Never, Iago. Like to the
   Pontic sea,
Whose icy current and compulsive
   course
Ne'er feels retiring ebb, but keeps
   due on

	To the Propontic, and the Hellespont;	
	Even so my bloody thoughts, with violent pace,	
	Shall ne'er look back, ne'er ebb to humble love,	
	Till that a capable and wide revenge Swallow them up.	
Take heed you prove this true.	Villain, be sure thou prove my love	
D'Av. My lord. (p. 69)	a whore.	359
Duke. If not,	Be sure of it; give me the ocular	
I'll tear thee joint by joint.—Phew! methinks	proof. . . .	360
	Make me to see 't.	364
It should not be:—Bianca! . . . . hell of hells!	. . . . or woe upon thy life!	366
See that you make it good.		

Secco . . . Keep your bow close, vixen.* [*Pinches Morosa.*]
            The Fancies, Chast and Noble. 1638. III. iii.
                    Ford's Works; ed. Dyce, 1869, ii. 277.

* "This is taken from Ancient Pistol's injunction to his disconsolate spouse at parting ['keep close' in Shakespeare's *Henry V*, act ii. sc. 3, where the 4to (not the folio) has "buggle boe."—Dyce], and with her it might have been safely left."—Gifford, *ib.*

            Crabbed age and youth †
              Cannot jump together;
              One is like good luck,
               'Tother like foul weather.
                    Fancies, Act IV. sc. i.   Ford's Works, 1869, ii. 291.

† This is patched-up from a despicable ditty in the *Passionate Pilgrim*, foolishly attributed to Shakespeare.—Gifford, *ib.* ii. 291.   I don't agree with Gifford's 'despicable.'—F.

            Neither the lord nor lady, nor the bawd,
            Which shuffled them together, Opportunity,§
            Have fasten'd stain on my unquestion'd name.
                    The Lady's Trial (licenst May 3, 1638, publisht
                    1639), Act III. sc. iii.   Ford's Works, ed.
                    Dyce, 1869, iii. 57.

§ Here Ford had in his thoughts some lines of Shakespeare's *Lucrece*,
        "O *Opportunity*, thy guilt is great! . . . .
         Thou foul abettor! thou notorious *bawd!*"—Dyce.

With frightful lightnings, amazing noises ;
But now, th' enchantment broke,‡ 'tis the land of peace,
Where hogs and tobacco yield fair increase.
  T. Middleton. *Anything for a Quiet Life*, V. iii. *Works*, iv. 499.

‡ Treated by Malone (*Variorum Shakspere*, 1821, xv. 424-5) as an allusion to Prospero's island, in *The Tempest*. The reference is Dyce's.

For the Middleton-*Witch* and Shakspere-*Macbeth* references, &c., see *Centurie*, p. 51.—F.

In Middleton's *Mayor of Queenborough*, (Works, i. 197,) which Dyce thinks 'was among the author's first attempts at dramatic composition,' but which mentions in Act V. sc. i. 'a play called the *Wild Goose Chase*, that may be Fletcher's,' produced about 1621, Reed says on the following passage, p. 197,

  Methinks the murder of Constantino
  Speaks to me in the voice of 't, and the wrongs
  Of our late queen, slipt both into one organ.

"Shakespeare seems to have imitated this in the Tempest, A. 3. S. 3.

 . . . Methought the billows, spoke, and told me of it ;
 The winds did sing it to me ; and the thunder,
 That deep and dreadful organ-pipe, pronounc'd
 The name of Prosper."

But, says Dyce, 'The date of *The Tempest* must be settled before we can determine whether Shakespeare or Middleton was the imitator.'

                F. J. F.

THO. RANDOLPH, 1634 (?).

Pen. VVho would carry you up to *London*, if the VVaggon-driver fhould think himfelf as good a man as his mafter?

Dic. VVhy we would ride thither on our own Hackney-Confciences.

Pen. Nay if this were fo, the very Tailers though they damn'd you all to hell under their fhop-boards, would fcorn to come to the making up of as good a man as *Pericles* Prince of *Tyre*.

Tho. Randolph. *Hey for Honesty*, ed. 1651.

(R. died 1634. See *Centurie*, p. 293-4)—J. O. H.-P.

ANONYMOUS, 1635.

Hufh, where is this fidle? in the ayre? I can perceave nothing.

The Lady Mother. 1635. Act II. sc. i. Bullen's *Old Plays*, vol. ii. p. 132.

Warme charity, no more inflames my breft
Than does the glowewormes ineffectual fire
The ha[n]d that touches it.

Ibid. Act IV. sc. i. p. 178.

The allusions are to *Tempest*, I. ii. 387, and *Hamlet*, I. v. 89-90. The 'file' = defile, *Macbeth* (III. i. 65), occurs later:

Send him (Death) to file thy house,
Strike with his dart thy Children and thyselfe.

Ibid. Act V. sc. ii. p. 193.

H. A. EVANS.

Till doomfday alters not complexion:
Death's the beft painter then: &c. &c.

Besides the other passages referred to in the *Centurie*, pp. 51 and 60, these may be added: *A Mad World*, III. i., with *Rom. and Jul.*, I. iv. 35; *The Honest Whore*, IV. i., with *Hamlet*, I. v. 29; *Ibid.* IV. iii., with Falstaff's exclamation, 1 *Henry IV.*, V. iii. 51.

One or two of these may be coincidences of expressions used at that time. But none can doubt that Middleton was influenced by Shakspere, and I add these references, because they bear on the question—Which was the more likely to borrow "Black spirits and white," &c.? though for my own part, I believe it can be shown that these lines were popularly known.—B. N.

SIR H. MILDMAY, 1635.

1635. . Maij. . 6: not farre from home all day att the bla : ffryers & a play this day Called the More of Venice.

Sir H. Mildmay's Diary, 1633-1651. *MS. Harl.* 454, *leaf* 10, *back*, 5 *lines from foot.*

Given mainly in Halliwell's *Folio Shakespeare*... where the editor says of *Othello*:

"It was acted before the King and Queen at Hampton Court on December 8th, 1636. . . . A year or two previously, an actress had appeared on the English stage in the character of Desdemona."

Unluckily there is no entry in Sir H. Mildmay's accounts at the other end of the MS., of what he paid to hear *Othello*, but I suppose it was 3s., or that some friend paid for him. In the account for April, 1635, MS. leaf 173, back, lines 11, 12, are the entries—

	£	s	d
Expended att the bla : fryers—28	00 =	03 =	00 =
for wine to Supper & before	00 =	01 =	00 =

And on turning back to the Diary, leaf 10, back, I find under April 28, "this after Noone, I spente att a playe wth good Company"—and so forgot to say what the play was: probably not one of Shakspere's, or it would have overpowerd the recollection of the 'good company.'

Two or three other items from the account (lf. 273, back), including 1s. for Fletcher's *Elder Brother*, may interest the reader.

	£	s	d
To Hughe Ap : Jones for the hire of : 2 : Coache horses to the Justice seate	00 =	10 =	00 =
To him for the haye of my horses	00 =	04 =	06 =
. . . .			
To Ann Mannfeilde for Cowe heeles	00 =	01 =	06 =
To Henry Pinsor In full for his pickture	01 =	00 =	00 =
To a playe eod*em* Called the Elder Brother	00 =	01 =	00 =
To the poore of bridewell with Mr. Caldewell	00 =	00 =	06 =
. . . .			
To Besse Preston In *parte* for a bottle of stronge waters : 2 : Maij	00 =	05 =	00 =
To El : Preston In full for stronge waters	00 =	06 =	00 =
. . . .			
To Mr. Lea : his Man for a shagge hatt and bands	00 =	14 =	00 =
Expences In boates etc. this : 10th [of May]	00 =	02 =	06 =

[F. J. F.]

THOMAS HEYWOOD, 1635.

CHAP. II.

A Catalogue of sundry Helluoes, *and great quaffers amongst the* Grecians : *Infamous for their vinosity.*

 Come now to speake of the ancient Carowsers: I will first begin with the merry *Greekes*. From whom the Good-fellowes of this age would borrow that name, and see what frollike healthers I can find amongst them . . . . He that dranke immoderately, and above his strength, had the denomination of *Philocothonista :* Among whom *Nestor* a great
* Old *Nestor*, even in his third age, was numberd; drinker.
He was observed to take his rowse freely, and more at the siege of *Troy*, then the Generall *Agamemnon*, whom *Achilles* upbraided for his immoderate drinking: Neither in the hottest of the battell, was hee ever knowne to venter further then within sight of his Bottle : To whom Sir *Iohn Falstaffe* may not unfitly be compared, who never durst ride [p. 11] without a Pistoll, charg'd with *Sacke*, by his side.

> Philocothonista, / Or, The / Drvnkard, / Opened, Dissected, and Anatomized. / [*woodcut: see next page*] London,/ Printed by *Robert Raworth:* and are to be sold at his house / neere the *White-Hart* Taverne in *Smithfield.* 1635./

THOMAS HEYWOOD, 1635.

"Curious if an allusion to old play of *Tr. & Cr.*" J. O. HILL.-P. Part sent by Dr. Ingleby. The Title to this little book has the well-known foreign cut of some old drunkards[1] at table. I got it from the Ballad Society some time ago to use elsewhere for certain swinish Shaksperans of our own day, whose performances it represents; but as the occasion has past by, I may as well add the cut here. Falstaff's pistol, or bottle of sack, is in 1 *Henry IV*, V. iii. 51-4.—F. J. F.

---

[1] There is an odd list of 25 euphemistic names of a Drunkard, on p. 44, 45.

WILLIAM SAMPSON, 1636.

Crof[*fe*]. Will he bedrunke?
Bal[*l*]. Moſt ſwine-like, and then by the vertue of his good liquor hee's able to convert any Browniſticall ſiſter.
Crof. An excellent quality!
Bal. Nay, in that moode, you ſhall have him, inſtead of preſenting *Pyramus*, and *Thiſbe*, perſonate *Cato Cenforious*, and his three ſons, onely in one thing he's out, one of *Cato's* ſons hang'd himſelfe, and that he refer's to a dumbe ſhow;

> *The | Vow | Breaker. | or, | The Faire Maide | of* Clifton. | In *Notinghamshire* as it hath beene diuers times Acted by | severall Companies *with great applause.| By William Sampson.|* . . . London.| *Printed by Iohn Norton and are to be sold by | Roger Ball at the signe of the* Golden | Anchor *in the Strand, neere Temple-| Barre*, 1636.| *Sign. I, back.*

Perhaps this alludes to the sub-play in *M. N. Dr.*—F. J. F.

JOHN TRUSSELL, 1636.

After the folemnitie [Henry V.'s Coronation] paſt, the next day hee cauſed all his wonted Companions to come into his preſence, to whom hee uſed theſe words; It is ſufficient, that for many yeares together, I have faſhioned my ſelfe to your unruly diſpoſitions, and have (not without ſome reluctation, in the very action) followed you in your deboſht and ſwaggering courſes, I have to my ſorrow and ſhame, I may ſay to thinke of it, irregularly wandered, in all rude and unſeemely manner in the vaſt wilderneſſe of ryot and unthriftineſſe, whereby I was almoſt made an alian, to the hearts of my Father and Allyes, and in their opinions violently carried away by your meanes from grace, by keeping you company, therein I have ſo vilified my ſelfe that in the eyes of men, my preſence was vulgar and ſtale, and like the Cuckow in Iune, heard but not regarded. One of you being convented before the Lord chiefe Iuſtice for miſuſing a ſob·r-minded Citizen, I went to the publique Seſſions houſe, and ſtroke him on the face, and being by him deſervedly committed to the *Fleet*, (for which act of juſtice I ſhall ever hold him worthy the place, and my favour, and wiſh all my Iudges to have the like undaunted courage, to puniſh offenders of what ranke ſoever) it occaſioned my Father to put mee from my place in Councell, appointing it to bee ſupplyed by my younger Brother, how often have I by your animation committed thefts, even on my Fathers and my owne Receivers, and robd them of the mony provided for publicke appointments, to maintaine your midnight revellings and noone beſelings; But it is time now to

Margin note: King *Henry* [V] taketh leave of his antient companions.

give a period to thefe exorbitant, and unbefitting courfes, and to falve the wounds my intemperance hath made in my [*p. 93*] reputation, and to turne over a new leafe, and not only to decline the company of fuch mifleaders of yours, but defert their conditions, of all therefore I ftraightly charge and command you, and every one of you, that from henceforth untill you haue fettled your felves in a more orderly courfe of life, and redeeme[d] your pawnd credits, with faire and regarded behauiour, hereafter upon paine of forfeiture of your heads, not to appeare in my prefence, nor to come within the verge of my Court; For what is paft I will grant you my pardon, and withall, becaufe I know fometimes neceffitie will cripple honefty, I will allow each of you a competency of maintenance, as a ftocke to begin a courfe whereby to live orderly hereafter; But take heed of relapfing, for the leaft complaint of ill-behauiour of any of you hereafter, if proved, fhall forfeit your pardons, and exclude my favour for ever: which refolution of mine I will never breake, and fo without attending any reply hee departed.

> A / Continuation / Of The Collection / Of The History of / *England*, Beginning Where / Samvel Daniell / Esquire ended, /.— *By* I. T. London, / Printed by *M. D.* for *Ephraim Dawson*, / and are to bee sold in Fleet-street at the signe of the Rainebowe / neere the inner Temple-/ gate. 1636./ p. 92-3.

The passages alluded to are (1) in the Prince's speech, as King, to Falstaff, 1 *Henry IV*, II. iv. 491, "hence forth nere looke on me, thou art violently carried awaie from grace, there is a diuell haunts thee in the likenesse of an olde fat man;" and (2) in Henry IV's speech to Prince Hal in 1 *Henry IV*, III. ii. 41 and 75-6:

> Had I so lauish beene,
> So common hackneid in the eyes of men,
> So stale and cheape to vulgar companie,
> Opinion that did helpe me to the crowne,

Had still kept loyall to possession,
And left me in reputelesse banishment, 44
A fellow of no marke nor likelihoode.
 . . . . .
So when he had occasion to be seene,
He was but as the Cuckoe is in Iune,
Heard, not regarded 76

That some, if not much of the speech put by Trussell into Henry V's mouth is due to the perversion of History in Shakspere's plays, few readers will doubt. How unjustly Prince Hal's character was represented in these plays, Mr. Alex. Ewald has shown, from contemporary documents, in his late book, *Stories from the Record Office*, a collection of articles that have appeared in divers journals. Mr. Hll.-P. noted the fact of there being a 1 *Hen. IV* allusion in the 1685 edition of Trussell.—F. J. F.

ANON., 1636.

One afkt another whether or no hee had ever read Venus & Diogenes.
  The Booke of Bulls baited with two Centuries of bold Jests, 1636.

J. O. Hll.-P.

*THO. HEYWOOD, 1637 (?).[1]

A young witty Lad playing the part of Richard *the third: at the
Red Bull: the Author becauſe hee was intereſſed in the Play
to incourage him, wrot him this Prologue and
Epilogue.*

The Boy the Speaker.
If any wonder by what magick charme,
Richard the third is ſhrunke up like his arme:
And where in fulneſſe you expected him,
You ſee me only crawling, like a limme
Or piece of that knowne fabrick, and no more . . . .
Let all ſuch know: . . . .
Hee's tearmed a man that ſhowes a dwarfiſh thing,
. . . . have you never read
Large folio Sheets which Printers over-looke,
And caſt in ſmall, to make a pocket booke?
So *Richard* is transform'd : . . . .

---

[1] Pleaſant / Dialogves / and / Dramma's, / selected ovt of / Lucian, Erasmus, Textor, / Ovid, &c./ With sundry *Emblems* extracted from / the most elegant *Iacobus Catsius.*/ As also certaine *Elegies, Epitaphs,* and / *Epithalamions* or *Nuptiall Songs; Anagrams* and / *Acrosticks;* With divers Speeches (upon severall / occasions) spoken to their most Excellent / Majesties, King Charles, and / Queene Mary./ With other *Fancies* translated from Beza, / Bucanan, and sundry Italian Poets./ *By* Tho. Heywood./ *Aut prodesse solent, aut delectare.*/ London, / Printed by *R. O.* for *R. H.* and are to be sold by *Thomas* / *Slater* at the *Swan* in *Duck-lane.* 1637./ p. 247.

THO. HEYWOOD, 1637 (?).

The Epilogue
Great I confeſſe your patience hath now beene,
To ſee a little *Richard :* who can win,
Or praiſe, or credit? eye, or thinke to excell,
By doing after what was done ſo well?

The Dramatic Works of Thomas Heywood, London, 1874,
vol. vi. pp. 352-3. *Prologues and Epilogues.*
p. 248.

This is partly quoted, with the extract in *Centurie,* p. 7, in Halliwell's *Folio Shakespeare,* xi. 333, where the editor says : " It may, however, be too much to assume that the two notices last mentioned refer to Shakespeare's play," inasmuch as there were other plays on the same king—*The True Tragedie of Richard the Third,* 1594, and that of Henslowe's Company about 1599, with Banister in it, and perhaps alluded to in " A New Booke of Mistakes, or Bulls with Tales, and Buls without Tales, but no lyes by any meanes," 1637. "As late as the year 1654, Gayton speaks of a play of Richard the Third in which the ghost of Jane Shore is introduced."—*ib.* p. 330.—F. J. F.

* SHAKERLEY MARMION, 1637.

You much diſſemble, or you have forgot
His forme, and function, or you know them not.

> A Morall Poem, / Intituled the Legend of / Cvpid / and Psyche./ Or Cvpid and his / *Mistris.*/ . . . *Written* by *Shackerley Marmion, Gent.*/ . . . London ; / Printed by *N.* and *I. Okes*, and are to be sold by / *H. Sheppard,* at his shop in *Chancery lane* neere / Serjants Inne, at the Bible. 1637./ sign. E 4.

Now if this uncouth life, and ſolitude
Pleaſe you, then follow it, and be ſtill ſlew'd
In the ranke luſt of a laſcivious worme :
sign. E 4, back.

["imitates a passage in *Hamlet*, Act III. sc. iv, and bears the trace of another (?) in Act II. sc. ii. ll. 582, 583." *Centurie,* p. 428.]

Tears in his eyes, distraction in's aspect
A broken voice, and his whole function suiting
With forms to his conceit.
Hamlet, II. ii. 528-530.

Nay, but to live
In the rank sweat of an enseamed bed,
Stew'd in corruption, honeying and making love
Over the nasty sty.
Hamlet, III. iv. 91-4 Camb.
C. M. I.

THOMAS CAREW, BEF. 1638.

Shep[herd].
See Love the blushes of the morne appeare . . .
Sweet, I must stay no longer here.

Nymph.
Those streakes of doubtfull light usher not day,
But shewe my sunne must s t : . . .
The yellow planet and the gray
Dawne shall attend thee on thy way . . . .
. . . . Shepherd, arise,
The sun betrayes us else to spies . . . . . .

Shep.
Harke! *Ny*. Aye me! stay. *Shep*. For ever? *Ny*. No, arise,
Wee must be gone.

Poems./ By / Thomas Carew / Esquire./ . . .
London . . . 1640. A Pastorall Dialogue.
p. 77 (ed. W. C. Hazlitt, Roxb. Libr. 1870,
p. 58).

"This Pastoral Dialogue seems to be entirely an Imitation of the Scene between *Romeo* and *Juliet*, Act iii. Sc. 7. The time, the persons, the sentiments, the expressions, are the same."—T. Davies. *Carew's Poems, Songs, and Sonnets*, 1772, p. 67-8, *n*. (with 3 of the following lines):—

 Rom. . . . . look, love, what envious streaks
 Do lace the severing clouds in yonder east . . . . .
 I must be gone and live, or stay and die.
 Jul. Yon light is not day-light, I know it, I :
 It is some meteor that the sun exhales,
 To be to thee this night a torch-bearer,
 And light thee on thy way to Mantua . . .
 Rom. . . . I am content . . . let's talk ; it is not day.
 Jul. It is, it is ; hie hence, be gone, away ! . . . .
 O, now be gone ; more light and light it grows.
     Noted in *Centurie*, p. 429. F J. F.

1638.

[Five Songs from the *Tempest* are in a little (? 12mo) paper MS., Egerton 2421 (dated 1638), in the British Museum, bought of " J. Harvey, 8 Dec. 1877." The 46 leaves of the volume contain epigrams and poems from Dr. Doune and other writers, some printed, others seemingly unprinted. On the first page are the following lines—

> "To the reader of this booke.
> Kind curteous reader looke not to behold
> Here Indian iewells set in [r]inges of gold,
> Or swanlike Musicke in assorted straines,
> or the rare issue of inspiring braines ; [1]
> No Orphan [2] aeries or Amphions laies
> Neither Orion nor yet Lucius swaies
> These rurall sonnets made for mirth & sport
> Fitting the Vulgar, not the wiser sort;
> But yet Kind Reader, if yu please to looke [y^u = thou]
> Within the couert of this idle booke,
> Then turne not critique, least thy iudgment be
> By nicer wits brought into obloquie.
> This booke is like a garden in wch growes
> Herbes good and bad : he that the goodnesse knows
> May freely gather, and the bad he may
> Vse at his leasure, or else cast away.
> Be not too cruell, then, in thine election,
> But please thou thine, thou pleasest mine affection."]

[leaf 6, Songes lack]   [out of]   Shakefpeare. &c.

1

The
   Tempeft   Ariel.
[beg.] Full fadome 5 thy father lies

---

[1] The writer's opinion of Shakspere was evidently not a high one.
[2] Orphean, of Orpheus.

1638.

[*ends*] Seanimphes hourely ring his knell
    Burthen——ding dong &c.
Hearke now I heare them ding, dong, bell

2

Ibid.   Stephano.
[*beg.*] The mafter yᵉ Swabber yᵉ Botefwaine & I
[*ends*] Then to fea boyes & let her go hange
    Then to fea &c.

3

Ib.   Caliban.
[*beg.*] No more dams Ile make for fifh
[*ends*] Ban Ban Cacalyban
    Has a new mafter get a new man.

[*leaf 7, headed* "Songes"]   4

Ibid.   Juno.
[*beg.*] Honor, riches, marriage, bleffing,
[*ends*] Ceres bleflings fo bie on you.

5

Ibid.   Ariel.
[*beg.*] Where yᵉ bee fucks there fuck I
(*ends*) Vnder yᵉ bloffome yᵗ hanges on yᵉ bowe.

6

[*No more given.* The reference to Shakspere's songs in this MS. is in the Additional MSS' Catalogue, Brit. Mus.—F. J. Furnivall.]

HENRY ADAMSON, 1638.

Forteviot. Right over to *Forteviot* did we hy,
And there the ruin'd caſtle did we ſpy
K. Malcolme Kenmore. Of *Malcolme Ken-more*, whom *Mackduff*, then *Thane*,
Of *Fife*, (ſo cald) from *England* brought againe,
And fiercelie did perſue tyrant *Makbeth*,
Uſurper of the Crowne, even to the death.
Theſe caſtles ruines when we did conſider,
We ſaw that waſting time makes all things wither.

> *The Muses Threnodie, | or, | Mirthfull Mournings, on the death | of Master* Gall / Containing varietie of pleasant Poeticall descriptions, historicall narra-*tions and divine observations, with the | most remarkable antiquities of* Scot / land, *eſpecially at* Perth. / *By Mr. H. Adamson | Horat. in Arte.* / Omne tulit punctum, qui miscuit utile dulci. / *Printed at* Edinburgh *in King* James *College, /* by *George Anderson,* 1638. *The eight Muse,* p. 82.

Neere this we did perceave where proud *Makbeth*,
Makbeths castle on Dunsinnen hill. Who to the furies did his ſoul bequeath,
His caſtle mounted on *Dunſinnen* hill,
Cauſing the mightieſt peeres obey his will,
And bow their necks to build his *Babylon* . . . .
Who had this ſtrange reſponſe, that none ſhould catch him
That borne was of a woman, or ſhould match him:
Nor any horſe ſhould overtake him there, [p. 83]
But yet his ſprite deceav'd him by a mare,
And by a man was not of woman borne
Makduf. For brave *Makduff* was from his mother ſhorne . . . .
Up to *Dunfinnen's* top then did we clim,
With panting heart, weak loynes and wearied limme.

Ibid. p. 84.

Quoted,—(2) before (1), and with no dots . . . at the omissions, in
I. O. IIII.-P.'s *Cursory Memoranda on Makbeth,* pp. 7-8.

JOHN CLARKE, 1639.

Thought is free. (p. 63.)
A trout hamlet with foure legs.
An honest man and a good bowler.
Fat paunches make leane pates and grosser bits enrich the ribs, but bankerupt quite the wits.

Soterichi lecti. (p. 71.)
Non licet asse mihi qui me non asse licetur. (p. 72.)
Pinguis venter non gignit sensum tenuem. (p. 135.)

Parœmiologia | Anglo-latina,| in usum Scholarum concinnata, | or | Proverbs | English, and Latine, methodically disposed according to the Common-place | heads, in ERASMUS *his | Adages.|* Very use-full and delightfull for all sorts / of men, on all occasions.| *More especially profitable for Scholars | for the attaining Elegancie, sublimitie, and | varietie of the best expressions.| . . . London,| Imprinted by* Felix Kyngston *for* Robert | Mylbourne, *and are to be sold at the signe of | the* Vnicorne *neere* Fleet bridge. 1639.

'*The Epistle to the Reader*' is sign'd '*John Clarke.*' He was Master of the Grammar-School at Hull, and wrote several school-books. The present one is not in the British Museum. Mr. Reynell of Forde House, Putney, the owner of the old staind glass from Charlecote House, has kindly lent me his copy. Clarke says: "I have gleaned and gathered these *Proverbs* out of all writers, I could read or meet withall, and have used herein the help of sundry *scholars*, and worthy friends : over and beside my owne observation of many golden proverbs, dropping now and then out of *vulgar* mouthes *imâ de plebe*." His book, he says, "hath lien by me now these *eight* yeares, and been so long in *fieri*: now 'tis thine (if thou please in *facto*; for to the Presse I manu-mise it, *nonum ut prematur in annum*)."

That Shakspere was one of the writers from whom Clarke or his helpers had gleand and gatherd, seems clear. "*Thought is free*" may well be Stephano's, in *The Tempest*, III. ii. 132,[1] while the 'honest man and good bowler' may be Costard's "*an honest man . . . and a very good bowler*," in *Love's Labours Lost*, V. ii. 585-8, which play, in its lines 26-7 of Act I. sc. i. also gave Clarke its couplet.

"Fat paunches have lean pates, and dainty bits
Make rich the ribs, but bankrupt quite the wits."

---

[1] '*A moone-calfe, or wind-egge.|* Menia columna.'—Clarke, p. 70.

Mr. J. P. Collier was the first to print the 2nd and 4th of the quotations above, in his *Further Particulars regarding Shakespeare and his Works*, London, T. Rodd, 1839, p. 68, and on the *hamlet* one he remarks — 'But there is one saying, where Hamlet is named, which I cannot understand; it is this :

"A trout, Hamlet, with four legs."—p. 71.

Can it have any reference to the scene between Hamlet and Polonius (Act III. Sc. ii. [l. 394-9]), where the latter humours the prince by saying that a cloud is like a camel, a weasel, or a whale ? Has it been some absurd interpolation of the players, substituting "trout" for "whale?" is it from the older *Hamlet*, or has it nothing whatever to do with either play?'[1]

Before trying to give an answer to these questions, one has first to ask, What does '*Soterichi lecti*' mean ?

Our member, the Rev. W. A. Harrison, of St. Ann's Vicarage, answers, by Forcellini's help [2] :—

"The phrase '*Soterici lecti*' is found in Aulus Gellius (xii. 2, § 5, Delph. Ed.). He is quoting as 'a joke' of Seneca's an opinion that he expresses on some verses of the poet Ennius. ' Qui hujuscemodi, inquit [Seneca] versus amant, liqueat tibi eosdem admirari et " *Soterici lectos*." Dignus sane Seneca videatur lectione se studio adolescentium : qui honorem coloremque veteris orationis Soterici lectis compararit, quasi minimæ scilicet gratiæ, et relictis jam contemptisque.'

"He who can admire the verses of Ennius, is capable even of admiring the couches of Sotericus."

The Scholiast says that Sotericus was a coarse, clumsy workman, who made and carved couches in such a rude, unfinished style, that the phrase "like Sotericus's couches" came to be applied to anything clumsy and rough, or to bad art generally. "Hæc locutio (*i. e.* Soterici lecti) in vulgarem jocum abiit de re vili."

As then the Latin was applied to *res vilis*, and Clarke puts his proverb into his section " *Contemptus & vilitatis* " (p. 68),[3] so was the English *trout* employd, says Mr. Hessels. Maria uses the word for Malvolio (*Twelfth*

---

[1] Mr. H.-P. quotes this passage from Collier, in his *Mem. on Hamlet*, p. 21, and agrees with Dr. Ingleby that 'it is in all probability taken from the older play of Hamlet.'

[2] "Sotericus, gen.—ci. m., artifex lignarius valde rudis, unde Soterici lectus ponitur pro impolito, et nulla arte facto." And he quotes Seneca [as above]. Erasmus conjectures that Sotericus was some workman whose productions were very primitive and rude. Afterwards, of course, it became a proverb.—J. H. HESSELS.

[3] The 2 sentences before, are, " *Goe shake your eares. I'le not foule my fingers with him ;* " the 2 after, " *I'le not medle with him hot or cold. A rogues ward-robe is harbour for a louse.*"

Night, II. v. 25-6) coming to be foold, "here comes the *trout* that must be caught with tickling ;" and Latham's Johnson follows up this quotation by two others : " This [*the trout*] is in some kinde a foolish fish, and an embleme of one who loves to be flattered : for when he is once in his hold, you may take him with your hands by tickling, rubbing, or clawing him under the bellie.—Swan, *Speculum Mundi*, 1635, ch. viii. § 1, p. 389. Leave off your tickling of young heirs like *trouts*.—Beaumont and Fletcher." [1]

Granting then that there is a sneer in the words, and that they are spoken to Hamlet of some third person, I would make them, if they were used in Shakspere's play,[2] a bit of gag in the mouth of the man who playd Horatio shortly before 1639, and I would apply them to Hamlet's "waterfly . . beast . . and chough . . spacious in the possession of dirt " (V. ii. 84-90), even Osric, and either put them in after the words last cited, or add them to one of Horatio's like remarks on the 'beast : '—"His purse is empty already ; all's golden words are spent " (l. 135-7) ; " This lapwing runs away with the shell on his head." Or they might follow Osric's " The carriages, sir, are the hangers," l. 164. (Possibly they might have been used of the Grave-digger, in answer to Hamlet's " Has this fellow no feeling of his business, that he sings at grave making ? ")

Of Clarke's other saws, " All shall be well, and Jack shall have Jill," p. 63, is hardly Puck's "Jack shall have Jill :/ Nought shall go ill." *Mids. N. Dr.* III. ii. 461-2 ; and under " *Magnifica Promissa*," p. 193, " *Court holy water/* Incantatione quavis efficacius " is probably not from *Lear*, III. ii. 10 ; as " He must have a long spoon that will eate with the Devill," p. 127, dates from before Dromio of Syracuse, *Errors*, IV. iii. 64 ; and " It's merry i' th' hall when beards wag all," from before 2 *Hen. IV.*, &c., &c.[3]

Mr. Collier says of Clarke's book : ' Farther on (p. 192) we have " Fat paunches and leane pates." [4] In the same volume we have " Much ado about

---

[1] Compare too, in Fletcher's *Rule a Wife and have a Wife* (licenst Oct. 19, 1624, pr. 1640), Act II. sc. iv. (B. & F.'s Works, ed. Dyce, 1845, vol. ix, p. 419), Estefania's
    What, dost thou think I fish without a bait, wench ?
    I bob for fools : he is mine own ; I have him :
    I told thee what would tickle him like a *trout ;*
    And as I cast it, so I caught him daintily ;
    And all he has, I have stow'd at my devotion.

[2] I don't take to the notion of their being part of the old play, because of the late date at which they were used. Surely all trace of the old *Hamlet* had disappeared from the currency by 1639.

[3] "Much water goes by th' milne, that the milner knowes not off," is before *Tit. Andron.* II. i. 85.

[4] " Pinguis venter, macer intellectus."

nothing,"[1] "All's well that ends well[2]," and "To take your ease in your inn,"[3] which were proverbial long before the time of Shakespere.'

On p. 34 of the *Parœmiologia* is an illustration of Buckingham's 'Tremble and start *at wagging of a straw*,' *Rich. III*, III. v. 7 :—

| Angry at the wagging of a straw | Nè move festucam, A lasso rixu quæritur. |

---

[1] p. 51, "*You make much adoe about nothing.*/ Quid de pusillis magna procemia ?"

[2] p. 117, "Finis non pugna coronat."

[3] The earliest use I know is ab. 1536, and is given in my Thynne's *Animadversions*, p. 77

G. RIVERS, 1639.

"They, as frolick as youth, and wine that made them fo; unlock the treafures of their hearts, their Wives, and their beauties to the admiration of unfound cares."

Heroine, pp. 45-46. [Shakspere's *Lucrece*, l. 16.]

"*Tarquin* divided between aftonifhment & rage, that *Collatine* his fervant, fhould be his Soveraigne in happineffe: mounted upon the wings of luft and fury, flies to *Rome*."

p. 46. [Sh., l. 2, and ll. 41-42.]

"shee affrighted at the fword and blafted by the light that luft gave life to, trembling like a prey with more horrour then attention, heares him thus befpeak her."

p. 47. [cf. Sh., ll. 442—460.]

This night I muft enjoy thee *Lucrecia*,

p. 48. [Sh., l. 512.]

The fin unknown is unacted,

p. 49. [Sh., l. 527.]

In *Tarquines* fhape I entertain'd you; wrong not the Prince fo farre, as to proftrate his fame to fo inglorious an action.

p. 50. [Sh., l. 596.]

Firft they faw her face ftand in that amazed filence, that they could read, not heare the full contents of forrow.

p. 52-3. [Sh., ll. 590-596.]

her foule too pure for her bodie, difclogg'd it felfe of clay, and broke the vault of mortalitie.

p. 56. [?]

now when the brother of death had fummon'd to ftill mufick all but foule ravifhers, theeves, and cares;

p. 61. [Sh., L 126.]

The / Heroinæ : / Or / The lives / of / Arria, / Paulina, / Lucrecia, / Dido, / Theutilla, / Cypriana, / Aretaphila. / *London*, / Printed by *R. Bishop* for *John Colby*, / and are to be sold at his Shop under the / Kings head Tavern, at Chancery-/ lane end in Fleet-street. 1639./

There may be other bits from Shakspere in the *Heroinæ*. This interesting little book is dedicated to the *Lady Dorothy Sydney*, Waller's 'Sacharissa,' and is written by G. Rivers, almost certainly one of the brothers Rivers of whom one is addressed by Milton in his line, long a crux in the *Vacation Exercise*,

"*Rivers* arise!"

E. DOWDEN.

ANONYMOUS, 1639.

One afked another what *Shakefpeares* works were worth all being bound together? he anfwered not a farthing; not worth a farthing faid he why so? he anfwered that his plays were worth a great deale of mony but he never heard that his works were worth any thing at all.

> *Conceits, Clinches, Flashes, and Whim ies. Newly studied, with some Collections but those never published before in this kinde. London. Printed by R. Hodgkinsonne for Daniel Frere and are to be sold at the signe of the red Bull in little britain. 1639. No. 196, sign. E 4.* (Old English Jest-Books, *ed. Hazlitt,* 1864, iii. 49.)—E. PHIPSON.

ANON. 1640 (? 1628).

The Gluttons *Speech.*

A Chaire, a Chaire, fweet Mafter Jew, a Chaire: All that I fay, is this, I'me a fat man it has been a Weft-Indian voyage for me to come reeking hither; A Kitchin-ftuffe-wench might pick up a living, by following me, for the fat which I loofe in ftradling: I doe not live by the fweat of my brows, but am almoft dead with fweating, I eate much, but can talke little; *Sir Iohn Old-castle* was my greatgrandfathers fathers Uncle, I come of a huge kindred, And of you defire to learne, whether my Fortune be to die a yeere, or two, hence, or to grow bigger, if I continue as I doe in feeding, (for, my victuals I cannot leave:) Say, fay, mercifull Jew, what fhall become of me.

The Wandering-Jew, | *Telling* | *Fortvnes* | *to* | *English-men,* | [*Woodcut*] *London* ; | *Printed by* Iohn Raworth, *for* Nathaniel Butter. 1640. 4*to.* (4°, A. 14. Art.), p. 38. *Reprinted in* Halliwell's Books of Characters, 1857, p. 42.

Sir John Old-castle was Shakspere's first name for Falstaff (*Centurie*, p. 269, &c.), and this passage evidently alludes to him by it. The passage (now re-read with the original by Mr. Parker) is quoted by Reed (*Variorum Shakspere*, xvi. 418) and in Mr. Halliwell's *Character of Sir John Falstaff*, 1841, p. 26-7, without reference to Reed.—F. J. F.

The Preface is signed "Thy wandring friend Gad Ben-arod, Ben Baalam Ben-Ahimuth, Ben-Baal, Ben-Gog, Ben-Magog."

The British Museum copy has a MS. note by E. Malone. "This tract

ANON. 1640 (? 1628).

must have been written before 1630, for in p. 52 Spinola and Tilly are spoken of as living. Spinola died in 1630, and Tilly in 1632.[1]

"In p. 39 'this plentiful year' is mentioned.[2] I believe therefore it was written in 1628, the most plentiful year between 1620 and 1640. Wheat was in that year sold in Windsor Market for 28s. a qr., and elsewhere in England probably for 22s."

Passages referred to by Malone above.

[1] p. 52. [The Banckrupts speech] "to be call'd a weathy Citizen, is my minde, as great an honour as to bee call'd *Bethlem-Gabor*, or Spinola, or Tilley, they fight for glory, (and we Citizens striue for Riches)

Bethlen Gabor, i.e. Gabriel Bethlen, Prince of Transylvania, died 15 Nov. 1629,
John Tzerclaes, Count of Tilly, died 30 Apr. 1632,
Marquis Ambrosio de Spinola died 25 Sep. 1630."

[2] p. 39. [The Glutton's Fortune] "Pray for a Famine, for if that Surgeon cannot worke upon your body, and eate away the proud flesh, such a plentifull yeere as this, must put you to the charge of a longer girdle."

P. A. LYONS.

*JAMES SHIRLEY, 1640.

The Arcadia.

Dame[tas]. Ime out of breath, let me walke my felfe a little.
Pam[ela]. What hafte does tire you?
Dam. Tire me, I am no woman, keepe your tires to your felfe Nor am I *Pericles* prince of *Tyre*.

> A / Pastoral / Called / The / Arcadia. / Acted by her Majesties Servants / at the *Phœnix* in *Drury* / Lane. / Written by *Iames Shirly* Gent. / *London*, / Printed by *I. D.* for *Iohn Williams*, and *E. Eglesfield* / and are to be sould at the signe of the *Crane* / in *Pauls* Church-yard. 1640. / sign. B 4 back.
>
> J. O. H.-P.

ANON., 1640.

Q. What Birds are thofe, that are called Prophets twice borne?
A. The Cocke: firft an egge from the Henne, after a Cocke from the Egge: they foretell feafons and changes of weather, according to the Verfe:

> Some fay for ever 'gainft that feafon comes,
> Wherein our Saviours birth is celebrated,
> The Bird of dawning fingeth all Night long,
> And then they fay no Spirit dares walk abroad,
> So facred and fo hallow'd is that tune. [*sic*]
>   *W.* Shakefp.
>
> *A Helpe to Discourse.* 1640.
>   C. M. I.

(?) JAMES SHIRLEY, ab. 1640 or 1642.

Thomas, I muſt thinke how to provide mee of warlike accoutrements to accomodate, which comes of Accomodo: *Shakeſpeare*.

>*Captain Underwit, a Comedy;* printed in Mr. A. H. Bullen's *Collection of Old Plays*, London, 1882-3, vol. ii. p. 320.

[Referring of course to *Hen. IV.*, Pt II. Act III. sc. ii. ll. 72-78. The etymology being taken from the mouth of Mr. Shallow.]

Un. Theis things are very right, *Thomas*. Let me fee now the bookes of Martiall diſcipline.

Tho. I bought up all that I found have relation to warr and fighting. . . . .

Un. Shakeſpeares Workes.—Why *Shakeſpeares* Workes?

Tho. I had nothing for the pikemen before.

Un. They are plays.

Tho. Are not all your muſterings in the countrey ſo, Sir? Pray read on.

>*Ibid.* p. 342.

The play is anonymous, but Mr. Bullen confidently attributes it to Shirley, and supposes it to have been written about 1640 or 1642. At that date the volume that Thomas purchased for his master would probably have been the Folio of 1632. The jest on the title had already been made with reference to Ben Jonson's 1616 edition of his " Workes."—H. A. Evans.

[These extracts are given again, by oversight, more fully on p. 156-7. They were sent earlier from the MS by Mr. S. L. Lee.—F.]

RICH. GOODRIDGE, CHR. CH., 1640.

Were thy ſtory of as much direfull woe,
As that, of Iuliet *and* Hieronymo :
Here's that would cure you : . . .

('To the Authour upon his *Love-Melancholy.*') Commendatory Verses, sign. *a* 3, back, in

EPOTOMANIA / *or* / A Treatise / Discoursing of the Essence, / Causes, Symptomes, Prog-/nosticks, and Cure of / Loue, / or / *Erotique* / *Melancholy.* / *Written by* / Iames Ferrand[1] / Dr of Physick / [Englisht by E. Chilmead] *Oxford.* / Printed by *L. Lichfield* and are to be / sold by *Edward Forrest.* 1640./

[Two of the other Christ Church commendators mention 'Lucrece' (*b.* kk ; *b.* 5 bk), but evidently without reference to Shakspere. (Richard West of Christ Church, on sig. b 7, treats Ben Jonson as the great poet of the day :

"*As twere the only office of a Friend*
To Rhyme, and 'gainst his Conscience to commend ;
And sweare like Poets of the Post, This Play
Exceeds all Johnson's Works :"
Noted by Mr. Hll.-P.)

The extract abuv is printed in Hunter's *Illustrations*, i.]—F. J. F.

---

[1] Jacques Ferrand.

GEO. LYNN, 1640.

To his Friend the Author, on his *Fancies Theatre.*

* * * * * *

> For, when th' inticing pleafure of thy Line,
> And teeming *Fancies* unexhaufted *Myne*
> I view, me thinks the *Genius* of thofe *Three*
> Admired *Laureats* are eufphear'd in *Thee,*
> Smooth *Shakefpeare,* neat *Randolph,* and wittie *Ben,*
> Flow in a mutuall fweetneffe from *Thy* Pen:

> *The | Fancies | Theater. | by | Iohn Tatham | Gent.! ...
> London,| Printed by Iohn Norton, for | Richard Best,
> and are to be | sold at his Shop neere Grayes-Inne-| gate
> in* Holborne.| 1640.| *Sign.* (*) 8.

W. Ling, who writes the laft fore-praife poem to this play, doesn't deign (like so many other poetafters) to mention Shakfpere :—

> "Had I *Chapmans* Line or Learning, *Iohnsons* Art,
> *Fletchers* more accurate Fancie, or that part
> Of *Beaumont* that's divine, *Dun*'s profound skill,
> Making good Verfes live, and damning ill :
> I then would prayfe thy Verfes, which sho'd laft
> Whilft *Time* ha's sands to run, or *Fame* a blaft."
>
> F. J. F.

RICH. BRATHWAITE, 1641.

wee will now defcend to fuch particulars, wherein thefe cenforious *Timonifts* (whofe poore degenerate fpirits are ever delighted moft in detracting from women, or afperfing fome unworthy difgrace upon their fexe;) ufurpe this liberty, to lay upon their pureft reputes a lafting infamy. Wee fhall in every place heare calumnious tongues ... inveighing againft them in this manner: What vice is there extant, which is not in the practife of women frequent? .. If young, they are lafcivious: if old they are covetous. Their whole life a Comedy of errors: their formall feature a fardell of fafhions. Alas poore Girles! Have you no *Defence* againft fuch viperous tongues?

> A / Ladies / Love-Lecture : / Compofed, / and From The Choi- / ceft Flowers of / Divinitie and Humanitie / *Culled, and Compiled* : / As it hath beene by fundry Perfonages of emi- / nent qualitie, upon sight of some Copies di- / fperfed, modestly importuned : / To the memory of that Sexes honour ; for whose sweet / sakes he originally addressed this Labour. / By Ri. Brathwait *Esquire* . . . *London*, / Printed by Iohn Dawson, 1641. / *Section* VII. p. 419 of " *The English Gentleman* . . . The third *Edition* revised, corrected, and enlarged. 1641."

Reference to the book sent by Dr. Ingleby.—F. J. F.

148

*SHAKERLY MARMION, 1641.

Oh that I were a vail upon that face,
To hide it from the world; methinks I could
Envie the very Sun, for gazing on you!

> The / Antiquary. / A Comedy, / Acted by Her Maiestie's
> Servants / at / The Cock-Pit. / Written / By Shackerly
> Mermion, Gent. / London, / . . . 1641. Actus Secundus,
> sign. C 4 back

Probably referring to Romeo's
> O that I were a gloue upon that hand,
> That I might touch that cheeke!
> *Romeo and Juliet*, II. ii. 24.

J. O. HIL.-P.

ABRAHAM COWLEY, 1641.

1. *Bla[de]*. Fare ye well Gentlemen. I ſhall ſee thee *Cutter* a brave Tapſter ſhortly; it muſt be ſo i' faith, *Cutter;* thou muſt like *Bardolph* i' the play, the ſpiggot weild. (D 3, col. 2)

2. *Aur[elia]* * * * I ſhall never hear my Virginals when I play upon 'um, for her daughter *Tabytha's* ſinging of Pſalms. The firſt pious deed will be, to baniſh *Shakeſpear* and *Ben Johnſon* out of the parlour, and to bring in their rooms *Marprelate*, and *Pryn's* works. You'll ne'er endure 't, Sir. You were wont to have a Sermon once a quarter at a good time; you ſhall have ten a day now.

> The Guardian. / A Comedie / Acted before / Prince Charles His Highness / at *Trinity*-Colledge in *Cambridge*, / upon the twelfth of *March*, / 1641. Written by / Abraham Cowley : / London, Printed for *John Holden*, at the Anchor in / the New Exchange. 1650./

But it is worth noting that in his revision of the Guardian, "printed in 1663, the scene London in the year 1658" and called "Cutter of Coleman Street", (1) was wholly omitted, and the Shakespear of (2) altered to Fletcher.

In 1 (Act IV. sc. iii.) the reminiscence is to the *M. Wives of W.*, I. iii., and the last words to Pistol's

"O base Hungarian wight ! wilt thou *the spigot wield* ! "

In 2 (Act IV. sc. vii.) we have some evidence that Shakespeare and Ben Jonson were then the most popular dramatists, more popular than Beaumont and Fletcher, so often classed with them as the excelling tri- or quadr- umvirate. —B. N.

FRESH ALLUSIONS TO SHAKSPERE

THIRD PERIOD.
1642—1659.
(*From the Closing of the Theatres to the Stuart Restoration.*)

JAMES SHIRLEY, 1642, 1635.

"Stand off, gentlemen,—let me see—which? Hum! this?—
no; th' other! Hum! send for a lion and turn him loose; he
will not hurt the true prince."

> *The Sisters* (licenst in April, 1642, printed in 1652),
> Act V. sc. ii. *Works*, ed. Gifford, by Dyce,
> 1833, v. 421.

These are Piperollo's words when he's in doubt whether Farnese (the
Prince of Parma) or the disguised Frapolo, the chief bandit, is the true
prince. Gifford says ironically, "A *sneer* at Shakspeare! unnoticed by the
commentators." A good-humour'd allusion, there no doubt is,—to Falstaff's "but beware instinct: the lion will not touch the true prince"
(1 *Henry IV*, II. iv. 300),—but no sneer.

> *Arcadius.*   Thou art jealous now;
> Come, let me take the kiss I gave thee last;
> I am so confident of thee, no lip
> Has ravish'd it from thine.
>
>   1635. *The Coronation*, Act II. sc. 1. Works, ed.
>   Gifford, & Dyce. 1833, vol. iii. p. 474.

'This pretty thought,' says Gifford,—without any need for the remark,—
is from Shakespeare :

> "this kiss
> I carried from thee, dear, and my true heart
> Hath virgin'd it e'er since."—*Coriolanus*.'

The Coronation "was licensed in February 1634-5, as the production of
Shirley; but from some cause or other it is attributed to 'John Fletcher,'
in the title-page of the first edition, ("Written by John Fletcher, Gent.")
printed in 4to in 1640, though Fletcher had been dead ten years prior to
its first appearance on the stage."—*ib.* p. 457.

See too iv. 36, 437, 462 (Varges).—F. J. F.

JOHN MILTON, 1642.

(1). But fince there is fuch neceffity to the hear-fay of a Tire, a Periwig, or a Vizard, that Playes muft have bin feene, what difficulty was there in that? when in the Colleges fo many of the young Divines, and thofe in the next aptitude to Divinity, have bin feeue fo oft upon the Stage, writhing and unboning their Clergie limmes to all the antick and difhoneft geftures of Trinculo's, Buffons, and Bawds; proftituting the fhame of that miniftery, which either they had, or were nigh having, to the eyes of Courtiers and Court Ladies, with their Groomes and *Mademoifelles*.

p. 14, ed. 1642. (*Milton's Prose Works*, ed. Symonds, 1806, ii. 221.)

(2). I had faid, that becaufe the Remonftrant was fo much offended with thofe who were tart againft the Prelats, fure he lov'd toothleffe Satirs, which I look were as improper as a toothed Sleekftone. This Champion from behind the Arras cries out that thofe toothleffe Satyrs were of the Remonftrants making; and armes himfelfe here tooth and naile, and *horne* to boot, to fupply the want of teeth, or rather of gumms in the Satirs. And for an onfet tels me that the fimily of a Sleekftone *ſhewes I can be as bold with a Prelat as familiar with a Laundreſſe.*

> An / Apology / Against a Pamphlet / call'd / A Modest Confutation / of the Animadversions upon / the Remonstrant against / Smectymnuus./ [*in MS.* by m^r Milton / ex dono Authoris /] London, / Printed by E. G. for *Iohn Rothwell*, and are / to be sold at the signe of the Sunne / in *Pauls* Church-yard. 1642./ *Sect.* 6, p. 32. (M.'s *Prose Works,* Bohn's Stand. Libr. iii. 140.)

In (1)—sent by H. E. S.—Milton's *Trinculo* is from Shakspere's *Tempest ;* in (2) his Champion crying out from behind the Arras, is from Shakspere's Polonius, *Hamlet*, III. iv. 22.

"*Smectymnuus* was a pamphlet written by 5 Presbyterian divines— *S*tephen *M*arshall, *E*dmund *C*alamy, *T*homas *Y*oung, *M*atthew *N*ewcomen, *W*illiam *S*purstow (of whose initials the name is a compound)—against episcopacy." Bp. Hall answerd it. Milton answerd him. Then Hall (?) rejoind, declaring that Milton's phrazes showd he had pikt em up in Brothels and Playhouses. This malignant libel fired Milton, and he lasht his traducer in the way that such scoundrelly insinuations deservd. Milton's indignant vindication of the purity of his early manhood is very fine.—F. J. F.

SIR THOS. BROWNE, 1642.

If their[1] be any truth in Aftrology, I may outlive a Jubile, as yet I have not feene one revolution of *Saturne*, nor have my pulfe beate thirty yeares, and [yet[2]] excepting one, have feene the afhes, and left under ground, all the Kings of *Europe*, have been contemporary to three Emperours, foure Grand Signiours, and as many Popes; me thinkes I have out-lived my felfe, and begin to be weary of the Sunne.[3]

Religio Medici. Printed for Andrew Crooke. 1642. p. 78-9. (§ 40, p. 93, ed. 1643.)

Macbeth, V. v. 49 : I gin to be a weary of the sun.

E. PHIPSON and F. J. F.

---

[1] there. ed. 1643. [2] and yet. 1643.
[3] same, 1st. ed. 1642 (*spurious*). The first authorized edition of 1645, reads 'Sunne,' p. 87, § 40.

JOHN CLEVELAND, ? about 1644 (died 1658).

But once more to fingle out my embofs'd Committee-man; his Fate (for I know you would fain fee an end of him) is either a whipping Audit, when he is wrung in the Withers by a Committee of Examinations, and fo the Spunge weeps out the Moifture which he had foaked before; or elfe he meets his Paffing-peal in the clamorous Mutiny of a Gut-foundred Garrifon: for the Hedge-fparrow will be feeding the Cuckow, till he miftake his Commons and bites off her head.

The Character of a Country-Committee-man, with the Earmark of a Sequestrator. Clievelandi Vindiciæ ; *or Clieveland's Genuine Poems, Orations, Epistles,* &c. . . . London . . . 1677, p. 100.

The allusion is, I suppoze, to *Lear*, I. iv. 235—
"*Foole.* For you know Nunckle, the Hedge-Sparrow fed the Cuckoo so long, that it's had it head bit off by it young, so out went the Candle, and we were left darkling." 1 *Folio*, p. 288, col. 2.
For the probable date, see *Centurie*, p. 254.—F. J. F.

SIR RICHARD BAKER, 1645.

and therefore where he [Prynne, author of 'Hiftriomastix'] hath entituled his *Book*, A *Tragedie* of *Aftours;* he fhould, if he had done right, have entituled it, A *Comedie* of *Errours*.

Theatrum Redivivum, (a posthumously published work : Sir R. B. died in Feb. 1645). 1662. p. 96.

This book, an answer to Prynne, is singularly wanting in contemporary references or allusions of any kind, English or European.—B. N.

ANONYMOUS, ab. 1645 (?).

Act the first. [*leaf* 1]

Enter Captaine Vnderwit and his man Thomas.

* * * * *

Tho: and fo the Land has parted you, [*leaf* 1, *back*]

Vn. thou faift right, Thomas, it lies betweene both our houses [*leaf* 2] indeed, but now I am thus dignified, (I thinke that's a good word) or intituled is better, but tis all one, since I am made a Captaine—

Tho: by your owne defert, and vertue

Vn. thou art deceaud, it is by vertue of the Commiffion, the Commifion is enough to make any man an Officer without defert Thomas, I muft thinke how to prouide mee of warlike accoutrements, to accomodate, which comes of Accomodo. Shakefpeare the firft, and the firft

Tho: No Sir it comes of fo much money difburf'd

* * * * *

Vn: . . . . . . let me fee now, the bookes of Martiall difcipline. [*leaf* 18]

[*lf.* 18, *bk.*] Tho: I bought vp all, that I found haue relation to warr, and fighting . . .

Vn: . . . Item. the fword falue, . . . the Buckler of faith . . . A booke of mortification . . . Item the gunpowder treafon, and the Booke of Cannons . . . . Shakefpeares workes—why Shakefpeares workes?

Tho: I had nothing for the pikemen before,

Vn: they are playes,

ANONYMOUS, AB. 1645 (?).

Tho: Arc not all your mufterings in the Countrey, fo, fir? pray read on.

> Harleian MS. 7650 (in MS. at the end of the printed Catalog, vol. iii), formerly Sloane or Additional MS. 5,001: A Comedy without name or date, but probably soon after 1640, as it says, on leaf 2 back, "considering the league at Barwick[1], and the late expeditions wee may find some of these things [books on Tacticks] in the North, or else speake with some reform'd Captaine, though he be a Catholicke, and it may bee wee may haue them at cheaper rates."

The "accomodate, *accomodo*," is Shallow's comment on Bardolph's "a Souldier is better accommodated, then with a wife:" 2 *Henry IV*, III. i. 72: "Better accommodated, it is good, yea indeede is it : good phrases are surely, and euery where commendable. 'Accommodated', it comes of *Accommodo*: very good, a good Phrase."

The only treaty—called the Pacification—of Berwick known to me is dated June 18, 1639. When the Scotch, aided by the French, were in insurrection and had taken the Covenant, Charles advanced to the North with 23,000 men. The camp came to Berwick, and Charles himself negotiated a peace, and soon after disbanded his army.

The Scotch Parliament advanced, a few months later, other claims, and Charles had to renew the war, and in May 1640 an English army went North again to resist the Scotch advance into England.

The mention in the play of Tarleton, 'No Jokes since Tarleton died,' or something of the sort, would not be likely after 1660. —SIDNEY L. LEE.

---

[1] Supposed to refer to the Pacification of Berwick : Charles I's agreement with the Scotch in arms against him.

ROBERT WILD, 1646 (?).

Shakefpear.
Invent[*ion*]. His Quill as quick as Feather from the Bow!
O who can such another *Falftaff* fhow?
And if thy learning had been like thy Wit,
Ben would have blufht, and *Johnfon* never writ.
Fur[*or Poeticus*]. Pifh.—I never read any of him but in Tobacco papers and the bottom of Pigeon-Pies.—But he had been a Curate to the Stage fo long, that he could not choofe but get fome ends and bottoms;—I, and they were his Fees too;—
But for the fine and true Dramatick Law,
He was a Dunce and fcribled with a Straw.

The Benefice. A Comedy. By R[*obert*] *W*[*ild*] *D.D. Author of* Iter Boreale. *Written in his Younger Days: Now made Publick for Promoting Innocent Mirth . . . . London. MDCLXXXIX. p.* 10.

Internal political allusions prove this play to have been written about 1646. It is obviously imitated from the anonymous 'Returne from Pernassus' first published in 1606. Besides the Shakfperean criticism, are passages dealing with Ben Jonson, Beaumont and Fletcher, and 'Tom Randolph's Poems.' For an account of the author see *Poems by Robert Wilde, D.D.*, one of the ejected ministers of 1662, with a historical and biographical preface and notes by the Rev. John Hunt. London, 1870.—
S. L. LEE.

* SAM. SHEPPARD, 1647.

Suck[-dry]. We are in an excellent humour—lets have the tother quart.

Com[mon-curſe]. Rare rogue in Buckram—thou ſhalt goe out a wit, and vie with *Martin Parker*,[1] or *John Tailor*.[2]

> *The | Committee-|Man Curried. A Comedy presented to the view of all Men.* Written by *S. Sheppard*, ... *Printed* Anno Dom. 1647. 4to. Act. 3, p. 7.
>
> F. J. F.

Having regard to the great popularity of *Hen. IV*, this may be an allusion to Falstaff's 'rogues in buckram': though a buckram lord, rogue, man, &c. was a common phrase. C. M. I.

---

[1] The Ballad-Writer.   [2] The Water-Poet.

J. S., 1648.

With reference to Mr. Bullen's letter printed on the next page, and issued in my *Stubbes*, Part I, 1879, a note of mine appeard in the *Athenæum* of April 3, 1880, saying that I had chanst to take up *Wits labyrinth* " in the British Museum, and opening it at p. 19, my eye caught at once a line of Petruchio's remonstrance with Kate before she touches his meat :—

> The poorest service is repaid with thanks.
> *Taming of the Shrew*, IV. iii. 45.

As this line is not in the 'Taming of *a* Shrew,' 1594, it negatives Mr. Bullen's supposition that J. S., the compiler of 'Wit's Labyrinth,' had access only to Shakspere's historical plays and 'Titus.' That J. S. was Shirley the dramatist I don't for a moment believe. There are other J. S. initial books in 1639, 1643, 1660, 1664, &c."—F. J. F.

1648. J. S.

"'Wit's labyrinth. Or a briefe and compendious Abstract of most witty, ingenious, wise and learned Sentences and Phrases. Together with some hundreds of most pithy, facetious and patheticall, complementall expressions. Collected, compiled, and set forth for the benefit, pleasure, or delight of all, but principally the English Nobility and Gentry. *Aut prodesse aut delectare potest.* By J. S. Gent. London, printed for M. Simmons, 1648,' 4to, 53 pages.

"The quotations which [this volume] contains are strung together apparently without any order or arrangement, and without any indication of the sources from which they are derived. No name, in fact, of any author whatever is mentioned. The following, however, I have identified as being from Shakspeare, and, with the aid of Mrs. Cowden Clarke's valuable Concordance, I have appended to them the exact positions which they occupy in the Shakspearean dramas:—

'Suspicion always haunts the guilty mind.'—3 *Henry VI.*, Act v. sc. 3.
'Discretion is the better part of valour.'—1 *Henry IV.*, Act v. sc. 4.
'Uneasie lyes the head, that wears a Crowne.'—2 *Henry IV.*, Act iii. sc. 1.
Thieves are 'Diana's Foresters or Gentlemen of the Shade.'—1 *Henry IV.*, Act i. sc. 2.
'No beast so fierce but knows some touch of pity.'—*Richard III.*, Act i. sc. 2.
'That wrens may prey where eagles dare not perch.'—*Richard III.*, Act i. sc. 3.
'O Tiger's heart wrapped in a woman's hide.'—3 *Henry VI.*, Act i. sc. 4.
'Better than he have yet worn Vulcan's badge.'—*Titus Andronicus*, Act ii. sc. 1.
'Even such kin as the parish heifers are to the town-bull.'—2 *Henry IV.*, Act ii. sc. 2.
'The Fox barks not when he would steal the lamb.'—2 *Henry VI.*, Act iii. sc. 1.
'Did ever Raven sing so like a Lark?'—*Titus Andronicus*, Act iii. sc. 1.
'The Raven doth not hatch a Lark.'—*Titus Andronicus*, Act ii. sc. 3.
'Thanks, the exchequer of the Poor.'—*Richard II.*, Act ii. sc. 3.

"I have thus verified thirteen distinct quotations from Shakspeare in this little work, and I believe that there are still more. Of those which I have traced, it is singular that all except three are from the English historical plays, and that the three exceptions are from 'Titus Andronicus.' This would almost show that the compiler, whoever he was, had access only to those particular dramas, and not to any complete edition of Shakspeare's plays, either the 1623 edition or the 1632 edition. Otherwise we might have expected passages from the greater dramas, 'Hamlet,' 'Macbeth,' 'Lear,' 'Romeo and Juliet,' 'Othello,' 'The Tempest,' &c.

"And now the question arises, Who was the compiler? Who was 'J. S. Gent.'? The first name one thinks of is that of James Shirley, a dramatist himself, and the last of the glorious band in whom there survived somewhat of the genius of Shakspeare,—Marlowe, Webster, and Beaumont and Fletcher.

"Shirley, besides being a dramatist, was a clergyman of the Church of England who turned Catholic. He was also a schoolmaster, and the Latin quotation of the title-page, together with another Latin quotation in the preface, might lead one to suppose that the compilation was his. But the style and manner of the preface are altogether unworthy of him. Here is a passage from it:—

"'And lastly although this Poem [work?] is but a collection of divers sentences, phrases, &c., as appeareth in the Title (not methodically composed or digested), it being unpossible in a subject of this nature so to doe, but promiscuously intermixt with variety and delight, which many yeares since, in times of my better prosperity, I gathered out of some hundreds of Authors, never having the least thought of putting it to Presse: yet now,' &c. Then he goes on, in the style usual then as at present, to say that he was prevailed on by the importunities of friends 'to put it into print,' &c.

"Perhaps some one else may be more fortunate in discovering the name of the compiler."

[*Athenæum*, Sept. 6, 1879.]   G. BULLEN.

HENRY TUBBE, 1648-54.

Th' Example of his Converſation
With ſuch an high, illuſtrious vigour ſhone,
The blackeſt Fangs of baſe Detraction
Had nothing to traduce or faſten on.
His very Lookes did fairely edifie;
Not maſk'd with forms of falſe Hypocriſie:
A gracefull Aſpect, a Brow ſmooth'd wth Love,
The Curls of Venus, with the Front of Jove;

An Eye like Mars, to threaten & command
More than the Burniſh'd Scepter in his Hand:

A Standing like the Herald Mercurie;
A Geſture humbly proud, & lowly high;
A Mountaine rooted deepe, that kiſſ'd the Skie,
A Combination and Formalitie
Of reall Features twiſted in a String
Of rich Ingredients, fit to make a King.

Harleian MS. 4126, *leaf* 50 (*or* 51 *by the 2nd numbering*), *back. Epiſtles, Poems, Characters, &c.,* 1648-1654, *by Hy. Tubbe of St. John's College, Cambridge: from Eleg. VI on* "*The Roiall Martyr,*" *Charles I.*

[The Passage was firſt pointed out by Mr. Halliwell, and was ſent by me to the firſt number of the new monthly, the *Antiquary*. It is ſomewhat odd, that though Tubbe uſes Shakſpere's lines on Hamlet's Father—

See what a grace was ſeated on his Brow,
Hyperions curles, the front of Ioue himſelfe,
An eye like Mars, to threaten or command
A Station, like the Herald Mercurie

> New lighted on a heauen-kissing hill:
> A Combination and a forme indeed,
> Where euery God did seeme to set his Seale,
> To giue the world assurance of a man.
>   *1st Folio, Trag.*, p. 271, col. 1,

yet he doesn't name Shakspere as one of the Learned Ghosts who are to greet him and his friend in Elysium, lf. 37 (or 39), back : "the great Shadow of Renowned BEN," and "Ingenious Randolph"[1] are the only two specified for that honour.—F. J. F.]

---

[1] Epistles I. f. 37, 39.

> Our Spirits shall intermix, & weaue their knots;
> Free from the trouble of these earthly Grotts;
> Thence winged flie to the Elysian groves,   [*back*]
> Where, whilst wee still renew our constant Loves,
> A Thousand Troops of Learned Ghosts shall meet
> Us, and our Comming thither gladly greet.
>   First the Great Shadow of Renowned BEN
> Shall giue us hearty, joyfull Wellcome : then
> Ingenious Randolph from his lovely Arms
> Shall entertaine us with such mighty charms
> Of Strict Embraces, that wee cannot wish
> For any comforts greater than this Blisse.

ANON. 1649.

*Here to evince that scandal has been thrown
Upon a name of honour; charactred
From a wrong perfon, coward and buffoon;
Call in your eafy faiths, from what you've read
To laugh at* Falſtaffe; *as a humour fram'd
To grace the ſtage, to pleaſe the age, mifnam'd.*

*No longer pleaſe yourſelves to injure names
Who lived to honour: if, as who dare breathe
A fyllable from Harry's choice, the Fames,
Conferr'd by Princes, may redeem from death?
Live* Faſtolffe *then; whoſe* Truſt *and* Courage *once
Merited the firſt Government in France.*
Stanza 136. 139

Τριναρχωδια: <i>The several Reigns of Richard II, Henry
IV, and Henry V, MS.</i> 8vo., 1649, <i>in Hen. V.</i></p>

*howe'er the heaps
May crowd, in hungry expectation all,
To the ſweet* Nugilogues *of* Jack *and* Hal.
ib. Stanza 138.

*Then, from his bounty, blot out what may rife,
Of comic mirth, to Falſtoff's prejudice.*
Stanza 140.

The first two stanzas above are from William Oldys's Life of Sir John
Fastolf in "A General / Dictionary, / Historical and Critical : / in which /
A New and Accurate Translation / of that of the Celebrated / Mr. Boyle, /

with the Corrections and Observations printed / in the late Edition at *Paris*, is included, and interspersed / with several thousand Lives never before published. / . . . London, M D CC XXXVII. vol. 5, p. 195, note. Oldys says that as Shakspere's trespass was poetical, we shall end with a poetical animadversion taken from an original *Historical Poem* on *Three* of our *Kings*; in the possession of the writer of this article. Herein the Poet has five stanzas of reproof for this liberty taken on the Stage in derogation of our Knight; but, for brevity, shall at present repeat only these two," those above.

In his article on Fastolff[1] in the *Biographia Britannica*, 1793, Oldys quotes the few more lines, given above, from two more of the 5 stanzas he names in his first article. Yowell, in his account of Oldys in 3 *N. & Q.* i. 85 (Feb. 1, 1862), has a note by Bolton Corney, saying that the MS. of the *Trinarchodia* passt into the hands of "J. P. Andrews: Park describes it, *Restituta*, iv. 166."

The first 2 stanzas above were quoted by Mr. Halliwell in his *Character of Falstaff*, 1841, p. 44, as from "An anonymous and inedited poet of the early part of the seventeenth century, whose MS. works were formerly in the possession of Oldys," with no other reference. This designedly vague way of referring to other men's quotations—when he refers to em at all—is Mr. Halliwell's normal one, and cannot be too strongly condemnd. It is unfair to the original quoter, and unfair to the reader, on whom is thrown the nuisance of a long search when he wants to find the original quotation, and remove Mr. H.'s later needless alterations of italics, &c. in it.—F. J. F.

---

[1] Said in the B. Mus. Cat. to be revised and enlarged by Nicols.

1651.

This champion from behind the arras cries out, ...
    Milton's *Smectymnuus*. Bohn's Edⁿ. of Pr. Works, p. 140.

An allusion to Polonius in *Hamlet*. Sent by H. E. S.

RICHARD WHITLOCK, 1652.

The Index

Mans ſpeculation a comedy of errours, and imployments much ado about nothing, 319

> ZΩOTOMI'A, / Or / Observations / On The / Present Manners / Of The / English : / *Briefly Anatomizing the Living / by the Dead.* / With / an Usefull Detection / Of The / Mountebanks of both Sexes. / By *Richard Whitlock*, M.D. Late Fellow of / *All-Souls* Colledge in *Oxford.* / *London,* / Printed by *Tho. Roycroft,* and are to be sold by / *Humphrey Moseley,* at the Princes Armes in / St. *Pauls* Church-yard, 1654. / (The 4 of 1654 is crost thru, and the day of buying, Jan. 24, 1653 [-4], written in.)

There is no allusion to Shakspere's plays abuv-named, at p. 319, and the book is so full of classical references, tho' alluding to Lord Bacon, Ben Jonson, Rabelais, &c., that I doubt Shakspere allusions occurring elsewhere than in its Index. Dr. Ingleby named the book to me as having an Allusion.

—F. J. F.

FRANCIS KIRKMAN, 1652.

TO
His much honored Friend
WIL. BEESTON Esq;.

Worthy Sir,

*D*Ivers times (in my hearing) to the admiration of the whol Company, you have most judiciously discoursed of Poësie: which is the cause I presume to chuse you for my Patron and Protector; who are the happiest interpretor and judg of our English Stage-Playes this Nation ever produced; which the Poets and Actors of these times, cannot (without ingratitude) deny; for I have heard the chief, and most ingenious of them, acknowledg their Fames & Profits essentially sprung from your instructions, judgment and fancy. I am vers'd in Forraign tongues and subscribe to your opinion, that no Nation ever could glory in such Playes, as the most learned and incomparable Johnson, the copious Shakespear,* or the ingenuous Fletcher compos'd; but I beleeve the French for amorous language, admirable invention, high atchievments, honorable Loves inimitable constancy, are not to be equalled: and that no Nation yeilds better Arguments for Romance Playes (the only Poëms now desired) then the French: Therefore, and for you have I translated the Adventures and Loves of Clerio and Lozia; and I doubt not though they fail to receive incouragement from you, your son Mr George Beeston (whom knowing men conclude a hopeful inheritor of his Fathers rare ingenuity) may receive them with a gracious allowance.

> The Epistle Dedicatory to *The | Loves | and | Adventures | of |* Clerio & Lozia./ A / Romance./ *Written Originally in French, and | Translated into English | By* Fra. Kirkman, *Gent.* London [Aug. 3] *Printed by* J. M. *and are to be sold by |* William Ley, *at his shop at* Pauls / Chain. 1652./ Sign. A 2, A 3. —F. J. F.

The Epistle Dedicatory is signd 'Fra. Kirkman, jun.'

* Catchword. Sheak-

RO. LOVEDAY, 1652.

Vpon BELLEY'S IPHIGENES, better'd into *English* by the Ingenious Pen of His Dear Brother, Major *WRIGHT*.

I Need not injure Truth *to Blazon thee*
  (*Wer't in my pow'r*) *with* Wit's falſe Heraldrie:
For, but to give thee all thy due, would ſwell
Too high, and turne the Reader Infidell.
I'le onely tell him, hee'll finde nothing here,
But what is Manly, Modeſt, Rich and Cleare.
No Dropſi'd Monſter-words, *all ſweet, and cleane*
Aſ the ſmooth Cheeke of baſhfull Iphigene;
Who, as thy Pen has made her woo'd and wooe,
Might paſſè for Venus *and* Adonis *too.*

J. O. IIII.-P.

NATHANIEL HOOKE, 1653.

The Heavens court thee, Princely *Oberon*
And *Mab* his Emp'retle both expect thee yon,
They wait to fee thee, fport the time away,
And on green beds of dazies dance the hay;
In their fmall acorn pofnets, as they meet
Quaffe off the dew, left it fhould wet thy feet."
Hooke's *Amanda*, 1653, p. 47.

Possibly an allusion to Shakspere's Fairy King and Queen.—R. ROBERTS.

" If *Owen Tudor* prais'd his Madams hue
'Caufe in her cheeks the *rofe* and *lilie* grew,
Thou'rt more praife-worthy then was *Katherine*,
There's frefher *York* and *Lancafter* in thine:
    Had thy fweet features with thy beauty met
In *William de*-la-pool's faire *Margaret*,
The *Peers* furpriz'd had never giv'n confent,
For th' *Duke of Suffolks* five years banifhment,
For the Exchange of *Manns*, *Anjou*, and *Main*,
T' haue giv'n a kingdom for thee had been gain : "
Hooke's *Amanda*, 1653, p. 71.

Possibly an allusion to the Shaksperean Henry VI. Plays.—R. R.

1653. RICHARD FLECKNOE, 1656.

1653.

THE HISTORY OF CARDENIO. A Play, by Mr. Fletcher and Shakspeare. Entered on the book of the Stationers' Company, Sept. 9, 1653; but we believe never printed. It has been suggested that this play may possibly be the same as *The Double Falsehood*; afterwards brought to light by Mr. Theobald. 1812. Baker's *Biogr. Dram.*, ii. 306, col. 1.

RICHARD FLECKNOE, 1656.

On the Play of the life and death of Pyrocles, / *Prince of* Tyre.

A *Rs longa, vita brevis*, as they fay,
But who inverts that faying, made this Play.

The / *Diarium*, / or / *Journall* :[1] / 1656 [*p.* 96]. Halliwell's *Folio Shakespeare*, xvi. 70. See too *Centurie*, p. 173.

[1] Divided into 12. *Jornadas* / in / Burlesque Rhime, / or / Drolling Verse, / With divers other pieces of the / same Author./ . . . *London*, / Printed for *Henry Herringman* at the sign of / the Anchor in the lower walk of the New-/ Exchange, 1656 [March 28]. "I . . take thee aside from the Title-page, & tell thee my name is *Richard Fleckno*." Sign. A 4.—F. J. F.

1660.

DAVENPORT, ROBERT . . was also the author of the following :
9. *Henry I.* and *Henry II.*
It does not appear whether these are one or two plays. In the book of the Stationers' Company, they are said to be written by Shakspeare and Davenant.
1812. Baker's *Biogr. Dram.*, vol. I. Pt. 1, p. 176-7.

EDMUND GAYTON, 1654.

Unà Eurufque Notufque ruunt, Creberque procellis,
Affricus, & vaftos volvunt ad littora Fluctus,
Qua data porta ruunt, & terras turbine perflant.

Which in plaine Englifh read you thus,

Suppofing *Sancho Æolus:*
And with both hands his belly preffing,
Blow winds faith he, upon my bleffing;
VVhen that the Port-hole opes, or his back door,
Out goe the Winds, Eaft Eaft, Nore and by Nore.
Thefe fly about, and like the Bawdy wind,
(Sweet breath'd or no) kiffe all they meet or find;
There is no guard againft 'um, though you compaffe
Your Nofe, they have priviledge (as the Trump *has)*
To goe about:

<blockquote>Pleasant / Notes / upon / Don Quixot./ By Edmund Gayton, Esq;/ [motto from Juvenal.] London, / Printed by William Hunt. MDCLIV. p. 106.</blockquote>

The quotation is from *Othello,* IV. ii. 78:

"What committed?
Heauen stoppes the Nose at it, and the Moone winks:
The baudy winde that kisses all it meetes,
Is hush'd within the hollow Myne of Earth,
And will not hear 't. What committed?"

Part sent-in by Mr. Hll.-P.
For several other Allusions in Gayton, see *Centurie,* p. 299.—F. J. F.

ALEXR. BROME, 1654.

Val[*entia*]. What are you fir? whence are you? what's your name?

Pro[*fpero*]. I am your friend, fhould you defire to know
What my name is, alas my name's your foe.

Val. Being my friend, and court me in this kind,
You fhould have come and left your name behind.

Pro. I fhould indeed, my name is *Profpero*.

Val. Prince *Profpero*, and the Duke *Verona's* Son,
Our profeft Foe?

Pro. Give me fome other name,
Call me your friend and I am not the fame.

Val. Y' are not the fame, you are th' adven'trous Knight
That from the forreft-treafon fav'd my Father.

Pro. I was Prince *Profpero* when I refcu'd him,
And fo continued till I faw your face;
But as my heart within your eye was toft,
At once my hatred and my name I loft.

> The | Cunning | Lovers.| A | Comedy.| As it was Acted with great Applause, | by their Majesties Servants | at the private House | in Drury Lane.| VVritten by | Alexander Bromes, Gent.| London, Printed for Will. Sheares, at the Bible in S. Pauls | Churchyard, neare the little North doore, 1654.| Act II. Scene I. p. 24.

[*ib*. Act IV. Scene I. p. 44-5]. *Clo*[*wne*]. I have a fute to your Grace.

Man[*tua*]. Thy bufinefs Groome?

Clo. That for the good news I have brought you I may have fome guerdon, fome remuneration, as they fay.

Man. This thy reward be, since by thy occasion
My Dutchefs of her beſt wits is depriv'd,
Wander for ever like a baniſh'd *Caine*,
Till of her fence ſhe be poſſeſt againe
Dare not ſo neare our Court . . . . . .

   Clo. Baniſh, what's that? can any man tell me what it means? let me fee; Baniſh'd . . . the meaning of it may be, give him a hundred Crowns . . . Baniſh'd? I will go feek out fome wife man or other to tell me what the word meanes, and what fum of money I may demand of the Duke's Treafurer; Baniſh'd——

                                    Enter Montecelfo.

. . . my friend, what are you?

   Mon. Sir I profeſſe my felfe to be a wife man.

   Clo. Then you are the man that I defire to meet, for I was feeking a wife man to tell me the meaning of a ſtrange word . . . . . . it was my fate to bring the news to the Court . . . now demanding reward for my news, the Duke out of his bounty faid, he would baniſh me the Court; now I would faine know what fum of money the word baniſh'd fignifies.

"The conversation between Valentia and Prospero recalls that between *Romeo and Juliet*, Act II. sc. ii. ll. 33—61. The scene with the Clown and Mantua as to 'guerdon' and 'banish' seems founded on Costard's 'remuneration' in *Love's Labours Lost*, Act III."—*Centurie*, p. 429.
                                                        —F. J. F.

J. QUARLES, 1655.

"The Rape of

LUCRECE,

Committed by

TARQUIN the Sixt;

AND

The remarkable judgments that befel him for it.

BY

The incomparable Master of our *English Poetry,*

WILL: SHAKESPEARE Gent.

Whereunto is annexed,

The Banishment of TARQUIN:

Or, *the Reward of Lust.*

By J. QUARLES.

[woodcut, wreath round I·S W G]

LONDON.
Printed by *J. G.* for *John Stafford* in George-yard
neer Fleet-bridge, and *Will: Gilbertſon* at
the Bible in Giltspur-ſtreet, 1655."

[In the Brit. Mus. Case Copy of this book, there is a Portrait of Shakſpere on the frontispiece.—F. J. F.]

SAMUEL HOLLAND [1], 1656.

They had no fooner finifhed their Ditty, but behold, Madam *Gylo* (apparelled in a loofe veftment, her haire bound up in a carnation Cawl, which excellently became her) appeared (like another *Juliet* ready to receive her beloved *Romeo*) on the Battlements.

> Don Zara Del Fogo : / A / *Mock-Romance./* Written Originally in the *Brittish* / Tongue, and made *English* by a / person of much Honor, / *Basilios Mvsophilvs./* With a Marginall Comment / Expounding the hard things of / the History/. *Si foret in terris rideret Democritus.* / *London,* Printed by *T. W.* for *Tho. Vere,* / at the sign of the Angel without / Newgate. 1656. p. 58.

A skit on Don Quixote by Samuel Holland. (Noted by Mr. IIII.-P.)

F. J. F.

---

[1] See *Centurie,* p. 302.

T. GOFF, 1656.

In T. Goff's *Careless Shepherdess*, a Tragi-Comedy,[1] 1656, there is " An exact and perfect Catologue of all *Playes* that are Printed." It gives to Shakspere, by name, only—

As you like it.
Comedy of errors.
Coriolanus.
Cinebiline [so]
Edward 2.
Edward 3.[2]
Edward 4.
Henry the 4. both parts.
Henry 5.
Henry 6 three parts.

Hen[r]y 8.
Julius Cæfar.
London Prodigall.
Leyre and his three daughters.
Meafure for Meafure.
Mackbeth.
Moor of Venice.
Richard the 3.
Taming of a Shrew.
Tempest.

But it mentions also, without any author's name,

Alls well that ends well.
Antonio and Cleopatra.
Gentleman of verona.[3]
Hamlet Prince of Denmark.
Loves labor loft.
Marchant of Venice.
Midfommer nights dream.
Much adoe about nothing.
Pericles Prin[c]e of Tire.

Richard the 2.
Rome[o] and Juliet.
Titus and Andronicus.
Troiles and Crefida.
Two Gentlemen of Verona.[3]
Two Noble Kinfmen.
Twelfth night.
Timon of Athens.
Winters Tale.

[1] The / Careles Shepherdess. / A Tragic Comedy. / * * * / Written by T. G. M[r] of Arts / * * * With an Alphebeticall Catologue of all such Plays / that ever were Printed./ London printed for *Richard Rogers* and *William* Leg, / and are to be sould at *Pauls* Chaine / nere Doctors commons, / 1656./ 8vo.

[2] So here's an assignment of this 'Pseudo-Shakspere' play to our great dramatist, nearly a hundred years before Capel in 1760. But it is of little or no worth, as *Edward II.* is Marlowe's, and *Edward IV.* Heywood's.

[3] Are these not the same?

? EDWARD ARCHER, 1656.

An Exact and perfect CATALOGUE of all the PLAIES that were ever printed; together, with all the Authors names; and what are Comedies, Histories, Interludes, Maſks, Paſtorels, Tragedies: And all theſe Plaies you may either have at the Signe of the *Adam and Eve*, in Little Britain; or, at the *Ben Jhnſon's* Head in Thredneedle-ſtreet, over againſt the Exchange.

Arraignment of Paris	T	*Will. Shakſpeare*.....
As you like it	C	*Will. Shakeſpeare*.....
All's well that ends well	I	*Will. Shakeſpeare* ....
Antonio and Cleopatra	T	*Will. Shakeſpeare*.....
Comedy of errors	C	*William Shakeſpear* ...
Cymbelona	T	[no name]
Coriolanus	T	*William Shakeſpear* ...
Chances [Beaumont & Fletcher. Fol. 1647.]	C	*Will Shakeſpear* .....
Cromwells hiſtorie	H	*William Shakeſpere* ...
Gentleman of Verona	C	*William Shakeſpeare* ...
Hoffman [Hy. Chettle]	T	*William Shakeſpeare* ...
Hamblet prince of den	T	
Henry Fourth, both parts	H	
—— Fifth	H	} *Will. Shakeſpeare* ...
—— Sixth 3 parts	H	
—— Eight	H	
Hieronimo, both paits [Kyd's]	H	*Will. Shakeſpeare* ....
Julius Cæsar	T	*Will. Shakeſpeare* ....

? EDWARD ARCHER, 1656.

John, K. of England, both parts [1]		*Will. Shakefpeare.* ...
London prodigall	C	*Will. Shakefpear* .....
Loves labor loft [2]	C	*Will. Shakefpeare* .....
Merry divell of Edmond [? T. Brewer]	C	*William Shakefpeare* ...
Mucidorus	C	*Will. Shakefpeare* ....
Merchant of Venice	C	*William Shakefpeare* ...
Merry wives of windfor	C	*William Shakefpear* ...
Midfommer nights dream	C	*William Shakefpear* ...
Much a doe about nothing	C	*Will. Shakefpear* .....
Meafure for Meafure	C	*Will. Shakefpear* .....
Magbeth	T	*Will. Shakefpeer* .....
Othello	T	*Will. Shakefpeare* ....
Puritan Widow	C	*Will. Shakefpeare* ....
Pyrocles prince of Tyre	C	*Will. Shakefpeare* ....
Roman actor [Massinger]		*William Shakefpere* ....
Romeo and Juliet	T	*William Shakefpear* ...
Richard 2d.	T	*Will. Shakefpeare* ....
——— Third	T	*Will. Shakefpeare* ....
Troilus and Creffida	T	[no name]
Twelfth-night	C	*William Shakefpere* ....
Tempeft	C	*Will. Shakefpeare* ....
Timon of Athens	I	[no name]
Two noble kinfmen	C	*Will Shakefpear* .....
Titus Andronicus	T	*Will. Shakefpeare* .....
Taming of a fhrew [3]	C	*Will. Shakefpeare* .....

---

[1] The old *Troublesome Raigne* which Shakespeare re-wrote for his *King John*.

[2] Another "Loves labor lost | C | " is put to *Will. Sampson*.

[3] The foundation-play on which Shakspere and the man he helpt, workt.

? EDWARD ARCHER, 1656.

Trick to catch the old one [Middleton]	C	Will. Shakeſpeare ....
Winters Tale	C	Wil. Shakeſpear .....
Yorkſhire Tragedie	T	Will. Shakeſpeare ....

The / Excellent Comedy, called / The Old Law: / or / A new way to please you. By Phil. Massinger. / Tho. Middleton. / William Rowley./ Acted before the King and Queene at Salisbury House, / and at severall other places, with great Applause./ Together with an exact and perfect Catalogue of all / the Playes, with the Authors Names, and what are / Comedies, Tragedies, Histories, Pastoralls, / Masks, Interludes, more exactly Printed / than ever before. / London, / Printed for Edward Archer, at the signe of the Adam and Eve, in Little Britaine. 1656./ [The last '6' of 1656 has been crosst thro with a pen; '5' put in its place, and 'August 6' written above.]

Neither Shakspere's *King Lear* nor the older *Leir* is in this Catalogue. Among the other entries are,

Arden of Feverſham	I	Rich. Bernard ......
Edward Third	T	
* 2 Noble Kinſman [an earlier entry]	C	

The dots after Shakspere's name mark that a line or more is left out between it and the next quotation.

—F. J. F.

In the list of 'Poems and Plays, Printed for Tho. Bennet,' at the end of Charles Burnaby's *Reform'd Wife*, 1700, are Cowley's Works, Waller's Poems, Suckling's Works, Hon. Rob. Howard's Five new Plays, T. Killigrew's Comedies and Tragedies ; then 9 'Plays by Mr. Dryden,' and then, plays "By Others"—authors evidently not worth mentioning [1]— "Æsop a Comedy ... *Hamlet* Prince of *Denmark*, *Mackbeth*. ... *Tempest*, or the *Inchanted Island*."—F. J. F.

[1] The other unnamed authors are Vanbrugh, Etherege, Shadwell, Aphra Behn, Brady and Porter.—P. A. L.

SIR WM. DUGDALE, 1656.

Befides all this, here is 𝕾tratforð, a fair Bridg of ftone, over 𝕬bon, containing xiiii· arches, with a long Caufey at the weft end of it, walled on both fides: which Bridg and Caufey were fo built[h] in *H.* 7. time *Lel.* }h
by the before fpecified *Hugh Clopton*, whereas before *Itin. f.*
there was[i] only a timber Bridg and no Caufey, fo 167. }i
that the paffage became very perillous upon the overflowing of that River. One thing more, in reference to this antient Town is obfervable, that it gave birth and fepulture to our late famous Poet *Will. Shakefpere*, whofe Monument I have inferted in my difcourfe of the Church.

> Antiquities / of / Warwickshire / Illustrated ; / From Records, Leiger-Books, Ma- / nuscripts, Charters, Evidences, / Tombes, and Armes : / Beautified / With Maps, Prospects and Portraitures / By *William Dvgdale.* / [Latin Motto.] London, / Printed by Thomas Warren, in the year of our Lord / God, M.DC.LVI, p. 523, col. 2.
>
> J. O. IIII.-P. (revized).

ANON. 1656.

To the Memory of
BEN : JOHNSON.

[Begins p. 129.] As when the veſtall hearth went out, no fire
  Leſſe holy than the flame that did expire
[Ibid.]
  Though the Prieſt had tranſlated for that time
  The Liturgy, and buried thee in rime;
  So that in meeter we had heard it ſaid
  Poetique duſt is to Poetique laid :
  And though that duſt being *Shakeſpeares* thou mighſt have
  Not his room but the Poet for thy grave;
  So that as thou didſt Prince of numbers dye
  And live ſo now thou mighſt in number lye;
  Twere fraile ſolemnity.
[Ends p. 133]
  Who without Latine helps, hadſt been as rare
  As *Beaumont, Fletcher*, or as *Shakeſpeare* were :
  And like them from thy native ſtock couldſt ſay
  Poets and Kings are not born every day.

> *Parnassus Biceps,* | or | *Severall Choice Pieces* | of | *Poetry,* | *Composed by the best Wits* | *that were in both the* | *Universities* | *before their* | *Dissolution.* | With an *Epistle* in the behalfe of | those now doubly secluded and sequestred | *Members,* by One *who himselfe is none.* | London : | *Printed for* George Eversden *at the Signe* | *of the* Maidenheade *in St.* Pauls | *Churcyard.* 1656. |

The Epistle to the Ingenious Reader is signed Ab: Wright.
                                    —PONSONBY A. LYONS.

ANON. 1658.

"*To his ingenious Friend, the Author,
on his incomparable Poems.
Carmen Jocoferium.*"
    SW. W.C.C. *Oxon.*

" To thee compar'd, our Englifh Poets all ftop,
And vail their Bonnets, even *Shakefpear's* [1] *Falftop*. [" It should have been *Falstaff*, if the rhyme had permitted it."]
Chaucer the firft of all wafn't worth a farthing,
Lidgate, and Huntingdon, with Gaffer *Harding*.[2]
Non-fenfe the *Faëry Queen*, and *Michael Drayton*,
Like Babel's Balm; or Rhymes of *Edward Paiton*,[3]
Waller, and *Turlingham*, and brave *George Sandys*,
Beaumont, and *Fletcher*, *Donne*, *Jeremy Candish*,
Herbert, and *Cleeveland*, and all the train noble
Are *Saints-bells* unto *thee*, and *thou* great *Bow-bell*."

    Naps upon Parnassus, 1658, B. v.

"*Naps upon Parnassus*" is a small book of 43 leaves. It consists mainly of " Preliminary " leaves; which are joking poems upon Austin the imputed author, in the style of the Commendatory Poems in Tom Coryat; only they are not so good. I say "imputed" author, for it is most probable that the whole thing is a joke. As to Turlingham and Jeremy Candish,—most likely they were fellow-students of Austin, and it was part of the joke to class them with Donne, Herbert, &c. They were probably something like Dr. Grosart's friend, "*Mr* Thomson, of Edinburgh," whose opinion he so gravely quotes on disputed literary matters.—R. ROBERTS.

---

[2] The Chronicler.
[3] ? Sir E. Peyton, author of 'The divine Catastrophe of the Kingly Family of the House of Stuarts.' 1652. See *Ath. Oxon.* 1692, ii. 87.

ANON. 1658.

The rest of the title is "A Sleepy Muse nipt and pincht, though not awakened. Such Voluntary and Jovial Copies of Verses, as were lately receiv'd from some of the *Wits* of the Universities, in a Frolick, dedicated to *Gondibert's* Mistress by Captain Jones and others. Whereunto is added for Demonstration of the Author's prosaick Excellency's, his Epistle to one of the Universities, with the Answer, together with two Satyrical Characters of his *Own*, of a *Temporizer*, and an *Antiquary*, with Marginal Notes by a Friend to the Reader. Vide *Jones* his *Legend*, Drink Sack and Gunpowder, and so fall to 't. [A Greek Quotation.] London, Printed by express Order from the *Wits*, for N. Brook, at the Angel in *Cornhill*, 1658, 8vo." (Hazlitt's *Handbook*, p. 17.)

Antony Wood, *Ath. Oxon.* (folio, 1692, ii. 232), gives the following account of the book :—

"SAMUEL AUSTIN a *Cornish* man born, was entred a Commoner of *Wadham* Coll. under the tuition of *Gilb. Stokes* Chapl. of that house in 1652, aged 16 years, took one degree in Arts, compleated it by *Determination*, and then went to *Cambridge* for a time. But such was the vanity of this Person, that he being extremely conceited of his own worth, and overvaluing his poetical fancy, more than that of *Cleveland*, who was then accounted by the Bravadoes the *Hectoring Prince of Poets*, fell into the hands of the Satyrical wits of this University, who having easily got some of his prose and poetry, served him as the wits did *Tom. Coryat* in his time, and published them under these titles.

"*Naps upon Pernassus.* A sleepy muse nipt and pincht, though not awakened, &c. *Lond.* 1658. oct.

"*Characters*—Printed with the former. Both which were usher'd into the world by more than twenty Copies of verses (advantaging the sale of the book) by such that had the name of, or at least pretended to be, Poets. Among them were *Tho. Flatman*, *Tho. Sprat*, and *Sam. Woodford*, since noted and famed for their Poeticall works, *Silvanus Taylour* and *George Castle* of Alls[ouls] Coll. the former better at Musick, the other at lying and buffooning, than Poetry. And among others, not now to be named, must not be forgotten, *Alexander Amidei* a Jew and Florentine born, then a Teacher of Hebrew and other Tongues in the University, afterwards a converted Christian and Reader of a Hebrew Lecture in *Sion* Coll. *Lond*.". . .

—F. J. F.

GILBERT SWINHOE, 1658.

Dæm[osthenes]. I was inseparable in life,
And will not be disjoyn'd in death.
Oh! oh!   *He stretches himself down by the Corps and with the same dagger kills himself.*
All. Oh! Loyal Servant!   *Dyes.*

    This is a Spectacle of like Woe
    To that of *Juliet,* and her *Romeo.*
                           Exeunt omnes.

    The | Tragedy | of | The unhappy Fair | Irene.| By Gilbert Swinhoe, *Esq ; |* London :| *Printed by* J. Streater, *for* J. Place ; | *at* Furnifals Inn *Gate, in* Holborn, | *M.DC.LVIII.* |[1] *p.* 30.

The last two lines of Shakspere's *Romeo and Juliet* are :—
' For neuer was a Storie of more wo
  Then this of *Juliet* and her *Romeo.*" First Folio. *Tragedies,* p. 79, col. 2.
                                                       F. J. F.

[1] The title-page (644, f. 63) is dated in MS. 8ber 29.

1658, W. LONDON.

Romances, Poems and Playes.

Poems.

Mr *Shaksper's* Poems (sign. F)
$12°$

Playes. (sign. F4)

Mr. *Shakspear's* Playes. *folio.*
— King *Leare*, and his three Daughters, with the unfortunate life of *Edgar*. $4°$
— The life and death of *Rich.* the 2°. $4°$
. . . .
The merry wines [so] of *Windsor*. $4°$

> *A | Catalogue | Of | The most vendible Books in* England, | *Orderly and Alphabetically Digested; | Under the Heads of | Divinity, History, Physick, and Chy-|rurgery, Law, Arithmetick, Geometry, Astro-|logie, Dialling, Measuring Land and Timber, Gage-'ing, Navigation, Architecture, Horsmanship, | Faulconry, Merchandize, Limning, Military | Discipline, Heraldry, Fortification and Fire-works, Husbandry, Garden-|ing, Romances, Poems, | Playes,* &c. | *With | Hebrew, Greek, and Latin Books, | for Schools and Scholars. | The like Work never yet performed by any. |* Varietas Delectat. | *London, | Printed in the Year* 1658. |

[The Dedication is signed 'W^m. London'. The book is evidently an extension of Andrew Maunsell's Catalogue of 1595, of which unluckily only two Parts were publisht ; the third, of Plays, &c., never appeard.—F.]

ANON., 1658.

[In a Memorandum endorst on a letter among the Isham Correspondence (still in MS., and belonging to Sir Chas. Isham, Bart.), dated 31 May, 1658, is this entry]

      remember as to
  Shakefpere   Ufhers Analls, &c.

          WALTER RYE.

[Mr. Rye has been long engaged in abstracting and calendaring this Isham Correspondence. See under 1660, and 1677, below.—F.]

*ANON., 1659.

Oh that I were a worm to crawl on that face of thine, or a flee.—Hee'd bite me, fure.—To flip about my neck.
       The London Chaunticleres, 1659.
          J. O. HILL.-P.

Possibly imitated from Romeo's
    'O that I were a gloue vpon that hand,
    That I might touche that cheeke.'
     Rom. and Jul. II. ii. 23-4, Qo. 2.

"The tragedy of Romeo and Juliet is mentioned in a list of 'some of the most ancient plays that were played at Blackfriars,' a manuscript written in 1660." HILL.-P. *Outlines*, p. 106.

Till the MS. is identified and produced, this statement must be receivd with caution.—F.

FRESH ALLUSIONS TO SHAKSPERE.

FOURTH PERIOD.
1660—1693.
(From Charles II. to Dryden.)

1660.

I muft to *Rumford* ride (ud's nigs)
I've rid my felf quite off my legs.
Jack *Falftaffe* vildly did abate,
But never furely, at the rate
That I have done, fince action laft
I'me no mans length of life i' th' wafte.
My leg is not fo big by th' half,
Im'e but ill *Effex't* in the Calf.

From a Poem entitled "Friend," beginning
"For guilded Pill and Pill was not," dated *March* 27. 1660.
printed in "Choyce / Poems, / being / Songs, Sonnets,
Satyrs and Elegies./ By the Wits of both / Universities./
London, / Printed for *Henry Brome* at the *Gun* in *Ivy-
lane*./ 1661, / 8vo, p. 8."
—PONSONBY A. LYONS.

In 2 *Notes & Queries*, viii. 285, Oct. 8, 1859, Ithuriel writes:—
Amongst a collection of poems, sixteenth and seventeenth century,
formerly in the possession of Dr. Bliss, and noted by him as collected
by Clement Paman, we find one called "A Poetical Revenge," which
alludes to the plays of Shakspeare:—

"But ere I farre did goe
I flunge ye darts of wounding poetrie
These two or three sharpe curses backe. May he
Be by his father in his study tooke,
At Shakespeare's Playes instead of the Ld Cooke."—F. J. F.

LADY DOLLY LONG, 1660.

Dame Quickly would faine turne mercury to communeate
Scotch affaires but for Sir Cautelus in the Chimney corner . . .

A Valentine from Lady Dolly Long to (?) Justinian Isham, Esq.,
in the Isham Correspondence (still in MS.). See p. 184, above.
WALTER RYE.

ANON. AB. 1661.

Prologue to Richard *the third.*

Lock up your doores and bring the keys to me,
 From henceforth learn to value liberty.
This day we Act a Tyrant, ere you go
I fear that to your cost you'l find it so.
What early haft you have made to pass a Fine,
To purchase Fetters, how you croud to joyne
With an Usurper, be advis'd by me
Ne're serve Usurpers, fix to Loyalty
For you will find, at latter end ot'h day
It is your noblest and the safest way.
Who steers that course, needs fear nor wind, nor tide,
He wants no Pilott who has such a guide.
Tyrants (like Childrens bubbles in the Air)
Puft up with pride, still vanish in despair.
But lawful Monarchs are preserv'd by Heaven,
And 'tis from thence that their Commissions given.
Though giddy Fortune, for a time may frown,
And seem to eclipse the lustre of a Crown,
Yet a King can with one Majestick Raye
Dispearse those Clouds and make a glorious day.
This blessed truth we to our joy have found,
Since our great Master happily was Crown'd.
So from the rage of *Richards* Tyranny,
Richmond himself will come and set you free.

> *Covent Garden* / Drolery, / or A / Collection, / Of all the Choice *Songs, Poems,* / *Prologues,* and *Epilogues* (Sung and / Spoken at *Courts* and *Theaters*) never in / Print before./ *Written by the refined'st Witts of the Age. And Collected* by A. B. *London.* Printed for *James Magnes* neer the *Piazza in Russel-street.* 1672. p. 13-14.

This must be a Prologue to Shakspere's *Rich. III*, and must have been written soon after Charles II's coronation, April 23, 1661. A. B. may be Alexander Brome, as he died June 30, 1666 (Baker, i. 68).

The *Covent Garden Drollery* is ascribed to him by Lowndes and by the British Museum Catalogue. —F. J. F.

The following extract was sent me as an allusion to Shakspere in 1654:—

"An *Inigo Jones* for scenes ; a *Shakespeare* and a *Johnson* for plays, produced great improvements on the stage. The pieces these great poets wrote, had language, dependency of parts, possibility of plot, &c., and were not to be equalled : nor were they ashamed to permit their being printed, since which they are read with as much satisfaction, as they gave in the representation.—Edmund Gayton, *Festivous Notes on Don Quixote*, p. 236. Pub. 1654. Ed. 1768."

But on comparing it with the original of 1654, the latter was found to be this :

"An *Inigo Iones* for scenes, and a *Ben Iohnson* for Playes, would have wrought great cures upon the stage, and it was so well reform'd in *England*, and growne to that height of Language, and gravity of stile, dependency of parts, possibility of plot, compasse of time, and fulnesse of wit, that it was not any where to be equall'd ; nor are the contrivers asham'd to permit their playes (as they were acted) to the publick censure, where they stand firme, and are read with as much satisfaction, as when presented on the stage, they were with applause and honour. Indeed their names now may very wel be chang'd & call'd the works not Playes of *Iohnson, Beaumont and Fletcher, Cartwright*, and the rest, which are survivers of the stage ; that having faln, not into Court-Reformers, but more severe correctors, who knowing not how to amend or repair, have pluckt all downe, and left themselves the only spectacle of their times."—*Pleasant Notes upon Don Quixote*, by Edmund Gayton, Esq. London, 1654, fol. p. 273-4. ("Festivous Notes Upon Don Quixot" is the running title.)

So 6 or 8 Shakspere quotations from the notes of a modern edition of Burton's *Anatomy*, seemingly of Burton's writing, and sent to me as such, proved to be the modern editor's.—F. J. F.

1661.

The / Merry conceited Humors / of / Bottom / The Weaver, as It hath been often publikely / Acted by fome of his Majefties Co-/medians, and lately, privately, prefented, / by feveral Apprentices for their / harmlefs recreation, / with / Great Applaufe./ *London* / Printed, for *F. Kirkman* and *H. Marſh,* at the *Io. Fletchers* Head, on the backſide of St. *Clements,* and the *Princes Arms* in *Chancery* Lane nere *Fleetſtreet.* 1661. (A.)

The Stationers to the Reader. (A 2.)

Gentlemen, the entreaty of feveral Perfons, our friends, hath enduced us to the publiſhing of this Piece, which (when the life of action was added to it) pleaſed generally well. It hath been the defire of feveral (who know we have many pieces of this nature in our hands) that we ſhould publiſh them, and we confidering the general mirth that is likely, very fuddainly to happen about the Kings Coronation; and fuppofing that things of this Nature, will be acceptable, have therefore begun with this which we know may be eafily acted, and may be now as fit for a private recreation as formerly it hath been for a publike. If you pleafe to encourage us with Your acceptance of this, you will enduce us to bring you forth our ftore, and we will affure you that we are plentifully furniſhed with things of this Nature; Receive this then with good will as we intend it, and others ſhall not only fucceed it but you ſhall continue us

Your Servants,
FRANCIS KIRKMAN,
HENRY MARSH.

The Names of the Actors. (A 2, back.)

Quince the Carpenter who speaks the Prologue.

Bottome the Weaver.
Flute the Bellowfmender.
Snout the Tinker.
Snug the Ioyner.
Starveling the Taylor.

{ *Pyramus.*
Thifle.
Wall.
Lion.
Moonfhine. } who likewife may prefent three Fairies.

Oberon King of the Fairies, who likewife may prefent the Duke.

Titania his Queen the Dutcheffe.

Pugg. a Spirit a Lord.

[The Play consists of nearly all the Rustics' and Fairies' parts, but begins with a new speech from Bottom :—]

" *Bottome.* Come Neighbours let me tell you, and in troth I have fpoke like a man in my daies, and hit right too, that if this bufinefs do but difpleafe his Graces fancy, we are all made men for ever.

Quince. I believe fo too neighbour, but is all our company here ?

Bott. You had beft to call them generally man by man according to the Scrip. . . . ."

(When) *Enter Oberon King of the Fayries and Pugg a Spirit,* (Oberon begins with—)

" I am refolved and I will be revenged
Of my proud Queen *Titania's* injury,
And make her yeild me up her beloved page ;
My gentle Pugg come hither thou Remembereft
Since that I fat upon a Promontory, ..."

The Play is 12 leaves, and ends on D 4. Fra. Kirkman reprinted it in his *Wits*, 1673, Pt. 2, or *Droll Humours*, p. 29—57 :—in the 4º edition of The Wits, part 2, 1673. 4º British Museum, C. 12, b. 8, pp. 18—39. This volume contains only the Second Part of the Wits.—See *Centurie*, p. 354. —F. J. F.

FRANCIS KIRKMAN, 1661.

At the end of the 1661 reprint of the old Interlude of *Tom Tyler:* "Tom Tyler / and / His Wife./ An Excellent Old / Play,/ as / It was *Printed* and *Acted* about a / hundred Years ago. / Together, with an exact *Catalogue* of all the playes / that were ever yet printed./ *The second Impression./ London,* / Printed in the Year, 1661./" Francis Kirkman, the publisher of the Drolls (see p. 132, 133), has printed.

"A True, perfect, and exact Catalogue of all the Comedies, Tragedies, Tragi-Comedies, Pastorals, Masques, and Interludes, that were ever yet printed and published, till this present year 1661. all which you may either buy or sell at the several shops of *Nath. Brook* at the Angel in *Cornhil, Francis Kirkman* at the *John Fletchers Head,* on the Back-side of St. *Clements, Tho Johnson* at the Golden Key in St. *Pauls* Churchyard, and *Henry Marsh* at the Princes Arms in *Chancery-lane* near Fleetstreet. 1661."

But as I could not find the Museum copies[1]—*Tom Tyler* being as yet catalogued only in the King's Pamphlets, and its Catalogue, without the Play, being under the heading 'Catalogue,' I printed Kirkman's list from his 2nd ed^a of 1671; and as it is hardly worth while to print the same thing twice over, I let the -71 print stand, noting only that in the -61 Catalogue, Shakspere's name is often spelt in its full printer's form "Shakespeare" (but not under H, I, M, O (1), T, W, Y), not dockt of its final *e* as in the -71 Catalogue; and that in the -61 list, *Locrine* is not set down to Shakspere, but only to "*W. S.*" The -61 list also puts the names of many other plays between the spurious plays—'The Arraignment of Paris,' 'Cromwels History,' 'John K. of England 1st part' and '2d. part,' 'Leir & his three daughters,' 'The London Prodigal,' 'Merry Divel of Edmonton,' 'Mucidorus,' 'Old Castles life and death,' 'The Puritan Widow,'—and Shakspere's genuine works. Also 'Pericles Prince of Tyre,' and the 'Yorkshire Tragedy,' tho given to Shakspere, are not put first under their respective letters, as his name and genuine plays are put. This looks as if all these plays had been first treated as anonymous, and Shakspere's name afterwards added to them. "Titus Andronicus" is enterd as the other genuine plays are.—F. J. F.

---

[1] Mr. Lyons afterwards found em for me.

FRA. KIRKMAN, 1661—1671.

[Kirkman's 1671 Catalogue is printed at the end of (643. d. 75 Corneille) "Nicomede A Tragi Comedy translated out of the French, of Monsieur Corneille By John Dancer, London, 1670, 4°. As it was Acted at the Theatre-Royal in Dublin. Together with an exact catalogue of all the English Stage Plays printed till this present year 1671." See note, p. 343, below.]

A True, perfect, and exact Catalogue of all the Comedies, Tragedies, Tragi-Comedies, Paftorals, Mafques, and Interludes, that were ever yet Printed and Publifhed, till this prefent year 1671. all which you may either buy or fell, at the Shop of *Francis Kirkman*, in *Thames-ftreet*, over-againft the Cuftom Houfe, *London*.

A   p. 1.

Names of the Authors.	Names of the Playes.	
Will. Shakefpear	As you like it.	C
Will. Shakefpear	All's well that ends well	C
Will. Shakefpear	Anthony & Cleopatra.	T
Will. Shakefpear	Arraignment of Paris.[1]	P

(p. 2) C

Will. Shakefpear	Comedy of Errors.	C
Will. Shakefpear	Coriolanus.	T
Will. Shakefpear	Cymbeline.	T
Will. Shakefpear	Cromwels History.	H

(p. 6) G

| *Will. Shakefpear* | Gentleman of Verona | C |

[1] 'Arden of Feversham, T.' is enterd without any author's name. It is 'too childish foolish for this world' to make it Shakspere's.

FRESH ALLUSIONS.

H

Will. Shakespear	Henry the 4th 1ſt. part.	H
Will. Shakespear	Henry the 4th. 2d. part.	H
Will. Shakespear	Henry the 5tb.	H
Will. Shakespear	Henry the 6th. 1ſt. part.	H
Will. Shakespear	Henry the 6th. 2d. part.	H
Will. Shakespear	Henry the 6th. 3d. part.	H
Will. Shakespear	Henry the 8th.	H
Will. Shakespear	Hamlet.	T

(p. 7) I

Will. Shakespear	John King of England.	H
Will. Shakespear	Julius Cæſar.	T
Will. Shakespear	[1] John K. of England, 1ſt. part.	H
Will. Shakespear	[1] John K. of England, 2d. part.	H

(p. 8) L

Will. Shakespear	Locrine, Eldest Son of K. Brutus.	T
Will. Shakespear	Loves labour loſt.	C
Will. Shakespear	[2] Leir and his three Daughters.	T
Will. Shakespear	London Prodigal.	C

(p. 9) M

Will. Shakespear	Merry Wives of Windſor.	C
Will. Shakespear	Meaſure for meaſure.	C
Will. Shakespear	Much adoe about Nothing.	C
Will. Shakespear	Midſomer nights Dream.	C
Will. Shakespear	Merchant of Venice.	C
Will. Shakespear	Mackbeth.	T
Will. Shakespear	Merry Devil of Edmonton.	C
Will. Shakespear	Mucedorus.	C

[1] The old *Troublesome Raigne*, which Shakspere rewrote.
[2] This does not mean the real *Lear*, but the old *Leir*, I fear.

FRA. KIRKMAN, 1661—1671.

(p. 11) O

| *Will. Shakespear* | Othello, the moor of Venice. | T |
| *Will. Shakespear* | Old-Castle's Life and Death. | H |

P

| *Will. Shakespear* | Pericles Prince of Tyre. | H |
| *Will. Shakespear* | Puritan Widow. | C |

(p. 12) R

Will. Shakespear	Richard the Second.	H
Will. Shakespear	Richard the 3d.	H
Will. Shakespear	Romeo & Juliet.	T

(p. 14) T

Will. Shakespear	Tempest.	C
Will. Shakespear	Twelf night, or what you will.	C
Will. Shakespear	Taming of the Shrew.	C
Will. Shakespear	Troylus and Cresida.	T
Will. Shakespear	Titus Andronicus.	T
Will. Shakespear	Tymon of Athens.[1]	T

(p. 15) W

| *Will. Shakespear* | Winters tale. | C |

(p. 16) Y

| *Will. Shakespear* | Yorkshire Tragedy. | T |

[See next page, and the extract under F. Kirkman, 1673.]

[1] '*John Fletcher* | Two Noble Kinsmen | T C.' is the entry for that play.

An Advertisement to the Reader (p. 16).

IT is now just ten years since I Collected, Printed, and Published, a Catalogue of all the *English* Stage-Playes that were ever till then Printed; I then took so great care about it, that now, after a ten years diligent search and enquiry I find no great mistake; I only omitted the Masques and Entertainments in *Ben. Johnsons* first Volume. There was then in all, 690. several Playes; and there hath been, since that time, just an hundred more Printed; so, in all, the Catalogue now amounts to (those formerly omitted now added) 806. I really believe there are no more, for I have been these twenty years a Collector of them, and have conversed with, and enquired of those that have been Collecting these fifty years. These, I can assure you, are all in Print, for I have seen all them within ten, and now have them all by me within thirty. Although I took care and pains in my last Catalogue to place the Names in some methodical manner, yet I have now proceeded further in a better method, having thus placed them. [*No break in original.*]

First, I begin with *Shakespear*, who hath in all written forty-eight.[1] Then *Beaumont* and *Fletcher* fifty-two, *Johnson* fifty, *Shirley* thirty-eight, *Heywood* twenty-five, *Middleton* and *Rowley* twenty-seven, *Massenger* sixteen, *Chapman* seventeen, *Brome* seventeen, and *D'Avenant* fourteen; so that these ten have written in all, 304. The rest have every one written under ten in num-

---

[1] This includes the 11 spurious ones: *Arraignment of Paris*; *Thomas, Lord Cromwell*; 2 Parts of *The Troublesome Raigne of K. John*; *Locrine*; *London Prodigal*; *Merry Devil of Edmonton*; *Mucedorus*; *Old-Castle's Life and Death*; *Puritan Widow*; *Yorkshire Tragedy*.

ber, and therefore I pafs them as they were in the old Catalogue, and I place all the new ones laft. I have not only feen, but alfo read all thefe Playes, and can give fome account of every one; but I fhall not be fo prefumptuous, as to give my Opinion, much lefs, to determine or judge of every, or any mans Writing, and who writ beft; . . . (643, d. 75. Brit. Mus.)

In "*A Catalogue of some plays Printed for* R. Bentley, *in* Russel-street *in* Covent Garden," at the end of George Powell's version of Fletcher's *Bonduca*, 1696, is "*Beaumont* and *Fletcher's* Plays : In all 51. in large Fol. Mr. *Shakespear's* Plays : in one large Fol. Volume, containing 43 Plays." The 36 of Folios 1 & 2, plus *Pericles* and the 6 spurious plays put into the 1664 issue of the 3rd Folio (1663), 4th. edition, 1685.—F. J. F.

"The first Catalogue that was printed of any worth was that Collected by *Kirkman*, a *London* Bookseller, whose chief dealing was in Plays ; which was published 1671, at the end of *Nicomede* a Tragi-comedy, Translated from the *French* of Monsieur *Corneille*. This Catalogue was printed *Alphabetically*, as to the Names of the *Plays*, but *promiscuously* as to those of the authors (*Shakspeare, Fletcher, Johnson*, and some others of the most voluminous Authors excepted) each Authors Name being placed over against each Play that he writ, and still repeated with every several Play, till a new Author came on. About *Nine* years after, the Publisher of this Catalogue, Reprinted *Kirkman's* with emendations, but in the same Form. Notwithstanding the *Anonimous* Plays, one would think easily distinguishable by the want of an Author's Name before them ; yet have both these charitable kind Gentlemen found Fathers for them, by ranking each under the Authors Name that preceded them in the former Catalogues. (Langbaine, *Momus Triumphalis*, London, Sam. Holford, 1688, 4°. Preface, sig. A3.)"

PONSONBY A. LYONS.

ROBT. DAVENPORT, 1661.

              I throw the pawn
Of my afflicted honour, and on that
I openly affirm your abſent Lady
Chaſtitie's well-knit abſtract, ſnow in the fall,
Purely refin'd by the bleak Northern blaſt,
Not freer from a ſoyl, the thoughts of Infants;
But little neerer heaven.

> The / City-Night-Cap : / Or, / *Crede quod habes & habes.*/ A / Tragi-Comedy./ By *Robert Davenport.* As it was Acted with great Applause, / by Her Majesties Servants, at / the Phœnix in *Drury Lane.*/ *London:* / Printed by *Ja : Cottrel,* for *Samuel Speed,* at the Signe of the / Printing-Press in St. *Paul*'s Church-yard, 1661./ p. 27.

Davenport's snow metaphor is from Shakspere's simile in *Winter's Tale*, IV. iv. 375,

              I take thy hand, this hand,
As soft as dove's down, and as white as it,
Or Ethiopian's tooth, or the fann'd snow that's bolted
By the northern blast twice o'er.

It was first noted in 1 *Notes & Queries,* i. 330.—EMMA PHIPSON.

*THOMAS FULLER, 1661.

MARGARET PLANTAGENET Daughter to *George* Duke of *Clarence*, and *Ifabel Nevile* Eldeft Daughter and Co-heir of *Richard Nevile* Earl of *Warwick*, was born *Auguſt* 14. 1473.* at *Farrley-Caſtle* in this County. Reader, I pray thee, let her paſs for a Princeſſe, becauſe Daughter to a Duke, Neece to *two* Kings, (*Edward* the fourth, and *Richard* the third,) Mother to Cardinal *Reginale Pole*.

> The / History / of the / Worthies / of / England. / Endeavoured by / Thomas Fuller, D.D. / *London*, / Printed by *J. G. W. L.* and *W. G.* MDCLXII. [Part III]. sign. T t t back, p. 146.

* Mr. *Dugdale* in his ¹Alluſtration of *Warwickshire*, page 335.

I suppose the "pass for a Princesse" is a recollection of Portia's "God made him, and therefore let him passe for a man," in *The Merchant*, I. ii. 60. Compare the Duke in *Mids. N. Dr.*, V. i. 219. "If we imagine no worse of them, then they of themselues, they may passe for excellent men."

The *Worthies* was brought out after Fuller's death on Aug. 15, 1661, by his son.—F. J. F.

¹ So in the original side-note.

ANONYMOUS, 1662.

Nor need you doubt, in this our *Comick* Age,
Welcome acceptance for them from the *Stage:*
For, if 'tis true the *Proverb* doth exprefs,
That . * . *He's beft Prophet, who doth neareft guefs,*
This I'le dare to foretell, although no Seer,
That *Thorny-Abbey* will out-dare King *LEAR.*

.˙. Μάντις ἄριστος, ὅστις εἰκάζει καλῶς. †

Theatro-Philos. To his worthy Friend Mr. R. F. *upon his publifhing his Ternary of* English Plays . . *sign.* * 4, *back, of* Gratiæ Theatrales, / *or / A choice Ternary of / Englifh Plays,** / (1. Thorny Abbey, 2. The Marriage-Broker, and 3. Grim the Collier of Croydon.) 1662. Sig * 4, back.—F. J. F.

---

* The full title is: "GRATIÆ THEATRALES, / or / A choice Ternary of / ENGLISH PLAYS, / Composed upon especial occasions / by several ingenious persons ; / viz. / *THORNY-Abbey*, or *The LON-/DON-*Maid ; a Tragedy, by T. W. / The Marriage-Broker, or The Pan-/der ; a Comedy, by *M. W.* M. A. / *GRIM the Collier of CROYDON,* / or *The Devil and his Dame ;* with / the *Devil* and St. *Dunstan*: a Co/medy, by I. T. / Never before published : but now printed / at the request of sundry inge-/nious friends. / LONDON, / Printed by R. D. and are to be sold at / the sign of the *Black Bear* in *S. Paul's* / Church-yard, 1662 / "

† The Greek quotation is a line from a lost play of Euripides, the name of which is unknown. It is quoted by Plutarch, *De defectu oraculorum,* c. 40, and by Cicero in his letters to Atticus (vii, 13, 4). Cicero translates it (*De Divinatione,* II, 5, 12), "Bene qui conjiciet, Vatem hanc perhibeto optimum " (Wagner, *Fragmenta Euripidis,* p. 844).

EDMUND GAYTON, 1662.

Thereupon calling a Court at home, and to the beſt of my underſtanding having acted *Pyramus* and *Thiſbe*, the Lion and the Moon-ſhine (with leſſe partiality perhaps one way, then would have appeared the other in the Votes on your ſide the water) *I* ſtood clearly acquitted upon the whole matter

> Coll. Henry Marten's / Familiar / Letters / to / His Lady / of / Delight./ Also / Her kinde Returnes, / With / His Rivall R. Pettingalls Heroicall / Epistles./ Printed by *Edmundus De Speciosâ Villâ*./ Bellositi Dobunorum./ Printed for *Richard Davis*, 1662./ p. 2.

F. J. F.

WM. HEMINGS, before 1662.

Enter Eleazer.

Elea. To be, or not to be, I there's the doubt
For to be Sovereign by unlawful means,
Is but to be a flave to bafe defire,
And where's my honour then?

> The / Jewes / Tragedy, / Or, / Their Fatal and Final / Overthrow / By / Vespatian and Titus his Son. / Agreeable / To the Authentick and Famous History / of Iosephus. / Never before Published, / *By* William Hemings, *Master of Arts of Oxon.* / *London,* / Printed for *Matthew Inman,* and are to be sold by *Richard Gam-/mon,* over-against *Excester-House* in the *Strand,* 1662. / *Actus tertius, Scena secunda.* p. 37.

Ib. p. 40. *Enter the Watch.*

(p. 41.) 1 *W.* Well, come let us take our ftand here, we fhall fee fome vacant fellow, rambling this way anon, I warrant you.

2 What muft we do then neighbour?

1 Marry we muft remit um to prifon, and then afk um whither they were going.

3 But what if they run away neighbour?

1 Why then we muft knock um down, and bid um ftand. Nay I warrant ye neighbour, I have all ye r points of law Barbatim.

[The whole scene is imitated from *Much Ado,* III. iii. (or iv, in Spedding's arrangement); and "The Mechanicks bit" in *The Jewes Tragedy,* I. ii. p. 9-10, is also from Dogberry.]

ib. *Actus Quartus*, p. 51.

Enter Peter

Call ye this Honour ? a pox of honor,
Giue me honefty, down-right honefty :
Souns, break ones head, and give him no warning!
I woo'd not have Honor come fo fatt upon me neither.
                                            Looks who comes
I'me pepperd with a vengeance : Farewel Honor,
Ile to my Lady agen.   *Exit*

On other pages are seeming recollections of Shakspere, as on p. 7, "See where's the prologue to the bloody Scœne"[1]; on p. 9:

"How my distemper'd doubts disturb my brain,
Puzzle my will,[2] excrutiate my soul."

on p. 38, the dispute between Jehochanan and Eleazer—probably that pointed out by Mr. Collier as founded on the quarrel between Brutus and Cassius. *J. Cæsar*, IV. iii ; and on p. 56.

Dr. Ingleby sent me the information that Mr. J. P. Collier [*] notes the abuv quotations of "A pox of honour," &c., and "To be or not to be," and also 'a sort of copy of the quarrel scene between Brutus and Cassius'.

The play was printed some years after the death of its writer, the son of Wm. Heminge, Shakspere's fellow-player.—F. J. F.

---

[*] In his "Trilogy-Conversations between three friends on the Emendations of Shakespeare's Text contained in Mr. Collier's Corrected Folio, 1632, and employed by recent Editors of the Poet's Works," London. T. Richards, 37 Great Queen Street (*no date*), p. 21.

T. S. (GENT,) * 1662.

K. Hen. 8.

A Company of little Boyes were by their Schoolmaſter not many yeares ſince appointed to Act the play of King *Henry the eight*, and one who had the preſence (or the abſence rather) as being of a whining voice, puling ſpirit, conſumptive body, was appointed to perſonate King *Henry* himſelfe, only becauſe he had the richeſt cloaths, and his Parents the beſt people of the pariſh, but when he had ſpoke his ſpeech rather like a Mouſe then a Man, one of his fellow Actors told him; If you ſpeak not *HOH* with a better ſpirit and voyce, your Parliament will not grant you a Farthing.

> Fragmenta Aulica, / *or, Court / and / State Jeſts / in / Noble Drollery.*/. *True and Reall.*/ *Aſcertained to their* Times, / Places *and* Persons. *By T. S. Gent.*/ London, / *Printed for* H. Marsh *at the /* Princes Armes *in* Chancery-lane *near /* Fleetstreet; *and* Joſ. Coniers *at / the* Black-Raven *in the long / Walk near Christ Church, /* 1662./ p. 1.

The same story is told also in Fuller's *Worthies.*—Halliwell's *Folio Shakeſpeare*, xii. 59.

THO. FULLER, 1672.

HENRY the Eighth . . . Indeed he was a Man of an Uncomptrolable ſpirit, carrying a MANDAMUS in his mouth, ſufficiently ſealed when he put his hand to his Hilt. He awed all into *Obedience*, which ſome impute to his ſkilfulneſſe to Rule, others aſcribe to his *Subjects* ignorance to reſiſt.

Let one pleasant passage (for Recreation) have its Pass amongst much serious Matter. A company of little boyes were by their School-Master not many years since appointed to act the Play of *King Henry the Eighth*, and one who had no presence but (an absence rather) as of a *whyning voice, puling spirit, Consumptionish body* was appointed to personate *K. Henry* himself, only because he had the richest Cloaths, and his parents the best people of the parish: but when he had spoke his speech rather like a *Mouse* than a *Man*, one of his fellow Actors told him; *If you speak not* Hou *with a better spirit your Parliament* will not grant *you a penny of Money*.

> The | History | of the | Worthies | of | England. | Endeavoured by | Thomas Fuller, D.D. | London, | Printed by J. G. W. L. *and* W. G. MDCLXII. | Part II., Kent, *p*. 66.

Tho *Ha!* is markedly Henry's word in Shakspere and Fletcher's play—see III. iii. 61, 62 ; I. ii. 186 ; II. ii. 64, 73 ; V. i. 66, 81, 87 ; V. ii. 25—while Cranmer says *Ho!* V. ii. 3, and tho in the same play Henry asks no Parliament for a penny, yet as I know no other *Henry VIII.* of the time, I give these extracts for what they are worth.—F. J. F.

J. KELYNGE, 1663.

On the Incomparable LOVE à la MODE.

C Riticks approach, view what a ftreame of Wit
Through this one Poem runs; examine it:
I dare engage, each Act, each *Scœne*, each line,
Of pureft Wit and Mirth's the richeft mine
Ere fprung from *Englifh* Pen ....
Were *Shakefpeare, Fletcher,* or renowned *Ben*[1]
Alive, they'd yield to this more happie pen
Thofe lawrells that bedeckt their brows; and fay,
Love à la mode's the beft-accomplifh'd Play.

J. Kelynge Efquire.

A fore-praise Poem to "*Love a la Mode.*/ *A
Comedy.* / *As it was lately Acted with great* /
Applause at Middlesex-House. / *Written* / *By
a Person of Honour.*/ .... London, / *Printed
by* J. C. *for* John Daniel, *at the three Hearts* /
in St. Paul's Church-yard, *near the* / *West-
end.* 1663./ 4to.

F. J. F.

---

[1] *W. K.*, in the next fore-praise poem '*On the Composure of* LOVE à la MODE,' also says—

"all just Wits agree
In commendation of this Comedie.
And for its worth, I thus far dare ingage,
Since the revival of the English Stage;
No modern Muse hath yet produced such:
Were *Johnson* living, he would swear as much."

THOS. JORDAN, 1663 (?).

We have been so perplext with Gun and Drum,
Look to your Hats and Clokes, the Red-coats come,
D'amboys is routed, Hotspur quits the field,
Falstaff's out-filch'd, all in Confusion yield,
Even Auditor and Actor, what before
Did make the Red Bull *laugh, now makes him roar.*

> A Prologe to the King, in "Tricks / of Youth, / or, / The Walks of / Islington / and / Hogsdon, / with / The Humours of *Woodstreet*-Compter./" A Comedy, / As it was pu[b]lickly Acted nineteen dayes together / with Extraordinary Applause./ Never printed before. / Written by *Tho. Jordan*, Gent. /. . . *London*, Printed by Authority for the use of the Author./ (?) 1663.

This Prologue is not in the earlier edition of 1657. At the end of the play, the Comedy is said to have been licenst by Henry Herbert on Aug. 2, 1641. The extract above is printed in the *Centurie*, p. 330, from Mr. Collier's reprint, with 'Cloaks' for 'Clokes' (G. Chapman's), 'D'Ambois' for 'D'amboys,' 'it' for 'him.'

To explain line 2, Mr. Ponsonby Lyons gives me the following interesting bit : "Thus were these Compositions [the Drolls] liked and approved by all, and they were the fittest for the Actors to Represent, there being little Cost in Cloaths, which often were in great danger to be seized by the then Souldiers ; who, as the Poet sayes, *Enter the Red Coat, Exit Hat and Cloak*, was very true, not only in the Audience, but the Actors too, were commonly, not only strip'd, but many times imprisoned, till they paid such Ransom as the Souldiers would impose upon them ; so that it was hazardous to Act any thing that required any good Cloaths, instead of which painted Cloath many times served the turn to represent Rich Habits."—FRANCIS KIRKMAN, *The Wits*, 1673, 4to, Preface. Sign. A 3.—F. J. F.

HENRY BOLD, 1664.

(1) Well! hear fam'd *Ancient Piſtol* tel ye once
What falls on *thoſe*, confront, the *Helicons!*
He ſayes that *Gaping, ghaſtly wounds* and *Bliſters*,
(Look to it) ſhall *untwine* the *fatal-ſiſters*.
Poems, 1664, p. 169

(2) But thou muſt put me to the *purchaſe*
Of ſuch a *pipe*, which uſed in *Churches*,
Hath brought to *pulpit*, Roger *Korum*,
(As Bumkin ſwears) who long before um
Knew not (*Jack Falſtaf*wiſe) ſince ever born
Church inſide more, then does a *peppercorn*.

Poems / Lyrique / Macaronique / Heroique, &c. / *By* Henry Bold / *Olim è* N. C. *Oxon.* / (quotation from Horace, 2. l. 2. Ep. 11.) *London*, / Printed for *Henry Brome*, at the Gun in / *Ivy-lane*, 1664. / To my Friend, V. O. &c. p. 169, p. 170. See p. 281, below.

The allusion in (1) is to Pistol's mouthing in 2 *Henry IV*, II. iv. 211-213,
    " Then Death rocke me asleepe, abridge my dolefull dayes!
    Why then let grieuous, gastly, gaping Wounds,
    Vntwine the Sisters three! Come *Atropos*, I say!"
in (2) to 1 *Henry IV*, III. iii. 8-12, Falstaff's
    "An I haue not forgotten what the in-side of a Church is made of, I am a Pepper-Corne, a Brewers horse! the inside of a Church! Company, villanous Company hath beene the spoyle of me!"
Quotations and one reference sent by J. O. Hll.-P.; revized by F. J. F.

ANONYMOUS, 1666.

Great *MONK* ſo *thundered*, that 'twas hard to ſay
Whether 'twas *He*, or *Fate*, that got the Day.
Smith ſent ſuch *Thunderbolts* as ne'r were made
By *Vulcan*, ſince he firſt wrought of his Trade;
Who gaz'd, but durſt not come within a Shot,
For fear his other *Legg* had gone to *Pott*. . . . . . .
  Had *Goffe*,[1] *Ben. Johnſon*, or had *Shakeſpear* been . ⎫
Spectators there, ſuch *Acts* they ſhould have ſeen, . . ⎬
As they ne'r *acted* in an *Engliſh* Scean : . . . . ⎭
Theſe fought with Blows, they only claſh'd in Words;
They fought with Foyls, but theſe with naked Swords.
Here ſhould they've ſeen an angry Sea their *Stage*,
Cover'd with rolling Billows, Foam and Rage;
Now ſunk to Hell, anon with Pride ſo high,
As if it gave defiance to the Skie.
There ſhould they've ſeen *retiring Rooms* of VVar,
Such *Rooms* as farr excells *Romes Theater*:
A Ghaſtfull *Scean*, not *Thebes*, but *Thetis* VVomb,
VVherein the Actors did themſelves intomb.

> The Dutch Gazette :/ or, / The Sheet of Wild-Fire, that
> Fired the / Dutch Fleet./ *Licenſed* Aug. 20 *Roger
> L'Estrange. London,* Printed by *T. Leach,* in *Shooe-
> Lane,* 1666. A Broadside. Brit. Mus. 83t. l. 9,
> (now marked C. 20. f.) art. 70.—F. J. F.

[1] See p. 175 above.

W. DAVENANT, BEF. 1668.

Before April 17, 1668, when Sir William Davenant died, he mixt *Measure for Measure* and *Much Ado* up into his *Law against Lovers*, first printed in his Works, 1673, ii. 273. (See *Centurie*, p. 408.)

"Act I. Scene I.
Enter Duke, Angelo, and Attendants.
Duke. I M fure in this your fcience does exceed
The meafures of advice; and to your skill,
By deputation, I refolve to leave a while
My place and ftrength."

Baker's entry of the play (*Biogr. Dram.* ii. 364, col. 2) is "THE LAW AGAINST LOVERS, Tragi-Com. by Sir W. Davenant. Fol. 1673. This play, which met with great success, is a mixture of the two plots of Shakspeare's *Measure for Measure*, and *Much Ado about Nothing*. The characters, and almost the language of the piece, are borrowed from that divine author,—all that Sir William has done, being to blend the circumstances together, so as to form some connexion between the plots, and to soften and modernize those passages of the language which appeared rough or obsolete. The scene, Turin."

—F. J. F.

THO. SHADWELL, 1668.

I have endeavour'd to reprefent variety of Humours (moſt of the perfons of the *Play* differing in their Characters from one another) which was the Practife of *Ben Johnfon*, whom I think all Dramatick *Poets* ought to imitate, though none are like to come near; he being the onely perfon, that appears to me to have made perfect Reprefentations of Humane Life: moſt other Authors, that I ever read, either have wilde Romantick *Tales*, wherein they ſtrein Love and Honour to that Ridiculous height, that it becomes Burlefque: or in their lower Comœdies content themfelves with one or two Humours at moſt, and thofe not near fo perfect Characters as the admirable *Johnfon* alwayes made, who never wrote Comedy without feven or eight confiderable[1] Humours. I never faw one except that of *Falftaffe*, that was in my judgment comparable to any of Johnfon's confiderable Humours: You will pardon this digreſſion when I tell you he is the man, of all the World, I moſt paſſionately admire for his Excellency in Drammatick-*Poetry*.

> The *Preface to* ' The / Sullen Lovers : / or, the / Impertinents. / A / Comedy / Acted[2] by his Highness the Duke of / Yorkes Servants. / Written by / Tho. Shadwell. / . . . . In the Savoy, / Printed for Henry Herringman at the Sign of the Anchor in the Lower-Walk of the New-Exchange. 1668. 4to.

For further praife of Ben Jonson by Shadwell, see his Preface to his *Humourifts*, Works, G 3, back, and his Epilogue to it ; his Epistle Dedicatory to his *Virtuoso* (Mr. J. ' was incomparably the best Dramatick Poet that ever was, or, I believe, ever will be ') ; his Prefaces to his *Royal Shepherdess* ('the incomparable Johnson '), and *Psyche;* his Prologue to his *Squire of Alsatia*, to his *Lancashire Witches* ('the most admirable Johnson '), &c.—F. J. F.

---
[1] Excellent, in *Works*, 1720.
[2] at the / Theatre Royal / by / Their Majesties Servants.—*Works*, 1720, vol. 1.

SIR W. DAVENANT, 1668.

In this year was publisht a play founded, more or less, on *The Two Noble Kinsmen* by Shakspere and Fletcher. Its title is "The / Rivals. / A / Comedy. / Acted by His Highnes the / Duke of York's Servants. / Licensed September 19. 1668. / *Roger L'Estrange*. / *London*, / Printed for *William Cademan*, at the *Pope's Head* in / the Lower Walk of the *New Exchange*, 1668."

"The Actors Names" are   [2 N. K.]

" Arcon   *The Prince of* Arcadia.   [*for*   Theseus
Polynices   *His General*.   Pirithous
Provost   *Mr. and keeper of the Cittadel*.   Gaoler
Theocles }   *Rivals to the Princess* Heraclia   { Palamon
Philander }   { Arcite
Cunopes   *The* Provost's *Man*
Heraclia   *Neece to the Prince*   Emilia
[Cleone,   her waiting-woman]   Her waitingwoman
Celania   *Daughter to the* Provost   Gaoler's Daughter]
Leucippe   Celania's *Maid*.
             Attendants and Guards."

The parts of the play uz'd are mainly Fletcher's. Theocles and Philander are kinsmen of the tyrant Harpacus, and have been taken prisoners in the battle in which Arcon has killd Harpacus.

In this part, *The Rivals* borrows a bit from Shakspere's Act I. sc. iv. of the 2 *Noble Kinsmen*.

Rivals, I. ii. p. 3.

Arcon. They are not wounded much?
Provost. Not mortally;
But yet their wounds are not Contemptible.
Arcon. Let 'em have Noble usage:
   Summon all
Our Surgeons to their Cure; Their
   Lives concern us
Much more then Millions do of Common rank.
I value pris'ners of their quality

2 *N. K.* I. iv. : ed. Littledale.

Theseus. . . . They are not dead? 24
Herald. Nor in a state of life : . . .
   yet they breathe,
And have the name of men.   28
Theseus. Then like men, use 'em
. . . all our surgions   30
Convent in their behoofe . . . their
   lives concerne us   32
Much more than Thebs is worth :
   rather then have 'em
. . . Sound and at liberty, I would
   'em dead ;   35

Too much to let 'em Captives be to
  death.
Yet *Prevost* let their persons be se-
  cur'd
I' th' Cittadel, till we give further
  order.

But, forty thousand fold, we had
  rather have 'em
Prisoners to us then death. Beare
  'em speedily
From our kinde aire,—to them un-
  kinde,—and minister
What man to man may doe.   39

Theocles and Philander are confin'd in the Citadel, and while walking on
the Tarras (terrace), talk Fletcher (among other things):

The Rivals, Act I. p. 6, 7.
Theo. Cosin, How d'you? . . .
Phi. I'm strong enough I hope for
  Misery,
Although I fear, we are for ever
  pris'ners.
Theo. My thoughts are of the same
  complexion too. . .
Philan. O, Cosin *Theocles*, How
  are we lost?
Where are our kindred, friends and
  Country now,
Those comforts we shall never meet
  agen.
No more shall we behold the games
  of Honour
Where Youths (with painted favours
  hung
Like tall Ships under Sail) striving
  for fame,   [p. 7.]
Rival each others glory. We no
  more
Like twins of honour e're shall exer-
  cise
Our arms agen. Our Swords which
  Lightn'd in
The peoples Eyes, must now, like
  Trophy's, hang
To deck the Temples of the Gods
  that hate us,
And signify our ruine and defeat.

2 *N. K.* II. ii. 1—55 : ed. Littledale.
Palamon. How doe you, noble
  cosen? . .
Why, strong inough to laugh at
  misery.
. . . . We are prisoners   3
I feare for ever cosen. *Arcite.* I be-
  leeve it. . . .
Pal.   Oh cosen Arcite,
Where is Thebs now? where is our
  noble country?
Where are our friends and kindreds?
Never more   8
Must we behold those comforts,
  never see
The hardy youthes strive for the
  games of honour,
Hung with the painted favours of
  their ladies,
Like tall ships under saile ;
. . . whilst Palamon and Arcite
Out-stript the people's praises . . .
O, never   16, 17
Shall we two exercise, like twyns of
  honour,
Our armes againe . . . Our good
  swords now—
. . . . like age, must run to rust,
And decke the temples of those gods
  that hate us. . . .

Theo. Our hopes are pris'ners with us, we review Our former happiness in vain. Our Youth Too soon will wither into age, and prove Like a too timely Spring, abortive. Here (Which more afflict us) we shall both expire Unmarryed; No imbraces of a Wife, Loaden with Kisses and a thousand *Cupids,* Shall ever clasp our necks, no issue know us, No figures of our selves shall we e're see To glad our age, and like (young Eagles) teach 'em To look against bright arms.	*Arcite.* No, Palamon, 26 Those hopes are prisoners with us: here we are, And here the graces of our youthes must wither, Like a too-timely spring; here age must finde us, And, which is heaviest, Palamon, unmarried; The sweete embraces of a loving wife, 30 Loden with kisses, armd with thousand cupids, Shall never claspe our neckes; no issue know us, No figures of our selves shall we e'er see, 33 To glad our age, and like young eagles teach 'em Boldly to gaze against bright armes... 35
Phila. No more shall we e're hollow to our Hounds Which shook the aged Forrest with their Eccho, All pleasures here shall perish, and at last (Which is the Curse of Honour,) We shall dye Children of grief and ignorance.	*Pal.* 'Tis too true, Arcite. To our Theban houndes 46 That shooke the aged forest with their ecchoes, No more now must we halloa;.. all valiant uses... In us two here shall perish: we shall die— 52 Which is the curse of honour—lastly, Children of greife and ignorance. 55

In the rest of the scene, and in Act II, more of Fletcher is borrowd. Heraclia and Celania overhear the prisoners' talk, and Celania evidently falls in love with Philander. The latter, in Act II, first sees Heraclia in the garden, and shows her to Theocles, who proclaims his love to her, and is reproacht by Philander, and they quarrel. Theocles is set free (tho' banisht) at the asking of Polynices, whose life he had saved in the battle. But he disguises himself, and in Act III, sc. i, (p. 24,) which is from Fletcher's II. v. of 2 *N. K.*,* is, as victor in the country games, assignd to

---

* *Arcon.* May I demand wherein? *Theocles.* In somewhat of all Noble qualities;   *Theseus.* ... What prooves you? 9 *Arcite.* A little of all noble qualities:

Heraclia as her attendant. Meantime Philander has been set free by Celania, who gets the prison-keys from her father's man Cunopes, who loves her. In Act III. sc. ii, modelld on 2 *N. K.* III, i.—Shakspere, toucht by Fletcher,—the rivals meet. As in 2 *N. K.*, Theocles loses the King and his niece in the wood, and thus apostrophises her (p. 27):

O *Heraclia!*	O queene Emilia, 4
Sweeter than Spring and all the golden buttons On her fresh boughs; How fortunate am I in such a Mistress?	Fresher then May, sweeter Then hir gold buttons on the bowes . . . . . . thrice blessed chance To drop on such a mistris. . . (14) . . . Alas, alas 22
Alas, poor pris'ner! poor *Philander!*	Poore cosen Palamon, poore prisoner! thou
Thou little dream'st of my success: thou think'st Thy self more bless'd to be near *Heraclia.*	So little dream'st upon my fortune, that 24 Thou think'st thy selfe the happier thing, to be
Me thou presum'st most wretched, though I'm free; Because thou think'st me in my Country, but Wer't thou acquainted with my happiness, How I enjoy the lustre of her Eyes, What passion, Cosin, wou'd possess thee?	So neare Emilia; me thou deem'st at Thebs, And therein wretched, although free; but if Thou knew'st my mistris breathd on me, and that 28 I car'd her language, livde in her eye, O coz, What passion would enclose thee!
Enter Philander *out of a bush.*	*Enter* Palamon *as out of a bush* . . .
Phila. Traitor Kinsman! thou shoud'st perceive my Passion, were this hand but owner of a Sword;	*Pal.* Traytor kinsman! Thou shouldst perceive my passion, if these signes Of prisonment were off me, and this hand 32

I could have kept a Hawk and hollow'd well To a deep Cry of doggs. I dare not praise My Horse-man-ship, yet those who know me well Gave me a Character I blush to own. But I am most ambitious to be thought a Soldier.	I could have kept a hawke, and well have holloa'd To a deepe crie of dogges; I dare not praise 12 My feat in horsemanship, yet they that knew me Would say it was my best peece; last and greatest, I would be thought a souldier. 15

And were my strength a little re-   But owner of a sword . . . . . give
  inforc'd with one   me a sword,   72
Meals-meat, Thy wounds shou'd   Though it be rustle, and the charity
  shew the justice of my Love, &c.   Of one meale lend me ; come before
                                      me then . . . .

Theocles agrees to bring him food and a sword, and fight him. The next scene, Celania's Soliloquy, is adapted from that of the Gaoler's daughter, 2 N. K. III. ii. : Shakspere, toucht by Fletcher (Littledale). Then Fletcher's scenes iii.—vi. of the 2 N. K.[1] are more or less taken for the rest of Act IV. of the *Rivals*, in Theocles feeding Philander, the country sports, the two rivals' fight, the discovery of them by Arcon, and his judgment that he will reverse his sentence of death on both, for that one of them whom Heraclia will marry. After Celania's mad scene in Act V. sc. i., which is taken from Fletcher's V. ii. of the 2 N. K., the writer of the *Rivals* devises a new ending to his Play. He makes Arcon try, by offering first to save Theocles, and then Philander, to find out which of the two Heraclia likes best. This failing, he tries which of the doom'd men will say the most generous things of his rival when that rival is accused of unworthy acts. But in this trial of generosity, the rivals are equal, each defending his former friend most warmly. Then the crazed Celania comes in, mourning Philander's supposed death. He is brought to her alive ; she proclaims her love for him ; and on this, Heraclia givz him up ; Arcon bestows Heraclia on Theocles ; and Philander, as he has lost Heraclia, out of gratitude to Celania for saving his life, takes her. It is obvious that all this end of Act V. has nothing to do with Shakspere.

Langbaine, in his *Momus Triumphans* or " Catalogue of Plays with their Known or Supposed Authors, &c." of 1688, put *The Rivals* among the plays by " Unknown Authors," p. 32, line 1. In his recast of this book, his " Account of the English Dramatick Poets," 1691, he still kept *The Rivals*, at p. 547, under the head of " Unknown Authors," p. 524, entering it thus : " *Rivals*, a Tragi-Comedy in quarto, which at present I have not ; but have heard Mr. *Cademan*,[2] for whom (as I think) it was printed, say it was writ by Sir *Will. D'Avenant*."

C. Gildon, who revizd Langbaine in 1699, and profest to correct his mistakes, cut out the attribution of the play to Davenant, and merely enterd it in the 'Unknown Authors' class ; but Downes, who was, from 1662 to 1706, Davenant's ' Book-keeper[3] and Prompter,' says in his

---

[1] With help from Ben Jonson's *Sad Shepherd*, says T. Davies.

[2] Waldron's note on p. 40 of his *Downes* suggests that Wm. Cademan the publisher might have been the same man as Cademan the actor.

[3] Thos. Davies's note to Downes : *Book-Keeper* means here, not one who *keeps accounts*, but the person who is *entrusted with*, and *holds a book of the*

Roscius Anglicanus (1708, p. 23-4), ed. 1789, p. 32-3: "*The Rivals**, a Play; wrote by *Sir William Davenant;* having a very fine interlude in it, of vocal and instrumental music, mixt with very diverting dances; Mr *Price* introduced the dancing by a short comical prologue, gain'd him an universal applause of the town ... all the Women's Parts admirably acted; chiefly Ce[lan]ia, a Shepherdess, being mad for Love; especially in singing several wild and mad songs; *My Lodging is on the Cold Ground*, &c. She performed that so charmingly, that not long after, it rais'd her from her bed on the cold ground, to a Bed Royal.† The Play, by the excellent Performance, lasted uninterruptedly Nine Days, with a full audience."

Oldys adds, in his MS. note in Utterson's interleavd copy of Langbaine's *Engl. Dram. Poets* in the Brit. Mus. (p. 547, C. 45. d.), "The Song she sings in her phrenzy, *My lodging* is on the cold ground, &c, became very famous from' her charming the King [Charles II.] in it." On Downes's authority, then, I put *The Rivals* down to his master Davenant.

Play, in order to furnish the Performers with written parts, and to prompt them when necessary. In "*The Spanish Tragedy:* or *Hieronimo is mad again*," a play is introduced, as in *Hamlet*, and this is spoken relative to it,

"Here, brother, you shall be the *book-keeper*,
This is the argument of that they show."
Old Plays, 1780, Vol. 3, Page 224.

Ben Jonson, in his Induction to *Cynthia's Revels*, calls this retainer to the stage, *the Book-holder.*—p. iii. ed. 1789.

* I know not on what authority this Play of *The Rivals* is ascribed to *Davenant;* it is not in the Folio collection of his works, nor does the 4to edition of it, 1668, bear his name. It is a very indifferent alteration of *Shakspeare* and *Fletcher's* TWO NOBLE KINSMEN, and contains several Songs, &c. not in the Original; particularly a hunting-dialogue sung by Forresters, Hunters, and Huntresses: the ideas and hunting-terms in which are entirely borrowed from *Ben Jonson's* Pastoral of *The Sad Shepherd*. [T. Davies.]
An alteration of The Two Noble Kinsmen, by the Editor of this Tract, was performed at the Theatre-Royal, Richmond, 1779.—F. G. Waldron's 1789 ed. of Downes, with T. Davies's Notes, p. 32, 33.

† Charles II. had by this Mrs. Davis or Moll Davis a daughter, 'who was named *Mary Tudor*, and was married to *Francis* Lord *Radcliffe*, afterwards Earl of *Derwentwater*.'—Evans's *Ballads*, 1784, iii. 285.—*ib*. p. 33.

Nell Gwyn got rid of Moll Davis by giving her some sweetmeats made up with aperients one night before she went to the King.—*Lives of the most celebrated Beauties*, &c., 1715, quoted by Davies, *ib*. p. 33. Nell Gwyn's son was made Duke of St. Albans, and his issue are among our hereditary legislators, I suppose.

JOHN DRYDEN, 1668.

The Master-piece of *Seneca* I hold to be that Scene in the Troades, where *Ulysses* is seeking for *Astyanax* to kill him; There you see the tenderness of a Mother, so represented in Andromache, that it raises compassion to a high degree in the Reader, and bears the nearest resemblance of any thing in their Tragedies to the excellent Scenes of Passion in *Shakespeare*, or in *Fletcher:—Of Dram. Poesie*, p. 44.

The unity of Action in all their [the French] Plays is yet more conspicuous, for they do not burden them with under-plots as the English do; * * * * From hence likewise it arises that the one half of our Actors are not known to the other. They keep their distances as if they were *Mountagues* and *Capulets*, and seldom begin an acquaintance till the last Scene of the Fifth Act, when they are all to meet upon the Stage.—(p. 28.)

On the other side, if you consider the Historical Playes of *Shakespeare*, they are rather so many Chronicles of Kings, or the business many times of thirty or forty years, crampt into a representation of two hours and a half, which is not to imitate or paint Nature, but rather to draw her in miniature, to take her in little; to look upon her through the wrong end of a Perspective, and receive her Images not onely much less, but infinitely more imperfect then the life: this instead of making a Play delightful, renders it ridiculous.

Quodcunque ostendis mihi sic, incredulus odi.

For the Spirit of man cannot be fatiffied but with truth, or a leaft verifimility; and a Poem is to contain, if not τὰ ἐτυμα, yet ἐτύμοισιν ὁμοῖα, as one of the Greek Poets has expreffed it.

(p. 29, 30.)

Hence the reafon is perfpicuous, why no French Playes, when tranflated, have, or ever can fucceed upon the Englifh Stage. For, if you confider the Plots, our own are fuller of variety, if the writing ours are more quick and fuller of fpirit: and therefore 'tis a ftrange miftake in thofe who decry the way of writing Playes in Verfe, as if the Englifh therein imitated the French. We have borrow'd nothing from them; our Plots are weav'd in Englifh Loomes: we endeavour therein to follow the variety and greatnefs of characters which are deriv'd to us from *Shakefpeare* and *Fletcher*: the copioufnefs and well-knitting of the intrigues we have from *Johnfon*, and for the Verfe it felf we have Englifh Prefidents of elder date then any of Corneille's Playes: (not to name our old Comedies before *Shakefpeare*, which were all writ in verfe of fix feet, or *Alexandrin's*, fuch as the French now ufe) I can fhow in *Shakefpeare*, many Scenes of rhyme together, and the like in *Ben. Johnfons* Tragedies :—(p. 46.)

But to return from whence I have digreff'd, I dare boldly affirm thefe two things of the Englifh Drama: Firft, That we have many Playes of ours as regular as any of theirs; and which, befides, have more variety of Plot and Characters: And fecondly, that in moft of the irregular Playes of *Shakefpeare* or *Fletcher* (for *Ben. Johnfon's* are for the moft part regular) there is a more mafculine fancy and greater fpirit in all the writing, then there is in any of the French. I could produce even in *Shakefpeare's* and *Fletcher's* Works, fome Playes which are almoft exactly form'd, as the Merry Wives of *Windfor*, and the Scornful *Lady:*

JOHN DRYDEN, 1668.

but becaufe (generally fpeaking) *Stakefpeare*, who writ firſt, did not perfectly obferve the Laws of Comedy, and Fletcher, who came nearer to perfection, yet through careleſſneſs made many faults; I will take the pattern of a perfect Play from *Ben. Johnſon*, who was a careful and learned obferver of the Dramatique Lawes, and from all his Comedies I ſhall ſelect *The Silent Woman;* of which I will make a ſhort Examen, according to thoſe Rules which the French obferve.

As *Neander* was beginning to examine the Silent Woman, *Eugenius*, looking earneſtly upon him; I befeech you *Neander*, ſaid he, gratifie the company and me in particular fo far, as before you ſpeak of the Play, to give us a character of the Authour; and tell us franckly your opinion, whether you do not think all Writers, both French and Engliſh, ought to give place to him?

I fear, replied Neander, That in obeying your commands I ſhall draw a little envy upon my felf. Befides, in performing them, it will be firſt neceſſary to ſpeak ſomewhat of *Shakefpeare* and *Fletcher*, his Rivalls in Poefie; and one of them, in my opinion, at leaſt his equal, perhaps his ſuperiour. — (p. 46, 47.)

[Then follows p. 47, 48, the paſſage "To begin then with *Shakespeare*," etc. printed in the *Centurie*, p. 341.]

Their Plots [i. e. Beaumont and Fletcher's] were generally more regular than *Shakefpeare's*, eſpecially thoſe which were made before *Beaumont's* death; and they underſtood and imitated the converſation of Gentlemen much better; whoſe wilde debaucheries, and quickneſs of wit in repartees, no Poet can ever paint as they have done. * * * * Their Playes are now the most pleaſant and frequent entertainments of the Stage; two of theirs being acted through the year for one of *Shakefpheare's* or *Johnſons:* the reaſon is, becauſe there is a certain gayety in their Comedies, and Pathos in their more ſerious Playes, which ſuits generally with all mens humours. *Shakespeares* language is likewise a little obfolete, and *Ben. Johnson's* wit comes fhort of theirs.—(p. 48, 49.)

If I would compare him [Ben Johnfon] with *Shakespeare*, I muft acknowledge him the more correct Poet, but *Shakespeare* the greater wit. *Shakespeare* was the Homer, or Father of our Dramatick Poets; *Johnson* was the *Virgil*, the pattern of elaborate writing; I admire him, but I love *Shakespeare*.

(p. 50.)

I am affur'd from diverfe perfons, that *Ben. Johnson* was actually acquainted with fuch a man, one altogether as ridiculous as he[1] is here reprefented. Others fay it is not enough to find one man of fuch an humour; it muft be common to more, and the more common the more natural. To prove this they inftance in the beft of Comical Characters, Falftaff: There are many men refembling him; Old, Fat, Merry, Cowardly, Drunken, Amorous, Vain, and Lying: But to convince thefe people I need but tell them, that humour is the ridiculous extravagance of converfation, wherin one man differs from all others. If then it be common or communicated to many, how differs it from other mens? or what indeed caufes it to be ridiculous fo much as the fingularity of it? As for Falftaffe, he is not properly one humour, but a Mifcellany of Humours or Images, drawn from fo many feveral men; that wherein he is fingular in his wit, or thofe things he fayes, *præter expectatum*, unexpected by the Audience; his quick evafions when you imagine him furpriz'd, which as they are extreamly diverting of themfelves, fo receive a great addition from his perfon; for the very fight of fuch an unwieldy old debauch'd fellow is a Comedy alone.—(p. 51, 52.)

---

[1] Morose in *The Silent Woman*.

You [Lisideius and Neander] have concluded, without any reason given for it, that Rhyme is proper for the Stage. I [Crites] will not dispute how ancient it hath been among us to write this way; perhaps our Anceftours knew no better till *Shakefpeare's* time. I will grant it was not altogether left by him, and that *Fletcher* and *Ben. Johnfon* us'd it frequently in their Paftorals, and fometimes in other Playes * * * To prove this [that Rhyme is not allowable in ferious Playes], I might fatiffie myfelf to tell you, how much in vain it is for you to ftrive againft the ftream of the peoples inclination; the greateft part of which are prepoffefs'd fo much with thofe excellent Playes of *Shakefpeare, Fletcher,* and *Ben. Johnfon,* (which have been written out of Rhyme) that except you could bring them fuch as were written better in it, and thofe too by perfons of equal reputation with them, it will be impoffible for you to gain your caufe with them, who will ftill be judges.—(p. 57.)

And this, Sir, calls to my remembrance the beginning of your difcourfe [p. 56, 57], where you [Crites] told us we fhould never find the Audience favourable to this kind of writing, till, we could produce as good Playes in Rhyme, as *Ben. Johnfon, Fletcher,* and *Shakefpeare,* had writ out of it. But it is to raife envy to the living, to compare them with the dead. They are honor'd and almoft ador'd by us, as they deferve; neither do I [Neander] know any fo prefumptuous of themfelves as to contend with them. Yet give me leave to fay thus much, without injury to their Afhes, that not onely we fhall never equal them, but they could never equal themfelves, were they to rife and write again. We acknowledge them our Fathers in wit, but they have ruin'd their Eftates themfelves before they came to their childrens hands. There is fcarce an Humour, a Charaêter, or any kind of Plot, which they have not blown upon: all comes fullied or wafted to us: and were they to entertain this Age, they could not make fo plenteous treatments out of fuch decay'd Fortunes. This therefore will be a good Argument to us either not to write at all, or to attempt fome other way. There is no bayes to be expected in their Walks; *Tentanda via est quâ me quoque possim tollere humo.*—(p. 64, 65.)

> Of / Dramatick Poesie, / an / Essay./ By John Dryden Esq; / * * * * London, / Printed for *Henry Herringman*, at the Sign of the / *Anchor*, on the Lower-walk of the New /*Exchange.* 1668./ 4to.

1669.

But I fear leaft defending the receiv'd words, I fhall be accus'd for following the New way, I mean, of writing Scenes in Verfe: though to fpeak properly, 'tis not fo much a new way amongft us, as an old way new reviv'd; For many Years before *Shakepears* Plays, was the Tragedy of Queen *Gorboduc*[1] in *Englifh* Verfe, written by that famous Lord *Buckhurft*, afterwards Earl of Dorfet, * * * *S'hakefpear* (who with fome Errors not to be avoyded in that Age, had, undoubtedly a larger Soul of Poefie than ever any of our Nation) was the firft, who to fhun the pains of continuall Rhyming, invented that kind of Writing, which we call blanck Verfe, but the *French* more properly, *Profe Mefuree:* into which the *Englifh* Tongue fo naturally Slides, that in writing Profe 'tis hardly to be avoyded.

> Dedication " *To the Right Honorable* Roger *Earl of* Orrery." Sig. A3 back.
>
> The / Rival / Ladies / A / Tragi-Comedy / As it was Acted at the *Theatre-/Royal./ Nos hæc Novimus esse nihil./* Written by / *John Driden*, Esquire./ *London,* / Printed for *H. Herringman*, and are to be sold at his shop in / the Lower walk in the *New* Exchange. 1669./ 4to.

---

[1] *Ferrex and Porrex*, by Thomas Norton and Thomas Sackvile, afterwards Lord Buckhurst and Earl of Dorset, was sometimes called the tragedy of *Gorboduc* (Halliwell, Dict. of Old Eng. Plays). Gorbogudo, king of Britain, had two sons, Ferrex and Porrex. Their mother's name was Widen (Geoffrey of Monmouth, *British History*, Book II. chap. 16).

JOHN DRYDEN, 1669.

It [the play] was originally *Shakefpear's*: a Poet for whom he [Sir W. Davenant] had a particularly high veneration, and whom he firſt taught me to admire. The Play it felf had formerly been acted with fuccefs in the *Black-Friers:* and our excellent *Fletcher* had fo great a value for it, that he thought fit to make ufe of the fame defign, not much varied, a fecond time. Thofe who have feen his *Sea-Voyage*, may eafily difcern that it was a Copy of *Shakefpear's Tempeſt:* the Storm, the Defert Ifland, and the Woman who had never feen a Man, are all fufficient Teftimonies of it. But *Fletcher* was not the onely Poet who made ufe of *Shakefpear's* Plot: &c. &c. [See *C. of P.* p. 211.]

* * * * *

I am fatisfi'd I could never have receiv'd fo much honour, in being thought the Author of any Poem, how excellent foever, as I fhall from the joyning my imperfections with the merit and name of *Shakefpear* and Sir *William Davenant*.

> *Preface to* " *The | Tempest, | or the | Enchanted Island. |* A *|* Comedy *|* As it is now Acted *|* At his *|* Highness *|* the *|* Duke of York's Theatre, *|* London, *|* Printed by *J. Macock*, for *Henry Herringman* at the Sign of the *| Blew Anchor* in the Lower Walk of the *New* Exchange. *|* M.DC.LXXVI. (*by* Sir *William Davenant and John Dryden*), *4to.* [signed *J. Driden.* Decem. 6. 1669].

[B. N.]

1671.

*I would haue the characters well chosen, and kept distant from
interfering with each other; which is more than* Fletcher *or*
Shakespear *did* :—(Preface, Sig. a 1 back.)

Yet, as Mr. Cowley, *(who had a greater portion of it than any
man I know) tells us in his Character of Wit, rather than all wit
let there be none; I think there's no folly so great in any Poet of
our Age as the superfluity and wast of wit was in some of our predecessors: particularly we may say of* Fletcher *and of* Shakespear,
what was said of Ovid, In omni ejus ingenio, facilius quod rejici,
quàm quod adjici potest, invenies. *The contrary of which was
true in* Virgil *and our incomparable* Johnson[1].—(Preface, Sig. a 2.)

*Some enemies of Repartie have observ'd to us, that there is a great
latitude in their Characters, which are made to speak it: And that
it is easier to write wit than humour; becaufe in the characters of
humour, the Poet is confin'd to make the person speak what is only
proper to it. Whereas all kind of wit is proper in the Character of
a witty person. But, by their favour, there are as different characters
in wit as in folly. Neither is all kind of wit proper in the mouth
of every ingenious person. A witty Coward and a witty Brave must
speak differently.* Falstaffe *and the* Lyar, *speak not like* Don John
in the Chances, *and* Valentine *in* Wit without Money. *And*
Johnson's Truewit *in the* Silent Woman, *is a character different
from all of them* . . . . (Pref. sign. a 2.—F. J. F.)

Most of Shakespear's *Playes, I mean the Stories of them, are to
be found in the* Hecatommuthi, *or hundred Novels of* Cinthio. *I*

---

[1] *Johnson* was the only man of all Ages and Nations w[h]o has perform'd
it [humour] well. . . . *Ben Johnson* is to be admir'd for many excellencies; and can be tax'd with fewer failings than any *English* Poet.
sign. a.

haue, my felf, read in his Italian, *that of* Romeo and Juliet, *the* Moor of Venice, *and many others of them.*—(Preface, Sig. a 4.)

> An / Evening's Love. / or the / Mock-Astrologer. / Acted at the Theatre-Royal / By His / Majesties Servants. / Written By / *John Dryden* / Servant to His Majesty. / *Mallem Convivis quàm placuisse Cocis.* Mart. / In the *Savoy*, / Printed by *T. N.* for *Henry Herringman*, and are / to be sold at the *Anchor* in the Lower / walk of the *New Exchange*, 1671. / 4to.

1672.

You have loft that which you call natural, and have not acquir'd the laft perfection of Art. But it was onely cuftome which cozen'd us fo long: we thought, becaufe Shakefpear and Fletcher *went no farther, that there the Pillars of Poetry were to be erected. That, becaufe they excellently defcrib'd Paffion without Rhyme, therefore Rhyme was not capable of defcribing it. but time has now convinced moft men of that Error.*

> "Of Heroick Playes. An Essay" prefixed to the First Part of The Conquest of Granada. 1672, Sign. a 2 and a 2 back.

There will be Praife enough: yet not fo much,
As if the world had never any fuch:
Ben Johnfon, Beaumont, Fletcher, Shakefpear, are
As well as you, to have a Poets fhare.
You who write after, have befides, this Curfe,
You muft write, better, or, you elfe write worfe:

> "On *Mr.* Dryden's *Play*, The Conquest of GRANADA." signed "*Vaughan*" prefixed to the First Part (Sig. b 3) of—
> The Conquest / of / Granada / by the / Spaniards: In Two Parts. / Acted at the *Theater-Royall.* / Written by *John Dryden* Servant / to His Majesty. / * * * / In the *Savoy*, / Printed by *T. N.* for *Henry Herringman*, and are to / be sold at the *Anchor* in the Lower Walk / of the *New Exchange*. 1672. /

1673.

If in the feaver of his writing he [Dryden] has difcovered any paffion, the impertinency of the age is to be blam'd for troubling him, otherwife he is more to be efteem'd for his judgment than cenfur'd for his heat. If he tells us that *Johnfon* writ by art, *Shakefpeare* by nature; that *Beaumont* had judgment, *Fletcher* wit, that *Cowley* was copious, *Denham* lofty, *Waller* fmooth, he cannot be thought malitious, fince he admires them, but rather fkilful that he knows how to value them.—(p. 32.)

> A / Description of the Academy / of the / Athenian Virtuosi: with *A* Discours *held there in* Vindication *of* / *Mr.* Dryden's Conquest of Grenada; / *Against the Author of the* Censure / of the Rota. / * * * *London.* / Printed for *Maurice Atkins.* 1673. / 4to, 36 pages.

1677.

And Poets may be allow'd the like liberty, for defcribing things which really exift not, if they are founded on popular belief: of this nature are Fairies, Pigmies, and the extraordinary effects of Magick; and thus are Shakefpeare's Tempeft, *his* Midfummers nights Dream, *and* Ben. Johnfons Mafque of Witches *to be defended*.—(The Preface, Sign. C.)

> The / State of Innocence, / and / Fall of Man: / an / Opera. / Written in Heroique Verse, / And Dedicated to Her *Royal Highness*, The Dutchess. / By *John Dryden*, Servant to His Majesty. / * * * / *London:* Printed by *T. N.* for *Henry Herringman,* at the / Anchor in the Lower-Walk of the *New Exchange*, 1677. / 4to.

1683.

Am I tyed in *Poetry* to the ftrict rules of *Hiftory ?* I haue follow'd it in this Play more clofely, than fuited with the Laws of the *Drama,* and a great Victory they will haue, who fhall difcover to the World this wonderful Secret, that I haue not obferv'd the Unities of *place* and *time;* but are they better kept in the *Farce* of the *Libertine deftroy'd?* 'Twas our common bufinefs here to draw the *Parallel* of the Times, and not to make an *Exact Tragedy:* For this once we were refolved to erre with honeft *Shakefpear.*—(p. 12.)

But *thefe Lyes* (as Prince *Harry* faid to *Falftaffe*) *are as groffe as he that made them.* More I need not fay, for I am accufed without witnefs.—(p. 21.)

For your Love and Loyalty to the King, they who mean him beft amongft you, are no better Subjects than *Duke Trinculo:* They wou'd be content he fhou'd be *Viceroy,* fo they may be *Viceroys* over him.—(p. 42.)

> The / Vindication : / or the / Parallel / of the / French Holy-League, / and the / English League and Covenant, / Turned into a Seditious Libell against the / King and his Royal Highness, / by / *Thomas Hunt* and the Authors of the *Reflections* upon / the Pretended Parallel in the Play called / The Duke of *Guise.*/ Written by Mr. Dryden./ * * * London, / Printed for *Jacob Tonson* at the *Judges Head* in *Chancery-Lane;* / near *Fleetstreet*, MDCLXXXIII./ 4to, 60 pages.

1685.

It was Originally intended only for a Prologue to a Play, Of the Nature of the Tempeft; which is, a Tragedy mix'd with *Opera;* or a *Drama* Written in blank Verfe, adorned with Scenes, Machines, Songs and Dances.—(*The Preface,* Sig. b 2.)

> Albion / and / Albanius: / an / Opera./ Perform'd at the Queens Theatre, / in *Dorset* Garden./ *Written by Mr.* Dryden./ *Discite justitiam moniti, & non temnere Divos.* Virg./ London, / Printed for *Jacob Tonsen,* at the *Judge's Head* in / *Chancery-lane,* near *Fleet-strect.* 1685 : / fol.

[This alludes to the recast of Shakspere's play.—P. A. LYONS.]

1693.

The Subject of this Book confines me to Satire : And in that, an Author of your own Quality, (whofe Afhes I will not difturb,) has given you all the Commendation, which his felf-fufficiency cou'd afford to any Man : *The beft Good Man, with the worft-Natur'd Mufe.*[1] In that Character, methinks I am reading *Johnfon's* Verfes to the Memory of *Shakefpear:* An Infolent, Sparing, and Invidious Panegyrick : Where good Nature, the moſt God-like Commendation of a Man, is only attributed to your Perfon, and deny'd to your Writings :

> The / Satires of / Decimus Junius Juvenalis./ Translated into / English Verse, / By / Mr. *Dryden*, / And / Several other Eminent Hands./ Together with the / Satires / of / Aulus Persius Flaccus, / Made English by Mr. *Dryden*./ With Explanatory Notes at the end of each Satire./ To which is Prefix'd a Discourse concerning the Original and Progress / of SATIRE. Dedicated to the Right Honorable *Charles* Earl of / *Dorset*, &c. By Mr. *Dryden*./ *Quicquid agunt homines, votum, timor, Ira, voluptas, / Gaudia, discursus, nostri est farrago libelli*./ London, / Printed for *Jacob Tonsen*, at the *Judge's Head* in *Chancery Lane*, near / Fleetstreet. MDCXCIII./ Where you may have Compleat Sets of Mr. *Dryden's* Works, in Four Volumes / in Quarto, the Plays being put in the order they were written./ folio xxxix, 407 pages. Dedication, p. iii.
>
> PONSONBY A. LYONS.

But fuppofe that *Homer* and *Virgil* were the only of their Species, and that Nature was fo much worn out in producing them, that fhe is never able to bear the like again ; yet the

[1] Alluding to Rochester's well-known couplet :

For pointed satire I would Buckhurst chuse ;
The best good man, with the worst natured muse.

Allusion to Horace's 10*th Satire, Book I.* (Dryden's Works, ed. Sir Walter Scott, xiii. 7).

Lord Rochester died 16 July 1680.

Example only holds in Heroick Poetry: In Tragedy and Satire I offer my felf to maintain againſt fome of our Modern Criticks, that this Age and the laſt, particularly in *England*, have excell'd the Ancients in both thofe kinds; and I wou'd inſtance in *Shakeſpear* of the former, of your Lordſhip in the latter fort.—
Ib. (Dryden's *Juvenal*, 1693), *The Dedication,* p. vii.
J. O. IIII.-P.

What then would he [Homer] appear in the Harmonius Verſion, of one of the beſt Writers, Living in a much better Age than was the laſt? I mean for verſification and the Art of Numbers; for in the *Drama* we have not arriv'd to the pitch of *Shakeſpear* and *Ben Johnſon*.

The Dedication to "The Third Part of Miscellany Poems," London, 1693, 8vo. Sig. B 6.

The following extract may be a year after our limit, 1693 :—
"After I haue confess'd thus much of our modern heroick poetry, I cannot but conclude with Mr. Rymer, that our English comedy is far beyond anything of the Ancients : and notwithstanding our irregularities, so is our tragedy. Shakspeare had a genius for it; and we know, in spite of Mr. Rymer, that genius alone is a greater virtue (if I may so call it) than all other qualifications put together. You see what success the learned critick has found in the world, after his blaspheming Shakspeare. Almost all the faults which he has discover'd are truly there; yet who will read Mr. Rymer, or not read Shakspeare? For my own part I reverence Mr. Rymer's learning, but I detest his ill-nature and his arrogance. I indeed, and such as I, have reason to be afraid of him, but Shakspeare has not."

John Dryden to John Dennis [probably Mar. 1693-4, in answer to John Dennis's letter dated Mar. 3.] Printed among Dryden's Letters in Malone's *Critical and Miscellaneous Prose Works of John Dryden,* Vol. I, part ii, p. 34, 35.
PONSONBY A. LYONS.

1694.
Prologue to his laſt play.

He leaves his Manners to the Roaring Boys,
Who come in Drunk, and fill the House with noise.
He leaves to the dire Critiques of his Wit,
His Silence and Contempt of all they Writ.
To Shakespear's Critique, he bequeaths the Curse,
To find his faults; and yet himself make worse.

"Prologue. Spoken by Mr. *Betterton :*" sig. A back. Love Triumphant; / or, / Nature will Prevail./ A / Tragi-Comedy./ As it is Acted at the / Theatre Royal, / By Their Majesties Servants,/ * * * * * Written by Mr. *Dryden./ London*, Printed for *Jacob Tonsen*, at the *Judges Head* near / the *Inner-Temple-Gate* in *Fleet-street.* 1694./ 4to.

? — WATSON, 1670.

An Elegy on Sʳ W Davenant   [p 57, leaf 33]
& his Buriall amongst the Ancient
    Poet*es*.

[*verse 9*]

Firſt in the broad Elyſian ſtreets   [p. 58, lf. 33, bk.]
Him his old father Iohnſon greets;
Next him his Couſen Shakeſpear meets,
And his friend Sucklin lends him ſheets.

(10)

Cowley a fair apartment keeps;   [p. 59, lf. 34]
Receiving him with joy he weeps;
Into his bed Sʳ William creeps;
And now in Abraham's boſome ſleeps.

* * * * *

Communica*tum* a fratre Tho : Watson
Januar : 20 : 16⁵⁰⁄₇₁

Addit. MS. Brit. Mus. 18,220, lf. 33-4.

The compiler had at least one other 'frater'—Ben Whiting (leaf 102, back), and another, Ben Watson (leaf 60), but as Sir Frederic Madden's note on a fly-leaf says, the little volume was "Apparently compiled by one Watson."

—F. J. F.

W. RAMESEY, 1672.

(p. 127) But the Nobleſt exerciſe of the mind within doors, and moſt befitting a Perſon of Quality, is Study, ſometimes one, and ſometimes another, for Diverſion, were not amiſs. {Study commended.} Which are moſt commendable, and becoming a *Gentleman*, you have been taught before.* And, as I hinted there; *A few good Books is better than a Library, and a main part of Learning.* I ſhall here contract his Study into theſe few Books following; in which he may indeed reade all that is requiſite, and of Subſtance . . . .

(p. 129) . . . *Homer, Horace, Virgil, Ovid, Buchanan* the *Scot,* not inferiour to any Poet. And among our ſelves, old Sr. *Jeffery Chaucer, Ben Johnſon, Shakeſpeare, Spencer, Beaumont* and *Fletcher, Dryden,*† and what other Playes from time to time you find beſt Penn'd; And for a Diverſion you may read *Hudebras,* and *Don Quixot,* and *Quevado* for proſe; As alſo for General Readings, *Burton's Melancholy,* and our famous *Selden* his works.

> The / *Gentlemans* / Companion : / Or, A / *Character* / of *True Nobility,* and *Gentility.* / In the way of Essay / [By Wm. Ramesey (in MS.)] *By A Person of Quality.* / Written at first for his own Private Use, / and now Published for the Benefit of all. / London, / Printed by *E. Okes,* for *Rowland Reynolds,* at / the Sun and Bible in the Poultery, 1672. / Division IV. p. 129. (The Title is black and red : the red is in italic here.)

---

* Chap. 1. Memb. 1, Part 1.
† A sidenote in MS. adds ' Cleveland, Howel,' but who is *instar omnium* our Cowley of Cambridge.

The Allusion to Shakspere, Spenser, &c. was noted by Mr. W. C. Hazlitt in the second Series of his valuable *Bibliographical Collections and Notes,* 1882, under the *Gentleman's Companion.*—F. J. F.

ANONYMOUS, 1672.

In Country Beauties as we often fee
Something that takes in their fimplicity
Yet while they charm, they know not they are fair,
And take without their fpreading of the fnare;
Such Artlefs beauty lies in *Shakefpears* wit,
'Twas well in fpight of him what ere he writ.
His excellencies came and were not fought,
His words like cafual Atoms made a thought:
Drew up themfelves in Rank and File, and writ,
He wondring how the Devil it were fuch wit.
Thus like the drunken *Tinker*, in his Play,
He grew a Prince, and never knew which way.
He did not know what trope or Figure meant,
But to perfwade is to be eloquent,
So in this *Cæfar* which this day you fee,
Tully ne'r fpoke as he makes *Anthony*.
Thofe then that tax his Learning are too blame [sic]
He knew the thing, but did not know the Name:
Great *Johnfon* did that Ignorance adore,
And though he envi'd much, admir'd him more,
The faultlefs *Johnfon* equally writ well.
Shakefpear made faults; but then did more excel.
One clofe at Guard like fome old Fencer lay,
Tother more open, but he fhew'd more play.
In Imitation *Johnfons* wit was fhown,
Heaven made his men but *Shakefpear* made his own.

Wife *Johnson*s talent in obferving lay,
But others follies ftill made up his play.
He drew the like in each elaborate line,
But *Shakefpear* like a Mafter did defign.
Johnfon with fkill diffected humane kind,
And fhow'd their faults that they their faults might find
But then as all Anatomifts muft do,
He to the meaneft of mankind did go.
And took from Gibbets fuch as he would fhow.
Both are fo great that he muft boldly dare,
Who both of 'em does judge and both compare.
If amongft Poets one more bold there be,
The man that dare attempt in either way, is he.

> Covent Garden Drollery, or a Collection, Of all the Choice Songs, Poems, Prologues, and Epilogues, (Sung and spoken at *Courts* and *Theaters*) never in Print before. *Written by the refinad'st Witts of the Age and Collected by A. B...* 1672.

Line 15 and its context show that the play was Shakspere's *Julius Cæsar*. The bold poet alluded to in the last couplet is no doubt Dryden, whose judgment and comparisons of Shakspere and Ben Jonson (1668-72) may be seen on pages 216-224 above. In the British Museum Catalogue A. B. is marked A[lex] B[rome].—B. N.

ANONYMOUS, 1673.

To all thefe Reafons, our Farce-monger might have added another, which is a *non pareillo*, namely, that which Mr. *Bays* returned when it was demanded of him, Why in his grand Show (grander than that in *Harry* the VIII.[1]) two of the Cardinals were in Hats, and two in Caps, *becaufe*. - - - - - *By gad I won't tell you*, which after a paufe, is a reafon beyond all exception.

> *The | Transproser | Rehears'd : | or the | Fifth Act | of Mr. Bayes's Play.*[2] 12mo. *Oxford,* 1673 [*p.* 7]. Halliwell's *Folio Shakespeare, xii.* 61

---

[1] See Downes below, p. 353.

[2] Being a Postscript to the | Animadversions on the | Preface to Bishop *Bramhall's* | Vindication, &c. | shewing | *What Grounds there are of Fears and Jealousies of Popery.* | *Oxford,* Printed for the Assignes of *Hugo Grotius,* and *Jacob Van Harmine,* on the North-side of the Lake *Lemane.* 1673. (Mr. Bayes was Samuel Parker, Bp. of Oxford.)

See Dryden's "*S'too him Bayes:*"[3] | On Some | Observations | Upon the | Humour of Writing | *Rehearsal's Transpros'd* | ... *Oxon:* | Printed in the year 1673.|

[3] ? Here Bayes = Jn. Dryden.

F. J. F.

SIR W. DAVENANT, 1673.

SONG.

O Thou that *ſleep'ſt like Pigg in Straw*,
Thou Lady dear, *ariſe;*
Open (*to keep the* Sun *in awe*)
Thy pretty *pinking eyes.*

News from Plimouth, Act III. Additions to *Works*, 1673, p. 14, coL 1, B bbb 3 back.   J. O. HlL.-P.

The / Works / of / Sr William Davenant K^t / Consisting of / *Those which were formerly Printed,* / And / *Those which he design'd for the Press :* / Now Published / Out of the Authors / Originall Copies. / *London :* / Printed by *T. N.* for *Henry Herringman,* at the Sign of the / *Blew Anchor* in the Lower Walk of the *New* / *Exchange,* 1673. /—F.

The reference is to Cloten's serenade to Imogen, in *Cymbeline,* II. iii. 27.

MR. ARROWSMITH, 1673.

Pif[auro]. Come Sir you are a judge, what opinion have you of the laft new Play?

Tut[or to Pacheco]. Faith - - - well for an effay, I guefs the Gentlemans but a beginner. I my felf - - -

Pis. Now he's in. (*Afide.*)

Tut. Writ with the fame much fuccefs at firft, 'twas induftry and much converfe that made me ripe; I tell you Gentlemen, when I firft attempted this way I underftood no more of Poetry than one of you.

Ped[ro]. This is ftrange impudence. } *Aside.*
Ant[onio]. 'Tis nothing yet.

Tut. There are many pretenders but you fee how few fucceed; and bating two or three of this nation as *Taffò*, *Ariofto* and *Guarini*, that write indifferently well, the reft muft not be named for Poefy: we have fome three or four, as *Fletcher*, *Iohnfon*, *Shakefpear*, *Davenant*, that have fcribbled themfelves into the bulk of follies and are admired to, but ne're knew the laws of heroick or dramatick poefy, nor faith to write true Englifh neither.

> The / Reformation./ A / Comedy./ Acted / At the / Dukes Theater./ . . . London,/ *Printed for* William Cademan, *at the Popes-Head, in the / Lower Walk of the New* Exchange *in the Strand.* MDCLXXIII./ 4to. Act IV. *Scene* i. p. 46-47.

"This Play is ascribed to Mr. *Arrowsmith* and is a very good comedy." —*Langbaine*, 1691, p. 546.

"But being too free wth the Laws of Morality & Vertue, was soon laid aside." (MS. note by Wm Oldys in the Brit. Mus. copy, C. 28. g 1.)

"This Play is accounted to be written by Mr. *Arrowsmith*." Gildon's *Langbaine*, 1699, p. 167.—F. J F.

ANON., 1673.

A Critick continuing on the difcourfe, faid, he was forry that Mr *Dryden* when he charged every page of *Shakefpeer* and *Fletcher* with fome *Solecifm* of Speech or fome notorious *flaw* in fence, did not read their writings and his own with the fame fpeƐtacles, for had he, he would never have left fo incorreƐt a line as this in that *Epilogue*, where he taxes the Antients fo fuperciliouſly;

> *There Comedy was faultleſs, but 'twas courfe.*
> [Epilogue to the Second Part of the Conquest of Grenada.]

'tis a favour to call this but a *flaw* ; (p. 7.)

In another place in *Maximin*, he feems fully to have anfwer'd his *Prologue*, in not *fervilely ſtooping fo low as Sence;*

> To bind Porphyrius *firmely to the S'ate*,
> *I will this day my Cæfar him create,*
> *And, Daughter, I will give him you for wife*,

here, in making *Porphyrius* a Bride, he has *reacht an excellence*, and juftify'd his reprefentation of *big-belly'd Men* in the *Wild Gallant*, a greater impoſſibility, then any *Shakfpear* can be cenfur'd for (for impofybility's in Mr *Drydens* charge are fence, but in anothers nonfence) though he wants not thefe fmaller *indecorum's* neither ; (p. 9.)

He was the man Nature feem'd to make choice of to enlarge the Poets Empire, & to compleat thofe Difcovery's others had begun to *ſhadow:* that SHAKESPEAR and *Fletcher* (as fome think) ereƐted the *Pillars* of Poetry is a groſſe errour ; (p. 13.)

The / Censvre / of the / Rota./ On M Driden's *Conquest* of / Granada./ *Oxford*, / Printed by *H. H.* for *Fran. Oxlad* junior./ *An. Dom.* 1673./ 4to. 21 pages.

PONSONBY A. LYONS.

RICHARD WARD, 1673.

(p. 207) ¶ Some *Words* are contrary to *Prudence, Difcretion*
and *Wifdom:* as
Firft, foolifh and undifcreet *Words* . . . .
(p. 208.) Secondly, there are Ignorant *Words*.
Thirdly, there are unprofitable, and ineffectual *Words*; as one
faith,
You may as well go ftand upon the beach,
And bid the main flood bate his ufual height,
Or even as well vfe queftion with the Wolf.
Or the poor Ewe bleat for the fimple Lamb.
You may as well forbid the Mountain Fines
To wag their high tops, and to make no noife,
When they are fretted with the gufts of heaven; As
to perfwade fuch or fuch an one, to fuch or fuch a thing, &c.

> *Two very Usefull and | Compendious | Theological Treatises: | The First shewing | The Nature of Wit, | Wisdom and Folly.| The Second describing | The Nature, Use, and Abuse | of the | Tongue | and Speech, | Whereby principally Wisdom and | Folly are expressed.| Wherein also are divers Texts of Scripture | touching the respective Heads explained.| By* Richard Ward, *Preacher of the | Gospel at* Bushey *in* Hartford-shire. . . . . . London, | *Printed for* William Miller *at the Gilded Acorn in St.* Pauls Church-yard, *near the little North Door,* 1673.| . . . . .
> (*p.* 147) *The Second | Treatise, | of the | Nature, Use, and Abuse | of the | Tongue | and | Speech.|* . . . . London, | *Printed by* E. T. *and* R. H. *for* Will. Miller | *at the gilded Acorn in St.* Pauls *Church-yard, | over against the little North Door.* 1673.| *p.* 208.

Noted in *Centurie*, p. 429, no. 16.—F. J. F.
(*Merchant of Venice*, IV. i. 71-7.)

237

FRANCIS KIRKMAN, 1673.

In "The Wits or Sport upon Sport. 4to. 1673." Another edition of the second part. The Preface [A.2. second paragraph] is :—"The most part of these Pieces were written by such Penmen as were known to be the ablest Artists that ever this Nation produced, by Name, *Shake-spear*, *Fletcher*, *Johnson*, *Shirley*, and others; and these Collections are the very Souls of their writings, if the witty part thereof may be so termed: And the other small Pieces composed by several other Authors are such as have been of great fame in this last Age. When the publique Theatres were shut up, and the Actors forbidden to present us with any of their Tragedies, because we had enough of that in earnest; and Comedies, because the Vices of the Age were too lively and smartly represented; then all that we could divert our selves with were these humours and pieces of Plays, which passing under the Name of a merry conceited Fellow, called *Bottom the Weaver*, *Simpleton the Smith*, *John Swabber*, or some such Title, were only allowed us, and that but by stealth too, and under pretence of Rope-dancing, or the like; and these being all that was permitted us, great was the confluence of the Auditors; and these small things were as profitable, and as great get-pennies to the Actors as any of our late famed Plays. I have seen the *Red Bull* Playhouse, which was a large one, so full, that as many went back for want of room as had entred; and as meanly as you may now think of these Drols, they were then Acted by the best Comedians then and now in being;"

[A List of "*Books Printed for Francis Kirkman*" following the Preface says]. "The exact price of this Book stitch'd is 1 s."

[The Wits or Sport upon Sport, is said to be] in Quarto: price stitcht 1.s. Or more at large, in Octavo; price bound 2s. 6d.

PONSONBY A. LYONS.

[As the Title-page of Kirkman's book also bears witness to the great popularity of *Bottom*, &c., and is very curious, it is added here from the 4to copy.—P. A. L.]

THE
WITS
OR,
SPORT upon SPORT.
BEING A
Curious Collection of several
DROLS and FARCES,
Presented and Shewn
For the
MERRIMENT and DELIGHT
OF
Wise Men, and the Ignorant:
As they have been sundry times Acted
In Publique, and Private,

In *LONDON* at *BARTHOLOMEW* } FAIRES.
In the Countrey at other

In HALLS and TAVERNS,
On several MOUNTEBANCKS STAGES,
At Charing Cross, Lincolns-Inn-Fields, and other places,
BY
Several Stroleing PLAYERS,
FOOLS, and FIDLERS.
And the Mountebancks ZANIES.
With Laughter, and great Applause.
[in *MS*, Robt Cox]

Written I know not when, by several Persons, I know not who;
But now newly Collected by your Old Friend to please you,
FRANCIS KIRKMAN.

London, Printed for *Fran. Kirkman,* and are to be Sold by most Book-Sellers. 1673.

ANON, 1674.

On the World.

The World's a City,
furnisht with spacious streets,
And Death's the market place,
whereat all creatures meet.

Loves | Garland: | or, | Posies for Rings, Hand-ker-|chers, & Gloves: And such pretty To-| kens that Lovers send their Loves.| London, *Printed by* Andrew Clark, *and are | to be sold by* Tho. Passenger *at the Three | Bibles upon* London-Bridge, 1674.*/ sign. B* 3 *back*, the last page but one.

This is a variation of two lines in Act I. sc. v. of " *The | Two | Noble | Kinsmen* : / Presented at the Blackfriers / by the Kings Maiesties servants, / with great applause : / Written by the memorable Worthies / of their time ; /
{ Mr. *John Fletcher*, and }
{ Mr. *William Shakspeare* } Gent. / Printed at *London* by *Tho. | Cotes,* for *John Waterson :* / and are to be sold at the signe of the *Crowne* | in *Pauls* Church-yard. 1634. /" sign. D. p. 17 :—

3 *Qu[eene.]* This world's a Citty full of straying Streetes,
And Death's the market place, where each one meetes.
(Part II. p. 22, l. 15—16, ed. Littledale, N. Sh. Soc. 1876.
Mr. L. unluckily turns the capitals into ' lower case.')

Spalding assignd this scene to Shakspere. Hickson doubted about it. Littledale inclines to make it Fletcher's. The scene is only 16 lines, and surely Shakspere never wrote the 9 lines of Dirge in it. But as his name is on the title of the 2 *N. K.*, the Posy must be here, till it has been shown to be an old saw before Shakspere's time.

The quotation, and the title of the book suit well Jaques's sneer at Orlando : " You are ful of prety answers : haue you not bin acquainted with goldsmiths wiues, & cond the*m* out of rings." (Fol. p. 196, col. 2.)

F. J. F.

THOMAS DUFFETT, 1674.

[To this writer's " The / Emprefs / of / Morocco./ A Farce./ Acted / By His Majefties Servants./ London, / Printed for/ *Simon Neal*, at the Sign of / the three Pidgeons in *Bedford-ftreet* / in *Covent-Garden*. 1674./ 4to is]
"An Epilogue fpoken by Witches, / after the mode of *Macbeth*" [half-title, p. 25. The full title, p. 27, is]
"Epilogue. / Being a new Fancy after the old, / and moft urprifing way / of / M A C B E T H, / Perform'd with new and coftly / Machines, / Which were invented and managed / by the moft ingenious Operator / Mr. *Henry VVright*. P. G. Q./ *London*, Printed in the Year 1674./"

[After 'the Actors Names' (6), p. 28, comes, on p. 29]

" An / Epilogue / Spoken by / *Heccate* and the three Witches,/ According / To the Famous Mode of / M A C B E T H./"

[In the text of the Epilogue, some of Shakspere's words are us'd with slight change, and burlesqued. Hecate's 2nd and 3rd lines are]
" What have you been at Hot-Cockles I fee,
  Beldames ! how dare you traffick thus, and not call me ?
  'Tis I muft bear the brunt."
[from *Macbeth*, III. v. 2—8, "beldames . . . How did you dare To trade and traffic with Macbeth . . . And I . . . was never call'd to bear my part. . . ."
On the next page, the 2nd Witch, after Shakspere's first in *Macbeth*, I. iii, says]

THOMAS DUFFETT, 1674.

"I pick't Shop-keeper up, and went to th' Sun.
He Hounch't . . . and Hounch't . . . and Hounch't;
And when h' had done,
Pay me, quoth I,
Be damn'd you VVhore! did fierce Mechanick cry, . . .
Hec. His shop is in *Fleetstreet*——
2. *Witch.* In *Hackney* Coach, I'le thither sail,
Like wanton VVife with sweeping Tail;
I'le do! I'le do! and I'le do!"
(p. 34) 1 Witch. *Fih! Fah! Fum!*
By the itching of my Bum,
Some wicked Luck shou'd that way come.
{ *pointing to the Audience.*"

[At the end, p. 41, is]

"An

Epilogue.

"THis Farce————
Not like your Country Girl made proud at Court,
Because she there first learn'd the naughty sport,
She'd now take place of all, and's grown so haughty,
Those that debauch't her, dare not say she's faulty,
Asham'd to own she jilted them with low drefs,
As stroling Punk did once in Somers progrefs:
No, this like Sutler's Doxie, came from *Black-heath*,
Long'd but to be as fine as Witch in *Mackbeth*."

Lock's music to *Macbeth* was written before 1672, as it was playd in that year. I cannot find any print of it then. See note to *Lock*, 1675, below.
—F. J. F.

THOMAS DUFFETT, 1675.[1]

[As pearls before swine, so were Shakspere's plays in the eyes of the hog Duffett. Not content with degrading *Macbeth*, he went on to turn *The Tempest*—thro its Davenant-adaptation—into a bawdy burlesque,]

"The / Mock-Tempeſt : / or the / Enchanted Caſtle./ acted at the / Theatre Royal./ Written by T. Duffett./ *Hic totus volo rideat libellus*. Mart./ *London*,/ Printed for *William Cademan* at the *Popes-Head* in the lower / Walk of the *New Exchange* in the *Strand*. 1675./"

[The Prologue in its "You fee our Study is to pleafe you all;" evidently aims at Prospero's Epilogue, "my project . . was to pleafe." The "Perfons Reprefented" are]

---

[1] "Thomas Duffet. He was, before he became a Poet, a Milliner in the New Exchange : he has writ four Plays, two of them in a Burlesque Stile. . .

The Mock Tempest, or, The *Enchanted Castle*, a Farce, 4to. 1675. Acted at the Theatre Royal by his Majesty's Servants. Writ on purpose to draw Company from the other Theatre, where was great resort about that time, to see that reviv'd Comedy, call'd, *The Tempest*, then much in vogue." (1699) Gildon's *Langbaine*, p. 48. See Downes, below, p. 353.

Langbaine, 1691, p. 177-8. *Mock Tempest*, or *The Enchanted Castle*, a Farce acted at the Theatre-Royal, printed in quarto, *Lond*. 1675. The Design of this Play was to draw the Town from the Duke's Theatre, who for a considerable time had frequented that admirable reviv'd comedy call'd *The Tempest*. What success it had may be learnt from the following lines,

    The dull Burlesque appeared with Impudence,
    And pleased by Novelty for want of Sence.   1°   s5
        Boyleau's Art of Poetry, p. 5 [see p. 245, below].

A Burlesque piece of Ribaldry designed to ridicule Dryden's 'Tempest.' MS. note by Oldys in C. 28. g. 1.

"Prospero—*a Duke, Head-keeper of the Enchanted Castle.*
Alonzo—*a Duke, his mortal Enemy.*
Quakero—*Son of Alonzo.*
Gonzalo—*a subject of Alonzos.*
Antonio—*his Friend.*
Hypolito—*Infant Duke of* Mantua, *Innocent and ignorant.*
Hectorio—*a Pimp.*
Miranda——
Dorinda—— } *the harmless daughters of* Prospero.
Stephania—— *a Baud.*
Beantosser
Moustrappa } *Wenches.*
Drinkallup
Ariel—— *a spirit waiting on* Prospero.
A Plenipotentiary.

Wenches, Bridewell - *Keepers, Spirits, Devils, Masquers, and Prisners.*
       The Scene in LONDON."

[The first scene opens with "a great noyse" of men breaking into a brothel, and with occasional use of Shakspere's words, "What care these Roarers for the worshipful Pin-makers?" (p. 2) &c. Scene ii. burlesques Shakspere's:]

(p. 10) "*Pros.* . . Thy Father, *Miranda,* was 50 years ago a man of great power, Duke of my Lord Mayors Dogg-kennel. . . Thy Mother was all mettle. . . canst thou remember when thou wert Born, sure thou canst not, for then thou wert but three days old.

Mir. I' fads, I do remember it Father, as well as 'twere but yesterday.

Pros. Then scratch thy tenacious Poll, and tell me what thou findest backward in the misty black and bottomless Pit of time.

Mir. Pray Father had I not Four, or Five Women waiting upon top of me, at my Mother's groaning, pray?

Pros. Thou hadſt, and more, *Miranda*, for then I had a Tub of humming ſtuff would make a Cat ſpeak.

Mir. O Gemine! Father how came we hither?

Pros. While I, deſpiſing mean, and worldly buſ"neſs, as miſ-becoming my grave Place, Quality, did for the bett'ring of my mind, apply myſelf, to the ſecret and laudable ſtudy of Nine-pins, Shovel-board and Pigeon-holes—do'ſt thou give ear Infant? (p. 11) *Mir.* I do, moſt Prudent Sir. . . . ."

[In Act II. sc. ii. Devils,[1] and then Fraud and Rapine, frighten Alonzo and Gonzalo. On p. 18 "Enter *Murther*," (from *Macbeth*).—]

"A man dreſt all in Red, with two Bloody Daggers in his hands, and his Face and Hands ſtain'd with blood.

Sings.

Murther. *Wake Duncan! would thou couldſt.*
 Diſguiſ'd with blood, I lead them on,
 Vntil to Murther they arrive." (p. 18.)

[In Act III, sc. ii, Ariel's songs are parodied, and Act IV, sc. i. (p. 31) opens with]

"*Pros.* Now does the charm'd impoſtume of my Plot Swell to a head, and begin to ſuppurate,
 If I can make *Mantua's* Infant Duke,
 Switchel my young giglet *Dorinda."* (p. 31.)

[In Act V, Sc. ii. Shakspere's beautiful "Advance the fringëd curtains of thine eyes," &c., appears thus (p. 41) :—]

---

[1] In his Epilogue to *the Armenian Queen*, Duffett alludes to these Devils:
"When Tempests and Enchantments fly the Town,
 When *Prosp'ro's* Devils dare not stand your frown;
 They to the Country strole with painted ware,
 Where mighty sums of precious time they share;"

 New / Poems, / Songs, / Prologues and Epilogues. Never before printed./ Written by / *THOMAS DUFFETT*, / And Set by / The most Eminent Musicians about / the Town./ *Qui fugit Molam fugit Farinam.*/ *London* : / Printed for *Nicholas Woolfe* at the End of / *Breadstreet*, next to the Red Lion in / *Cheap-side.* 1676, / p. 86.

"*Pros.* Advance the frizled frouzes of thine Eyes, and glout on yon fair thing.

Mir. O dear fweet Father, is that a ho ho ho a Horfe-man, Hufband?

Pros. It is my Girle, and a yerker too; . . .

Mir. 'Tis a moſt crumptious thing; i' vads if you'l let me have it, I'll make no more dirt Pies, nor eat the Chalk you score with." . . . (p. 44) [and so on, the vulgar beast *!—F. J. F.]

> The dull Burlesque appear'd with impudence,
> And pleased by Novelty in Spite of Sence,
> All, except trivial points, grew out of date;
> *Parnassus* spoke the Cant of *Bellinsgate;*
> Boundless and Mad, disorder'd Rhyme was seen:
> Disguis'd *Apollo* changed to *Harlequin.*
> This Plague, which first in Country Towns began,
> Cities and Kingdoms quickly over-ran;
> The dullest Scriblers some Admirers found,
> And the *Mock Tempest* was a while renown'd:
> But this low stuff the Town at last despis'd,
> And scorned the Folly that they once had pris'd;
> Distinguish'd Dull, from Natural and Plain,
> And left the Villages to Fleckno's Reign.
>> The / Art / of / Poetry, Written in *French* by The *Sieur de Boileau,* / Made English./ *London,* / Printed for R. *Bentley*, and *S. Magnes*, in *Russel-Street* in *Covent-Garden*, 1683,† p. 5-6. Canto I, ll. 81—94. The Works of John Dryden, ed. Sir Walter Scott. Vol. xv. p. 233. (The Art of Poetry.)—P. A. L.

---

* He was a Milliner in the New Exchange before he set up for a Poet (MS. note by Oldys in C. 28-9, 1). He has written three Plays: "Two of which were purposely design'd in a Burlesque Stile: but are intermixed with so much Scurrility, that instead of Diverting, they offend the modest Mind. And I have heard that when one of his Plays, *viz. The Mock Tempest*, was acted in *Dublin*, Several Ladies, and Persons of the best Quality left the House: such Ribaldry pleasing none but the Rabble " (Langbaine, *Ibid.*).

† Republished as The / Art / of / Poetry, / Written in *French* by / The Sieur *de Boileau.*/ In Four Canto's./ Made *English*, / By Sir *William Soames.*/ Since Revis'd by John Dryden, Esq.; / *London:* / Printed and Sold by *H. Hills*, in *Black-fryars* near / the Water-side. 1710, / (Price three Pence) / in which edition this passage occurs (p. 5-6) word for word except that line 91 has "at least" instead of "at last."

W. WYCHERLEY, 1675.

Next you Fallſtaffs *of fifty, who beſet*
Your Buckram Maidenheads, which your friends get ;
And whilſt to them, you of Atchievements boaſt,
They ſhare the booty, and laugh at your coſt.

    Epilogve spoken by Mr. *Hart*, to 'The / Country-Wife, / A / Comedy, / Acted at the / *Theatre Royal.*/ Written by Mr. Wycherley / . . . *London*, / Printed for *Thomas Dring*, at the *Harrow*, at the / Corner of *Chancery-Lane* in *Fleet-ſtreet*. 1675.'/ 4°.

[B. N. and F. J. F.]

SIR FRANCIS FANE, junior, 1675.

Players turn Puppets now at your defire,
In their Mouth's Nonfence, in their Tails a Wire,
They fly through Clouds of Clouts, and fhowers of Fire.
A kind of loofing Loadum *is their Game,*
Where the worft Writer has the greateft Fame.
To get vile Plays like theirs, fhall be our care;
But of fuch awkard Actors we defpair.
Falfe taught at firft ————
Like Bowls ill byaff'd, ftill the more they run,
They're further off, then when they firft begun.
In Comedy their unweigh'd Action mark,
There's one is fuch a dear familiar fpark,
He yawns, as if he were but half awake;
And fribbling for free fpeaking, does miftake.
Falfe accent and neglectful Action too
They have both fo nigh good, yet neither true,
That both together, like an Ape's mock face
By near refembling Man, do Man difgrace.
Through pac'd ill Actors, may perhaps be cur'd,
Half Players like half Wits, can't be endur'd.
Yet thefe are they, who durft expofe the Age
Of the great Wonder *of our Englifh Stage.*
Whom Nature feem'd to form for your delight,
And bid him fpeak, as fhe bid Shakefpeare *write.*
Thofe Blades indeed are Cripples in their Art
Mimmick his Foot, but not his fpeaking part.

Let them the Traytor *or* Volpone *try,*
Could they ————
Rage like Cethegus, *or like* Caffius *die,*
They ne'er had fent to Paris *for fuch Fancies,*
As Monfter's heads, and Merry Andrew's *Dances.*[1]

> Love in the Dark,/ or | The Man of Bus'ness. | A Comedy :/ Acted at the Theatre Royal / By His Majesties Servants,/ Written By | Sir *Francis Fane, Junior;* Knight of the *Bath.*/ Naturam expellas furcâ, licet, usque recurret. Hor./ In the Savoy./ Printed by *T. N.* for *Henry Herringman,* and are to be sold / at the Anchor in the Lower Walk of / the *New Exchange.* 1675 / 4°. Epilogue, as it was spoken by Mr. *Haines,* p. 95-6.

F. J. F.

---

[1] Cp. Mrs. Mary Pix's Prologue to her *Double Distress,* 1701 :—

Nor Wit nor Nature now can plense alone,
When French *Jack-pudding* so delight the Town :
Instruction on the Stage is thrown away,
And *Jegg* does more then charming *Dryden* say :
Our ancestors without Ragou's or Dance,
Fed on plain Beef, and bravely conquer'd *France :*
And *Ben* and *Shakespear* lasting Laurels made
With Wit alone, and scorn'd their wretched Aid :

Nicholas Rowe has a like complaint in the Epilogue to his *Ambitious Stepmother,* 1701 :—

Show but a mimick Ape, or *French* Buffoon,
You to the other House in shoals are gone,
And leave us here to Tune our Crowds alone.
Must *Shakespear, Fletcher,* and laborious *Ben,*
Be left for *Scaramouch* and *Harlequin ?*
Allow you are unconstant, yet 'tis strange,
For sense is still the same, and ne'er can change ;

MATTHEW LOCK, 1675.

The / *Englifh Opera;* / or / The Vocal Mufick / in / Pfyche, / With the / Inftrumental / Therein Intermix'd. / To which is Adjoyned / The Inftrumental Mufick / in the / Tempeft. / By / Matthew Lock, Compofer in Ordinary / to His Majefty, and Organift to the Queen. / Licenfed 1675. ROGER L'ESTRANGE. / London, / Printed by *T. Ratcliff,* and *N. Thompfon* for the / Author, and are to be Sold by *John Carr* at his Shop at / the *Middle Temple Gate* in *Fleet-Street.* MDCLXXV. /

(A 4.) *The Inftrumental Mufick before and between the Acts, and the Entries in the Acts of* Pfyche *are omitted by the confent of their Author,* Seignior Gio. Baptifta Draght. *The Tunes of the Entries and Dances in the* Tempeft *(the Dancers being chang'd) are omitted for the fame reafon.*

[p. 62.] The *Inftrumental Mufick ufed in the* Tempeft.

[*Introduction, p.* 62. *Second Galliard, p.* 63. *Gavot, p.* 64. *The Second Musick, p.* 65. *Lilk* . . *The end of the Second Musick, p.* 67.]

[p. 68.] *Curtain Tune in the* Tempeft.

[*The First Act Tune, p.* 71. *The Second Act Tune. The Third Act Tune, p.* 72. *The Fourth Act Tune, p.* 73. *The Conclusion, p.* 71.]

Lock's Music to *Macbeth* was not publisht till 1770 by Dr. Boyce, tho the play was acted with the Music in 1672. See the articles on *Lock* by Mr. W. H. Husk and on *Macbeth Music* by Mr. Wm. Chappell [1] in Grove's *Dict. of M. II.* 157, 183.—F. J. F.

---

[1] Music for witches was not well suited for private use, and the Macbeth music remained in manuscript until after his death in [Aug]. 1677 (art. *Macbeth Music*, p. 183).

R. BENTLEY, 1675.
The Bookseller to the Reader.

This Play was left in Mr. Dryden's hands many years since: The Author of it was unknown to him, and return'd not to claim it; 'Tis therefore to be presum'd that he is dead. After Twelve years expectation, Mr. Dryden gave it to the Players, having upon perusal of it, found that it deserv'd a better Fate than to be buried in obscurity [1]: I have heard him say, that finding a Scene wanting, he supply'd it [2]; and many have affirm'd, that the stile of it [3] is proper to the Subject, which is that the French call Basse Comedy. The turns of it are natural, and the resemblance of one man to another, has not only been the foundation of this, but of many other Plays. Plautus his Amphitrion, was the Original of all, and Shakespear and Moliere have copied him with success. Nevertheless, if this Play in it self should be a trifle, which you have no reason to suspect, because that incomparable Person would not from his Ingenious labours lose so much time as to write a whole Scene in it, which in it self sufficiently makes you amends, for Poetry being like Painting, where, if a great Master have but touch'd upon an ordinary Piece, he makes it of Value to all understanding Men; as I doubt not but this will be by his Additions: As it is, I am resolv'd to detain you no longer from it, but subscribe.my self,

Your very Humble Servant,

R. BENTLEY.

The / Mistaken Husband. / A / Comedie, / as it is Acted by / His Majesties Servants / At the / Theatre-Royall. / By a Person of Quality. —Hæc placuit semel.—[*Hor.*] / London, / Printed for *J. Magnes* and *R. Bentley* / in *Russel-street* in *Coven*[4]*-Garden* near / the *Piazza's*, Anno Domini, MDCLXXV./

Quoted by Mr. Algernon C. Swinburne in "A Relic of Dryden" in the *Gentleman's Magazine*, Oct. 1880, p. 417.—F. J. F.

[1] *Obscurity*, orig.—F.   [2] Act IV. sc. v.—A. C. P.
[3] Of the play, that is, in general; not by any means of the additional scene.—A. C. P.   [4] So.—F.

ANON., about 1675.

My *Nelde* (quoth fhe) fince I have thee here,
I will be a Port for to pleafe my Dear; [*read* Park.]
And in the foft Circuit of my Pale
feed either upon the high Hill or Dale;
Graze on my foft Lypis, if thofe Hills be dry
stray [lower] down where Fountains lye :

> Ballad of *The New Married Couple; Or, A Friendly Debate between the Country Farmer and his Buxome Wife. Roxburghe Ballads*, vol. iv. p. 17. (Ballad Society, 1881.) Douce Collection, ii. 165, verso.

These lines, all but the first, are l 230-4 of *Venus and Adonis*, slightly altered for the sake of the metre and rhyme. Hence the change of the evident misprint 'Port' into 'Park,' and the insertion of [lower] in the last line, instead of the previous insertion [further]. 'Dear' also should be 'Deer,' with the double meaning.

The words 'circuit' and 'Pale' (l. 3) show that 'Port' must have been 'Park,' and 'Dear' 'Deer.'—B. N.

RICHARD HEAD, 1675.

[1] Inculcate frequently the Proverb, and comment upon it, *That one pair of legs is worth two pair of hands;* That to fly is better than to die, commending *Falſtaff* in the Play, deriding Sir *Henry Blunt* that was ſlain; there lies grinning Honour, &c. In ſhort, let ſafety and ſecurity be above all things applauded. p. 75.

[2] Would it not be ridiculous * * to talk of nothing for an hour together to a *Quaker,* but what rare ſport there was the other day at the *Bear-Garden,* or, to tell him what excellent Scenes there are in *Macbeth,* and the late rectified inimitable *Tempeſt?* p. 147.

> Proteus Redivivus: / or the / Art of *Wheedling,* / or / *Insinuation, obtain'd by General Conversation,* / and / *Extracted from the several Humours,* / *Inclinations, and Passions of both Sexes,* / *reflecting their several Ages, and* suit- / *ing each* Profession *or* Occupation. / *Collected and Methodized by the Author of the First Part of the* English Rogue . . . *London, Printed by* W. D. *and are to be sold at the / Sign of the Ship in St.* Mary Axe, *and by / most Bookſellers,* 1675.

The version of the *Tempest* was Dryden's and Davenant's; the *Macbeth* was probably that now called Davenant's, though I incline to think wrongly.
B. N.

ANON. 1676.

And above all the rest, the poet, with a ring of admirers about him of the chiefest wits of the town, was tearing his throat with telling them he had seen *Shakespear, B. Johnson, Fletcher, Corneille,* had drunk many a quart with Saint *Amant, Davenant, Shirley,* and *Beys;* and lost good friends by the death of *Rotrou, Denham,* and *Cowly.*

> *Scarron's Comical Romance: or a facetious History of a Company of Strowling Stage-players interwoven with divers choice novels, rare Adventures, and amorous Intrigues, written originally in French, by the famous and witty poet Scarron, and now turn'd into English.* London: 1676, fol. chap. viii. p. 17.

The translator, who has added to his original many allusions to London, to "the famous Mr. Hobbes," etc., inserts the passage above. In Scarron's text, of course, only Frenchmen, such as Corneille, Rotrou, etc., are named.—J. J. JUSSERAND.

253

WILLIAM CAVENDISH, DUKE OF NEWCASTLE, 1676-7.

Codſh [*ead*]. Good Sir, try ſome Engliſh Poets, as *Shakeſpear*. *Doct*[*or*]. You had as good give him preſerv'd Apricocks, he has too much Wit for him, and then *Fletcher* and *Beaumont* have ſo much of the Spaniſh Perfume of Romances and Novels....

The laſt Remedy, like Pigeons to the ſoles of the feet, muſt be to apply my dear Friend Mr. *Johnſon's* Works, but they muſt be apply'd to his head.

Codſh. Oh, have a care, Doctor, he hates *Ben. Johnſon*, he has an Antipathy to him.

Cramb[o]. Oh, I hate *Johnſon*, oh oh, dull dull, oh oh no Wit *Doct*. 'Tis you are dull .... dull! he was the Honour of his Nation, and the Poet of Poets ....

> *The | Triumphant Widow, | or the | Medley of Humours. | A | Comedy, | Acted by His | Royal Highnes's | Servants. | Written by | His Grace the Duke of* Newcastle. / London, / Printed by J. M. *for* H. Herringman, *at the Sign of | the* Blew Anchor *in the Lower-Walk of the |* New-Exchange, 1677[1] / *p.* 60, 61.
>
> [F. J. F.]

---

[1] 'Licensed Nov. 27. 1676.' MS. note on title-page.

OCTAVIAN PULLEYN, 1677.

I believe Puckle and ye other witches in Mackbeth haue had a meeting here in thunder lightning and Raine.

> Letter from Octavian Pulleyn, dated 'Siena' 30 June 1677, to Sir Thos. Isham. Among the Isham Correspondence. See p. 184, above.
>
> WALTER RYE.

THO. SHADWELL, 1678.

Prologue to Timon.

* * * * *

In the Art of Judging you as wife are grown,
As in their choice fome Ladies of the Town.
Your neat fhap't Barbary Wits you will defpife,
And none but lufty Sinewy *Writers prize.*
Old Englifh Shakefpear-ftomachs *you have ftill,*
And judge as our Fore-fathers writ with Skill.
You Coin the Wit, the Witlings of the Town
Retailers are, that fpread it up and down ; [Sign. A. 4.]

Epilogue. (sign. M4.)

I F *there were hopes that ancient folid Wit*
Might pleafe within our new fantaftick Pit ;
This Play might then fupport the Criticks fhock,
The Scien *grafted upon* Shakefpears *Stock ;*
For join'd with his our Poet's part might thrive,
Kept by the vertue of his Sap alive. . . .

* * * * *

Though Sparks to imitate the French think fit
In want of Learning, Affectation, Wit,
And which is moft, in Cloaths wee'l ne'er fubmit.
Their Ships or Plays o're ours fhall ne're advance,
For our Third Rates fhall match the Firft of France,

*With Englifh Judges this may bear the Teft,
Who will for Shakefpear's part forgive the reft.*

> The | Hiftory | of | Timon of Athens, | the | Man-Hater. | As
> it is Acted at the | Duke's Theatre. | Made into a | Play. |
> By Tho. Shadwell. | Licensed, Feb. 18, 16¾. R. L'Eftrange. |
> London, | Printed by J. M. for Henry Herringman, at the
> Blue Anchor, | in the Lower Walk of the New-Exchange,
> 1678. | 4to. (The later edition has for 'at the *Blue
> Anchor*,' "*and are to be sold | by* Richard Bentley *at the
> Post-House in* Russel-street | *Covent-Garden*, 1688./")

Had this edition been consulted before, the extracts above would no doubt have come on p. 365 of the *Centurie*.—F. J. F.

THOMAS OTWAY, 1678.

Go bid the Coachman haften, and get all things ready; I am uneafy till I am gone. 'Tis time we were fet out.

> *The Wolves have prey'd, and look the gentle Day,
> Before the Wheels of* Phœbus, *all about
> Dapples the droufy Eaft with fpots of gray.*
>
> Friendfhip in Fafhion, Act V. sc. i. Works, ed. 1768,
> vol. ii. p. 101.

[The quotation is from *Much Ado*, V. iii. 25-27.—H. A. EVANS.]

Why, you fweet perfum'd Jeffamine knaves! you Rogues in Buckram! were there a Dozen of you, I'd beat you out of your artificial Sweetnefs into your own natural Ranknefs.—*Ibid.* p. 111.

[Another Falstaff reminiscence, 1 *Hen. IV.*, II. iv. 213.—H. A. E.]

JOHN OLDHAM, 1678.

Words new and forein may be beſt brought in,
If borrow'd from a Language near akin :
Why ſhould the peeviſh Criticks now forbid
To *Lee* and *Dryden*, what was not deny'd
To *Shakeſpear*, *Ben*, and *Fletcher*, heretofore,
For which they Praiſe, and commendation bore.

> " Upon the Works of Ben Johnson. Written in 1678. Ode," in ' Poems, / and / Translations, / By / *John Oldham.*/ *London* : / Printed for *Joſ:* Hindmarsh, Bookseller to his Royal / Highness, at the Black Bull in Cornhil, 1683.' pp. 69 to 89.[1]

The triumvirate of the last line are also mentioned by others as seemingly *the* three poets of the preceding age. But it is right to remark that elsewhere Oldham praises Ben supremely, especially in a very long Ode to him, addressing him as "Great Thou ! whom 'tis a Crime almost to dare to praiſe," and—

Hail mighty Founder of our Stage ! (p. 69)

and—

Never till thee the Theater possest
A Prince with equal Pow'r, and Greatness blest. (p. 71)

B. N.

[1] The Ode is also printed in "Poems / and / Translations./ By / *John* Oldham./ *London* : / Printed for *Joseph Hindmarsh*, at the *Golden Ball*, / in Cornhil. MDCLXXXIV./" 8vo, p. 6. Horace his Art of Poetry Imitated in English ; and in " Some New / Pieces / Never before Publish'd./ By the Author of the / *Satyrs upon the Jesuites*, * * * * London : Printed by *M. C.* for *Jo. Hindmarsh*, Bookseller to his Royal Highness, at the Black Bull in *Cornhil*, 1684, 8°. p. 6;"—a different and probably earlier edition of the *Poems & Transl.* of 1684 ;—and in ' The Works of Mr. John Oldham, together with his Remains,' 8vo. 1698, p. 6.

ELIAS TRAVERS, 1678-83.

This Nonconformist Minister was for many years chaplain and tutor in the family of Sir Thomas Barnardiston of Ketton Hall, Suffolk. He kept a Latin diary of how he spent his time, and this was described in an article in the *British Quarterly Review* for January 1872, entitled "An English Interior in the Seventeenth Century." The writer says that in the ordinary life of the chaplain, came 'after dinner, conversation and a reading in Shakspeare till about three.' Also that Travers's reading was "so strangely alternated that from a long reading of the Psalms he falls back on Shakspeare's comedies ; nay, once even confesses, 'prius Shak[s]peare quam sacras literas legi.' (*B. Q. Rev.*, lv. 63.)

" But Shakspeare gives our chaplain his highest intellectual treat, and hours are spent over his historical plays and comedies, including those which he describes ' ominosorum titulorum,' Multum laboris circa nihil [Much Ado about Nothing] et 'Amoris labor perditus' [Loves Labours lost]. The course of reading was not a little grotesque. Three or four Psalms are immediately succeeded by *King Lear*, that again by the meditations of M. de Brieux, '*On the Vanity of Human Wishes.*'" (*B. Q. Rev.*, lv. 64.)

Noted by ' Bibliothecary' in 6 *N. & Q.*, i. 453, col. 1, June 5, 1880.

—F. J. F.

THO. SHADWELL, 1679.

Nor are your Writings unequal to any Man's of this Age, (not to ſpeak of abundance of excellent Copies of Verſes) you have in the Mulberry-Garden[1] *ſhown the true Wit, Humour, and Satyr of a Comedy ; and in* Antony *and* Cleopatra,[2] *the true Spirit of a Tragedy, the only one (except two of* Johnſon's *and one of* Shakeſpear's) *wherein* Romans *are made to ſpeak and do like* Romans.[3]

> A / *True Widow,* / A / *Comedy,* / *Acted by the* Duke's Servants./ *Written by* / *Tho. Shadwell.*/ Odi profanum Vulgus & arceo./ London, / *Printed for* Benjamin Tooke, *at the* Ship *in St. Paul's Church-*/*yard* 1679. 4to / *The Epistle Dedicatory to Sir Charles Sedley, signd* '*Tho. Shadwell, London, Feb.* 16, 167⅞.'
> (*Works,* 1720, *ii.* 110.)

---

[1] The / Mulberry-Garden, / A / Comedy./ As it is Acted by / His Majestie's Servants / at the / Theatre-Royal./ Written by the Honourable/ Sir *Charles Sidley.*/ London, / Printed for *H. Herringman*, at the Sign of the *Blew Anchor* in the / Lower Walk of the *New Exchange*, 1668./ 4to., 76 pages.

[2] Antony / and / Cleopatra : / A Tragedy./ As it is Acted at the Dukes / Theatre./ Written by the Honourable / Sir Charles Sedley, Baronet./ Licensed *Apr.* 24, 1677. Roger L'Estrange./ London, / Printed for *Richard Tonson* at his Shop under *Grayes Inne-Gate* next Grayes-Inne-lane. MDCLXXVII. A Play after Shakspere : a very long way.

[3] Nicholas Rowe, in the Prologue to his *Ambitious Stepmother*, 1701, notes how little of classic antiquity Shakspere has dealt with :

> Majestick Tragedy shou'd once agen
> In purple pomp adorn the swelling Scene
> Her search shou'd ransack all the Ancient's store,
> The fortunes of their loves and arms explore,
> Such as might grieve you, but shou'd please you more.
> What *Shakespear* durst not, this bold Age shou'd do,
> And famous *Greek* and *Latian* Beauties show.

THOS. SHADWELL, 1679.

On Dryden's *Antony and Cleopatra*, just after his death, I find these lines written :—
"Ah ! see the Place where thy *Ventidius* stood,
Bending with Years, and most profusely good,
Unmov'd by Fate, and of unshaken Truth,
His Counsels those of Age, His Courage that of Youth ;
Where mourning *Anthony* contesting strove
Which to relinquish, *Honour*, or his *Love*,
As ev'ry Hearer's Sorrows took his Part,
And truly wept for him who griev'd with Art."

The / Patentee : / or, / Some Reflections in Verse on Mr. *R- - -'s* forgetting the Design of his / Majesty's *Bear-Garden* at *Hockly in the Hole*, and Letting out the Theatre in *Dorset-Garden* to the same Use, on the Day when / Mr. *Dryden's* Obsequies were perform'd ; And both Play-houses / forbore Acting in Honour to his Memory./ A folio Broadside. Printed in the year, 1700.

F. J. F.

ANON., 1679.

3

But lo! amidſt this furious Train
Of matchleſs Wights, appeared one
With Courage and with Proweſs main
As ever yet was ſhown.

4.

Of Viſage dark as day of Doom,
Moſt pittifully rent and tore,
Shews him a Warrior in the Womb
That Wounds receiv'd e're he was bore,

5.

His Breaſt all Steel, of Temper tuff,
And *Falſta's* Belly deckt with Charms,
VVith *Brandon's* Head, all clad in Buff,
Secure from Scottiſh Arms.

> A New Scotch Ballad : / call'd / Bothwel-Bridge : / or, / Hamilton's Hero./ To the Tune of *Fortune my Foe.*/ London, Printed for T. B. 1679, (Brit. Mus. 839. m. 22. art. 4.)
>
> PONSONBY A. LYONS.

T. DURFEY, 1680.

The following can hardly allude, I suppose, to Shakspere's 'Sir Pandarus of Troy' (*My. Wives*, I. iii) and drunken 'Sir Toby' (*Much Ado*).

Nokes.   Ye lye.
        And you're a Pimp, a Pandarus of *Troy*
        A Gripe, a Fumble.
Lee.   Nay, and you 'gin to quarrel,
        Gad ye're a Swaſh, a Toby in a Barrel.
        Would you were here.
             Prologue to *The Virtuous Wife.* A 2, back.

JOHN CROWNE, 1680.

Prologue.

For by his feeble Skill 'tis built alone,
The Divine *Shakeſpear* did not lay one Stone.

[This—placed after eight other lines from the prologue to *Henry the Sixth, the First Part*, at p. 389 of the *Centurie of Prayse*, and wrongly dated—is from the Prologue to *Henry the Sixth, the Second Part*, which, under the title *The Misery of Civil War*[1], was published before the First Part, from the Prologue to which, the other lines are taken. Langbaine, p. 96, is right when he says, "Part of this play likewise is borrowed from *Shakespear*." Cade's part is somewhat amplified and sometimes slightly altered; further I have not looked.

On the Prologue to the First Part, Langbaine also says that Crowne has borrowed; "tho' Mr. Crown, with a little too much assurance, affirms that he [Sh.] has no Title to the Fortieth part of it." 1691, p. 96. Whence [from Epis. Dedic. to Part i. See the extract, p. 306] Langbaine got this assertion I do not know; it is not so said in the printed copy.—B. N.]

Oldys's MS. note (C. 288. 1. p. 96) runs: "Oldmixon, in one of his histories, sais, Crown the poet told him that K. Cha. 2ᵈ gave him two Spanish Plays, and bad him joyn them together to form one, which he did, & showd his Majesty the Plan for his Comedy of Sir Courtly Nice," &c. (*a long MS. note*).

---

[1] The / Misery / of Civil - War. / A / Tragedy, / As it Acted at the / Duke's Theatre by His Royal Highnesses Servants, / written by Mr Crown / London, / Printed for *R. Bentley* and *M. Magnes* in *Russel-/Street* in *Covent-Garden*, 1680, / 4°.

Henry the Sixth, / The Second Part. / or the / Misery / of / Civil War, / As it was Acted at the / Dukes Theatre./ written by Mr Crown./ London, / Printed for *R. Bentley*, and *M. Magnes*, in *Russel-Street*, in Covent Garden, 1681./ 4°.

Henry the Sixth, The First Part. With the / Murder / of Humphrey / Duke of Glocester./ As it was Acted at the / Dukes Theatre / Written by Mr. Crown./ London, / Printed for *R. Bentley*, and *M. Magnes*, in *Russel-Street*, / in Covent-Garden. 1681 / 4ᵗᵒ.

THOMAS DURFEY, 1680.

Sir Lubb. Madam, for ever I'll inclofe you here, with the Circuit of this Ivory pale—What's next Sirra?

Boy. You'll be the Park—

Sir Lub. I'll be the Park, and you fhall be the Deer:
Feed where you will, on Mountain, or in Dale,
Graze on my lips, and when thofe Hills are dry—
When thofe—Hills are dry—hum—are dry,
What's next you Dog?

Boy. Stray tarther where the pleafant Fountains lie—

Sir Lubb. Stray further where the pleafant Fountains lie.

L[ady] Beard[ly]. Very well . . . . I vow there's a great deal of pleafure in being Courted . .

> The / Virtuous / Wife; / Or, / Good Luck at last. / A / Comedy. / As it is Acted at the / Dukes Theater, / By his *Royal Highness* / His Servants. / Written / by *Thomas Dvrfey*, Gent. / In the *Savoy*: / Printed by *T. N.* for *R. Bentley*, and *M. Magnes*, in *Russel- / Street*, near the Piazza, / at the Post-house. / *Anno Dom.* 1680. /

The first 3 lines were sent in by Mr. Hll.-P. as from *Good Luck at Last*. The passage is from *Venus and Adonis*, l. 230-2:

> 'Fondling', she saith, 'since I have hemm'd thee here
> Within the circuit of this ivory pale,   230
> I'll be a park, and thou shalt be my deer;
> Feed where thou wilt, on mountain or in dale;
>   Graze on my lips, and if those hills be dry,
>   Stray lower, where the pleasant fountains lie.'

—F. J. F.

NATHANIEL LEE, 1680—1685.

He [Sir Philip Sidney] was at once a *Cæsar* and a *Virgil*, the leading Souldier, and the foremost Poet, all after this must fail: I have paid just Veneration to his Name, and methinks the Spirit of *Shakefpear* push'd the commendation.

Cæsar Borgia, 1680, 4to. *Dedication to Philip Earl of Pembroke and Montgomery.* Sign. A 2 back.

There are fome Subjects that require but half the strength of a great Poet, but when *Greece* or Old *Rome* come in play, the Nature Wit and Vigour of foremoft *Shakefpear*, the Judgment and Force of *Johnfon*, with all his borrowed Maftery from the Ancients, will fcarce fuffice for fo terrible a Grapple. * * * but Johnfon's *Catiline* met no better fate * * * Nay *Shakefpear's* Brutus with much adoe beat himfelf into the heads of a blockifh Age, fo knotty were the Oaks he had to deal with.

Lucius Junius Brutus, 1681, 4to. *Dedication to Charles, Earl of Dorset and Middlesex.*

I have indeavour'd in this Tragedy to mix *Shakefpear* with *Fletcher*; the thoughts of the former, for Majefty and true *Roman* Greatnefs, and the foftnefs and paffionate expreffions of the latter, which makes up half the Beauties, are never to be match'd: How then have I endeavour'd to be like 'em? O faint Refemblance! (Sign. A 2 back.)

For *I* have many times found fault with an Expreffion, as *I* pretended was in a Play of my own, and had it dam'd by no indifferent Criticks, tho the immortal *Shakefpear* will not blufh to own it. (Sign. A 3.)

Mithridates King of Pontus, 4to, 1685. *London. Licensed, March* 28, 1678. *Epistle Dedicatory to the same.*

[It must be remembered that Lee is here addressing a Sidney in the adulatory strains of the day.—B. N.]

JOHN CROWNE, 1681.

Now fome fine things perhaps you think to hear,
But he who did reform this Play does fwear
He'l not beftow rich Trappings on a Horfe,
That will want Breath to run a Three-days Courfe;
And be turn'd off by Gallants of the Town,
For Citizens and their Wives to Hackney on.
Not that a Barb that's come of *Shackfpear's* breed,
Can e'er want Mettle, Courage, Shape, or Speed;
But you have Poetry fo long rides Poft,
That your delight in Riding now is loft.
Epilogue to Henry the Sixth, Part I., 4to. (See the full title on p. 3 above.)

[The age was so desirous of novelty that many plays, even if successful, did not run more than the third or author's day. Twelve representations was an acme of success seldom attained.[1] This may in part account for the remodelling of Shakespeare's plays.—B. N.]

---

[1] See Downes's numbers below, p. 349, 354.—F.

(*The Epiftle Dedicatory*)—In fhort, Senfe is fo great a ftranger to the moft, that it is never welcome to Company for its own fake, but the fake of the Introducer. For this reafon I ufe your Name [Sir Charles Sidley] to guide that fhare of it is in this Play through the Prefs, as I did *Shakefpear's* to fupport it on the Stage, I called it in the Prologue *Shakefpear's* Play, though he has no

Title to the 40th part of it. The Text I took out of his Second Part of *Henry* the Sixth, but as moſt Texts are ſerv'd, I left it as ſoon as I could. For though *Shakeſpear* be generally very delightful, he is not ſo always. His Volumn is all up-hill and down; *Paradiſe* was never more pleaſant than ſome parts of it, nor *Ireland* and *Greenland* colder, and more uninhabitable than others. And I have undertaken to cultivate one of the moſt barren Places in it. The Trees are all Shrubs, and the Men Pigmies, nothing has any Spirit or ſhape; the Cardinal is duller then ever Prieſt was. And he has hudled up the Murder of Duke *Humphry*, as if he had been guilty of himſelf, and was afraid to ſhew how it was done: But I haue been more bold, to the great diſpleaſure of ſome, who are it ſeems aſhamed of their own myſteries,— (Sign. A 3 back.)

PONSONBY A. LYONS.

NAHUM TATE, 1681.

[The notice in *The Centurie*, p. 380, note, of Tate's recast of Shakspere's *Rich. II.* as *The Sicilian Usurper*, 1681, is insufficient. The 2 short extracts are therefore reprinted here, with additions.]

I fell upon the new-modelling of this Tragedy (as I had juft before done on the Hiftory of King Lear) *charm'd with the many Beauties I difcover'd in it, which I knew wou'd become the Stage; with as little defign of Satyr on prefent Tranfactions, as Shake-fpear himfelf that wrote this Story before this Age began.*

[From the Epistle Dedicatory "To my esteemed Friend George Raynsford, Esq;" (Sign. A.) On A, back, is]

Our Shakefpear *in this Tragedy, bated none of his charaćters an Ace of the Chronicle; he took care to fhew 'em no worfe Men than They were, but reprefents them never a jot better. His* Duke of York *after all his buify pretended Loyalty, is found falfe to his Kinfman and Sovereign, and joyn'd with the* Confpirators. *His King* Richard *Himfelf is painted in the worft colours of Hiftory. Diffolute, Unadvifeable, devoted to Eafe and Luxury. You find old* Gaunt *fpeaking of him in this Language—*

───────────Then there are found
Lafcivious Meeters to whofe Venom found
The open Ear of Youth do's always Liften.
Where doth the World thruft forth a Vanity,
(So it be New, there's no refpect how Vile)
That is not quickly buzz'd into his Ear?
That all too late comes Counfel to be heard.
[Rich. II. ii. 1.]

without the leaft palliating of his Mifcarriages, which I have done in the new Draft with fuch words as Thefe.

Your Sycophants bred from your Childhood with you,
Have fuch Advantage had to work upon you,
That fcarce your Failings can be called your Faults.
[II. i., p. 14.]

NAHUM TATE, 1681.

His Reply in Shakefpear *to the Hunt honeft Advifer runs thus—*

And thou a Lunatick Lean-witted-fool, &c.
Now by my Seat's right Royal Majefty,
Wer't Thou not Brother to great *Edward's* Son,
The Tongue that runs thus roundly in thy Head
Shou'd run thy Head from thy unreverent Shoulders.

On the contrary (though I have made him exprefs fome Refentment) yet he is neither enrag'd with the good Advice, nor deaf to it. He anfwers Thus—

Gentle Unkle;
Excufe the Sally's of my Youthfull Blood, &c. [p. 13.]
(Sign. A. back. On A 2 is)

Nor cou'd it fuffice me to make him fpeak like a King (who as Mr. Rhymer *fays in his* Tragedies of the laft Age confidered, are always in Poëtry prefum'd Heroes) but to Act fo too, viz. with Refolution and Juftice. Refolute enough our Shakefpear (copying the Hiftory) has made him, for concerning his feizing old Gaunt's Revennues, he tells the wife Difwaders,

Say what ye will, we feize into our Hands
His Plate, his Goods, his Money, and his Lands.

But where was the Juftice of this Action? This Paffage I confefs was fo material a part of the Chronicle (being the very Bafis of Bullingbrook's Ufurpation) that I cou'd not in this new Model fo far tranfgrefs Truth as to make no mention of it; yet for the honour of my Heroe I fuppofe the forefaid Revennues to be Borrow'd onely for the prefent Exigence, not Extorted.

Be Heav'n our Judge, we mean him fair,[1]
And fhortly will with Intereft reftore
The Loan our fuddain Streights make neceffary.

[1] Tate here misquotes himself.
King. Be Heav'n our Judge, we mean him nothing foul.
[Act II. Sc. i., p. 15.]
It is not surprising then that he should misquote Shakspere.

My Defign was to engage the pitty of the Audience for him in his Diftreſſes, which I cou'd never have compafs'd had I not before fhewn him a Wife, Active and Juft Prince. Detracting Language (if any where) had been excufable in the Mouths of the Con- fpirators: part of whofe Dialogue runs thus in Shakefpear:

> *North.* Now afore Heav'n 'tis fhame fuch wrongs are born
> In him a Royal Prince [etc. Act II. Sc. i.]

with much more villifying talk; but I wou'd not allow even Traytors and Confpirators thus to befpatter the Perfon whom I defign'd to place in the Love and Compaffion of the Audience. Ev'n this very Scene (as I have manag'd it) though it fhew the Confederates to be Villains, yet it flings no Afperfion on my Prince. (Sign. A 2 and A 2 back.)

Take ev'n the Richard of Shakefpear and Hiftory, you will find him Diffolute, Carelefs and Unadvifable: perufe my Picture of him and you will fay, as Æneas did of Hector, (though the Figure there was alter'd for the Worfe and there for the Better) Quantum mutatus ab illo!—[Sign. A 2 back.]

Once more, Sir, I beg your Pardon for digreffing, and difmifs you to the following Poem, in which you will find fome Mafter Touches of our Shakefpear, that will Vie with the beft Roman Poets that have fo defervedly your Veneration. (Sign. A 3 back.)

Nahum Tate's alteration of one of the first lines of the play may be useful as an illustration of one of the changes which had taken place in the language since Shakespeare's time. He alters Shakespeare's

"Th' accufer and th' accufed freely fpeak:"
to,
"Th' Accufer and the Accuf'd both freely fpeak."

PONSONBY A. LYONS.

*NAHUM TATE, 1681.

*Now we expect to hear our rare Blades say
Dam' me, I see no Sense in this dull Play ;
Tho' much of it, our older Judges know,
Was famous Sense 'bove Forty Years ago.*

> Epilogue to The / History / of / King Richard / The Second / Acted at the Theatre Royal / Under the Name of the / Sicilian Usurper./ With a Prefatory Epistle in Vindication of the / Author./ Occasion'd by the Prohibition of this / Play on the Stage./ By N. Tate./ Inultus ut Flebo Puer ? Hor./
>
> London, / printed for Richard Tonson, and Jacob Tonson, / at Grays-Inn Gate, and at the Judges-Head / in Chancery-Lane near Fleet-street, 1681./ 4to
>
> [B. N.]

NAHUM TATE, 1681.

*Well—since y'are All for blustring in the Pit,
This Play's Reviver humbly do's admit
Your abs'lute Pow'r to damn his Part of it ;
But still so many Master-Touches shine
Of that vast Hand that first laid this Design,
That in great Shakespear's Right, He's bold to say
If you like nothing you have seen to Day
The Play your Judgment damns, not you the Play.*

> Epilogue, Spoken by Mrs. Barry, p. 68, of 'The / History / of / King / Lear./ Acted at the / Duke's Theatre./ Reviv'd with Alterations./ By N. Tate./ London, / Printed for E. Flesher, and are to be sold by R. Bent-/ ley, and M. Magnes in Russel-street near Covent-Garden, 1681.' 4to

[Had the maker or verifier of the extracts on pages 390·1 of *Centurie* turn'd to the last page of Tate's book, the above lines would have followed *Centurie*, p. 391. (P.S. Furness of course has this passage on p. 477 of his admirable new Variorum *Lear*.)—F. J. F.]

THOMAS OTWAY, 1681, 1685.

1. But your true Jilt is a Creature that can extract Bawdy out of the chafteft fence, as eafily as a Spider can Poifon out of a Rofe: They know true Bawdy, let it be never fo much conceal'd, as perfectly as *Falftaff* did the true Prince by inftinct: They will feparate the true Metal from the Allay let us temper it as well as we can; fome Women are the Touch-ftones of filthinefs.

(*Dedication to The Soldiers Fortune*, 1681. 4to.[1])

Enter Sir Davy.

2. (p. 59). *Sir Da.* Hah! what art thou? approach thou like the rugged *Bank-fide Bear*, the *Eaftcheap-bull*, or Monfter fhewn in Fair, take any fhape but that, and I'll confront thee.

(A parody of *Macbeth*, III. iv. 102.—H. A. EVANS.)

3. (p. 62). *Lady.* Alas, alas, we are ruin'd, fhift for your felf, counterfeit the dead Corps once more, or any thing.

Sir Da. Hah! whatfoe're thou art, thou canft not eat me, fpeak to me, who has done this? thou can'ft not fay I did it.

(After *Macbeth*, III. iv. 50.—H. A. EVANS.)

4. *O Poets, have a care of one another,*
There's hardly one amongft ye true to to'ther:
Like Trincalo's *and* Stephano's *ye Play*
The lewdeft tricks, each other to betray.
Like Foes detract, yet flatt'ring friendlike fmile,
And all is one another to beguile
Of Praife, the Monfter of your Barren Ifle:

(*Epilogue to The Soldiers Fortune*, 1681.)

[1] The / Souldiers Fortune : / A / Comedy./ Acted by their / Royal Highnesses / Servants / At the / Duke's Theatre./ Written by *Thomas Otway.*/ *Quem recitas meus est O Fidentine libellus,* / *Sed male cum recitas incipit esse tuus.*/ London Printed for *R. Bentley* and *M. Magnes*, at the Post-House in / Russel-Street in *Covent-Garden*, 1681./ 4to.

THOMAS OTWAY, 1681, 1685.

5. Mercy's indeed the Attribute of Heav'n,
   For Gods have Pow'r to keep the balance ev'n.
   (*Windsor Castle, a poem*, 1685, p. 3.[1])

[In 1. he is defending his Play against the imputation of that vice; 5. is a reminiscence of *Merchant of Venice*, IV. i. 190.—B. N.]

[1] Windsor Castle, / In / A Monument / To our Late Sovereign / K. Charles II. / Of ever Blessed Memory./ A Poem./ By *Tho.* / *Otway*, / * * * * *London*, Printed for *Charles Brome*, at the *Gun*, / at the West-end of St. *Paul's*, 1685./ 4º.

THO. DURFEY, 1682.[1]

[His version of Shakspere's *Cymbeline* is entitled]
The / Injured Princefs, / or the / 𝕱𝖆𝖙𝖆𝖑 𝖂𝖆𝖌𝖊𝖗 : / As it was Acted at the / Theater-Royal, / By His Majefties Servants./ By *Tho. Durfey*, Gent. / *London* : / Printed for *R. Bentley* and *M. Magnes* in *Ruffel-ftreet* in / *Covent-Garden*, near the *Piazza*. 1682./ 4to.

The Prologue.

O Ld Plays like Miftreffes, long fince enjoy'd,
Long after pleafe, whom they before had cloy'd;
For Fancy chews the Cudd on paft delight,
And cheats it felf to a new Appetite.
But then this fecond Fit comes not fo ftrong,
Like fecond Agues, neither fierce nor long:
What you have known before, grows fooner ftale,
And lefs provokes you, than an untold Tale.
That but refreshes what before you knew,
But this difcovers fomething that is new;
Hence 'tis, that at new Plays you come fo foon,
Like Bride-grooms, hot to go to Bed ere noon!
Or, if you are detain'd fome little fpace,
The ftinking Footman's fent to keep your place.
But, when a Play's reviv'd, you ftay and dine,

---

[1] Durfey doesn't condescend to mention Shakspere in his performance. A later adapter of another play had more modesty. See the extract from John Sheffield, Duke of Buckingham, 1692, p. 334, below.

THO. DURFEY, 1682.

And drink till three, and then come dropping in;
As Hujband after abfence, wait all day,
And decently for Spoufe, till Bed-time flay!

Scene *Luds* Town, alias *London*.

The "Drammatis [Personæ]" are '*Cymbeline*, *King of Britain*. *Vrfaces* (= Pofthumus,) A noble Gentleman married to the Princefs *Eugenia*' (= Imogen). '*Pifanio*, Confident and Friend to *Vrfaces*.' *Cloten*, A Fool, Son to the Queen by a former Hufband. *Jachimo*, A roaring drunken Lord, his Companion; *Silvio*, Another Companion. *Shattillion* [for Shakspere's Iachimo], An opinionated *Frenchman*.

Beaupre, } His Friends.
Don Michael, }

Bellarius, An old Courtier banifh'd by *Cymbeline*.
Palladour [for Shakspere's } Two young Princes, Sons to
　　　　　　　Guiderius], } *Cymbeline*, bred up by *Bel-*
Arviragus, } *larius* in a Cave as his own.

Lucius, General to *Augufius Cæfar*. *Women*. The Queen, *Eugenia* [for Shakspere's Imogen], the Princefs. *Clarina*, Her Confident.

Sophronia, } Women, one to the Queen, the other to the
Aurelia, } Princefs.'

[Tho the Play is much alterd and fhortend from *Shakspere's*, much being new, it follows his main lines; but Shattillion (= Iachimo) is killd by Ursaces (= Pofthumus). As a sample of the Shakspere part revisd by Durfey, take the latter's version of Iachimo in Imogen's bedroom—all its fervour and beauty gone —Act II. Sc. iv. p. 20 : the italics in [ ] mark Durfey's work.]

" *Enter* Shatillion *from the Chefl*; *a Table-book*.

[Shatt. *All's fiill as Death, and hufh'd as Midnight filence:*
Now the Crickets fing, and mortal wearied Senfe

Repairs it felf by reft. Lewd] *Tarquin* thus
Did foftly [*tread and tremble,*] ere he wak'ned
The Chaftity he wounded. [*Oh Soul of Beauty !
Sure none but I cou'd fee thee thus, and leave thee
Thus in this lovely pofture, But no more ;
I've other bufinefs. Chill all my Bloud,
Ye Powers, and make me cold to her Allurements :
This is no loving minute ; Come, to*] my defign :
To note the Chamber : [*Here*] I'le write all down ;
Such and fuch Pictures ; there the Window ; fuch
The adornment of her Bed ; the Arras Figures :
Why fuch, and fuch, and the Contents o' th' Story.
Ay but fome natural Notes about her Body,
Above ten thoufand meaner [*Witneffes.*] { *She ftirs and
Wou'd teftifie to enrich my Inventory.   he ftarts back.*
[*What's there, a Bracelet on her Arm ?* 'Tis *fo,
Now*] fleep thou Ape of Death, lye dull upon her ;
And be her Senfe but as a Monument,
Thus in a Chappel lying. [*Fortune befriend me ;*]
'Tis mine, and this will witnefs outwardly,
As ftrongly as the Confcience does within,
To th' [*torture*] of her Lord : On her left Breaft,
A Mole Cinque, fpotted like the Crimfon drops
In the bottom of a Cowflip : Here's a Voucher
Stronger than ever Law cou'd make ; this fecret
Will force him think I've pick'd the Lock and ftoll'n
The Treafure of her Honour. No, [*now*] I have enough :
To th' [*Chest*] agen.
Swift, fwift, [*ye*] Dragons of the Night ; [*lov'd Phofpher,
Return the welcome day,*] I lodge in fear,
Tho' [*there's*] a heavenly Angel, Hell is here. [*Gets into the
                                                            Cheft.*"

[All the beautiful lamentation over Fidele, after IV. iii. 216 ('Anſwer'd my ſteps too loud') in Shakſpere is doubled up by Durfey into 3½ lines, p. 43.

"*Bellar.* Well, 'tis in vain to mourn, what's paſt recovery: Come Sons, let's lay him in our Tomb.
Arvir. Reſt there ſweet Body of a ſweeter Soul, [*They lay him* Whilſt we lament thy Fate. *in the Grave.*
   Enter Caius Lucius, Captains *and* Souldiers, *with Drum and Colours.*"]

See our friend Harold Littledale's interesting account of the acting of *Tara*, the Marathi version of Shakspere's *Cymbeline*, in Baroda, province of Bombay.—*Macmillan's Mag.*, May, 1880.

F. J. F.

ANONYMOUS, 1682.

He's one whoſe Works, in times to come,
Will be as Honour'd, and become
Deathleſs as *Ben's* or *Cowley's* are,
As *Beaumont*, *Fletcher*, or *Shakeſpear*
One he himſelf is pleaſ'd t'admire.
Nor could theſe Laureats living, be
Better prefer'd, or lov'd than he.

    1682.   *Poeta de Tristibus:* or | *the* | *Poet's Complaint.* A | Poem.| In four *Canto's.*| Ovid. de Trist.| Parve, nec invideo, sine me Liber ibis in Vrbem : | Hei mihi ! quò —— / London, | *Printed for* Henry Faithorne *and* John Kersey, *at the* | Rose *in St.* Pauls' Church-Yard. 1682./ 4º. (Third Canto), p. 21.

"The Authors Epistle" is Dated at *Dover* the Tenth day of January 168¾.

[E. DOWDEN.]

NAHUM TATE, 1682-5.

1. Yet he prefumes we may be fafe to Day,
   Since *Shakefpear* gave Foundation to the Play :
   'Tis Alter'd—and his facred Ghoft appear'd;
   I with you All as eafily were Pleaf'd :
   He only ventures to make Gold from Oar;
   And turn to Money, what lay dead before.

   > 1. *The | Ingratitude | of A | Common-Wealth : | or the Fall of | Caius Martius Coriolanus.| As It Is | Acted | at the | Theatre-Royal.| By N. Tate.| * * * * London, | Printed by T. M. for* Joseph Hindmarsh, *at the Black-Bull | in Cornhill.* 1682, 4to. *Prologue.*

2. Our Trinculo and Trapp'lin were undone,
   When *Lime's* more Farcy Monarchy begun.

   > 2. *Prologue to Cuckolds-Haven, or an Alderman no Conjurer.* 1685, 4to. (See p. 283.)

   [B. N.]

JO. HAINS, 1683.

Go then thou Emblem of their torrid Zeal,
Add flame to flame and their ſtiff tempers Neal,
'Till they grow ductile to the Publick Weale.
And ſince the Godly have eſpouſ'd thy Cauſe,
Don't fill their heads with Libertys and Laws,
Religion, Privilege, and lawleſs Charters,
Mind them of *Falſtaffs* Heir apparent Garters,
And keep their outward Man from *Ketches* Quarters.

   A / Satyr / against / Brandy. / *Written by* Jo. Hains, *as he saith himself.* /
   Printed for *Jos. Hindmarsh* at the *Black-Bull* in *Cornhill*, 1683.
   [A Broadside, 839. m. 22 (art. 19) Brit. Mus.]

F. J. F.

* THOMAS SOUTHERNE, 1684.

Alph[onso]. 'Tis enough you know him.

Rog[ero]. Know him! ah God help thee, and the quantity of thy Brains, by thy impertinent Catechifm.

Alph. Why then old Truepenny the Duke is now moft violently in labour.

Rog. In labour! Alas, I am in pain for thee.

> The | Disappointment | or the | Mother in Fashion.| A ç Play| As it was Acted | at the | Theatre Royal.| Written by | Thomas Sovtherne./ . . . London :/ Printed for Jo. Hindmarsh, Bookseller to his Royal Highness,| at the Black Bull in Cornhil. 1684.| 4to. Act III. sc. i. p. 31.

This is possibly a recollection of Hamlet's 'Truepenny' and 'old mole' (I. v. 150, 162), tho Truepenny is usd in Nashe's *Almond for a Parrat*, 1589 (Collier). Dr. Ingleby refers also to the *Returne from Pernassvs*, London, 1606, Act II. sc. iv. sign. C 3, back. Hazlitt's *Dodsley*, ix. 138 — "What haue we here, old true-penny come to towne, to fetch away the liuing in his old greasie slops? then ile none :"—and to *Wit's Interpreter*, 16.., p. 85, where one Margaretta says, "Thou art still old Truepenny."

But the reference to *Hamlet* in the quotation from Marston's *Malcontent*, 1604, III. iii. (due to Steevens), in the *Centurie*, p. 66, seems clear¹; and Mr. Aldis Wright says (Clarendon Press *Hamlet*, p. 146-7), Congreve probably had Hamlet in his mind "when he makes a son irreverently address his father as 'old True-penny,'" *Love for Love*, iv. 10, A.D. 1695.* See Forby's Vocabulary of East Anglia, p. 357, or Halliwell's Dict. which says: "Generally, ' Old-Truepenny,' as it occurs in Sh. Hamlet," that is, does not occur ; the *old* there belonging to *mole*.—F. J. F.

---

¹ It begins with " *Illo, ho, ho,*" and contains 5 misprints acc. to C. 34, l. 40, printed from C. 39, l.

"Illo, ho, ho, ho, arte there olde true penny?
Where hast thou spent thy selfe this morning? I see flattery in
Thine eies, and damnation in thy soule. Ha thou huge rascall !"

* "Val[entine]. A ha! Old Truepenny, say'st thou so?
Thou hast nick'd it."—Loue for Loue, 1695, p. 58.

HENRY BOLD, bef. 1685. ? bef. 1664, see p. 206 abuv.

On the Death of the late Tyrannical Ufurper,

Oliver Cromwel.

Gone with a Vengeance! had he twenty lives
He needs muft go (they say) the Devil drives.
Nor went he hence away, like Lamb fo mild
Or Falftaff-wife, like any Chrifome-Child
In *Arthur*'s Bofom, he's not hufh, yet dy'd
Juft as he did, at turning of the Tide,
But with it fuch [a] wind, the Sails did fwell,
Charon ne're made a quicker pafs to Hell.
  Now, as there muft be wonder to pretend
Every notorious Birth, or difmal end,
Juft as when Hotfpurs Grannams Cat (of Yore)
Did Kitten, or when *Pokins* loft a Bore,
So when this prodigy of Nature fell,
Her felf feem'd half unhing'd, Tempeft foretell
Direful Events, *Boreas* was out of Breath
Till by his Soul infpir'd at his Death.

> Latine Songs, / With their / English : / and / Poems. /
> By *Henry Bold*, / Formerly of N. Coll. in *Oxon*, after- /
> wards of the Examiners Office in / Chancery. / Collected
> and perfected by / Captain *William Bold*. / (*motto from*
> Hor. 2, L. 2. Ep. 11) *London*, Printed for *John Eglesfield*
> Bookseller at the / *Marigold* neai *Salsbury Court* in
> *Fleet-/ street*. MDCLXXXV. p. 159.

The first allusion is to Mrs. Quickly's account of Falstaff's death in *Henry V*, II. iii. 9—13,

"*Hostesse.* Nay sure, hee's not in Hell: hee's in *Arthurs* Bosome, if euer man went to *Arthurs* Bosome: a made a finer end, and went away and it had beene any Christome Child: a parted eu'n iust betweene Twelue and One, eu'n at the Turning o' th' Tyde:" I Folio, p. 75, col. 2.

The second is to Hotspur's speeches in I *Henry IV*, III. i. 18-21, 33-35,

"(*Glen.* . . . .   and at my birth
The frame and huge foundation of the earth
Shaked like a coward.)

Hot. Why so it woulde haue done at the same season if your mothers cat had but kittend, though your selfe had neuer beene borne. . . . . .

. . . . At your birth
Our Grandam earth, hauing this distemperature,
In passion shooke."

Hy. Bold of New, Antony Wood has only as writing forepraise verses to Wm. Cartwright's Poems. *Ath. Ox.* iii. 70. He may have been a relative of Henry Bold of Christ Church, as some ChristChurch men wrote forepraise "—— poems to his postumous volume then." Ant. Wood enters Henry Bold of Ch. Church as one of the Proctors, Apr. 9, 1662 (*Fasti* ii. 261, *Ath. Ox.* ed. Bliss, iv.), and under 1664 has "Batchelors of Divinity, July 5. HENRY BOLD of Ch. Ch. He was at this time chaplain to Henry lord Arlington, by whose endeavours he became not only fellow of Eaton Coll. but chaunter of the church at Exeter.[1] He died in France (at Montpelier as 'twas reported) either in the latter end of September, or beginning of Oct. 1677."

---

[1] He was succeeded in this post by Geo. Hooper, afterwards Dean of Canterbury. *Ath. Ox.* iv. 642. See also iv. 634.

NAHUM TATE, 1685.

Wyn[ny (Security's Wife)]. Ay, but there is a pretty play in *Moor-fields.*
Sec[urity]. Why, I will act thee a better Play my felf. What wilt thou have? The Knight of the Burning Peftle? or, the doleful Comedy of *Piramus* and *Thifbe*? That's my Mafter-Piece; when *Piramus* comes to be dead, I can act a dead man rarely, *The rageing Rocks, and fhivering Shocks, fhall break the Locks of Prifon Gates; and* Phœbus *Carr, fhall fhine from Far, to make and marr the foolifh Fates.*——Was not that lofty, now? Then there's the *Lion, Wall* and *Mounfhine,* three Heroick Parts; I play'd 'em all at School. I roar'd out the Lion fo terribly, that the Company call'd out to me to roar again.

<blockquote>
Cuckolds-Haven: | or, an | Alderman | No Conjurer.| A | Farce.| Acted at the Queen's Theatr | in Dorset Garden.| By N. Tate.| London, | Printed for J. H., and are to be sold by Edward Poole, | next door to the Fleece Tavern in Cornhill. 1685./ 4to. See p. 278, 1682. *p.* 16.
</blockquote>

[Quoted (without italics, &c.) in Mr. Halliwell-Phillipps's *Memoranda on the Midsummer Night's Dream,* 1879, p. 11. The passage is Bottom's:—
"I could play *Ercles* rarely, or a part to teare a Cat in, to make all split the raging Rocks; and shiuering shocks shall break the locks of prison gates, and *Phibbus* carre shall shine from farre, and make and marre the foolish Fates. This was lofty." *M. N. Dreame,* 1st Fol. p. 147, col. 2.
"Let mee play the Lyon too, I will roare that I will doe any mans heart good to heare me. I will roare, that I will make the Duke say, Let him roare againe, let him roare againe."—*ib.* F. J. F.]

N. TATE, 1686,

TO THE

AUTHOR [Sir Francis Fane].

When o'r the World the mild Auguſtus reign'a,
  Wit's Empire too the Roman Poets gain'd:
So when the firſt auſpicious James poſſeſt
Our Brittiſh World, and in Poſſeſſing bleſt;
Our Poets wore the Laurels of the Age,
While Shakeſpear, Fletcher, Johnſon Crown'd the Stage.
And tho' our Cæſar's ſince have raiſ'd the State,
Our Poetry ſuſtains the Roman Fate.
In leſs Eſſays ſucceſſful we have been,
But loſt the Nobler Province of the Scene:
Perverters, not Reformers of the Stage,
Deprav'd to Farce, or more fantaſtick Rage.
  How therefore ſhall we Celebrate thy Name,
Whoſe Genius has ſo well retriev'd our Fame?
Whoſe happy Muſe ſuch Wonders can impart,
And temper Shakeſpear's Flame with Johnſon's Art.
Whoſe Characters ſet juſt Examples forth;
Mix Humane Frailties with Heroick Worth:
Shunning th' Extreams in Modern Heroes ſeen,
Than God's more perfect, or more frail than Men.
With Reaſon, Nature, Truth, our Minds you treat,
And ſhew a Prince irregularly great,

N. TATE, 1686.

A generous Soul ſtorm'd by impetuous Love,
Which yet from Virtue's Centre ſcorns to move.
Thus while the Hero does himſelf defeat,
Your Tamerlane *is rendred truly GREAT.*
When by his Troops whole Empires were o'rthrown,
'Twas Fortune's Work, this Conqueſt was his own.
Your Monarch rages in Othello's *Strein,*
Iago *in* Ragalzan *lives again.*
Not Hecuba *like your* Deſpina *Rag'd,*
Like Her, for Empire and a Monarch's Fate engag'd:
With Iphigene *your Fair* Irene *vies,*
And falls a more lamented Sacrifice.
    Your Stile, tho juſt, ſubſervient to the Thought;
So Milton, *by* Aonian *Muſes taught,*
Your Numbers in Majeſtic Plainneſs wrought.[1] ...

. . . .
Thus, for a Theatre the World you find,
And your Applauding Audience, All Mankind.

                             N. TATE.

        The / Sacrifice./ A / Tragedy./ By the Honourable / Sir Francis Fane,/ Knight of the Bath./ Licensed,/ May 4, 1686./ *Ro. L'Estrange.*/ London, / Printed by *J. R.* for *John Weld* at the *Crown* / between the *Temple Gates* in *Fleetstreet,*/ 1686./ 4to.

Dramatis Personæ.—*Tamerlane* the Great: *Bajazet*, Emperor of the Turks. *Ragalzan*, one of Tamerlane's Chief Officers: a Villain. *Irene*, Tamerlane's Daughter: *Deſpina*, Bajazet's Wife.

---

[1] 'So Milton,' &c., omitted in 3d ed. 1687. 'Strein' is printed 'Strain.' —*Ib.*

[Sir Francis ought to have paid well for Tate's praise. F. J. F.]

THO. JEVON, 1686.

Therefore if in greater and more evident Points the Lawyer can no more be without his Fee, than the Lord Chancellour his Mace, or a Poet without Errors, (my felf alone exempted) why fhou'd the Judgment of a Man that is partially byafs'd againft the Banditti, *rule the Author's opinion in his own Hemifphere, and discufs at large the Virtues of* Jobfon's *Wife, without the Management of* Hobbs *his* Leviathan? *Why fhou'd* Shakefpear, Johnfon, Beaumont, Fletcher, *that are no way Adequate to the profound Intellects of my prefent Atonement, be rank'd above the Laborious, tho' dull States-man.*

—Sed Vaftum Vaftior Ipfe,
Suftulit Æg des,[1] &c.   Ov. Metam.

> The Preface to The / Devil of a Wife, / or a / *Comical Transformation.*/ As it is Acted by their Majeſties / Servants at the Queen's Theatre in / *Dorset* Garden./ *Vini, Vidi, Vici.* / Licensed *March* 30th. 1686. *R. L. S./ London,* / Printed, by *J. Heptinstall,* for *J. Eaglesfield* / at the *Marigold* over against the *Globe-Tavern* in / *Fleet-Street.* MDCLXXXVI./ 4to./

[In excuse of the chaff above, may be cited "The Epistle Dedicatory. To my Worthy Friends and Patrons at *Lockets* Ordinary.

"You are not to be told, that Poets are sawcy, very sawcy, mighty sawcy, but your (wou'd be) Poet, or Farce Snipper Snapper, such a Promiscuous Riddle me Re, as my self always super-abounding; Therefore do I heartily hope, but more humbly entreat, that with the Piercing Eye of Understanding, and through the Orbicuous Glass of Reason, you will perfectly discern, and then wholly attribute the bold Presumption of this sharp Epistle (as I may justly term it) to my Seeming self as Audacious *Jevon* the Poet, and not to my Real self as Modest Mr. *Jevon* the Player."—F. J. F.]

---

[1] 'Ægydes' (Theseus, son of Ægeas) in subsequent editions (1693, 1695, 1724, 1735) is printed incorrectly 'Ægynes.' The passage really is:
"Antiquus crater, quem vastum vastior ipsi
Sustulit Ægides;" (*Metam.* xii, 235-6.)

APHRA[1] BEHN, 1686.

Bred[*wel*]. 'Tis a pretty convenient Tub Madam. He may lie along in't, there's juft room for an old Joyn'd Stool befides the Bed, which one cannot call a Cabin, about the largenefs of a Pantry Bin, or a Usurer's Trunk, there had been Dornex[2] Curtains to't in the Days of *Yore;* but they were now annihilated, and nothing left to fave his Eyes from the Light, but my Land-ladies Blew Apron, ty'd by the ftrings before the Window, in which ftood a broken fixpenny Looking-Glafs, that fhow'd as many Faces, as the Scene in *Henry* the Eighth, which could but juft ftand upright, and then the Comb-Cafe fill'd it.

The | Luckey Chance, | or an | Aldermans | Bargain. | A | Comedy.| As it is Acted by their Majesty's | Servants.| Written by Mrs. *A. Behn*, | 1687.[3]/ 4to./ [*p.* 10]. Halliwell's *Folio Shakespeare, xii.* 61.

Is that any more than you fee in the moft celebrated of your plays ? as *City Politicks*, the *Lady Mayorefs*, and the *Old Lawyers Wife*. So in that lucky play of the *London Cuckolds*. And in that good comedy Sir Courtly Nice, Valentinian, * * * In *Valentinian*, fee the Scene between the *Court Bawds*. And *Valentinian* all loofe and rufl'd a Moment after the Rape and

---

[1] The Mus. Catalogue calls her 'Aphara.'

[2] Dormer (in Halliwell). But Dornex is in the Museum original. It is the Italian '*Spalliera* . . . a kinde of stuffe made for hangings called Darnix.' 1598. Florio.

Dornex too in Behn's Plays, Histories, and Novels, 6 vols. 1871, Vol. III. p. 178, and Behn, Plays, 4 vols. 1724. Vol. iii. p. 178.

[3] This may be Printed, April 23, 1686. R. P. / *London.| Printed by R. H. for W. Canning*, at his Shop in *Vine-Court, Middle-Temple*. 1687.

all this you fee without fcandal, and a thoufand others. The *Moor of Venice* in many places. The *Maids Tragedy*.— * * * All thefe I Name as fome of the beft Plays I know; If I fhould repeat the Words exprefs'd in thefe Scenes I mention, I might juftly be charg'd with courfe ill Manners, and very little Modefty, and yet they fo naturally fall into the places they are defigned for, and fo are proper for the Bufinefs, that there is not the leaft Fault to be found with them; though I fay thofe things in any of mine would damn the whole Peice, and alarm the Town. * * * And this one thing I will venture to fay, though againft my Nature, becaufe it has a Vanity In it : That had the Plays I have writ come forth under any Mans Name and never known to have been mine; I appeal to all unbyaft Judges of Senfe, if they had not faid that Perfon had made as many good Comedies, as any one Man that has writ in our Age; but a Devil on't the Woman damns the Poet.

ib. A 4. Mrs. A. Behn's *Preface to The Luckey Chance.*
[F. J. F.]

APHRA BEHN,[1] 1687.

The Defence of the firſt [the Pulpit] *is left to the Reverend Gown, but the departing Stage can be no otherwiſe reſtor'd, but by ſome leading Spirits, ſo Generous, ſo Publick, and ſo Indefatigable as that of your Lordſhip, whoſe Patronages are ſufficient to ſupport it, whoſe Wit and Iudgment to defend it, and whoſe Goodneſs and Quality to juſtifie it; ſuch Encouragement wou'd inſpire the Poets with new Arts to pleaſe, and the Actors with Induſtry.* 'Twas this that occaſioned ſo many Admirable Plays heretofore, as Shakeſpear's, Fletcher's *and* Iohnſon's, *and* 'twas this alone that made the Town able to keep ſo many Play-houſes alive, who now cannot ſupply one.

"Emperor / of the / Moon: / A / Farce./ As it is acted by Their / Maiesties Servants, / At the / Queens Theatre./ Written by Mrs *A. Behn.*/ *London :* / Printed by *R. Holt,* for *Joseph Knight,* and *Francis* / *Saunders,* at the *Blew Anchor* in the lower Walk of the / *New Exchange,* 1687./ 4to. Dedication "to the Lord Marquess of Worcester." sign. A3.

PONSONBY A. LYONS.

---

[1] Mrs Behn got more credit as an authoress than as a translatress :—
I'd let him take *Almanzor* for his Theme ;
In lofty Verses make *Maximin* Blaspheme,
Or sing in softer Ayres St. *Katharine*'s Dream.
Nay, I cou'd hear him damn last Age's Wit,
And rail at Excellence he ne'er can hit ;
His Envy shou'd at powerful Cowley rage,
And banish Sense with Johnson from the Stage ;
His Sacrilege should plunder *Shakespear*'s Urn,
With a dull Prologue make the Ghost return
To bear a second Death, and greater Pain,
While the Fiend's Words the Oracle prophane ;
But when not satisfy'd with Spoils at home,

The Pyrate wou'd to foreign Borders roam;
May he still split on some unlucky Coast,
And have his Works or Dictionary lost;
That he may know what Roman Authors mean,
No more than does our blind Translatress *Behn*.[1]

A Satyr on the Modern Translators. By Mr P——r. p. 119. Printed in *Pecunia obediunt Omnia*./ "Money / Masters all Things: or, Satyrical Poems, / shewing / The Power and Influence of Money / over all Men / of what Profession or / Trade soever they be./ To which are added, / *A Lenten Litany*, by Mr C——d, / a *Satyr* on Mr *Dryden*, and several / other Modern Translators; also a *Sātyr* on Women in general: Together with / Mr *Oldham's Character* of a cer/tain Ugly Old P...... [Preacher, see pp. 131, 132] * * * * * * Printed, and Sold by the Booksellers of / *London* and *Westminster*, 1698."

This Satyr is not in the edition of *Pecunia* published at York 1696, 4ᵗᵒ P——r, C—d, and P...... are conjectured in the British Museum Catalogue to be Prior, Coward, and Player. In the *Supplement to the Works of the Most celebrated Minor Poets*, London, F. Cogan, 1750, Part II. p. 12, it is placed first among "Poems by Mr Prior."—PONSONBY A. LYONS.

---

[1] Lycidus, or the Lover in Fashion, translated by Mrs A. Behn, 1688. 4ᵗᵒ.—Bohn's *Lowndes*, i. 147.

MARTIN[1] CLIFFORD, 1687.

But I might have fpared this Quotation, and you your avowing: For this Character might as well have been borrowed from fome of the Stalls in *Bedlam*, or any of your own hair-brain'd Coxcombs, which you call *Heroes*, and Perfons of Honour. I remember juft fuch another fuming *Achilles* in *Shakefpear*, one Ancient *Piftol*, whom he avows to be a man of fo fiery a temper, and fo impatient of an injury, even from Sir *John Falftaff* his Captain, and a Knight, that he not only difobeyed his Commands about carrying a Letter to Mrs. Page, but return'd him an anfwer as full of contumely, and in as opprobrious terms as he could imagine.*

> *Let Vultures gripe thy guts, for gourd and Fullam holds,*
> *And high and low beguiles the rich and poor:*
> *Tefter I'll have in pouch, when thou fhalt lack,*
> *Bafe Prygian Turk,* &c.

Let's fee e'er an *Abencerrago* fly a higher pitch. Take him at another turn quarrelling with Corporal *Nym*, an old *Zegri:* The difference arofe about mine Hoftefs *Quickly* (for I would not give a Rufh for a man unlefs he be particular in matters of this moment) they both aimed at her body, but *Abencerrago* Piftol defies his Rival in thefe words:

> *Fetch from the Powdring-Tub of Infamy*
> *That Lazar-Kite of Creffids kind,*

---

[1] The Brit. Mus. Catalog givs an alternativ 'Matthew', but 'Martin' is signd at the foot of p. 16 of the *Notes*.
* *Merry Wives of Windsor*.

Doll Tearsheet, *she by name, and her espouse: I have and
I will hold
The quondam* Quickly *for the onely she.*
And pauca . . . . .
There's enough.

> Notes / Upon / Mr. Dryden's Poems / In / Four Letters./
> By *M. Clifford,* late Master of the / *Charter-House,
> London.*/ To which are annexed some Reflections upon
> the / *Hind* and *Panther.* By another Hand./ [motto
> from] Juven. Sat. 7. *London.* Printed in the year
> .1687./ The Second Letter, p. 6-7.

But pray give me leave without any offence, to ask you why
it was a Fault in *Shakespear,* that *his Plays were grounded upon
Impossibilities, and so meanly written, that the Comedy neither
caused your Mirth, nor the* [p. 8] *serious part your Concernment?*
This you say in your Postscript . . . . . *ib.* p. 7-8.

Mr. *Dryden,*

THere is one of your Virtues which I cannot forbear to
animadvert upon, which is your excefs of Modefty; When
you tell us in your Poftfcript to *Granada,* That *Shakespear is
below* * *the Dulleft Writer of Ours, or any precedent Age.* In
which by your favour, you Recede as much from your own
Right, as you difparage *Almanzor,* becaufe he is yours, in pre-
ferring *Ben. Johnfon's Cethegus* before him; faying in your
Preface, that his Rodomontadoes are neither fo irrational as the
others, nor fo impoffible to be put in execution.

ib. The Third Letter, p. 10-11

*We follow Fate which does too faft purfue.
'Tis juft that Flames ſhould be condemn'd to Fire.*

You muft not take it ill, Mr. *Dryden,* if I fufpect both thofe
Verfes to have a ftrong tincture of Nonfenfe, but if you'l defend

'em, of all loves I beg of thee that thou would'ſt conſtrue them, and put them into ſenſe: for to me, as Parſon *Hugh* ſays in *Shakeſpear*, they ſeemed Lunacies, it is mad as a mad Dog, it is affeɛtatious.¹ *ib*. p. 12. . . . . —F. J. F.

[1] This was an adjective then new to the English language, I believe, made by the compositor turning the *n* of the Welsh Parson Evans's 'it is affectations' in *Merry Wives*, I. i. 150. The short extract containing it was the only one sent-in for the word for the Philological Society's new English Dictionary. As 'affectatious' has more ridicule in it than 'affected', it should be kept and uzed.

GERARD LANGBAINE, 1688.

[See the first allusion to Sh. in this volume, under Kirkman, 1661, above, p. 190.]

But before I quit this Paper, I desire my Readers leave to take a View of Plagiaries *in general, and that we may observe the different proceedings between the* Ancients *and our* Modern *Writers.* * * * [Sig. a]

But let us now observe how these Eminent Men [Virgil, Ovid, and Terence] *manage what they borrow'd; and then compare them with those of our times.* First, *They propos'd to themselves those Authors whose Works they borrow'd from, for their Model* Secondly, *They were cautious to borrow only what they found beautiful in them, and rejected the rest.* * * * Thirdly, *They plainly confess'd what they borrow'd, and modestly ascrib'd the credit of it to the Author whence 'twas originally taken.* * * * * [Sig. a, back]

Lastly, *Whatsoever these ancient Poets (particularly* Virgil) *copyed from any Author, they took care not only to alter it for their purpose; but to add to the beauty of it: and afterwards to insert it so* handsomly *into their Poems, (the body and Oeconomy of which was generally their own) that what they* borrow'd, *seemed of the same Contexture with what was* originally *theirs. So that it might be truly said of them;* Apparet unde sumptum sit, aliud tamen quàm unde sit, apparet.

If we now on the other side examine the proceedings of our late English *Writers, we shall find them diametrically opposite in all things.* Shakspear *and* Johnson *indeed imitated these Illustrious Men I have cited; the one having borrow'd the Comedy of Errours from the* Menechmi *of Plautus; the other has made use not only*

GERARD LANGBAINE, 1688.

of him, but of Horace, Ovid, Juvenal, Salust, *and several others, according to his occasions: for which he is commended by Mr.* Dryden, as having thereby beautified our Language: * * * Epist. to Mock A-*But for the most part we are treated far otherwise; not with* strologer. *round* Roman *Wit, as in* Ben's *time, but with empty* French *Kickshaws, which yet our Poetical Host's serve up to us for Regales of their own Cookery;* [Sig. a. 2]

'*Tis true indeed, what is borrow'd from* Shakspeare *or* Fletcher, *is usually own'd by our Poets, because every one would be able to convict them of Theft, should they endeavour to conceal it.* [Sig. a 3.]

Preface to **Momus Triumphans**: / Or the / Plagiaries / of the / English Stage ; / Expos'd in a / Catalogue / of all the / *Comedies, Tragi-Comedies, Masques, Tragedies, Opera's, Pastorals, Interludes,* &c. Both Ancient and Modern that were ever yet Printed in *English.* The Names of their Known and Supposed Authors./ Their several Volumes and Editions : With an Account of / the various Originals, as well English, *French* and *Italian* as / *Greek* and *Latine*; from whence most of them have Stole / their Plots./ By *GERARD LANGBAINE* Esq ; * * * * *London:* Printed for *N. C.* & are to be sold by *Sam. Holford,* at the Crown in the *Pall Mall.* 1688./ 4to.

At pp. 21, 22, is a catalogue of Shakespear's plays including Cromwell's History ; "John K. of England, 2 Pts. H. Fol."; Locrine's Tragedy; London Prodigal ; Old-Castle, Lord Cobham's Life and Death ; Puritan Widow ; Yorkshire Tragedy ; Birth of Merlin—41 entries—with notes of he sources of most of the plays. At the end of the thin volume is an Alphabetical Index of Plays.

PONSONBY A. LYONS.

GERARD LANGBAINE (?), 1691.

To day, the Poet does not fear your Rage,
Shakefpear by him reviv'd now treads the Stage :
Under his facred Lawrells he fits down
Safe, from the blaft of any Criticks Frown.
Like other Poets, he'll not proudly fcorn
To own, that he but winnow'd *Shakefpear's* Corn ;
So far he was from robbing him of's Treafure,
That he did add his own, to make full Meafure.

An Account of the English Dramatick Poets, p. 465, 1691 [8vo.].

[Langbaine on Shakespeare, speaking of Ravenscroft, and having given the words quoted from Ravenscroft's preface to *Titus Andronicus*, in *Centurie of Prayse*, p. 404, says, "I shall not engage in this Controversy, but leave it to [others] . . . But to make Mr. Ravenscroft some reparation, I will here furnish him with part of his Prologue, which he has lost ; [Ravenscroft states he had lost both Prologue and Epilogue] and if he desire it, send him the whole." The last lines seem to be a skit modelled on Ravenscroft's own words in his Epistle to the Reader—"Compare the Old Play with this, you'l finde that none in all that Authors [Sh.] Works ever receiv'd greater Alterations or Additions, the Language not only refin'd, but many Scenes entirely New : Besides most of the principal Characters heighten'd, and the Plot much encreas'd."—B. N.]

1688.

Plays Printed for *Henry Herringman,* and Sold by *Jofeph Knight,* and *Francis Saunders.*

*   *   *   *

By Mr. Shakefpear.

Hamlet.
Macbeth.
Julius Cæfar.

> List of Plays on p. 68 of " A / Fool's Preferment, / Or, The / Three Dukes of Dunstable. / A Comedy./ As it was Acted at the Queens Theatre in / *Dorset-Garden,* by Their Majesties Ser-/vants./ *Written by Mr. D'urfey./* Together, with all the Songs and Notes to 'em, / Excellently Compos'd by Mr. Henry Purcell. 1688. / Licensed, / May 21, 1688. *R. P.* / . . . . Printed for *Jos. Knight,* and *Fra. Saunders* at the *Blue Anchor* / in the *Lower Walk* of the *New Exchange* in the *Strand,* 1688./

Shakspere comes after Beaumont and Fletcher, the Duke of Newcastle, Earl of Orrery, Mr. Wicherly, Major Porter, Sir George Etherege, Mr. Dryden, Mr. Shadwell, Mr. Killigrew. He is before Mr. Cowley, Sir Charles Sydley, Sir Samuel Tuke, Sir Francis Fane, Mr. Caril, and Plays 'By Several.'—F. J. F.

T. BETTERTON, 1690.

Epilogue. p. 75.

* * * * *

When this is brought to pafs, I am afraid
That in a Play-houfe I shall dye a Maid;
That Miracles don't ceafe, an l I fhall fee
Some Players Martyrs for their Honefly.
J. H. - - - the greateft Bigot of the Nation,
And fee him burn for Tranfubftantiation.
Or hope to fee, from fuch a Mongrel breed,
Wit that the Godlike Shakefpear *fhall exceed;*
Or what has dropt from Fletcher's *fluent Pen,*
Our this days Author, or the Learned Ben.

    1690. Thomas Betterton. Epilogue to his alteration of Beaumont and Fletcher's *Prophetefs*, after the Manner of an Opera.[1]
    The Epilogue is anonymous.

Betterton's 'Godlike' Shakspere, matches Crowne's 'Divine' (p. 262 above), and Nat Lee's 'immortal' (p. 264). As there are not too many of such epithets in these Additions, or the *Centurie*, I add Powell's 'immortal' of 1696:—

'Now if the World has made so little Provision for the maintenance of the Muses, (as kind *Davenants* too true Oracle tells us,) I'm afraid upon due Examination, that little Bread they gather will be found almost all glean'd

---

[1] The / Prophetesse / or, the / History ' of / Dioclesian / Written by *Francis Beaumont* and *John Fletcher.*/ With / ALTERATIONS and ADDITIONS, / after the Maner of an / OPERA./ Represented at the / Queen's Theatre, / By their Majesties Servants./ *London,* / Printed for *Jacob Tonson* at the *Judges Head* in *Chancery Lane,* 1690.—Epilogue, p. 75.

from a Theatre; one kind honest Actor, that frets and struts his hour upon the Stage (as the Immortal *Shaksphear* has it,) is possibly a greater Benefactor to the Muses, then the greatest Family of Grandees that run Pedigrees, and track Originals up from the Conquest.'

1696. G. Powell. The Epistle Dedicatory to *The Treacherous Brothers:* A Tragedy. London, 1696, 4°.[1]

F. J. F.

---

[1] The / Treacherous Brothers : / A / Tragedy : / As it is Acted / At the / Theatre-Royal / By / His Majesty's Servants./ Written by / *George Powell.*/ London, / Printed for *W. Freeman,* at the *Bible,* over / against the *Middle-Temple-Gate* in *Fleet-Street,* 1696./ 4to.

T. D'URFEY, 1690.

Where Verſe has not the power to Influence,
What method ever can reform the Sence?
What would a *Cato*, or a *Virgil* be,
Johnſon, or *Shakeſpeare*, to the Mobile?
Or how would *Juvenal* appear at Court,
That writing Truth had his Bones broken for 't?

> A new / Essay / In Defence of / Verse. / With a Satyr / Upon the Enemies of / Poetry, *in* "New / Poems,/ Consisting of / Satyrs, / Elegies, / and / Odes: / Together with a / Choice Collection / Of the Newest / Court Songs,/ Set to Musick by the best Masters / of the Age./ All Written by Mr. *D'Vrfey.*/ .... *London*, Printed for *J. Bullord*, at the Old / Black Bear in St. *Paul's* Church-Yard, and / *A. Roper*, at the Bell near *Temple-Bar*, 1690." p. 5.—F. J. F.

? ANON., or WM. MOUNTFORT, 1690.

Here [says Wm. Mountfort] *is another facetious piece, as Ironically meant, as the former was serioufly defigned; it was fent me as from a Woman, to make it go down the glibber; and I think I could not do the Author juftice (any other way) but in Printing it.*

Hail thou the Shakfphear of our prefent age,
Who doft at once, fupply and grace the Stage
With different proofs of thy furprizing wit,
Vying with what the eftablifh'd Pens have writ.
                                                    (Sign. A 4.)
But to encreafe the wonder of thy pen,
Thou art not now, more learn'd then *Shakefpear* then,
Who to th' amaze of the more Letter'd men,
Minted fuch thoughts from his own Natural Brain,
As the great Readers, fince could ne're attain,
Though daily they the ftock of Learning drain,
                                                    (Sign. A 4 back.)
How long in vain, had Nature ftriv'd to frame
An acting Poet, till great *Shakpher* came;
And thou the next wil't Rival him in Fame.
                                                    (Sign. a.)

The Preface to the Reader, to *The | Successful Strangers, | a | Tragi-Comedy :|* . . . . *written | by William Mount-fort |* . . . . London | 1690, 4to.| (See also p. 235. Did Mountfort himself write this skit on himself?
                                                    F. J. F.

WILL: MOUNTFORT, 1691.

*But Virtue, tho' she suffer'd long at last,
Was Crown'd with a reward for what was past;
The honest thinking Heathen shew'd the way,
And handed Down the Moral call'd a Play:
Old Ben, and Shakespear copied what they writ,
Then Downright Satyr was accounted wit;
The Fox and Alchymist expos'd the Times,
The Persons then was loaded with their Crimes;
But for the space of Twenty years and more,
You've hiss'd this way of Writing out of door,
And kick and winch when we but touch the fore.*[1]
*But as some Fashions long since useless grown,
Are now Reviv'd and all the Mode o' th' Town.
Why mayn't the Antient way of Writing please,
And in its turn meet with the same Success?*

> Prologue to " King / Edward the Third, / with / the Fall of / Mortimer/ Earl of / March,/ An Historicall Play, / As it is Acted at the Theatre-Royall, / By their Majesties Servants./ London, Printed for J. Hindmarsh at the Golden-Ball against the / Royal Exchange. . . . . 1691. 4¹⁰.—F. J. F.

[1] Compare Caryl's earlier complaint :—
*A formal Critick with his wise Grimace
Will on the Stage appear with no ill grace:
Most of that Trade in this Censorious Age
Have little of the Poet, but his Rage:
Perhaps old Johnson's Gall may fill their Pen;
But where's the Judgment, and the salt of Ben?*

> 1667. Jn. Caryl. Epilogue to *The English Princess: or, The Death of Richard the III.* A Tragedy Written in the year 1666 and Acted at his Highness the Duke of York's Theatre. Licensed May 22 1667. London, T. Dring. 1667. 4'. p. 66.

WILLIAM MOUNTFORT, 1691

Indifferent Authors in moſt Ages have been incourag'd and preſerv'd under the Clemency of the Nobility, in hopes that they might be better: But the ſeverity of our Wits would have the firſt Plays which are now written, equal to the beſt of Ben Johnſon, *or* Shakeſpear: *And yet they do not ſhew that eſteem for their Works which they pretend to, or elſe are not ſo good Judges as they would be thought: When we can ſee the Town throng to a* Farce,[1] *and* Hamlet *not bring Charges: But notwithſtanding they will be Criticks, and will ſcarce give a man leave to mend;*

The Dedication of 'Greenwich-Park: / A / Comedy./ . . . Acted at the / Theatre-Royal / by Their / Majesties Servants./ *Written by* William Mountfort./ London. . . . . MDCXCI. to the Right Honourable *Algernon* Earl of Essex.'

---

[1] The author of *Tunbridge Wells, or a Days Courtship*, a Comedy, 1678, in his Prologue complains,
  Th' Old Engliſh Stage, confin'd to Plot and Sense,
  · Did hold abroad but small intelligence,
  But since th' invasion of the forreign Scene,
  Jack pudding Farce, and thundering Machine.
  Dainties to your graue Ancestour's unknown,
  (Who never disliked wit becauſe their own)
  There's not a Player but is turned a scout,
  And every Scribler sends his Envoys out
  To fetch from *Paris*, *Venice*, or from Rome,
  Fantastick fopperies to pleaſe at home.
  And that each act may rise to your desire,
  Devils and Witches must each Scene inſpire,
  Wit rowls in Waves, and showers down in Fire.—F. J. F.

THO. SHADWELL, 1691.

For the Magical Part, I had no hopes of equalling Shakespear *in fancy, who created his Witchcraft for the most part out of his own imagination (in which faculty no Man ever excell'd him) and therefore I resolv'd to take mine from Authority. And to that and, there is not one Action in the Play, nay scarce a word concerning it, but is borrow'd from some Antient, or Modern Witchmonger which you will find in the Notes,*

To the Reader. The | Lancashire Witches, | and | Tegue O Divelly | the | Irish Priest.| A | Comedy.| Written by Thomas Shadwell . . . | London, Printed * * * | 1691|. 4to. Sign. A 3. (Works, 1720, ii. 218.)

F. J. F.

ELKANAH SETTLE, 1691.

And now, after all my repented Follies, if an Unhappy Stray into Forbidden Grounds (like *Trinculo* from his Dukedom where he was almoſt ſtarv'd in't) may be permitted to return to his Native Province, I am refolved to quit all pretenſions to State craft, and honeſtly ſculk into a Corner of the Stage, and there die contented.

> *Distressed Innocence:* | *or,* | *the* | *Princess of Persia.* | *A Tragedy. As it is Acted at the Theatre Royal by Their Majesties Servants.* Written by E. Settle. | . . . | London | *Printed by* G. I. *for* Abel Roper *at the* Mitre *near* Temple-Bar *in* Fleet-Street. 1691, 4to. *Dedication to John Lord Cutts, Baron of Gowram.*

[Langbaine says it was printed 1690; possibly he put by mistake the year in which it was acted.—B. N.]

GERARD LANGBAINE, 1691.

[p. 67, *Dram. Poets*] and how flight an Opinion foever this Age may entertain of his [George Chapman's] Tranflations, I find them highly extoll'd in an Old Copy call'd *a Cenfure of the Poets*[1]: which having fpoke of the Eminent Dramatick Poets, as *Shakefpear, Johnfon, Daniel*, &c., it adds of Tranflators as follows, placing our Author in the firft Rank.

[2] p. 95. [Crowne's] *Henry the Sixth* the Firft Part, with the Death of the Duke of *Gloucefter*; a Tragedy acted at the Duke's Theatre, printed in quarto *Lond.* 1681, and dedicated to Sr. *Charles Sedley*. [p. 96] This Play is (if I miftake not) very much borrow'd from the Second Part of *Shakefpear's Henry the Sixth*; tho' Mr. *Crown* with a little too much affurance affirms, that he has no Title to the Fortieth part of it. This Play was oppof'd by the Popifh Faction, who by their Power at Court got it fuppreft: however it was well receiv'd by the Reft of the Audience.

[Crowne's] *Henry the Sixth* the Second Part, on the Mifery of Civil-War; a Tragedy acted at the Duke's Theatre, printed in quarto *Lond.* 1681. Part of this Play likewife is borrow'd from *Shakefpear*.

p. 103 [Sir Wm. Davenant's] *Law againft Lovers*, a Tragi-

[1] Michael Drayton's 'Of Poets and Poesie': Elegies, 1627. See *Centurie* p. 168.
[2] Denham's lines on Cowley, *Centurie*, p. 343, are quoted by Langbaine, p. 83.

Comedy made up of two Plays written by Mr. *Shakefpear*, viz. *Meafure for Meafure*, and *Much Ado about Nothing*. Tho' not only the Characters, but the Language of the whole Play almoſt, be borrow'd from *Shakefpear*; yet where the Language is rough or obfolete, our Author has taken care to polifh it: as to give, inſtead of many, one Inſtance. *Shakefpear*'s Duke of *Vienna*, fays thus [1]—

> *I love the People;*
> *But do not like to Stage me to their Eyes:*
> *Though it do well, I do not relifh well*
> *Their loud Applaufe, and Aves vehement:*
> *Nor do I think the Man of fafe difcretion,*
> *That does affect it.*

[p. 109] In Sr. *William*'s Play the Duke fpeaks as follows; [2]

> *I love the People;*
> *But would not on the Stage falute the Croud.*
> *I never relifht their Applaufe; nor think*
> *The Prince has true difcretion who affects it.*

[p. 133] But had he [Dryden] only extended his Conqueſts over the *French* Poets, I had not medled in this Affair . . . but when I found him fluſht with his Victory over the great *Scudery* . . . and not content with Conqueſts abroad, like another *Julius Cæfar*, turning his Arms upon his own Country; and as if the profcription of his Contemporaries Reputation, were not fufficient to fatiate his implacable thirſt after Fame, endeavouring to demolifh the Statues and Monuments of his Anceſtors, the Works of thofe his Illuſtrious Predeceſſors, *Shakefpear*, *Fletcher*, and *Johnfon*: I was refolv'd to endeavour the refcue and preferv-ation of thofe excellent Trophies of Wit, by raifing the *Poffe-comitatus* upon this Poetick *Almanzor*, to put a ſtop to his Spoils

---

[1] *Measure for Measure*, Act I, Sc. i.
[2] *Law against Lovers*, Act I, Sc. i.

upon his own Country-men. Therefore I prefent my felf a Champion in the Dead Poets Caufe, to vindicate their Fame, with the fame Courage, tho' I hope different Integrity than *Almanzor* engag'd in defence of Queen *Almahide*, when he bravely Swore like a *Hero*, that his Caufe was right, and She was innocent: [p. 134] tho' juft before the Combat, when alone, he own'd he knew her falfe:[1]

> *I have out-fac'd my felf, and juftify'd*
> *What I knew falfe to all the World befide.*
> *She was as Faithlefs as her Sex could be;*
> *And now I am alone, fhe's fo to me.*

But to wave this digreffion, and proceed to the Vindication of the Ancients; which that I may the better perform, for the Readers Diverfion, and that Mr. *Dryden* may not tell me, that what I have faid, is but *gratis dictum*, I fhall fet down the Heads of his Depofitions againft our ancient Englifh Poets, and then endeavour the Defence of thofe great Men, who certainly deferv'd much better of Pofterity than to be fo difrefpectively treated as he has ufed them.

Mr. *Shakefpear* as firft in Seniority I think ought to lead the Van, and therefore I fhall give you his Account of him as follows[2]: '*Shakefpear* who many times has written . . . [see *Centurie*, p. 351-2] e're you defpife the other.' Speaking of Mr. *Shakefpear's* Plots, he fays they were 'lame,[3] and that [p. 135] many of them [see *Centurie*, p. 350, 351] . . . your Concernment.' He fays further,[4] 'Moft of *Shakefpear's* Plays, I mean the Stories of them [see above, p. 226, 292] . . . and many others of them.'

He Characterizes Mr. *Fletcher*, who writ after Mr. *Shakefpear*,[5]

[1] Act V, Sc. i. [2] Poftscript to *Granada*, pag. 146. [3] *Ibid.* pag. 143.
[4] Preface to *Mock Aftrologer*, B. 4 [see *Cent.* p. 352].
[5] Poftscript, p. 144.

'As a Perſon that neither underſtood correct Plotting, nor that
'which they call *the Decorum of the Stage*.' . . . In another
place he ſpeaks of *Fletcher* thus [1]; ' Neither is the Luxuriance of
Fletcher a leſs fault than the Careleſsneſs of *Shakeſpear*; [2] . .
[p. 136] As to the great *Ben Johnſon* he deals not much better
with him.' . . .

Theſe are his own Words, and his Judgment of theſe three
Great Men in particular, now take his opinion of them all in
general, which is as follows; [3] 'But Malice and Partiality [p. 137]
ſet apart [see *Centurie*, p. 350], let any Man, who underſtands
Engliſh, . . flaw in Sence.' In the next Page, ſpeaking of their
Sence and Language, he ſays, ' I dare almoſt challenge any Man
'to ſhew me a Page together which is correct in both.' . .
Speaking of their Wit, he gives it this character [4], ' I have always
'acknowledg'd the Wit of our Predeceſſors, with all the Venera-
'tion that becomes me; but I am ſure, their Wit was not that
'of Gentlemen; there was ever ſomewhat that was Ill-bred and
'Clowniſh in it: and which confeſt the Converſation of the
'Authors.' Speaking of the advantage which acrues to our
Writing, from Converſation, he ſays,[5] 'In the Age wherein
'thoſe Poets liv'd, there was leſs of Gallantry, than in ours;
'neither did they keep the beſt Company of theirs. Their
'Fortune has been much like that of *Epicurus*, in the Retire-
'ment of his Gardens; to live almoſt unknown, and to be Cele-
'brated after their Deceaſe. I cannot find that any of them
'were Converſant in Court, except *Ben Johnſon*: and his Genius
'lay not ſo much that way as to make an Improvement by it.'
He gives this Character of their Audiences, [6] 'They knew no
'better, and therefore were ſatiſfied [p. 138] with what they
'brought. Thoſe who call theirs *The Golden Age of Poetry*,
'have only this Reaſon for it, that they were then content with

[1] Postscript, p. 146. [2] *Centurie*, p. 352. [3] Postscript, p. 143.
[4] *Ibid*. p. 148. [5] *Centurie*, p. 148. [6] *Ibid*. p. 144.

'Acorns, before they knew the ufe of Bread; or that Ἅλις ἑρνύς
'was become a Proverb.'

Thefe are Errors which Mr. *Dryden* has found out in the moft Correct Dramatick Poets of the laſt Age. . . .

I muſt do Mr. *Dryden* this juſtice, to acquaint the World, that here and there in this *Poſtſcript*, he interſperſes ſome faint Praiſes of theſe Authors; and beggs the Reader's Pardon for accuſing them, [1] 'Deſiring him to conſider that he lives in [an] Age where 'his leaſt faults are ſeverely cenſur'd, and that he has no way left 'to extenuate his failings, but by ſhewing as great in thoſe whom 'he admires.'

Whether this be a ſufficient Excuſe or no, I leave to the Criticks: but ſure I am that this [p. 139] procedure ſeems exactly agreeable to the Character which an ingenious Perſon draws of a Malignant Wit,[2] 'Who conſcious of his own Vices, 'and ſtudious to conceal them, endeavours by Detraction to 'make it appear that others alſo of greater Eſtimation in the 'world, are tainted with the ſame or greater: as Infamous 'Women generally excuſe their perſonal Debaucheries, by 'incriminating upon their whole Sex, callumniating the moſt 'Chaſt and Virtuous, to palliate their own diſhonour.' . . .

[p. 140] But . . I ſhall . . go on with the Thing I have undertook, (*to wit*) The Defence of the Poets of the laſt Age.

Were Mr. *Dryden* really as great a Scholar, as he would have the World believe him to be; he would have call'd to mind, that *Homer*, whom he profeſſeth to imitate, had ſet him a better pattern of Gratitude, who mentions with Reſpect and Kindneſs his Maſter *Phemis*, *Mentor* of *Ithaca*, and even *Tychius*, the honeſt Leather-dreſſer. Had he follow'd *Virgil*, whom he would be thought to eſteem; inſtead of Reproaches, he had heap'd Panegyricks on the Aſhes of his Illuſtrious Predeceſſors:

[1] Poſtſcript, p. 148.   [2] Dr. *Charleton's* Different Wits of Men, p. 120.

and rather than have tax'd them with their Errors in fuch a rude manner, would have endeavour'd to fix them in the Temple of Fame, as he did *Mufæus*, and the Ancient Poets, in *Elifium*, amongft the Magnanimous Heroes, and *Teucer*'s Off-fpring; ftiling them,[1] . . . . *Pii Vates, & Phœbo digna locuti.* Had he obferv'd *Ovid*'s *Elegy ad Invidos*,[2] he might have found that good-humour'd Gentleman, not only commending his Predeceffors, but even his Contemporaries. But it feems he has follow'd *Horace*, whom he boafts to have [p. 141] ftudied,[3] and whom he has imitated in his greateft Weaknefs, I mean his Ingratitude: if at leaft that excellent Wit could be guilty of a Crime, fo much below his Breeding; for the very fufpicion of which, *Scaliger* (who like Mr. *Dryden* feldome fpares any man), has term'd him Barbarous.[4] *Ingratus* Horatius, *atque animo barbaro atque fervili; qui ne à Mecenate quidem abftinere potuit: fiquidem quod aiunt, verum eft,* Malthinum *ab eo appellatum cujus demiffas notaret tunicas.*[5] Mr. *Dryden* having imitated the fame Fact, certainly he deferves the fame punifhment: and if we may not with *Scaliger* call him Barbarous, yet all ingenious Men, that know how he has dealt with *Shakefpear*, will count him ungrateful; who by furbifhing up an Old Play, witnefs *The Tempeft*, and *Troilus and Creffida*, has got more on the third Day, than it's probable, ever *Horace* receiv'd from his Patron for any One Poem in all his Life. The like Debt he ftands engag'd for to the French for feveral of the Plays, he has publifht; which if they exceed Mr. *Shakefpear* in Oeconomy, and Contrivance, 'tis that Mr. *Dryden*'s Plays owe their Advantage to his fkill in the French Tongue, or to the Age, rather than his own Conduct, or Performances [see *Centurie*, p. 408].

Honeft *Shakefpear* [see *Centurie*, p. 408: the quotation there should run on].

[1] *Æneid*, lib. 6.   [2] *Amorum*, l. 1, El. 15.
[3] Pref. *Relig. Laici.*, last Paragraph.   [4] *Poet.* L. 3, C. 97
[5] *Malthinus* tunicis demissis ambulat: *Satyrar.* L. 1, Sat. 2.

To conclude, if Mr. *Shakespear's* Plots are more irregular than those of Mr. *Dryden's* (which by some will not be allow'd) 'tis because he never read *Aristotle*, or *Rapin*; and I think *Tasso's* Arguments to *Apollo* in defence of his *Gierusalemme Liberata* may be pleaded in our Author's behalf.[2] . . The [p. 143] Sence of which is thus; That he had only observ'd the Talent which Nature had given him, and which his *Calliope* had infpired into him: Wherein he thought he had fulfill'd all the duties of Poetry, and that his Majesty having prescrib'd no Laws thereunto, he knew not with what Authority *Aristotle* had publiſhed any Rules to be obferved in it: and that he never having heard that there was any other Lord in *Parnaſſus* but his Majefty, his fault in not having obferv'd *Ariſtotle*'s Rules, was, an Error of Ignorance, and not of any Malice.

[p. 150][1] As to his Reflections on this Triumvirate [Shakspere, Fletcher, Jonson] in general: I might eafily prove, that his [Dryden's] Improprieties in Grammar are equal to theirs: and that He himfelf has been guilty of Solecifms in Speech, and Flaws in Sence, as well as *Shakefpear*, *Fletcher*, and *Johnfon*: but this [p. 151] would be to wafte Paper and Time.

p. 152 [Dryden's] *All for Love*, or *The World well Loft*; a Tragedy acted at the Theatre Royal; and written [p. 153] in imitation of *Shakefpear's* ftile, printed in quarto *Lond*. 1678. . . . . That our Author has nearly imitated *Shakefpear* is evident by the following Inftance. In the Comedy call'd *Much Ado about Nothing*[3] the Baftard accufes *Hero* of Difloyalty before the Prince, and *Claudio* her Lover: who (as furpriſ'd at

---

[1] Langbaine's justification of, or excuse for, Ben Johnson's Wit and Sir Philip Sidney's Word-play, 'playing with his Words,' will apply to Shakspere too.

[2] *I Ragguazli di Parnasso di Boccalini*, Ragg. 28. Or *Boccalini*'s Advertisements from *Parnassus*, Advertis. 28.

[3] Act 3, p. 101.

the News,) afks, Who! *Hero? Baft.* Even fhe, *Leonato's Hero*, your *Hero*, every Mans *Hero*. In this Play [of Dryden's],[1] on the like occafion, where *Ventidius* accufes *Cleopatra, Antony* fays, Not *Cleopatra! Ven.* Even fhe my Lord! *Ant.* My *Cleopatra? Ven.* Your *Cleopatra; Dollabella's Cleopatra:* Every Mans *Cleopatra. Ex homine hunc natum dicas.*

p. 169. In the mean time I muft acquaint the Reader, that however Mr. *Dryden* alleges that this Play [*Gorboduc*] was writ by the Lord *Buckhurft*, I can affure him that the three firft Acts were writ by Mr. *Thomas Norton:* and that the Play it felf was not written in Rime, but blank Verfe, or if he will have it, in *profe mefurée*, fo that Mr. *Shakefpear* notwithftanding our Author's Allegation, was not the firft beginner of that way of Writing.

p. 172 [Dryden's] *Tempeft*, or *The Inchanted Ifland*, a Comedy acted at his Royal Highnefs the Duke of *York's* Theatre, and printed in quarto, *Lond.* 1676. This play is originally *Shakefpear's* (being the [p. 173] firft Play printed in the Folio Edition) and was revif'd by Sr. [W.] *D'Avenant* and Mr. *Dryden* . . .

p. 173 [Dryden's] *Troilus and Creffida*, or *Truth found out too late;* a Tragedy acted at the Duke's Theatre, to which is prefixt a Preface containing the Grounds of Criticifme in Tragedy, printed in quarto, *Lond.* 1679. . . . This Play was likewife firft written by *Shakefpear*, and revif'd by Mr. *Dryden*, to which he added feveral new Scenes, and even cultivated and improv'd what he borrow'd from the Original. The laft fcene in the third Act is a Mafterpiece, and whether it be copied from *Shakefpear, Fletcher,* or *Euripides*, or all of them, I think it juftly deferves Commendation. The Plot of this Play was taken by Mr. *Shakefpear* from *Chaucer's Troilus and Creffida*. . .

p. 182 [Durfey's] *Injur'd Princefs*, or *The fatal Wager*, a

---

[1] Act 4, p. 54.

Tragi-Comedy acted at the Theatre-Royal by his Majesties Servants, printed in quarto *Lond.* 1682. The Defign and the Language of this Play is borrow'd from a Play call'd the *Tragedy of Cymbeline.* In this Play he is not content with robbing *Shakefpear*, but *tops* upon the Audience an old Epilogue to the *Fool turn'd Critick*, for a new Prologue to this Play. So that what Mr. *Clifford* faid of Mr. *Dryden*,[1] is more juftly applicable to our Author, 'That he is a ftrange unconfcionable Thief, that is not content to fteal from others, but robbs his poor wretched Self too.'

[p. 203] John FLETCHER, *and* Francis BEAUMONT, *Esq.*; I am now arriv'd at a brace of Authors, who like the *Diofcuri, Caftor* and *Pollux*, fucceeded in Conjunction more happily than any Poets of their own, or this Age, to the referve of the Venerable *Shakefpear*, and the Learned and Judicious *Johnfon.*

p. 214 [Fletcher's] *Sea Voyage*, a Comedy lately reviv'd by Mr. *Durfey*, under the Title of *The Common-wealth of Women.* This Play is fuppofed by Mr. *Dryden* (as I have obferv'd) to be copied from *Shakefpear's Tempeft.*[2]

*The Storm which vanifht on the neighbring fhore,
Was taught by* Shakefpears Tempeft *firft to roar,
That Innocence and Beauty which did fmile
In* Fletcher, *grew on this Enchanted Ifle.*

p. 215. *Two Noble Kinfmen*, a Tragi-Comedy. This Play was written by Mr. *Fletcher*, and Mr. *Shakefpear.*

p. 217 [Fletcher's] *Woman's Prize*, or *the Tamer tam'd*, a Comedy, written on the fame foundation with *Shakefpear's Taming of the Shrew*; or which we may better call a Second part or counter-part to that admirable Comedy. This was writ by *Fletcher's* Pen likewife.

[1] Notes on Mr. *Dryden's* Poems, p. 7. [2] *Dram. Essay*, p. 35.

GERARD LANGBAINE, 1691.

[p. 342] Chriftopher MARLOE.
An Author that was Cotemporary with the Incomparable *Shakefpear*, and One who trod the Stage with Applaufe both from Queen *Elizabeth*, and King *James*. [No: he was stabd in a Brothel-row on June 1, 1593.]

[p. 396] He [Thomas Otway] was a man of Excellent part and daily improved in his Writing: but yet fometimes fell into plagiary as well as his Contemporaries, and made ufe of *Shakefpear*, to the advantage of his *Purfe*, at leaft, if not his *Reputation*.

[p. 397] *Caius Marius his Hiftory and Fall*, a Tragedy [by Otway] acted at the Duke's Theatre, printed 4°. *Lond.* 1680, and dedicated to the L^d. Vifcount *Faulkland*. A great part of the Play is borrow'd from *Shakefpear's Romeo and Juliet;* as the Character [p. 398] of *Marius* Junior, and *Lavinia* the Nurfe, and *Sulpitius:* which laft is carried on by our Author to the end of the Play: though Mr. *Dryden* fays in his Poftfcript to *Granada*, 'That *Shakefpear* faid himfelf, that he was forc'd to 'kill *Mercurio* [so] in the 3d Act, to prevent being kill'd by 'him.' [*Centurie*, p. 352.]

[p. 424] I know nothing elfe of our Author's [Edward Ravenfcroft's] Writing without I fhould reckon his Alteration of *Titus Andronicus;* of which I fhall fpeak by and by, in the Account of *Shakefpear*.

[p. 451] [Shadwell's] *Timon of Athens, the Man-hater*, his Hiftory, acted at the Duke's Theatre; made into a Play, printed 4°. *Lond.* 1678, and dedicated to the late Duke of *Buckingham*. The Play is originally *Shakefpear's*; but fo imperfectly printed, that 'tis not divided into Acts. How much our Author has added, or expung'd, I muft leave to the Examination of the lefs bufie Reader; I not having time at prefent to inquire into particulars.

[p. 485. James Shirley's] *Triumph of Beauty*, perfonated by fome Young Gentlemen, for whom it was intended, at a private Recreation [1646]. The Subject of this Mafque, is that known Story of the Judgment of *Paris*, upon the Golden-Ball; which you may read in *Lucians Dialogues*. But our Author has imitated *Shakefpear*, in the Comical part of his *Midfummer Nights Dream*; and *Shirley*'s Shepheard *Bottle*, is but a Copy of *Shakefpear's Bottom, the Weaver*.[1]

p. 501 [N. Tate's] *Ingratitude of a Common-wealth*, or *The Fall of* Caius Martius Coriolanus; acted at the Theatre-Royal, printed 4°. *Lond*. 1682. . . . This Play is borrowed from *Shakefpear's Coriolanus*.

Lear King of England *his Hiftory*; acted at the Duke's Theatre: revived with Alterations; printed 4°. *Lond*. 1687. . . . This Play in the Original was writ by *W. Shakefpear*.

Richard the Third [*i.e.* Second], a Hiftory acted at the Theatre-Royal, under the name of *The Sicilian* [p. 502] *Ufurper*, with a Prefatory Epiftle, in Vindication of the Author; occafioned by the prohibition of this Play on the Stage, printed 4°. *Lond*. 1681. . . This Play owns [so] its Birth likewife to *Shakefpear*.

[p. 526] *Arraignment of* Paris, a Paftoral, which I never faw; but it is afcribed by *Kirkman* to Mr. *W. Shakefpear*.

[p. 528] *Contention between* York *and* Lancafter, *with the Death of the Good Duke* Humphry. . . . 4°. Lond. 1600. This Play is only the Second part of *Shakefpear's Henry the Sixth*, with little or no Variation.

[p. 541] *Merry Devil of* Edmonton, a Comedy acted fundry times by his Majefty's Servants at the *Globe* on the Bank-fide, and printed 4°. *Lond*. 1655. This Play is faid by *Kirkman*, to be writ by *Shakefpear*; tho' finding no Name to it, I have

---

[1] Yes; and the casting of the Play to be playd before the Prince, may have been suggested by that in *M. N. Dream*.

plac'd it amongſt thoſe that are anonymous. This Play is founded on the Hiſtory of One *Peter Fabel*, of whom ſee *Fuller's Worthies* in *Middleſex*, p. 186. . . . .

[p. 541] *Mucedorus, the King's son of* Valencia, *and* Amadine *the King's Daughter of* Arragon; *with* [p. 542] *the Merry Conceits of* Mouſe: a Comedy acted by his highneſs's Servants at the *Globe*, and before the King's Majeſty at *Whitehall* on *Shrove-Tueſday* Night; printed 4°. 1668. This Play is ſaid by former Catalogues to have been writ by *Shakeſpear;* and was, I preſume, printed before this Edition. It has been frequently the Diverſion of Country-people in *Chriſtmas* Time.

[p. 556] *Wits,* or *Sport upon Sport,* a Collection of Drolls and Farces, preſented at Fairs by Strolling Players; and printed laſt Edition octavo *Lond.* 1675. Theſe are moſt of them taken out of the Plays of *Shakeſpear, Fletcher, Shirley, Marſton,* &c. There is a former Edition, that has a Table prefixed, which ſhews from what Play each Droll is borrowed.

GERARD LANGBAINE, 1691.

[1] WilliaM Shakespear.

One of the moſt Eminent Poets of his Time; he was born at *Stratford* upon *Avon* in *Warwickſhire;* and flouriſhed in the Reigns of Queen *Elizabeth* and King *James* the Firſt. His Natural Genius to *Poetry* was ſo excellent, that like thoſe Diamonds,[2] which are found in *Cornwall*, Nature had little, or no occaſion for the Aſſiſtance of Art, to poliſh it. The Truth is, 'tis agreed on by moſt, that his Learning was not extraordinary; and I am apt to believe, that his Skill in the *French* and *Italian* Tongues, exceeded his Knowledge in the *Roman* Language: for we find him not only beholding to *Cynthio Giraldi* and *Bandello*, for his Plots, but likewiſe a Scene in *Henry* the Fifth, written in *French*, between the Princeſs *Catherine* and her Governante: Beſides *Italian* Proverbs ſcatter'd up and down in his Writings. Few Perſons that are acquainted with *Dramatick Poetry*, but are convinced of the Excellency of his Compoſitions, in all Kinds of it: and as it would be ſuperfluous in me to endea[3]vour to particulariſe what moſt deſerves praiſe in him, after ſo many Great Men that have given him their ſeveral Teſtimonials of his Merit; ſo I ſhould think I were guilty of an Injury beyond pardon to his Memory, ſhould I ſo far diſparage it, as to bring his Wit in competition with any of our Age. 'Tis true Mr. *Dryden*[4] has cenſured him very ſeverely, in his Poſt-

---

[1] Langbaine. Account of the English Dramatic Poets, 1691 (pp. 453—469).—F.
[2] Dr. *Fuller* in his Account of *Shakeſpear*.   [3] p. 454.
[4] See Mr. *Dryden's* Account.

script to *Granada* ; but in cool Blood, and when the *Enthuſiaſtick Fit* was paſt, he has acknowledged him [in his *Dramatick Eſſay*]. Equal at leaſt, if not Superiour, to Mr. *Johnſon* in *Poeſie*. I ſhall not here repeat what has been before urged in his behalf,[1] in that Common Defence of the Poets of that Time, againſt Mr. *Dryden's* Account of *Ben Jonſon* ;[2] but ſhall take the Liberty to ſpeak my Opinion, as my predeceſſors have done, of his Works; which is this, That I eſteem his Plays beyond any that have ever been publiſhed in our Language: and tho' I extreamly admire *Johnſon*, and *Fletcher* ; yet I muſt ſtill aver, that when in competition with *Shakeſpear*, I muſt apply to them what *Juſtus Lipſius* writ in his Letter to *Andræas Schottus*, concerning *Terence* and *Plautus*, when compar'd ; *Terentium amo, admiror, ſed Plautum magis*.

He has writ about Forty ſix Plays, all which except three, are bound in one Volume in Fol. printed *Lond.* 1685. The whole Book is dedicated to the Earls of *Pembroke* and *Montgomery:* being uſher'd into the World with ſeveral Copies of Verſes; but none more valued [p.455] than thoſe Lines made by *Ben Johnſon* ; which being too long to be here tranſcribed, I ſhall leave them to be peruſ'd by the Reader, with his Works, of which I ſhall give ſome Account as follows.

All's well, that ends well; a Comedy. This Play is founded on a Novel written by *Jean Boccacio* ; ſee his Nov. Day the 3. Nov. the 9. concerning *Juliet* of *Narbona*, and *Bertrand* Count of *Roſſilion*.

---

[1] A probable computation of the thousands of people of both sexes whom Shakespeare's Plays have maintained to this day would appear incredible to any one who did not maturely consider it.—MS. note by OLDYS. But few of the Notes in the interleavd copies of *Langbaine* in Brit. Mus. are given here. Utterson's copy, C. 45. d. is the fuller one.—F.

[2] "Ben Jonson" is scratched out, and "our author" written in a marginal note.—F.

Anthony and Cleopatra, a Tragedy. The ground of this play is founded on History: see Plutarch's Life of *Anthony;* *Appian, Dion Cassius, Diodorus, Florus* &c.

As you like it, a Comedy.

Comedy of Errors. This Play is founded on *Plautus* his *Mœnechmi:* and if it be not a just Translation, 'tis at least a Paraphrase: and I think far beyond the Translation, call'd *Menechmus*, which was printed 4° *Lond.* 1595.

Coriolanus, a Tragedy. This is founded on History: see *Livy, Dionysius Hallicarnassieus; Plutarch's* Life of *Coriolanus,* &c. Part of this play appear'd upon the Stage seven Years since, under the Title of *Ingratitude of a Common-Wealth.*

Cromwell, (*Thomas* L^d.) the History of his Life and Death. This Play is likewise founded on History: See *Fox's Martyrology; Fuller's Church History; Stow, Speed, Hollingshead, Herbert, Baker,* Dr. *Burnet* &c. The Story of *Cromwell,* and Mr. *Frescobald* the Merchant, is related in Dr. *Hakewell's* Apology, and *Wanley's History of Man,* Book 3. Ch. 20.

[p. 456] *Cymbeline his Tragedy.* This Play, tho the Title bear the Name of a King of *Brute's* Linage; yet I think ows little to the Chronicles of those Times, as far as I can collect, from *Grafton, Stow, Milton* &c. But the Subject is rather built upon a Novel in *Boccace, viz.* Day 2. Nov. 9. This Play was reviv'd

---

[1] Shakespeare was deeply delighted with the singing of Dowland the Lutanist, but Spencer's deep conceits he thought surpassed all others. See in his Sonnets *The friendly Concord.* That John Dowland and Thos. Morley are said to have set several of these Sonnets to musick, as well as others composed by Sir P. Sydney, S^r. Edwd. Dyer, S^r. Walter Raleigh, and Kit Marlow and Spencer. When the King of Denmark had heard that Dowland, he requested [as may be seen by his Letter in Harleian Library, No.] King James to part with him, and he had him over to Denmark where he died.—OLDYS.

Shakespeare's Poem called a *Lovers Affection* seems to be written to his beautiful Wife, under some Rumour of Inconstancy.—OLDYS.

by *Durfey* about seven Years since, under the Title of *The Injured Princess*, or *The Fatal Wager*.

Henry the Fourth, the First part; with the Life of *Henry Percy*, sirnamed *Hot-spur*. This Play is built upon our *English* History: see the four former years of his Reign, in *Harding Buchanan, Caxton, Walsingham, Fabian, Polydore Virgil, Hall, Grafton, Hollingshead, Heyward, Trussel, Martin, Stow, Speed, Baker,* &c. As to the Comical Part, 'tis certainly our Author's own Invention; and the Character of Sir *John Falstaff*, is owned by Mr. *Dryden,* to be the best of Comical Characters: and the Author himself had so good an opinion of it, that he continued it in no less than four Plays. This part used to be play'd by Mr. *Lacy*, and never fail'd of universal applause.

Henry the Fourth, the Second part; containing his Death and the Coronation of King *Henry* the Fifth. For the Historical Part, consult the forementioned Authors. The Epilogue to this Play is writ in Prose, and shews that 'twas writ in the Time of Q. *Elizabeth.*

Henry the Fifth, his Life. This play is likewise writ and founded on History, with a Mixture of Comedy. The Play is continued from the beginning of his Reign, to his Marriage [*p.* 457] with *Katherine* of *France.* For Historians, see as before, *Harding, Caxton, Walsingham,* &c. This Play was writ during the time that *Essex* was General in *Ireland*, as you may see in the beginning of the first [1] Act, where our Poet, by a pretty Turn, compliments *Essex,* and seems to foretell Victory to Her Majesties Forces against the Rebels.

Henry the Sixth, the First part.

Henry the Sixth, the Second part, with the Death of the good Duke *Humphrey*.

Henry the Sixth, the Third part, with the death of the Duke

---

[1] First is rightly scratcht but, and "fifth. O" writn in the margin.—F.

of *York*. Thefe three Plays contain the whole length of this King's Reign, *viz*. Thirty Eight Years, fix Weeks, and four Days. Altho' this be contrary to the ftrict Rules of *Dramatick Poetry*; yet it muft be owned, even by Mʳ. *Dryden*[1] himfelf, That this Picture in *Miniature*, has many Features, which excell even feveral of his more exact Strokes of Symmetry, and Proportion. For the Story, confult the Writers of thofe Times, *viz. Caxton, Fabian, Pol. Virgil, Hall, Hollingfhead, Grafton, Stow, Speed, &c.*

Henry the Eighth, the Famous Hiftory of his Life. This Play frequently appears on the prefent Stage; the part of *Henry* being extreamly well acted by Mʳ. *Betterton*. This Play is founded on Hiftory likewife. *Hollingfh. Hall, Grafton, Stow, Speed, Herbert, Martin, Baker, &c.*

Hamlet, Prince of *Denmark*, his Tragedy. I know not whether this ftory be true or falfe; but I cannot find in the Lift given by Dr. *Heylin*, [p. 458] fuch a King of *Denmark* as *Claudius*. All that I can inform: the Reader, is the Names of thofe Authors that have written of the Affairs of *Denmark* and *Norway;* and muft leave it to their further fearch : fuch are *Saxo-Grammaticus, Idacius, Crantzius, Pontanus* &c. This Play was not many years ago printed in quarto ; all being mark'd according to the Cuftom of the Stage, which was cut out in the Action.

John King of *England*, his Life and Death. For the Plot, fee *Matth. Paris, R. Higden, Walfingham, Weftminfter, Fabian, Pol. Virgil, Hollingfhead, Grafton, Stow, Speed, &c.*[2]

Julius Cæfar his Tragedy. This Play is founded on Hiftory ; fee *Livy, Plutarch, Suetonius, &c.* This Play was reviv'd at the Theatre-Royal about fifteen Years ago ; and printed 4ᵗᵒ London

[1] Drammat. Essay, p. 79.
[2] The Tragedy of King John was altered by Cibber and performed as a par'y piece in 1745, under the Title of Papal Tyranny, &c., but without success, &c. O. Derrick.—O[LDYS].

1684. There is an Excellent Prologue to it, printed in *Covent Garden Drollery*, p. 9.

Lear King of *England*,[1] his Tragedy. This Play is founded on Hiſtory; ſee ſuch Authors as have written concerning *Brutes* Hiſtory, as *Leland, Gloceſter, Huntingdon, Monmouth &c.* But the Subject of this Story may be read ſuccinctly in *Milton*'s Hiſtory of *England*, 4°. Book I, p. 17 *&c.* This Play about eight Years ſince was reviv'd with Alterations, by Mr. *Tate*.[2]

Locrine Eldeſt ſon to King *Brutus*, his Tragedy. This Tragedy contains his Reign, with the loſs of *Eſtrildis*, and *Sabra;* which according to *Iſaacſon*'s Chronology was twenty Years. For the Authors, conſult thoſe aforemention'd [p. 459] particularly *Milton*, Book I. p. 14. Supplement to *Theatre of Gods Judgments*, Ch. 6. *Ubaldino Le vite delle Donne Illuſtri*, p. 7.

London *Prodigal*, a Comedy. · This is One[3] of the Seven Plays which are added to this Volume; which tho' printed all of them in 4°. were never in Folio, till 1685. Two of theſe, *viz. Cromwell* and *Locrine*, we have already handled; the Remaining four, *viz. Old-caſtle, Pericles, Puritan Widow,* and *Yorkſhire Tragedy,* ſhall be treated in their order.

Loves Labour loſt, a Comedy : the Story of which I can give no Account of.

Meaſure for Meaſure, a Comedy, founded on a Novel in *Cynthio Giraldi; viz. Deca Ottava, Novella 5ª.* The like Story is in *Goulart's Hiſtoires Admirables de nôtre temps*, Tome 1. *page* 216. and in *Lipſii Monita* L. 2. C. 9. p. 125. This Play, as I have obſerved, was made uſe of with the Comedy *Much ado*

---

[1] 'England' scracht out and 'Britain' written over it.—F.

[2] The Play of Lear is said to have been prohibited acting by Lord Dorset in King Williams Reign.—O[LDYS].

[3] Of the 7 plays here mentioned some of them are much suspected to have been fathered falsely on this author.—O[LDYS].

about nothing by Sir *William D'Avenant*, in his *Law againſt Lovers*.

Merchant of Venice, a Tragi-comedy.

Merry Wives of Windſor, a Comedy; which M*r*. *Dryden* [1] allows to be exactly form'd; and it was regular before any of Ben Johnſon's. This is not wholly without tho Affiſtance of Novels; witneſs M*rs*. *Ford's* conveying out Sir *John Falſtaff* in the Batket of Foul Clothes; and his declaring all the Intrigue to her Huſband, under the name of M*r*. *Broom;* which Story is related in the firſt Novel of *The Fortunate Deceived, and Unfortunate Lovers:* which [p. 460] Book, tho' written ſince *Shakeſpear's* Time, I am able to prove ſeveral of thoſe Novels are tranſlated out of *Cynthio Giraldi*, others from *Malleſpini;* and I believe the whole to be a collection from old Novelliſts.

Mackbeth, a Tragedy, which was reviv'd by the Dukes Company, and re-printed with Alterations, and New Songs,[2] 4° *Lond.* 1674.[3] The Play is founded on the Hiſtory of *Scotland*. The Reader may conſult theſe Writers for the Story: *viz. Hector Boetius, Buchanan, Du Cheſne, Hollingſhead* &c. The ſame Story is ſuccinctly related in Verſe, in *Heywood's Hierarchy of Angels*, B. I, p. 508, and in Prose in *Heylin's* Coſmography, Book I. in the Hiſt. of *Brittain*, where he may read the Story at large. At the Acting of this Tragedy, on the Stage, I ſaw a real one acted in the Pit; I mean the Death of Mr. *Scroop*, who received his death's wound from the late Sir *Thomas Armſtrong*,

---

[1] Dram. Ess. p. 47.

[2] "By Sir W. Davenant." MS. note written over New Songs; and "The music composed by Matthew Locke" in marginal note.

[3] Betterton's Alteration of Macbeth is often acted with many new scenes & Dances, and a Scene between Macduff and his Lady, striking out some pretty gleams of fancy but 'tis much spoiled by being written in Rhime, which he endeavours to excuse as being the reigning taste.— O[LDYS].

and died prefently after he was remov'd to a Houfe oppofite to the Theatre in *Dorfet-Garden*.

Midfummer Nights Dream, a Comedy. The Comical part of this Play, is printed feparately in 4°. and ufed to be acted at *Bartholomew* Fair, and other Markets in the Country by Strolers, under the Title[1] of *Bottom the Weaver*.[2]

Much Ado about Nothing, a Comedy. I have already fpoke of Sir *William D'Avenant's* making ufe of this Comedy. All that I have to remark is, That the contrivance of *Borachio*, in behalf of *John* the Baftard to make *Claudio* jealous of *Hero* by the Affiftance of her Waiting-woman *Margaret*, is borrowed from Ariofto's [p. 461] *Orlando Furiofo:* fee Book the fifth in the Story of *Larcanio, and Geneuza:* the like Story is in *Spencer's Fairy Queen*, Book 2. canto 4.

Oldcaftle, the good Lord Cobham his Hiftory.[3] The Protagonift in this Play, is Sir *John Oldcaftle*,[4] who was executed in the Reign of King *Henry* the Fifth: See his Life at large in *Fox* his Martyrology; D^r. *Fuller*, and other Writers of Church Hiftory, as well as Chronologers.

Othello, the Moor of Venice *his Tragedy*. This is reckoned an Admirable Tragedy; and was reprinted 4°. *Lond.* 1680, and is ftill an Entertainment at the Theatre-Royal. Our Author

---

[1] "The Merrie Conceited humours of." Marginal note.

[2] From the Midsummer Night's Dream was taken the Fairy Queen a Dramatic Opera, 4°. 1692.—O.

N. B. The allusion to Mary Queen of Scots & Q. Elizabeth.—O[LDYS].

[3] 'his History' scracht out, and "The first part of the true & Hon. History of Sir John, acted by the Right Hon. the Earl of Nottingham's, Lord High Admiral of England, his Servants, 1600, 4to." added in marginal note.

[4] When Monsr. Vereiken Embassador to Q. Eliz. for the Archduke & the Infanta was entertained at London by the English Nobility, the Lord Chamberlain, after feasting at his House on March 6th, 1599, made his players act before him in the afternoon Sr John Oldcastle to his great contentment. Sidney's Letters, fol. 1746. Vol. 2. p. 175.—O. [query if it was not the character afterwards changed to Sr John Falstaff?—P.].

borrowed the Story from *Cynthio's* Novels, Dec. 3. Nov. 7. The truth is, *Salujtio Picolomini* in his letter to the Author, extreamly applauds thefe Novels as being moft of them fit Subjects for Tragedy; as you may fee by the following Lines. ' *Gli Heccathomithi voſtri, Signor* Cynthio, *mi fono maravigliofamente piaciuti. Et fra le altre cofe io ci ho veduti i più belli argomenti di Tragedie, che ſi poſſàno imaginare, & quanto a i nodi, & quanto alle folutioni, tanto felicemente ho viſte legate le difficultà, che pare ano impoſſibili ad eſſere ſlegate.* Mr. *Dryden* fays,[1] That moft of *Shakefpear's* Plots, he means the Story of them, are to be found in this Author. I muft confefs, that having with great difficulty obtained the Book from *London*, I have found but two of thofe mentioned by him, tho' I have read the Book carefully over.[2] [p. 462.]

Pericles Prince of Tyre; with the true Relation of the whole Hiftory, Adventures, and Fortunes of the faid Prince. This Play was publifh'd in the Author's Life-time, under the Title of The much Admired Play of *Pericles;* by which you may guefs the value the Auditors and fpectators of that Age had for it. I know not whence our Author fetch'd his Story, not meeting in Hiftory with any fuch Prince of *Tyre;* nor remembring any of that Name, except the Famous *Athenian,* whofe Life is celebrated by *Plutarch.*

Puritan, or The *Widow of Watling Street;* a Comedy fufficiently diverting.

Richard *the Second his Life and Death;* a Tragedy, which is extreamly commended even by M[r]. *Dryden,* in his Grounds of Criticifme in Tragedy, printed before *Troilus and Creſſida;* and Mr. Tate, who altered this Play in 1681, fays, That there are fome Mafter-touches in this Play, that will vye with the beft

---

[1] Preface *Mock Aftrol.*
[2] Jordan, the firſt woman who acted in this play of Othello.— O.

Roman Poets. For the Plot, confult the Chronicles of *Harding, Caxton, Walfingham, Fabian, Pol. Virgil, Grafton, Hollingfhead, Stow, Speed,* &c.

Richard *the Third his Tragedy, with the landing of the Earl of* Richmond, *and the Battle of* Bofworth *Field.* This Play is also founded on Hiftory. See *Fabian, Caxton, Pol. Virgil, Hollingfhead, Grafton, Truffel, Stow, Speed, Baker,* &c.

Romeo and Juliet, a Tragedy. This Play is accounted amongft the beft of our Author's Works. Mr. *Dryden* fays, That he has read the Story of it in the Novels of *Cynthio;* which [p. 463] as yet I cannot find, but fet it down in my former Catalogue, relying upon his Knowledge. But I have fince read it in *French,* tranflated by M. *Pierre Boifteau,* whofe Sir-name was *Launay;* who fays it was writ by *Bandello;* but not having as yet met with *Bandello* in the Original, I muft acquiefce in his Word. The *French* Reader may perufe it in the firft Tome of *Les Hiftoires Tragicques, extraiĉtes des œuvres Italiennes de Bandello, imprimé* 8°. *à Turin* 1570.

Taming of the Shrew, a very diverting Comedy. The Story of the *Tinker,* is related by *Pontus Heuteras, Rerum Bur[gun]dicarum,* lib. 4. and by *Goulart,* in his *Hift. Admirables.* Tom. 1. p. 360.

Tempeft, a Comedy. How much this Play is now in Efteem, tho' the Foundation were *Shakefpear's,* all People know. How it took at the *Black-fryars,* let M*r*. *Dryden's* Preface fpeak. For his Opinion of *Caliban,* the Monfter's Charaĉter, let his Preface to *Troilus and Creffida* explain. ' No man except *Shakefpear,* ever drew fo many Charaĉtars, or generally diftinguifh'd them better from one another, except only *Johnfon:* I will inftance but in one, to fhew the copioufnefs of his Invention: 'tis that of *Caliban,* or the Monfter in the *Tempeft:* He feems here to have created a Perfon, which was not in Nature; a boldnefs which at firſt fight would appear intolerable: For he makes him a *ſpecies* of himſelf, begotten by an *Incubus* on a *Witch:* but this is not wholly beyond the bounds of Credibility; at leaſt, the vulgar (I ſuppoſe) ſtill believe it. [p. 464] But this is not the only Character of this Nature that Mr. *Shakeſpear* has written; for *Merlin*, as he introduces him, is Cozen-german to *Caliban* by Birth; as thoſe may obſerve, who will read that Play. As to the Foundation of this Comedy, I am ignorant whether it be the Author's own Contrivance, or a Novel built up into a Play.

Titus Andronicus his Lamentable Tragedy: This Play was firſt printed 4° *Lond.* 1594. and acted by the Earls of *Derby, Pembroke*, and *Eſſex*, their Servants. 'Twas about the time of the *Popiſh-plot* revived and altered by Mr. *Ravenſcroft*. In his Preface to the Reader, he ſays[1] *That he thinks it a greater theft to rob the Dead of their Praiſe, than the Living of their Money:* Whether his Practice agree with his Proteſtation, I leave to the Compariſon of his Works with thoſe of *Molliere:* and whether Mr. *Shadwell's* Opinion of *Plagiaries*, reach not Mr. *Ravenſcroft*, I leave to the Reader. 'I (ſays he,[2] ingeniouſly) freely confeſs 'my Theft, and am aſham'd on't; tho I have the Example of 'ſome that never yet wrote a Play, without ſtealing moſt of it; 'and (like Men that Lye ſo long, till they believe themſelves) at 'length by continual Thieving, reckon their ſtollen Goods their 'own too: which is ſo Ignoble a thing, that I cannot but believe 'that he that makes a common practice of ſtealing other Men's 'Wit, would, if he could with the ſame Safety, ſteal any thing elſe, 'Mr. *Ravenſcroft*, in the Epiſtle[3] to *Titus*, ſays, That the Play was 'not originally *S'akeſpear's*, but brought by a private Author to 'be acted, and he only gave ſome Maſter-touches, to one or two 'of the Principal Parts or Characters: afterwards he boaſts his 'own pains; and ſays, That if the Reader compare the Old Play

[1] *Syneſius* his Opinion.   [2] Pref. *Sullen Lovers.*   [3] p. 465.

'with his Copy, he will find that none in all that Author's Works 'ever receiv'd greater Alterations, or Additions; the Language 'not only refined, but many Scenes entirely new : Befides moſt 'of the principal Characters heightened, and the Plot much 'encreaſed.' I ſhall not engage in this Controverſy, but leave it to his Rivals in the Wrack of that Great Man, Mr. *Dryden, Shadwell, Crown, Tate,* and *Durfey.* But to make Mr. *Ravenſ-croft* ſome Reparation, I will here furniſh him with part of his Prologue, which he has loſt; and if he defire it, ſend him the whole.

> To day the Poet does not fear your Rage,
> Shakeſpear *by him reviv'd now treads the Stage;*
> Under his ſacred Laurels he ſits down
> Safe, from the blaſt of any Criticks Frown.
> Like other Poets, he'll not proudly ſcorn
> To own, that he but winnow'd Shakeſpear's *Corn;*
> So far he was from robbing him of 's Treaſure,
> That he did add his own, to make full Meaſure.

Timon *of* Athens *his Life.* This Play was thought fit to be preſented on the Stage, with ſome Alterations by Mr. *Shadwell,* in the Year 1678. I ſhall ſay more of it in the Account of his Works. The Foundation of the Story [p. 466] may be read in *Plutarch's* Life of *M. Anthony;* ſee beſides *Lucian's Dialogues, &c.*

Troilus and Creſſida, a Tragedy. Of this Play I have already given an Account : ſee the Name, in the Remarks on M^r. *Dryden,* who altered this Play, in the Year 1679.

Twelfth-Night, or *What you will;* a Comedy. I know not whence this Play was taken ; but the Reſemblance of *Sebaſtian* to his Siſter *Viola,* and her change of Habit, occaſioning ſo many miſtakes, was doubtleſs firſt borrowed (not only by *Shakeſpear,* but all our ſucceeding Poets) from *Plautus,* who has made uſe of it in ſeveral Plays, as in *Amphitruo, Mœnechmi,* &c.

Two Gentlemen of Verona, a Comedy.

Winter's Tale, a Tragi-comedy. The Plot of this Play may be read in a little Stitcht-pamphlet, which is call'd, as I remember, *The Delectable History of* Doraſtus *and* Fawnia; printed 4º *Lond.*

Yorkſhire *Tragedy, not ſo new, as lamentable and true.* This may rather deſerve the Old Title of an Interlude, than a Tragedy; it being not divided into Acts, and being far too ſhort for a Play.

Theſe are all that are in Folio; there reſt yet three Plays to be taken notice of, which are in quarto, *viz.*

Birth of Merlin, *or The Child has loſt his Father;* a Tragicomedy ſeveral times acted with great applauſe, and printed quarto, *Lond.* 1662. This Play was writ by our Author and Mr. *W. Rowly;* of which we have already ſpoken. For the Plot, conſult the Authors of thoſe times: [p. 467] ſuch as *Ethelwerd, Bede, G. Monmouth, Fabian, Pol. Virgil, &c. Stow, Speed, &c. Ubaldino, Le Vite delle Donne Illuſtri,* p. 18.

John *King of* England *his troubleſome Reign;* the Firſt and Second Part, with the Diſcovery of King *Richard Cœur de lyon's* Baſe Son, (vulgarly named the *Baſtard Faucontridge*). Alſo the Death of King *John* at *Swinſtead* Abbey. As they were ſundry times acted by the Queens Majeſties Players, printed quarto *Lond.* 1611. Theſe Plays are not divided into Acts, neither are the ſame with that in Folio. I am apt to conjecture that theſe were firſt writ by our Author, and afterwards reviſed and reduced into one Play by him: that in the Folio, being far the better. For the Plot I refer you to the Authors aforementioned, in that Play which bears the ſame Title.

Beſides theſe Plays, I know Mr. *Kirkman* aſcribes another Paſtoral to him; *viz. The Arraignment of* Paris: but having never ſeen it, I dare not determine whether it belongs to him or no.

GERARD LANGBAINE, 1691.

Certain I am, that our Author has writ two fmall Poems, *viz.* *Venus and Adonis*, printed 8° *Lond.* 1602. and *The Rape of Lucrece*, printed 8° *Lond.* 1655. publifh'd by Mr. Quarles, with a little Poem annext of his own production which bear the Title of *Tarquin banifhed*, or *The Reward of Luft*, Sr. *John Sucklin* had fo great a value for our Author, that (as Mr. *Dryden* obferves in his *Dramatick Effay*) he preferred him to *Johnfon:* and what value he had for this fmall Piece of *Lucrece*, may appear from his Supplement which he writ, and[1] which he has publifht in his Poems: which becaufe it will give you a tafte of both their Mufes, I fhall tranfcribe. [Here follows a copy of the Poem, '*One of her Hands*,' &c., reprinted in the 'Centurie of Praife,' p. 205.]

I have now no more to do, but to clofe up all with an Account of his Death; which was on the 23^d of *April, Anno Dom.* 1616. He [*p.* 469] lyeth Buried in the Great Church in *Stratford* upon *Avon*, with his Wife and Daughter *Sufanna*, the Wife of Mr. *John Hall*. In the North Wall of the Chancel, is a Monument fixed which reprefents his true Effigies, leaning upon a Cufhion, with the following Infcription—'*Ingenio* . . . Apr.' [*See it printed in* Centurie, p. 125.]

Near the Wall where this Monument is Erected, lyeth a plain Free-ftone, underneath which, his Body is Buried, with this Epitaph

Good Friend, . . . *Bones* [&c.: see *Centurie*, p. 121].[2]

[1] p. 468.
[2] Charles Gildon, in " The Lives and Characters of the English Dramatick Poets—First begun by Mr. *Langbain*, improv'd and continued down to this Time, by a Careful Hand. London, 1698," says, p. 126 :—

William Shakespear.

He was born and buried in *Stratford* upon *Avon*, in *Warwickfhire*. I have been told that he writ the Scene of the Ghost in *Hamlet*, at his house which bordered on the Charnel-House and Church-Yard. He was both

Player and Poet; but the greatest Poet that ever trod the Stage, I am of Opinion, in spight of Mr. *Johnson* and others from him, that though perhaps he might not be that Critic in Latin and Greek as *Ben*; yet that he understood the former, so well as perfectly to be Master of their Histories, for in all his Roman Characters he has nicely followed History, and you find his *Brutus*, his *Cassius*, his *Anthony*, and his *Cæsar*, his *Coriolanus*, &c. just as the Historians of those times describe 'em. He died on the 23rd April, 1616, and is buried with his wife and daughter in *Stratford Church* aforesaid.

J. N.,[1] 1691.

*Shakespear &
Fletcher præ-
stantissimi Po-
etæ Dramatici
apud Anglos.*

*Hìc tamen, ut patriæ meritos folvamus Honores,
Dirigit obfcuros vatûm par nobile greffus,
Sublimes, quantùm non noxia tempora tardant,
Incultique hebetant mores, perituraque lingua:*

*   *   *   *   *

*Falstaff cele-
bris character
Comicus apud
Shakesperum.*

Fert palmam hìc, fenfa ut promam liberrima, † *Miles
Helluo, vanus, adulator, comes ufque facetus.*

*Tentamen | de | Arte Poetica, Authore | Comite de Mulgrave,
Regis nuper Jacobi II. | Hospitii Regii Camerario magno, à
Secretioribus | Consiliis, &c |ex | Anglico Latinè Redditum
*⁎*er J. N. A. M. (in the 2nd Edition* An Essay on
Poetry: | *London, J. Hindmarsh,* 1961,* *p.* 20, 22.)

* By the | Right Honourable, | the | Earl of Mulgraue./ The Second
Edition./ *London,* | Printed for Ja. Hindmarsh, at the *Golden-Ball* | over
against the *Royal Exchange* in | *Cornhil.* MDCXCL./ folio.

The English original of these passages, from the 1st edition of 1682, is
printed in the *Centurie,* p. 394, but in the 2nd Edition of 1691 the last line
of the *Centurie* quotation appears with a fresh side-note,

But || *Falstaff* seems inimitable yet.   ¶ An admirable
Character in
a lay of
Shakespear's.

[1] Said to be 'John Morris,' in the Brit. Mus. Catalogue. I doubt it.

[F. J. F.]

Jn. SHEFFIELD, DUKE OF BUCKINGHAM, 1692.

Hope to mend Shakefpear! or to match his Style!
'Tis fuch a Jeft, would make a Stoick fmile.
Too fond of Fame, our Poet foars too high;
Yet freely owns he wants the Wings to fly:
So fenfible of his prefumptuous Thought,
That he confeffes while he does the Fault:
This to the Fair will no great wonder prove,
Who oft in Blufhes yield to what they love.

> Jn. Sheffield, Duke of Buckingham (died 24 Feb. 1720-1).
> Prologue to his Alteration of *Julius Cæsar*, ed. 1723,
> 2 vols. 4°., I. 211.

His Works, London, E Curll, 1721, 8°. contain
"Four Chorus's to be Sung between the Acts of a Tragedy."
Written in the year 1692 (viz. Julius Cæsar), pp. 132—139.
Nothing is said of the date of his plays in Johnson's Series of the Poets;
Biogr. Brit. on Chalmer's Biogr. Dict.

SAMUEL JOHNSON, 1692.

By the Doctrine of an Ufurper *fet up by God, you have nothing left you : for a Kingdom of God's giving is* Nebuchadnezzar's *Kingdom ;* Dan. 5. 18, 19. Whom he would he flew, and whom he would he kept alive, and whom he would he fet up, and whom he would he put down. *So that it is the World's End with any or all of you, whenever the Court fends for your Lives, Liberties or Eflates. Such an Ufurper is a God upon Earth, which it is eafy for fome fort of Men to make. For fo* Calyban *made* Stephano *his God, and offered to lick his Foot; but it was for what he could get by him : And therefore it was* Trinculo's *Opinion, and it is alfo mine, that if his God were afleep, he would rob his Bottle.*

> An / Argument / proving / That the Abrogation of King *James* by / the People of *England* from the Regal Throne, / and the Promotion of the Prince of *Orange*, / one of the Royal Family, to the Throne of / the Kingdom in his stead, was according to / the Constitution of the English Government, / and Prescribed by it. / In Opposition to all the false and treacherous / Hypothesses, of Usurpation, Conquest, Desser-/tion, and of taking the Powers that *Are* upon / Content. / By *Samuel Johnson*. / *Nec Deus intersit nisi dignus vindice nodus* / *Inciderit.*—Horat. / *London*, / Printed for the Author. 1692. / p. 29.

BOOKSALE-CATALOGUES, 1678-92.

13 May 1678.

Catalogus / Librorum / In Quavis Lingua & Facultate insignium / Instructissimarum Bibliothecarum / Tum clarissimi Doctissimique Viri / D. Doctoris Benjaminis Worsley, / Tum , Duorum Aliorum Doctrina Præstantium : Quorum Auctio habebitur *Lon.tini* / in Œdibus è regione signi Gallinæ cum Pullis in / Vico vulgò dicto 𝔓ater 𝔣oster=𝔚o𝔴./ *Maii* 13. 1678./ Per *Joan. Dunmore* & *Ric. Chiswell*, Bibliopolas./ Catalogi gratis distribuentur ad Insigne Trium Bibliorum in V.co / dicto 𝔏ud𝔤ate=𝔰treet, & Rosæ Coronatæ / in Cæmeterio Paulino. 1678 4to. 2, 26, 51, 58, 13 pages. (The prices are marked in MS. in the British Museum copy.)

ENGLISH in Folio (p. 1—9, 364 nos.)

303. Shakefpear (W.) his Comedies, Hiftories and Tragedies.[1]
 (*a*)   0 — 16 — 0
304. ——— Idem iterum 1663. (*i*)   1 — 8 — 6

No explanation is given of the letters *a* and *i* which often occur throughout the catalogue. These were the first copies of Shakspere sold in England by Book Auction, and this was the fourth auction of books in England. The previous auctions were those of the libraries of Dr. Lazarus Seaman, 31 Oct. 1676 ; of Thomas Kidner, A.M., Rector of Hitchin, Herts, 6 Feb. 167⅞ ; and of William Greenhil, Vicar of Stepney, 18 Feb. 167⅞. Coke upon Littleton, London, 1670, fol. sold for 16s. ; Ben Johnson's Works, 2 vols. fol. 1640 for £1 13s. 6 ; King James Works, fol. 1616 for 19s. ; Raleigh's *History of the world*, 1614, fol. for 18s.; Spencer's *Fairy Queen*, &c., 1617, fol. for 15s. ; Stow's *Survey of London*, 1633, fol. 26s.; Speed's *Maps of Great Britain*, etc., 1676, fol. 35s. Holyoke's *Latin Dictionary*, 1677, fol. 24s. 6d. ; Plutarch's *Lives and Morals*, 2 vols. 1603, 1612, fol. for 27s. 6d.; The same 2 Vol, 1657, fol. 34s.; so that the two Shakspear folios sold for comparatively high prices.

---

[1] Dibdin, *Bibliomania*, p. 307, ed. 1876, says that this was the 2nd Folio of 1632 ; but the *Idem* of no. 304 implies that it was the 3rd Folio of 1663.

336 BOOKSALE-CATALOGUES, 1678, 1684.

Among the *English in Octavo*
822. Sport upon Sport, in Selected pieces of Drollerie. 1672 (a)
823. Scarronides, or *Virgil Travestie;* a Mock-Poem, 2 parts in 2 Vol. [no date]
824. Scoffer Scoft; Some of *Lucian*s Dialogues in *English*-Fustian. 1675 (a)
Sold for 3s.   PONSONBY A. LYONS.

14 Nov. 1678.

Catalogus / Variorum et Insignium Librorum Instructissimarum Bibliothecarum / Doctiss Clarissimorumq; Virorum / D. *Johannis Godolphin,* J. U, D, / et / D. *Oweni Phillips,* A.M. / & Scholæ *Wintoniensis* Hypo-Didascali, / Quorum Auctio habebitur *Londini* / in Vico Vulgo dicto 𝔚𝔢𝔰𝔱𝔪𝔬𝔯𝔩𝔞𝔫𝔡=𝔒𝔬𝔲𝔯𝔱 in St. *Bartho-/lomew*-Close Novembris 11, / Per *Gulielmum Cooper* Bibliopolum./ Catalogi Gratis Distribuentur ad Insigne Pelicani in Vico Vulgo / dicto *Little-Britain* 1678, / 4to, 52, 59 pages. The prices are marked in MS. in the British Museum copy.

Bundles of Pamphlets. (p. 36 to 59; 77 nos.)

26.
Elkan. Settles Love and Revenge, a Tragedy 1675
W. Shakefpears Tragedy of Hamlet Prince of Denmark 1676
The Tragedy of Macbeth with all the Additions . 1674
The Comical Revenge, or Love in a Tub 1664
The Wedding, written by James Shirley 1660
The Antipodes, A Comedy, by Rich. Brome 1640
The Unfortunate Favorite, a Tragedy 1664
A Cure for a Cuckold, by Jo. Webster and Will Rowley . 1661
The Converted Courtezan, by Th. Dekker 1604
Loves Victory, by Will Chamberlain 1658
Sold for 0—3—10.

Bundle 37 consisting of
Pericles Prince of Tyre by Will. Shakefpear . . . 1635
and 11 other plays sold for 0—5—6.
All the above appear to have been in Quarto.   P. A. L.

2 May, 1684.
Catalogus / Librorum / Reverendi Doctiq; Viri / *Matth. Smallwood,* S. T. P. / & Decani de *Lychfield* nuper Defuncti./ Quorum Auctio habebi-

tur *Londini* / in *Collegio Greshamensi* in Vico Vulgo dicto *Bishops-gate-street*, 2 die *Maii* 1684./ * * * Londini, 1684./ 4to 36 pages. The prices are marked in MS. in the British Museum Copy.

English in Folio (p. 23—25, 104 nos.)

99. Shakespear's (Will.) Comedies, Histories, and Tragedies, 3^d Edition. 1664. 0—15—6.

("Spenser's Fairy Queene, with other Works of Poetry, 1611., fol. sold for 4s. 1d. Ben Johnsons Works or Plays. First Vol, 1616, fol. 12s. Chaucer the Ancient Poet (Geffray) his Works perfect and fair, fol. 7s.)

(Ogilby's Virgil, 1654 (with Sculptures and gilt-Leafs, sold for 15s. 3d. Beaumont & Fletchers comedies and Tragedies, 1647, for 8s. Ben Johnsons Plays. First Volume, 1616. 12s.)

Matthew Smallwood succeeded as Dean of Lichfield in 1671, and died 26 April, 1693.   PONSONBY A. LYONS.

In 1684, 'A Catalogue of PLAYS, Printed for R. Bentley,' contains, out of 67 Plays, 4 of Shakspere's : nos.

30. Hamlet, Prince of Denmark, a *Tragedy* . . .
39. King Leare . . .
43. Moor of Venice . . .
95. Julius Cæsar . . .

(In Nat. Lee's *Constantine the Great*. Printed by H. Hills, jun. R. Bently, 1684.)—F. J. F.

Easter Term. 1685.

Reprinted.

4. Mr *William Shakespears* Comedies, Histories and Tragedies. Published according to the true original Copies. The fourth Edition. *Folio.* Printed for *H. Herringman*, and sold by *J. Knight*, and *F: Saunders* at the blew Anchor in the lower walk of the *New Exchange*.

A catalogue of Books Continued. (*Numb*. 19.) Printed and published at *London* in *Easter*-Term. 1685.

PONSONDY A. LYONS.

8 Sep. 1685.

Bibliotheca Sturbrigiensis, sive Catalogus Variorum Librorum, Antiquorum et Recentiorum Plurimis Facultatibus Insignium, Per Auctionem Vendendorum (In Gratiam Celeberrimæ Cantabrigiensis Academiæ) In Nundino Sturbrigiano, Prope Cambridg) Octavo die *Septembris*, 1685. Per *Edwardum Millingtonum*, Bibliopolam, Lond. Catalogues are gevin to all Gentlemen-Scholars, &c. at the several Coffee houses in Cambridg, 1685. 4to. 18 (Latin books), 12 (English). 1154 titles.

To the Reader. * * * This *Auction* will begin on *Tuesday* the 8th day of *September*, at the Auction-Booth in *Sturbridg*-Fair, from the Hours of Eight in the Morning to Eleven, and from One in the Afternoon to Five in the Evening ; and there continue daily until all the Books are sold.

Miscellanies in Folio ; viz. *History*, *Voyages*, *Travels*, *Military*, *Law*, Heraldry, &c. (p. 7—10, 101 nos.)

98 *Shakespears* Works ; *viz*. Comedies, Histories, Tragedies, 1685

Millington did not offer Shakspere for sale in his Catalogue for the fair of 1684.   PONSONBY A. LYONS.

---

19 Oct. 1685.

Catologus Variorum Librorum ex Bibliothecis Selectissimis Doctissim. Virorum Nuperime Defunctorum Quorum Auctio habebitur *Londini* in Ædibus *Johannis Bridge*, Vulgo dicto *Bridges* Coffee-House in *Popes Head Alley* in Cornhill 19 die Octobris 1685. 4°. 2,88 pages.

The title page of the British Museum copy is marked in a contemporary hand, "Thomas' Parkhursts booksellr." "This Sale consists of the Libraries of two Learned Men deceased" (Address to the Reader).

Among the "*Volumes of Miscellanies in* Quarto *bound*" is :—

53. Antonio's revenge, the 2d part. Tragedy of Andronicus. Cupids revenge by Fletcher ; with 8 more playes by Shakespear, &c. *wants the end*.
PONSONBY A. LYONS.

---

30 Nov. 1685.

A Catalogue Containing Variety of Ancient, and Modern English Books in Divinity, History, Philology, Philosophy, Physick, Mathematicks, &c. Together with Bibles, Testaments, Common Prayers, Singing Psalms, &c. of the best Prints in all Volumes ; Will be exposed to Sale (by way of Auction or who bids most) at Petty-*Canon*-Hall in *Petty-Canon*-Alley on the

BOOKSALE-CATALOGUES, 1685, 1686.

North side of St *Paul's* Church-yard, entring into *Pater-Noster-Row*, the 30*th* day of *November* 1685. *By* Edward Millington *Bookseller.* 4¹⁰.

English in Folio. (p. 1—7, 326 nos.)
288. Shakspear's Playes 1685
PONSONBY A. LYONS.

A Collection of Choice Books in Divinity, History, Philosophy, Heranldry, Horsemanship, Husbandry, with Variety of Books of Voyages, Travels, as also of Romances, Plays, Novels, &c. 𝕮𝖚𝖗𝖎𝖔𝖚𝖘𝖑𝖞 𝕭𝖔𝖚𝖓𝖉. Will be exposed to sale by way of Auction at *Bridges* Coffee-House in *Popes-Head-Alley* over-against the *Royal Exchange* in *Cornhill* on *Monday* the 8*th* day of February, 168²⁄₆. By *Edward Millington*, Bookseller. 4¹⁰. 48 pages.

Poetry, Plays, Romances, Novels, &c. Folio.

24. Shakespear (*Will*) his Comedies, Histories and Tragedies
    1685
    Bundles of Plays. Quarto. (30 nos.)

6 { Six Comedies and Tragedies (*viz.*) The Amorous Fryars. *Tamerlane* the Great. *Lucius Junius Brutus.* Wrangling Lovers. *Othello* the Moor of *Venice.* And the Modist Lovers . .

9 { Six Comedies and Tragedies (*viz.*) Wrangling Lovers. *Othello* the Moor of *Venice.* Sir *Fopling Flutter. Venice* preserved. *Gloriana* and the Plain Dealer . . . .

10 { Six Comedies and Tragedies (*viz.*) Modist Lovers. *Thyestes.* The Marchants Wife. The *London* Chanticleres. Madam *Fickle.* And the History of King *Lear* . . . .

17 { Six Comedies and Tragedies (*viz.*) The *Spanish* Rogue. The *French* Puritan. *Mithrodates* king of *Pontus*. History of *Richard* th 2*d*. Dame *Dobson.* And the heir of *Morocco* . .

19 { Six Comedies and Tragedies (*viz.*) The Mock-Tempest. The Atheist. The Virtuous Wife. *Macbeth.* The Wild Gallant. And Piso's Conspiracy. PONSONBY A. LYONS.

1686.

Catalogus / Variorum / in quavis / Linguo & Facultate / Insignium / *Tam Antiquorum quam Recentium*/ Librorum/ *Richardi Davis* Bibliopolæ./ Quorum Auctio (in gratiam & commodum Eru/ditorum) Oxoniæ habenda est è regione/ Ecclesiæ D. Michaelis, Aprilis. 19. 1686./ 4¹⁰. 212 pages. The prices are marked in MS. in the British Museum copy.

English Miscell.   Folios.   (p. 147)

450. *Shakespear's* (W.) Comedies, Histories and Tragedies [4th ed.] . . . *Lond.* 1685
Sold for "0. 18. 0."

English Folio (p. 211.)

68. William Shakespeares Comedies, Histories and Tragedies [2nd. ed.]. London. 1632
Sold for "0. 15. 1."

Among these English Folios, Bysshop Jo. Hackets Century of Sermons, 1675 sold for 15s. 6d. The works of the author of the Whole Duty of Man for 16s. The History of the Jews by Josephus, last edition with Sculpture, 1683, for 15s. 6d. Holyoake Latin Dictionary for 15s. 10d. Beaumont and Fletchers Fifty Comedies and Tragedies, 1672, for 15s. 10d.—P. A. L.

Catalogus Universalis Librorum in Omni Facultate, Linguaque Insignium, & Rarissimorum ; * * * Londini, apud JOANNEM HARTLEY Bibliopolam, exadversum *Hospitio Grayensi* in vico vulgo *Holburn* dicto. MDCXCIX. 12mo, 2 vols. Vol. II. p. G¹, 33.

English in Folio. [p. G 5.]

Shakspears (*W.*) Comedies, Histories, and Tragedies, *Best Edit. Lond.* 1685.   PONSONBY A. LYONS.

---

17 Feb. 1687.

A Catalogue of English Books : in Divinity, Humanity, Philology, History, &c. of Mr. *Charles Mearne's*, late Bookseller to His Majesty ; which will be exposed to Sale by Auction, at Richards' Coffee-House in *Fleetstret*, near the *Middle-Temple* Gate, on *Thursday*, the 17th day of this Instant February 168⅞. By Edward *Millington* Bookseller. 4to. 1818 nos.

English Miscellanies in Folio. (173 nos.)

156. Shakespear's (Will.) Comedies Histories and Tragedies.
1685

Appendix.—English Miscellanies in Folio. (200 nos.)

136. Shakespeare, &c. 1685.   PONSONBY A. LYONS.

21 Nov. 1687.

Bibliotheca Illustris sive Catalogus variorum Librorum * * * * Quorum Auctio habebitur Londini at Insigne Ursi in Vico dicto Ave Mary Lane, prope Templum D. Pauli. *Novemb.* 21. 1687. Per T. Bentley, & B. Walford, Bibliopolas, Lond. 4to, 94 pages, 4161 nos. The library of a great man deceased, price 6d.

(This seems to be the first auction catalogue for which a charge was made.)

English Folio *omitted*. (p. 94. 37 nos.)

27. *W. Shakespear's* Works, *viz.* Comedies Histories and Tragedyes, Oc. 4. Edit. . . . . *Lond.* 1685
PONSONBY A. LYONS.

13 Feb. 1688.

Catalogus Librorum Roberti Scott Bibliopolæ Regii *Londinensis* In quavis Linguo & Facultate Insignium Ex variis Europæ Partibus Advectorum, Quorum Auctio habenda est Londini, ad Insigne Ursi in Vico (vulgo dicto) *Ave-Mary-Lane*, prope *Ludgate-street*, Decimo Tertio Die *Februarii*, 168¾. Per *Benjaminum Walford*, Bibliopolam Londinensem. 4to, 176 pages. 8667 nos. A copy in the British Museum has prices marked in MS.

English Miscellanies in Folio. (p. 166—169, 166 nos.)

57. W. Shakespears Plays Collected into one Volume   1685
  —15—6

157. W. Shakesphears works . . . . . 1685 —15—4
PONSONBY A. LYONS.

1691.

821. i. 9.

Catalogus Variorum Librorum in Linguis et Facultatibus Omnigenis Insignium Sive Bibliotheca Instructissima Doctissimi cuiusdam Generosi Nuperrimme Defuncti * * * Quorum Auctio habebitur apud *TOM*'s Coffee-House junto *Ludgate* Die *Jovis* 26 Martii hora tertia post Meridian. [1691. p. 30.]

English Divinity, History, Poetry, Travels and Miscellanies in Folio.

56. *Shakespear's* Works, best Edition. . . London.   1664
—P. A. LYONS.

18 Ap. 1692.

Bibliotheca Ornatissima : or, A Catalogue of Excellent Books As well *Greek, Latin,* &c. as *English,* in all Faculties. As also of Divers Extraordinary, and choice Manuscripts which will be Sold by Auction at *Wills'* (lately *Roll's*) Coffe-house, over-against the *North* Door of St. *Pauls,* in St. *Paul's* Church-yard, *London,* on April 18. 1692. By Nathaniel Rolls. 4to. 72 pages.

English Miscellanies in Folio (220 nos).

15 Shakespears Comedies Histories and Tragedies.[1] . 1685
—PONSONBY A. LYONS.

(In 1726 we learn that only 15 of Shakspere's plays had been acted with applause : this from

"A Compleat Catalogue of all the Plays That were ever yet Printed In the English Language. Containing The Dates and Number of Plays Written by every particular Author : An Account of what Plays were Acted with Applause, and of those which were never Acted ; and also the Authors now Living. In Two separate Alphabets. Continued to the present year 1726. The Second Edition, London Printed for W. Mears, at the Lamb without Temple-Bar. MDCC.XXVI. Price One Shilling stitch'd.

N. B.—Those Plays that follow with this * Mark were acted with Applause. [I take out those only of]

---

[1] A later one, dated 29 June 1698, is this :—
Bibliotheca Levinziana sive Catalogus Diversorum Librorum Plurimis Facultatibus, Linguisque variis, præ-cæteris Excellentium, Quos Ingenti sumptu, & summa curâ sibi procuravit, Doct. G. Levinz M.D. in Academ. Oxoniensi S. Joh. Colleg. Præses dignissimus, nec non Ling. Græcæ Professor Regius. Quorum Auctio Habenda est in Gratiam Doctissim. Virorum Academ. Oxon. in Edibus Banisterianis prope Northgate (29) die Junii 1698. per Edwardum Millingtonum Bibliopol. Londin. 4to 76 pages. 3409 nos. "with about 200 more Volumes Bound, Stitcht in Bundles of all sorts Ancient and Modern ; * * * Of Plays and Poetry, History, &c."

Miscellanies in Folio, *History,* &c. (98 nos.)

54. Shakespear's Comedies, Histories and Tragedies . 1664 among *Miscellaneous Tracts.* No. 30 contained "The Tempest" with six other plays ; no. 38 "History of K. Richard II." with 8 others ; no. 40 "Timon of Athens" and 10 others ; no. 42 "Henry VI 2 parts" and 10 others ; no. 43 "Mackbeth" and 12 others ; no. 44 "Anthony and Cleopatra," "Troilus and Cresseida," and 9 others.

Note to KIRKMAN, *above*, p. 191.

William Shakespear.

* 1. The Tempest, a Comedy.
* 3. The Merry Wives of Windsor, a Comedy.
* 8. Midsummer Nights Dream, a Comedy.
* 11. The taming of the Shrew, a Comedy.
* 16. The Life and Death of King Richard II., a Comedy.
* 17. Henry the Fourth, an Hist. Play. The first Part.
* 23. The Life and Death of Richard the Third, with the landing of the Earl of Richmond and the Battle of Bosworth Field.
* 24. The life of king Henry the Eighth.
* 29. Timon of Athens, a Tragedy.
* 30. Julius Cæsar, a Tragedy.
* 31. Mackbeth, a Tragedy.
* 32. Hamlet Prince of Denmark.
* 34. Othello the Moor of Venice, a Tragedy.
* 35. Antony and Cleopatra, a Tragedy.
* 37. Pericles Prince of Tyre, an Historical Play.
* 39. The History of Sir John Old-Castle, the good Lord Cobham.

William Alexander, Earl of *Stirling*.

* 4. Julius Cæsar, a Tragedy.

(*Crown*, neither part of *Henry VI* has a star.)

John Dryden, Esq.

* 8. The Tempest or the Inchanted Island, a Comedy, 1676.

(Duffet's Mock Tempest has no asterisk.)

* 14. Troilus and Cressida, or Truth found out too late, a Tragedy, 1679.

Tho. Shadwell, Esq.

* 9. Timon of Athens, or the Man-hater, a Tragedy, 1678.

NOTE TO KIRKMAN, ABOVE, p. 191.

Sir Charles Sidley.
* 2. Antony and Cleopatra.

Nahum Tate, Esq.†
* 8. King Lear and his three Daughters, an Hist. Play.

† Tate's version of 1681 is given to N. Lee in a Catalogue of " Poems, Plays, &c., 1681 :
The History of King *Lear*, acted at the Dukes Theatre. Revived with alterations, by *N. Lee; quarto* price 1s."
> A Catalogue of Books continued, printed and published at *London*, in *Easter-Term*, 1681.

THE ATHENIAN MERCURY, 1691.

But fince we can't go through all the World, let's look home a little. *Grandfire Chaucer*, in fpite of the Age, was a Man of as much wit, fence and honefty as any that have writ after him. Father *Ben* was excellent at *Humour*, *Shakefpear* deferves the Name of *fweeteft*, which *Milton* gave him.—*Spencer* was a noble poet, his *Fairy-Queen* an excellent piece of Morality, Policy, Hiftory. *Davenant* had a great genius. Too much can't be faid of Mr *Coley*. *Milton's Paradife loft*, and fome other Poems of his will never be *equall'd*. *Waller* is the moft *correct* Poet we have.

The Athenian Mercury, Vol. 2. numb. 14, Saturday, July 11. 1691.
Answer to
Question 3. *Which is the beft* Poem *that ever was made and who in your Opinion, deferves the* Title *of the beft* Poet *that ever was.*

The Athenian Mercury began 17 Mar. 1691. under the title of "The Athenian Gazett, Resolving Weekly all the most *Nice and* curious Questions Proposed by the Ingenious." At the end of No. I. is the following

ADVERTISEMENT.

All Perfons whatever may be refolved gratis *in any Question that their own fatisfaction or Curiofity fhall prompt 'em to, if they fend their Queftions by a Penny Poft letter to Mr* Smith *at his Coffee-Houfe* in Stocks Market *in the* Poultry, *where orders are given for the Reception of fuch Letters, and care fhall be taken for their Refolution by the next Weekly Paper after their fending.*

PONSONBY A. LYONS.

ATHENIAN SOCIETY, 1692.

We are pretty confident, it wou'd not have been for the Difreputation of Sir *William Davenant*, if the World had never feen any thing of his, but his *Gondibert*, and the much more Excellent *Shakefpear* wou'd not have been lefs admir'd, if an abundance of thefe things which are Printed for his, were omitted, Mr *Cowly* is of this Opinion we are fure;

> *An Essay upon all sorts of Learning, Written by the* Athenian *Society*, (p. xii, xiii) prefixed to "The / Young = Students = Library, / containing, / Extracts and Abridgments / of the / Most Valuable Books / Printed / In *England*, and in the Forreign Journals, From the / year Sixty Five, to This Time, / To which is Added, / *A New Essay upon all sorts of Learning;* / Wherein / The Uses of the Sciences / Is Distinctly Treated on./ By the Athenean Society./ Also, A Large Alphabetical Table, / Comprehending / *The Contents of this Volume./* And of All / The *Athenian Mercuries* and *Supplements*, &c./ Printed in the Year 1691./ London, / Printed for *John Dunton*, at the *Raven* in the Poultry, Where is to be had the *Intire Sett* of *Athenian Gazetts*, and the *Supplements to 'em* for the Year, 1691. bound up all together, (*with the Alphabetical Table to the Whole Year*) or else in Separate Volumes, (Or single Mercuries to this Time.) 1692.' fol. pages, 2, xviii, 479, 32 = 531.

—P. A. LYONS.

347

1692.

The / Fairy-Queen : / an / Opera./ Reprefented at the / Queen's-Theatre / By Their / Majefties Servants./ London, / Printed for *Jacob Tonfon*, at the *Judges-Head* / in *Chancery-Lane*, 1692./

[This is Shakspere's *Midsummer Night's Dream*, with additions, Songs and Dances, 24 Chinese, and Juno "in a Machine drawn by Peacocks. . . While a Symphony Plays, the Machine moves forward, and the Peacocks spread their Tails, and fill the middle of the Theatre," &c., &c. Later, "Six Monkeys come from between the Trees, and Dance," "and the Grand Dance begins of Twenty four Persons."

Jn. Downes, Sir William Davenant's Prompter, &c., says of this Opera : "*The Fairy Queen*, made into an Opera, from a Comedy of Mr. *Shakespears:* This in Ornaments was superior to the other two [Operas, — Dryden's *King Arthur* and Betterton's *Prophetess* or *Dioclesian*, each with Music by Henry Purcel, and Dances by Jn. Priest] ; especially in Cloaths, for all the Singers and Dancers, Scenes, Machines and Decorations, all most profusely set off ; and excellently perform'd, chiefly the Instrumental and Vocal part Compos'd by the said Mr. *Purcel*, and Dances by Mr. *Priest*. The Court and Town were wonderfully satisfy'd with it : but the Expences in setting it out being so great, the Company got very little by it." 1708. Jn. Downes. *Roscius Anglicanus*, or an Historical Review of the English Stage, 1660—1706, p. 42-3

I give this entry here because so much of Shakspere's Play is kept in the Opera, very far more than there is of *Coriolanus* in N. Tate's *Ingratitude of a Common-Wealth: or, the Fall of Caius Martius Coriolanus*, 1682 (see *Centurie*, p. 392).—F. J. F.]

JOHN DOWNES, 1663—1693 (in 1708).

[Downes's book is entitled "*Roscius Anglicanus,* / or an / Historical / Review of the / Stage : / After it had been Suppres'd by means / of the late Unhappy Civil War, be-/ gun in 1641, till the Time of King / *Charles* the II^s. Restoration in *May* / 1660. Giving an Account of its Rise / again ; of the Time and Places the / Governours of both the Companies / firs Erected their Theatres/
"The Names of the Principal Actors and / Actresses, who Perform'd it the Chiefest / Plays in each House. With the Names / of the most taking Plays ; and Modern / Poets. For the space of 46 Years, and / during the Reign of Three Kings, and / part of our present Sovereign, Lady / Queen A N N E, from 1660 to 1706. / *Non Audita narro, sed Comperta.* / *London.* Printed and sold by *H. Playford*, at his House in / *Arundel-street*, near the Water-side, 1708. / "
And tho his account of Shakspere's Plays and their Actors should be excluded by the letter of the law which ends Shakspere's *Centurie* at 1693, yet as Downes was in Davenant's theatre in 1662, and Book-keeper and Prompter up to 1706, he was an eye-witness of what went on during 1660-93, and therefore I think his account of what he saw, tho not written down till 1708, may fairly come into our *Centurie* additions. This is Downes's account of himself :—]

TO THE READER.

THE *Editor of the enfuing Relation, being long Converfant with the Plays and Actors of the Original Company, under the Patent of Sir* William Davenant, *at his Theatre in* Lincolns-Inn-Fields, *Open'd there* 1662. *And as Book keeper*[1] *and Prompter, continu'd fo, till* October 1706, *He Writing out all the Parts in*

---

[1] "*Book-keeper* means here, not one who *keeps* accounts, but the person who is *entrusted with*, and *holds a book of the Play*, in order to furnish the Performers with written parts and to prompt them when necessary "(*Roscius Anglicanus* . . . with Additions by the late Mr Thomas Davies, author of the Life of Garrick and Dramatic Miscellanies, London, 1789, 8º. p. iii.

JOHN DOWNES, 1663—1693 (in 1708).   349

each Play ; and Attending every Morning the Actors Rehearſals, and their Performances in Afternoons ; Emboldens him to affirm, he is not very Erronious in his Relation. But as to the Actors of Drury-lane *Company, under Mr.* Thomas Killigrew, *he having the account from Mr.* Charles Booth, *ſometimes Book-keeper there ; If he a little Deviates, as to the Succeſſive Order, and exact time of their Plays Performances. He begs Pardon of the Reader, and Subſcribes himſelf,*
His very humble Servant,
John Downes.

[He then mentions the 6 Playhouses allowd in London in Charles I's. Reign, and says that

(p. 1, 2.) "The scattered Remnant of several of these Houses, upon King *Charles's* Restoration, Fram'd a Company, who acted again at the Bull [in St. John's Street. . . . .], and Built them a New House in *Gibbon's Tennis Court* in *Clare-Market ;* in which Two Places they continu'd Acting all 1660, 1661, 1662, and part of 1663. In this time they Built them a New Theatre in *Drury-lane :* Mr. *Thomas Killigrew* gaining a Patent from the King in (p. 2) order to Create them the King's Servants ; and from that time, they call'd themselves His Majesty's Company of Comedians in *Drury-lane.* Whose Names were,". . . . .

(p. 3) The Company [Sir Wm Davenant's] being thus Compleat, they open'd the New Theatre in *Drury-Lane,* on *Thurſday* in *Eaſter* Week, being the 8*th*, Day of *April* 1663, With the Humorous Lieutenant. . . *Note,* this Comedy was Acted Twelve Days Succeſſively.

[Among their Plays and Caſts were]

(p. 6) XII.
The Moor of *Venice.*

Brabantio,	*Mr. Cartwright.*	(p. 7) Iago,	*Major Mohun.*
Moor,	*Mr. Burt.*	Roderigo,	*Mr. Beeston.*
Cassio,	*Mr. Hart*	Deſdemona,	*Mrs. Hughs.*
		Emilia,	*Mrs. Rutter.*

XIII.
King *Henry* the Fourth.

King,	Mr. *Winterſel.*	Falstaff,	Mr. **Cartwright.**
Prince,	Mr. *Burt.*	Poyns,	Mr. **Shotterel.**
Hotspur,	Mr. *Hart.*		

(p. 8) XV.
Julius Cæfar.

Julius Cæsar,	Mr. *Bell.*	Anthony,	Mr. *Kynaston.*
Cassius,	Major *Mohun.*	Calphurnia,	Mrs. *Marshal.*
Brutus,	Mr. *Hart.*	Portia,	Mrs. *Corbet.*

Note, That thefe being their Principal Old Stock Plays; yet in this Interval from the Day they begun, there were divers others Acted,

As { Cataline's Confpiracy.
. . . .
The Merry Wives of *Windfor* [no. 2].
. . . .
(p. 9) *Titus Andronicus* [no. 21 and laſt].

Thefe being Old Plays, were Acted but now and then; yet being well Perform'd, were very Satisfactory to the Town.

(p. 16) I muſt not Omit to mention the Parts in feveral Plays of fome of the Actors; wherein they Excell'd in the Performance of them. *Firſt*, Mr. *Hart*, in the Part of . . . . *Othello Rollo. Brutus*, in *Julius Cæſar* . . . if he Acted in any one of thefe but once in a Fortnight, the Houfe was fill'd as at a New Play, efpecially *Alexander*, he Acting that with fuch grandeur and Agreeable Majefty . . . In all the Comedies and Tragedies, he was concern'd, he Perform'd with that Exactnefs and Perfection, that not any of his Succeffors have Equall'd him.[1]

(p. 17) Major *Mohun*, he was Eminent for . . . *Caffius* in *Julius Cæſar* . . .

[Next follows an Account of the Rife and Progreffion, of the Dukes Servants; under the Patent of Sir *William Davenant* who upon the faid Junction in 1682, remov'd to the Theatre Royal in *Drury Lane*, and Created the King's Company . . . .]

[no. 6. 13 named] *With divers others.*

(p. 18) *The Plays there Acted were* . . . . *Pericles* Prince of

[1] 'This is imported, without acknowledgment, into Betterton's *Hiſtory of the Stage.* 1741. p. 90.

Tyre. Mr. *Betterton*, being then but 22 years Old, was highly Applauded for his Acting in all thefe Plays, but efpecially, For . . . . *Pericles* . . . his Voice being then as Audibly ftrong, full and Articulate, as in the Prime of his Acting.

(p. 19) Mr. *Kynafton* . . . being then very Young made a compleat Female Stage Beauty, performing his Parts fo well, . . . that it has fince been Difputable among the Judicious, whether any Woman that fucceeded him fo Senfibly touch'd the Audience as he. . . .

In this Interim, Sir *William Davenant* gain'd a Patent from the King, and Created Mr. *Betterton* and all the reft of Rhodes's Company, the King's Servants, who were fworn by my Lord Manchefter then Lord Chamberlain, to ferve his Royal Highnefs the Duke of *York*, at the Theatre in Lincolns-Inn-Fields.

(p. 20) And in Spring 1662, Open'd his Houfe [the Theatre in Lincoln's Inn-Fields] with the faid Plays, having new Scenes and Decorations, being the firft that e're were Introduc'd in *England*. [The 'Siege of Rhodes' was playd for 12 days, then "The Wits" for 8, and then]

(p. 21) The Tragedy of *Hamlet*; *Hamlet* being Perform'd by Mr. *Betterton*, Sir *William* (having feen Mr. *Taylor* of the *Black-Fryars* Company Act it, who being Inftructed by the Author Mr. *Shakfepeur* [so]) taught Mr. *Betterton* in every Particle of it; which by his exact Performance of it, gain'd him Efteem and Reputation, Superlative to all other Plays. *Horatio* by Mr. *Harris*; The King by Mr. *Lilliflon*; The Ghoft by Mr. *Richards* (after by Mr. *Medburn*), Polonius by Mr. *Lovel*; *Rofencrans* by Mr. *Dixon*; *Guilderftern* by Mr. *Price*; 1ft, Grave. maker, by Mr. *Underhill*: The 2d, by Mr. *Dacres*; the Queen, by Mrs. *Davenport*; Ophelia, by Mrs. *Sanderfon*: No fucceeding Tragedy for feveral Years got more Reputation, or Money to the Company than this. . . . .

(p. 22) *Romeo* and *Juliet*, Wrote by Mr. **Shakefpear**: *Romeo*, was Acted by Mr. *Harris*; *Mercutio*, by Mr. **Betterton**; Count *Paris*, by Mr. *Price*; The *Fryer*, by Mr. *Richards*; Sampfon, by Mr. Sandford; *Gregory*, by Mr. *Underhill*; *Juliet*, by Mrs. *Saunderſon*; Count Paris's [? Montague's] Wife by Mrs. *Holden*.

Note. There being a Fight and Scuffle in this Play, between the Houſe of *Capulet*, and Houſe of *Paris* [? Montague]; Mrs. *Holden* acting his Wife, enter'd in a *Hurry*, Crying, O my dear *Count!* She Inadvertently left out, O, in the pronuntiation of the Word *Count!* giving it a Vehement Accent, put the Houſe into ſuch a Laughter, that *London* Bridge at low Water was ſilence to it.[1]

This Tragedy of *Romeo* and *Juliet*, was made ſome time after into a Tragi-Comedy, by Mr. *James Howard*,[2] he preſerving *Romeo* and *Juliet* alive; ſo that when the Tragedy was Reviv'd again, 'twas Play'd Alternately, Tragical one Day, and Tragi-comical another; for ſeveral Days together. . . . .

(p. 23) Twelfth Night, Or what you will; Wrote by Mr. *Shakeſpear*,[3] had mighty Succeſs by its well Performance: Sir *Toby Belch*, by Mr. *Betterton*; Sir *Andrew Ague-Cheek*, by Mr. *Harris*; *Fool*, by Mr. *Underhill*; *Malvolio* the Steward, by Mr. *Lovel*; *Olivia*, by Mrs. *Ann Gibbs*; All the Parts being juſtly Acted Crown'd the Play. Note, *It was got up on purpoſe to be Acted on Twelfth Night.* . . . .

(p. 24, quoted in *Centurie*, p. 324) King *Henry* the 8*th*. This Play, by Order of Sir *William Davenant*, was all new Cloath'd

---

[1] The old bridge, with a very steep fall between the massive stirlings of the narrow arches. So dangerous was the fall, that it gave rise to the old saying, 'London Bridge was built for wise men to go over, and fools to go under.' See a fine coloured print of the Bridge in my *Harriſon*, Pt. III.

[2] It's not among the Hon. James Howard's Plays in the British Museum, nor under Shakespeare, *Romeo and Juliet*.

[3] It's "Mr. Chaucer" too, as our little friend Edmund Matthew of one and three-quarters says: (p. 30) "The *M*an's the *M*aster, Wrote by Sir *William Davenant*, being the last Play he ever Wrote, he Dying presently after; and was Bury'd in *Weſtminſter-Abby*, near *Mr. Chaucer's M*onument, our whole Company attending his Funeral."

in proper Habits [fee p. 232 above [1]]: The King's was new, all the Lords, the Cardinals, the Bithops, the Doctors, Proctors, Lawyers, Tip-ftaves, new Scenes: The part of the King was fo right and ruffly done by Mr. *Betterton*, he being Inftructed in it by Sir *William*, who had it from Old Mr. *Lowen*, that had his Inftructions from Mr. *Shakefpear* himfelf, that I dare and will aver, none can, or will come near him in this Age, in the performance of that part: Mr. *Harris*'s performance of Cardinal *Wolfey*, was little Inferior to that, he doing it with fuch juft State, Port and Mein, that I dare affirm, none hitherto has Equall'd him: The Duke of *Buckingham*, by Mr. *Smith*; Norfork [to], by Mr. *Nokes*; *Suffolk*, by Mr. *Lillifton*; Cardinal *Campeius* and *Cranmur* [to], by Mr. *Medburn*; Bithop *Gardiner*, by Mr. *Underhill*; Earl of *Surry*, by Mr. *Young*; Lord *Sands*, by Mr. *Price*; Mrs. *Betterton*, Queen *Catherine*: Every part by the great Care of Sir *William*, being exactly perform'd; it being all new Cloath'd and new Scenes; it continu'd Acting 15 Days together with general Applause.....

(p. 26) Thefe being all the Principal, which we call'd Stock-Plays; that were *Acted* from the Time they Open'd the Theatre in 1662, to the beginning of *May* 1665, at which time the *Plague* began to Rage: The Company ceaf'd *Acting*; till the Chriftmafs after the Fire in 1666. Yet there were feveral other Plays *Acted*, from 1662, to 1665, both Old and Modern: As... *The Tragedy of King* Lear, as Mr. *Shakefpear* Wrote it; before it was alter'd by Mr. *Tate*...[2]

[1] And *Centurie*, p. 346.
[2] After Christmas 1666 were acted, "*Richard* the Third, or the *English Princess*, Wrote by Mr. Carrol," (p. 27) and " King *Henry* the 5*th*, Wrote by the Earl of *Orrery*.... This play was Splendidly Cloath'd: The King, in the Duke of *York's* Coronation Suit: *Owen Tudor*, in King *Chale's*: Duke of Burgundy, in the Lord of Oxford's, ... and the rest all New. It was Excellently Perform'd, and Acted 10 Days Successively." Neither play is in the B. Mus. Catalogue. "There is a manuscript copy of this play [Hen. V.] in the Bodleian Library. Rawl. Poet. 2" (Halliwell *Dict. of O. Eng. Plays*, p. 17).

(p. 31) The new Theatre in *Dorfet-Garden* being Finifh'd, and our Company after Sir *William's* Death, being under the Rule and Dominion of his Widow the Lady *Davenant*, Mr. *Betterton*, and Mr. *Harris*, (Mr. *Charles Davenant*) her Son, *Acting* for her) they remov'd from *Lincoln's-Inn-Fields* thither. And on the Ninth Day of *November* 1671, they open'd their new Theatre . . . Among the Plays acted, were]

(p. 33) The Tragedy of *Macbeth*, alter'd by Sir *William Davenant*; being dreft in all it's Finery, as new Cloath's, new Scenes, Machines, as flytngs for the Witches; with all the Singing and Dancing in it: The firft compof'd by Mr. *Lock*, the other by Mr. *Channell* and Mr. *Jofeph Preift*; it being all Excellently perform'd, being in the nature of an Opera, it Recompenc'd double the Expence; it proves ftill [1708] a lafting Play.

Note, That this Tragedy, King *Lear* and the *Tempeft*, were *Acted* in *Lincolns-Inn-Fields*; *Lear*, being *Acted* exactly as Mr. *Shakefpear* Wrote it; as likewife the *Tempeft* alter'd by Sir *William Davenant* and Mr. *Dryden*, before 'twas made into an Opera.

(p. 34, 1672) The Jealous Bridegroom, Wrote by Mʳˢ. *Bhen* [Aphra Behn[1]], a good Play and lafted fix days; but this made its Exit too, to give Room for a greater, *The Tempeft*.

Note, *in this Play, Mr.* Otway *the Poet having an Inclination to turn Actor; Mrs.* Bhen *gave him* the King *in the Play, for a Probation Part, but he being not uf'd to the Stage; the full Houfe put him to fuch a Sweat and Tremendous, Agony, being dafh't,*

[1] The Forc'd Marriage, or the Jealous Bridegroom. T. C. 1671. 4to. The first Play she writ. Gildon's *Langbaine*. Acted at his Highness the Duke of *York's* Theatre and printed in quarto, *Lond.* 1671. This, if I mistake not, was the first Play that our Authress brought on the Stage.—*Langbaine*, 1691. p. 20. The Forc'd Marriage, / or the / Jealous Bridegroom./ A Tragi-Comedy./ As it is Acted at His Highnesse / The / Duke of York's / Theatre./ Written by A. Behn./ *Va mon enfant!* prend la fortune—/ *London*, / Printed by *H. L.* and / *R. B.* for *James Magnus* in *Russel*-Street, / near the Piazza./ 1671./ 4ᵗᵒ.

JOHN DOWNES, 1663—1693 (in 1708).

fpoilt him for an Actor. Mr. Nat. Lee, had the fame Fate in Acting Duncan in Macbeth, ruin'd him for an Actor too. . .

The Year after in 1673. The Tempeft, or the Inchanted Ifland, made into an Opera by Mr. Shadwell [1], having all New in it; as Scenes, Machines; particularly one Scene Painted with *Myriads of Ariel* Spirits; and another flying away, with a Table Furnifht out with Fruits, Sweet meats, and all forts of Viands, juft when Duke *Trinculo* and his Companions, were going to Dinner: all was things perform'd in it fo Admirably well, that not any fucceeding Opera got more Money . . . .

After the Tempeft, came the Siege of *Conftantinople*, Wrote by Mr. *Nevill Pain*.

(p. 39) All the preceding Plays, being the chief that were *Acted* in *Dorfet Garden*, from *November* 1671, to the Year 1682; at which time the Patentees of each Company United Patents; and by fo Incorporating, the Duke's Company were made the King's Company, and immediately remov'd to the Theatre Royal in *Drury-Lane*.

The mixt Company then Reviv'd the feveral old and Modern Plays, that were the Propriety of Mr. *Killigrew* as, . . . (p. 40) *The Moor of* Venice.

(p. 41) About this time, there were feveral other new Plays *Acted*. As . . . *Troilus and Creffida*.[2]

(p. 42) *The Fairy Queen*, made into an Opera, from a Comedy

---

[1] See p. above.
[2] No doubt " *Troilus and Cressida*, or, *Truth found out too late*," a Tragedy 4to., 1679. Acted at the Duke's Theatre. One of Mr. *Shakespear's* altered by Mr. *Dryden*. Gildon's *Langbaine*, 1699, p. 47.
This Play was likewife firft written by *Shakespear*, and revis'd by Mr. *Dryden*, to which he added several new Scenes, and even cultivated and improv'd what he borrowed from the Original.—*Langbaine*, 1691. p. 173. Troilus / and / Cressida, / or, *Truth Found too late*./ A / Tragedy / as it is acted at the / Duke's Theatre./ To which is Prefixed, A Preface Containing / the Grounds of Criticism in Tragedy./ Written by John Dryden / Servant to his Majesty./ London . . . Jacob Tonson . . . 1679. 4º.

of Mr. *Shakefpears*[1]: This in Ornaments was Superior to the other Two; efpecially in Cloaths, for all the Singers and Dancers, Scenes, Machines and Decorations, all moſt profufely fet off; and excellently perform'd, chiefly the Inſtrumental and Vocal part Compof'd (*p.* 43) by the faid Mr. *Purcel*, and Dance, by Mr. *Prieſt*. The Court and Town were wonderfully fatiffy'd with it; but the Expences in fetting it out being fo great, the Company got very little by it.

Note, Between these Opera's there were feveral other Plays Acted, both Old and Modern. *As*, ... *The Taming of a Shrew.* . . .

[(p. 46) *Note*, From *Candlemas* 1704, to the 23*d* of April 1706. There were 4 Plays commanded to be *Acted* at Court at St. *James's*, by the *Actors* of both Houses, *viz.*

(p. 47) [3] The next was, *The Merry Wives of* Windsor, *Acted* the 23*d*, of *April*, the Queens Coronation Day: Mr. *Betterton*, Acting Sir *John Falstaff*; Sir Hugh, by Mr. *Dogget*; Mr. *Page*, by Mr. *Vanbruggen*; Mr. *Ford*, by Mr. *Powel*; Dr. *Caius*, Mr. *Pinkethman*; the Host, Mr. *Bullock*; Mrs. *Page*, Mrs. *Barry*; Mrs. *Ford*, Mrs. *Bracegirdle*; Mrs. *Ann Page*, Mrs. *Bradshaw*.]

(p. 50) *Next follows the Account of the prefent Young Company (which United with the Old, in* October 1706) *now Acting at* Drury Lane; *Her Majefly's Company of Comedians, under the Government of Col.* Brcet.

(p. 52) Mr. *Dogget*. On the Stage, he's very Afpectabund, wearing a Farce in his Face; his Thoughts deliberately framing his Utterance Congruous to his Looks: He is the only Comick Original now Extant: Witnefs, *Ben Solon, Nikin*, The *Jew of Venice*,[2] *&c*.

I muſt not Omit Praifes due to Mr. Betterton, *The firſt and now* [1708] *only remain of the old Stock, of the Company of Sir*

[1] See page 347, abuv.
[2] This was the play alterd from Shakspere by Lord Lansdowne in 1701: see Baker, *Biogr. Dram.* ii. 345: "as Rowe remarks, the character of Shylock (which was performed by Dogget) is made comic, and we are prompted to laughter instead of detestation."

JOHN DOWNES, 1663—1693 (in 1708).

William Davenant *in* Lincolns-Inn-Fields; *he like an old Stately Spreading Oak now ſtands fixt, Environ'd round with brave Young Growing, Flouriſhing Plants: There needs nothing to ſpeak his Fame, more than the following* [16] *Parts.*

Pericles Prince of *Tyre*	*Macbeth*
. . . .	*Timon* of *Athens*
Richard the Third	*Othello*
King *Lear*	. . . .
Hamlet	King *Henry* the Eighth
. . . .	Sir *John Falstaff.*

F. J. F.

NOTES.

p. 267-270. Tate's *Lear* and *Richard II.*

·1681. *Numb.* 3.

A CATALOGUE of BOOKS continued, Printed and published at *London*, in *Easter-Term*, 1681.

Poems, Plays, &c.

The History of King *Lear*, acted at the Duke's Theatre. Revived with alterations, by *N. Lee, quarto*, price 1s. (sign. F2, col. 2)
[Reprinted in 1689, CATALOGUE, No. 34, sign. Iiii 2, col. 2]

Numb. 4.

A CATALOGUE of BOOKS continued, Printed and Published at *London*, in *Trinity-Term*, 1681.

Poems, Plays.

The History of King *Richard* the Second, acted at the *Theatre Royal*, with a Prefatory Epistle, in Vindication of the Author, occasioned by the Prohibition of this Play on the Stage. By *N.* Tate. quarto, price 1s.
[Crown's *Henry VI.* Parts I and II are in No. 5 of the 'Catalogue', sign. L, col. 2. Shadwell's *Timon* is in No. 31, sign. Xxx. col. 2, and in No. 32, as 'Reprinted.']

p. 335. The entry should be "303 *Shakespear* (W.) his Comedies, Histories and Tragedies, 1632." The 'Idem iterum, 1663,' which follows means only "the same book again, but of the 3rd edition, 1663."

p. 336, lines 6 and 4 from foot. The Bundle is '34', not '37' (p. 48), and it contains 12 other plays, not only '11'.

p. 338. Entry 1. In the volume 821. i. 5, containing this Catalog, art. 8, is another entry in 1698 :
"54 Shakespear's Comedies, Histories and Tragedies. 1664."
This is on p. 9 of the English part of *Bibliotheca Levinsiana*: sale on 29 June, 1698.

I. GENERAL INDEX

TO '*THE CENTURIE OF PRAYSE*' AND THIS '*FRESH ALLUSIONS.*'

*The '*Centurie*' references are in old-style type; the '*Fresh Allusions*' ones in modern type.*
The items to which a * *is prefixed index the notes and general matter; the rest indicate '*allusions.*'*

ACHERLEY, Thomas, *Ce.* 52
*Actor, vocation of, *Ce.* 58, 277, 411
*Actors of Shakspere, practices of early, *Ce.* 132, 451
Actors of Shakspere, Downes on, *Fr. Al.* 348-357
Adamson, Henry, *Fr. Al.* 134
*Affectations, *Fr. Al.* 293
*Alexander, W., Earl of Stirling, *Ce.* 423
Allot, Robert, *Ce.* 437
*Alterations of Shakspere's plays after the Restoration, *Ce.* 324, 356, 365, 369-70, 380, 381, 389, 390, 391, 392; *Fr. Al.* 208, &c. See 'Davenant, Dryden, Tate,' &c.
'Ancient Funerall Monuments', *Fr. Al.* 105
'Angliæ Speculum Morale', *Ce.* 429
Anthropophagus, *Ce.* 159
'Antidote against Melancholy', *Ce.* 325
Anton, Robert, *Ce.* 115
Archer, E., *Fr. Al.* 176-8
Armin, Robert, *Fr. Al.* 57, 59
'Arraignment of Paris', *Fr. Al.* 316, 330
Arrowsmith, Mr., *Fr. Al.* 234
'Athenian Society', *Fr. Al.* 316
„ Mercury', *Fr. Al.* 345

Aubrey, John, *Ce.* 383
*Auctions of books, early, *Fr. Al.* 335-342
Austin, Samuel, *Ce.* 309
Aylward, Paul, *Ce.* 257
B. (R), 'Greene's Funeralls', *Ce.* 3
Bacon, Lord, 'Conference of Pleasure', *Ce.* xvi note
'Of Tribute' MS, *Fr. Al.* 2
*Bacon, Lord, at Gray's Inn with Shakspere on Dec. 28, 1594, *Fr. Al.* 1
Baker, Sir Richard, *Ce.* 250, 315; *Fr. Al.* 154
*Ballads, *Ce.* 56, 63, 330, 387, 419
Bancroft, Thomas, *Ce.* 227; *Fr. Al.* 110
Banks, John, *Ce.* 395
'Banquet of Jeasts', *Ce.* 181
Barkstead, William, *Ce.* 76
Barnes, Barnabe, *Fr. Al.* 45
Barnfeild, Richard, *Ce.* 26
Baron, Robert, *Ce.* 279
Barrey, Ludovic, *Ce.* 95; *Fr. Al.* 73
*Bartas, Du, *Ce.* 142 note
Basse, William, *Ce.* 136, 151 note, 432
Beaumont and Fletcher—
Booksellers' Preface to Works, *Ce.* 377
'Custom of the Country', *Fr. Al.* 23

I. GENERAL INDEX.

'King and no King', *Fr. Al.* 62
'Knight of the Burning Pestle', *Ce.* 78 note, 89 note, 117
*Langbaine on, *Fr. Al.* 314
'Maid's Tragedy', *Fr. Al.* 61
'Philaster', *Fr. Al.* 61.
'Scornful Ladie', *Ce.* 117
'Ten Players' Epistle to First Folio of,' *Ce.* 262
'The Woman Hater', *Fr. Al.* 52
Behn, Mrs. Aphra, *Fr. Al.* 287, 289, *354
Bell, William, *Ce.* 288
'Belvedere', *Fr. Al.* 13
Benson, John, *Ce.* 229
Bentley, R., *Fr. Al.* 250
Bergerac, C. de, *Ce.* 416
Berkenhead, J., *Ce.* 271
Betterton, T., *Fr. Al.* 298, *322, 324, 351-7
'Birth of Merlin,' *Fr. Al.* 330
*Black Book, *Ce.* 423
Bodenham, John, *Ce.* 433; *Fr. Al.* 13
Bold, Henry, *Fr. Al.* 206, 281
Bolton, Edmund, *Ce.* 91
'Both-wel Bridge', Ballad, *Fr. Al.* 261
'Bottom the Weaver, Merry conceited Humors of', *Fr. Al.* 188, 237, 325
Brathwaite, Richard—
 'English Gentleman', *Ce.* 224
 'English Gentlewoman', *Fr. Al.* 104
 'Strappado for the Divell', *Ce.* 112, 113
Breedy, Daniel, *Ce.* 257
Breton, Nicholas, *Ce.* 457
Brome, Alexander, *Ce.* 296, *429; *Fr. Al.* 171
Brome, Richard, *Ce.* 225, 297
Brome's Plays, preface to, *Ce.* 308
Brooke, Christopher, *Ce.* 109
Browne, Thomas, *Ce.* 406
Browne, Sir Thomas, *Fr. Al.* 153

Buck, George, *Ce.* 272
*Buckingham, Duke of, *Fr. Al.* 101
 „ *Fr. Al.* 334
Burbadge, Elegy on, *Ce.* 131, xvii
*Burbage, *Ce.* 58, 62, 67, 84, 132
Burton, Robert, *Ce.* 161; *Fr. Al.* 85
*Bust of Shakspere, *Ce.* 125, 154
Butler, Charles, *Ce.* 243
Butler, Samuel, *Ce.* 276 note

C. (I), 'St. Marie Magdalen's Conversion', *Ce.* 57
C. (I), 'Epigrames', *Ce.* 63
Camden, William, *Ce.* 59
'Cardenio, History of', *Fr. Al.* 160
Carew, Richard, *Ce.* 20
*Carew, Thomas, *Ce.* 429; *Fr. Al.* 131
*Carrol, Mr., 'Rich. III.' *Fr. Al.* 353
Cartwright, William, *Ce.* 270
Caryl, John, *Fr. Al.* 302
Cavendish, Margaret, *Ce.* 332
 „ Wm., Duke of Newcastle, *Fr. Al.* 253
Censure of the Poets, *Ce.* 168
 „ „ Rota, *Fr. Al.* 235
Chamberlain, Robert, *Ce.* 226
Chapman, George, *Ce.* 69, 186; *Fr. Al.* 110; Allusion to, *Fr. Al.* 146
'Bussy d'Ambois', *Fr. Al.* 23, 49
'Byron's Tragedie', *Fr. Al.* 49
'Eastward Hoe', *Ce.* 69; *Fr. Al.* 41, 42
*Chaucer, *Fr. Al.* 181, 231, 313, 345, 352
Chester, Robert, *Ce.* 43, 44
Chettle, Henry—
 'England's Mourning Garment', *Ce.* 55
 'Kind Hart's Dream', *Ce.* 4
Chetwood, Knightley, *Ce.* 399
*Chetwood, William R., *Ce.* 426
Chillingworth, William, *Ce.* 223

'Choyce Drollery', *Ce.* 134
'Choyce Poems', *Fr. Al.* 185
Clarke, John, *Fr. Al.* 135
Clarke, William, *Ce.* 15
Cleveland John, *Ce.* 254; *Fr. Al.* 154
Cokaine, Sir Aston—
  'A Preludium to Richard Brome's Plays', *Ce.* 297
  'To Clement Fisher', *Ce.* 307
  'To John Honyman', *Ce.* 306
  'To Philip Massenger', *Ce.* 196
  'To William Dugdale', *Ce.* 305
'Conceits, Clinches', &c., *Fr. Al.* 141
Condell, Henry, *Ce.* 143
'Contention between York and Lancaster', *Fr. Al.* 316
Cook, J., *Ce.* 276
Cooke, John, *Fr. Al.* 79
*Cooke, Joshua, *Fr. Al.* 22, 24
Cope, Sir Walter, *Ce.* 62
Corbet, Richard, *Ce.* 128
Cornwallis, Sir William, *Ce.* 41
Cotton Charles, *Ce.* 336
'Covent Garden Drollery', *Ce.* 348-9; *Fr. Al.* 186, 231*
Cowley, Abraham, *Ce.* 170, 303; *Fr. Al.* 169
Cranley, Thomas, *Ce.* 204
'Cromwell, Thomas Lord', *Fr. Al.* 320
Crown, J., *Ce.* 389; *Fr. Al.* 262, 265
*Current Elizabethan phrases, *Ce.* 19, 27, 54, 61, 82-3, 117, 155

DANIEL, George, of Beswick, *Ce.* 265, 266
Daniel, Samuel, *Ce.* 427
*Davenant, Charles, *Ce.* 398 note
Davenant, Sir William, *Ce.* 216
  Elegy on him, *Fr. Al.* 230
  *his abilities, *Ce.* 339 note; *Fr. Al.* 234, 346
  *his operas and alterations of Shakspere, *Ce.* 323, 356, 397, 408; *Fr. Al.* 169, 208, 222, 351, &c.
  his 'Rivals,' 1668, from 'The 2 Noble Kinsmen', *Fr. Al.* 210-215
  'Law against Lovers', *Fr. Al.* 324
  'News from Plimouth', *Fr. Al.* 233
  *reputed son of Shakspere, *Ce.* 385
Davenport, Anthony, *Ce.* 281
  ,,   Robert, *Fr. Al.* 169, 196
Davies, John, of Hereford—
  'Civill Warres of Death and Fortune', *Ce.* 84
  'Microcosmos', *Ce.* 58, *277
  'Paper's Complaint', *Ce.* 96, *423
  'Scourge of Folly', *Ce.* 28, *94, *155 note
Day, John, *Ce.* 82; *Fr. Al.* 56
Decker, Thomas—
  'A Knight's conjuring', &c., *Ce.* 74
  'Eastward Hoe', *Ce.* 69; *Fr. Al.* 41, 42
  'Honest Whore', *Fr. Al.* 11, 12
  'King's Entertainment', *Fr. Al.* 11
  'Lanthorne and Candle Light', *Ce.* 453
  'Northward Hoe', *Fr. Al.* 12
  'Old Fortunatus', *Fr. Al.* 10
  'Satiro-Mastix', *Ce.* 50; *Fr. Al.* 22
  'Shoomaker's Holiday', *Fr. Al.* 10
  'Sir Thomas Wyat', *Fr. Al.* 24, 53
  'The Dead Terme', *Fr. Al.* 55
  *'Westward Hoe', *Fr. Al.* 52
  'Wonder of a Kingdome', *Fr. Al.* 12
*"Delighted" in 'Measure for Measure', *Ce.* 217
Denham, Sir John—
  Poems, *Ce.* 343
  Verses on John Fletcher, *Ce.* 253
*Des Maizeaux, P., *Ce.* 199, 397 note
Digges, Leonard, *Ce.* 154, 231
*Dogget, Mr., as 'the only Comick Original' Shylock, *Fr. Al.* 356
Dolarney's Primerose, *Ce.* 451
Don Quijote, *Ce.* 428
Don Zara del Fogo, *Ce.* 302

I. GENERAL INDEX.

Dowdall, Mr., *Ce.* 417
Downes, Jn., *Ce.* 323-4, 356
Downes, John, *Fr. Al.* 348-357
Drayton, Michael—
  Barrons Wars, *Ce.* 53
  Elegies, *Ce.* 168
  Legend of Mathilda, *Ce.* 13
  Polyolbion, *Ce.* 428
*Drolls and Drolleries, *Ce.* 354
Drummond, Sir William, *Ce.* 71, 111, 116, 129
Drummond, W., *Fr. Al.* 82
Dryden, John—
  'Albion and Albanius', *Fr. Al.* 226
  An Evening's Love, *Ce.* 352 note
  * 'Antony and Cleopatra', *Fr. Al.* 260
  'Athenian Virtuosi', *Fr. Al.* 225
  Conquest of Granada, *Ce.* 352; *Fr. Al.* 224
  Criticism of, *Fr. Al.* 232*, 235, 291-3, 295, 310-13, 318, 322, 325, 327
  Dedic. to 'Rival Ladies', *Fr. Al.* 221
  Essay of Dramatic Poesie, *Ce.* 341; *Fr. Al.* 216-221
  'Letter to Jn. Dennis', *Fr. Al.* 223
  Lines to Congreve, *Ce.* 349 note
  'Miscellany Poems', Pt. III, Dedic. to, *Fr. Al.* 228
  Preface to 'All for Love', *Ce.* 368; *Fr. Al.* 312
  Pref. to 'Evening's Love', *Fr. Al.* 223
  Pref. to 'The Tempest', *Fr. Al.* 222, 311, 313
  Preface to 'Troilus and Cressida': Criticism on Tragedy, *Ce.* 369-377
  Prologue to 'Aurungzebe', *Ce.* 362
  Prologue to C. Davenant's 'Circe', *Ce.* 398
  Prologue to Harris's 'Mistakes', *Ce.* 411
  Prologue to 'Julius Cæsar', *Ce.* 348
  Prolog to 'Love Triumphant', *Fr. Al.* 229
  Prologue to 'Troilus and Cressida', *Ce.* 376; *Fr. Al.* 311, 313
  Prologue to University of Oxford, *Ce.* 357
  Satires of Juvenal and Persius, *Ce.* 413; *Fr. Al.* 227, 228
  'State of Innocence', *Fr. Al.* 225
  Tempest, *Ce.* 211, 338, 339
  'The Vindication', *Fr. Al.* 226
  To Sir Godfrey Kneller, *Ce.* 414
*Du Bartas, *Ce.* 142 note
Duffett, Thomas—
  'Empress of Morocco', *Fr. Al.* 240
  'The Mock-Tempest', *Fr. Al.* 242-5
Dugdale, Sir William, *Ce.* 298, 305; *Fr. Al.* 179
Dunton, John, *Ce.* 367 note
Durfey, T., *Fr. Al.* 261, 263, 273-6 and 314 ('Cymbeline'), 300, 314, 321
'Dutch Gazette', *Fr. Al.* 207

EDMONTON, Merry Divel of', *Ce.* 73
Education, Of, *Ce.* 353
Edwardes, Thomas, *Ce.* 17
Egerton MS. 2246, *Fr. Al.* 100
'England's Parnassus', *Ce.* 430-438
*Epigram, supposed, by Jonson and Shakspere, *Ce.* 410 note
Epigrames by I. C., *Ce.* 63
Essex Rebellion, examinations—
  Augustine Phillipps, *Ce.* 36
  Sir Gelly Meyricke, *Ce.* 35
Evelyn, John, *Ce.* 326, 407
Evremond, St., *Ce.* 396

'FAIRY-QUEEN, the', *Fr. Al.* 347, 355
Fane, Sir Francis, *Fr. Al.* 247
Feltham, Owen, *Ce.* 180, 213
*Ferrers, George, *Ce.* 22 note
Field, Nathaniel, *Ce.* 127
Fisher, To Clement, *Ce.* 307
*Fitzgeoffry, H., *Ce.* 233 note, 290
Flecknoe, Richard, *Ce.* 314, 345; *Fr. Al.* 169

I. GENERAL INDEX. 363

Fletcher, John (see 'Beaumont')—
Allusions to, *Fr. Al.* 116, &c. ; 217,
218, 219, 220, 222, 223, 224, 225,
231, 234, 235, 237, 248, 253, 257,
264, 277, 284, 286, 287, 289, 295,
298, 307, 308, 309, 312, 313, 314,
317, 319 (and see All. to 'Jonson,
Ben')
'Beggar's Bush', *Fr. Al.* 88*
*'Cupid's Revenge', *Fr. Al.* 338
Denham's Verses on, *Ce.* 263
'Elder Brother', *Fr. Al.* 125
'History of Cardenio', *Fr. Al.* 169
'Knight of Malta', *Ce.* 166
'Little French Lawyer', *Fr. Al.* 62
'Noble Gentleman', *Ce.* 167
'Sea Voyage', *Fr. Al.* 314
'The Captain', *Fr. Al.* 62
*The Prophetesse, *Fr. Al.* 98
'The Woman Hater', *Ce.* 72
'The Woman's Prize, or The Tamer
Tam'd', *Ce.* 135 ; *Fr. Al.* 314
'Wild Goose Chace', *Ce.* 135

Fletcher, Joseph, *Ce.* 101
Folio, first, verses prefixt to, *Ce.*
145-155
Folio Second, verses prefixt to, *Ce.*
189, 190
Ford, John, *Fr. Al.* 116
*Foreign plays got for England, *Fr.
Al.* 303
Forman, Simon, *Ce.* 97
Freeman, Thomas, *Ce.* 106
*French writers, first notices of
Shakspere by, *Ce.* 396, 415
Friend, one, to another, *Ce.* 40
Fuller, Thomas—
Church History, *Ce.* 249 note
Worthies, *Ce.* 246, 249 ; *Fr. Al.* 197,
202-3
Fulman, William, *Ce.* 405

GAYTON, Edmund, *Ce.* 299 ; *Fr.
Al.* 170, 199
Gee, John, *Ce.* 160
Gell, Robert, *Ce.* 169

FRESH ALLUSIONS.

*German writer, first mention of
Shakspere by, *Ce.* 342 note
*Germany, English Actors in. *Ce.*
342
'Gesta Grayorum', *Fr. Al.* 1
*Gildon, Charles, *Ce.* 198 note
*Globe Theatre, burning of, *Ce.* 102,
455
*Globe Theatre, 'Henry VIII.' at,
Fr. Al. 101
Golf, T., *Fr. Al.* 175
*Gosson, Stephen, *Ce.* 421
'Gratiæ Theatrales', *Fr. Al.* 198
Greene, Robert, *Ce.* 2
*Greene's Funeralls, *Ce.* 3
'Guerdon', 'L. L. Lost', *Fr. Al.* 4
*Guzman de Alfarache, *Ce.* 155

H., Elegy on Burbage, *Ce.* 131
Habington, William, *Ce.* 200
'Hæc Vir, or the Womanish Man',
Fr. Al. 85
Hains, Jo., *Fr. Al.* 279
Hales of Eton, John, *Ce.* 198, 208,
341
Harbert, Sir W. (?), *Ce.* 12
Harvey, Gabriel—
*Four Letters, &c., *Ce.* 422
(late) MS note in Speght's Chaucer,
Ce. 30
Hayward, Sir John, *Fr. Al.* 77
Head, Richard, *Fr. Al.* 252
'Hectors (the), or the False Challenge', *Fr. Al.* 301
Helmes, Henry, *Fr. Al.* 1
'Helpe to Discourse,' *Fr. Al.* 141
Heminge, John, *Ce.* 143
Hemings, William, *Ce.* 429 ; *Fr.
Al.* 200
Heraclitus Ridens, *Ce.* 388
Herbert, Sir Gerrard, *Fr. Al.* 82
Herbert, Sir Henry, *Ce.* 157, 173

C C

I. GENERAL INDEX.

'Hermeticall Banquet drest by a Spagiricall Cook', *Ce.* 290
Herringman, Henry, *Fr. Al.* 297
Heylyn, Peter, *Fr. Al.* 104*
Heywood, Thomas—
  'Apology for Actors', *Ce.* 99
  'Fayre Mayde of the Exchange', *Ce.* 80; *Fr. Al.* 47
  'Hierarchie of the Blessed Angels', *Ce.* 202
  'K. Edward IV.', *Fr. Al.* 40
  'Philocothonista', *Fr. Al.* 122
  'Pleasant Dialogues', *Fr. Al.* 128
  'Woman killed with Kindness', *Ce.* 427
Hind, Capt. James, *Ce.* 291
*'Histrio-Mastix', *Ce.* 200, 248
*Holden, Mrs., and 'Count', *Fr. Al.* 352
Holland, Hugh, *Ce.* 153
Holland, Samuel, *Ce.* 302; *Fr. Al.* 174
Honyman, To, John, *Ce.* 306
Hooke, Nathaniel, *Fr. Al.* 168
Horse in 'Ven. and Ad.', *Fr. Al.* 8
Howard, James, his 'Romeo and Juliet', *Fr. Al.* 352
Howell, James, *Ce.* 264
Howes, Edmund, *Ce.* 108
Howes, John, *Ce.* 411 note
Hubburd's Tales, Father, *Ce.* 60
'Humphrey, Duke of Glocester', *Fr. Al.* 19
I. M. S., see 'S'
'Isham Correspondence', *Fr. Al.* 184, 185, 254
Isham, Thomas, *Ce.* 355

J. (W.), Whipping of the Satyre, *Ce.* 47
*James I., his letter to Shakspere, *Ce.* 217
James, Richard, Dr., *Ce.* 164
Jefferies, Judge, *Ce.* 296 note
Jevon, Tho., *Fr. Al.* 286

'John, K., The Troublesome Raigne of', *Fr. Al.* 330
Johnson, John, *Ce.* 238
Johnson, Samuel, *Fr. Al.* 334*
Jonson, Ben—
  'Bartholomew Fair',* *Ce.* 61, 105
  Conversation with Drummond, *Ce.* 129
  *'Cynthia's Revels', *Ce.* 54, 151 note
  'Eastward Hoe', *Ce.* 69
  'Epicœne', *Ce.* 90
  *Epigram in his 'Life', *Ce.* 233, 234
  'Every Man in his Humour', *Ce.* 118
  'Every Man out of his Humour', *Ce.* 31
  'Fortunate Isles', *Fr. Al.* 99
  *New Inn, *Ce.* 423
  Ode appended to the New Inn, *Ce.* 172
  *Poetaster, *Ce.* 49, 423, 424, 425; *Fr. Al.* 21
  *'Sejanus', *Ce.* 119
  *Spurious Epigram by, *Ce.* 426
  'Staple of News', *Ce.* 163
  'Timber', *Ce.* 174
  Verses on Droeshout's Portrait of Sh. in Folio of 1623, *Ce.* 141
  Verses on Shakspere in Folio of 1623, *Ce.* 147
Jonson, Ben, MS. Epitaph on, *Ce.* 277
Jonson, Ben, allusions to, *Fr. Al.* 109, 110, 146, 149, 162, 165, 166, 180, 187, 194, 204, 207, 209, 217, 218, 219, 220, 223, 224, 225, 227, 228, 231, 232*, 234, 237, 248, 253, 257, 259, 264, 277, 284, 286, 289, 292, 294, 298, 300, 302, 306, 307, 309, 312, 314, 319, 327, 331, 332, 345
Jordan, Thomas, *Ce.*, 330; *Fr. Al.* 205
KEELING, Captain, *Ce.* 79
Kelynge, J., *Fr. Al.* 204
*Kempe's Jig, *Ce.* 27
Kirkman, Francis, *Ce.* 354; *Fr. Al.* 166, 190-5 (p. 343), 205, 237, 316, 330

'Lady Mother, The', *Fr. Al.* 120
Lambard, William, *Ce.* 449
Lane, John, *Ce.* 32
Langbaine, Gerard, *Ce.* 408; *Fr. Al.* 195, 294-6, 306-332
L'Estrange, Sir Nicholas, *Ce.* 282
Lee, Nathaniel, *Fr. Al.* 264, *355
Ligon, Richard, *Ce.* 304
Lock, Matthew, *Fr. Al.* 249
*'Locrine', *Fr. Al.* 323
*Lodge, Thomas, *Ce.* 294 note, 422
London, W., *Fr. Al.* 183*
*London Bridge, *Fr. Al.* 352
'London Post', *Ce.* 251
'London Prodigal', *Fr. Al.* 323
Long, Lady Dolly, *Fr. Al.* 185
Lorkins, Thomas, *Ce.* 102
'Love à la Mode', *Fr. Al.* 204
Loveday, Ro., *Fr. Al.* 167
Lovelace, Elegy on, *Ce.* 313
*'Lover's Affection', *Fr. Al.* 320 note
'Loves Garland', *Fr. Al.* 239
'Love's Hospitall', *Fr. Al.* 0
*Lucy, Sir Thomas, song on, *Ce.* 426
Lynn, George, *Fr. Al.* 146

M. (L.), Lines prefixed to first folio of Shakspere, *Ce.* 155
M. (L.), *Fr. Al.* 4
M. (J.), New Metamorphosis, *Ce.* 98
M. (T.), Father Hubburd's Tales, *Ce.* 60
*Mabbe's Guzman de Alfarache, *Ce.* 155
Machin, Lewis, *Ce.* 81
*Macklin the comedian, *Ce.* 426
Manningham, John, *Ce.* 45
Maresnests re 'L. L. Lost', *Fr. Al.* 5
Markham, Jarvis, *Ce.* 81
*Marlowe, Christopher, *Fr. Al.* 315
*Marlowe alluded to, *Fr. Al.* 285

Marmion, Shakerley, *Ce.* 428; *Fr. Al.* 130
Marston, John—
  * 'Antonio and Mellida', *Fr. Al.* 28
  'Dutch Courezan', *Fr. Al.* 10*
  'Eastward Hoe', *Ce.* 69
  'Insatiate Countess', *Ce.* 428; *Fr. Al.* 103
  'Malcontent', *Ce.* 66; *Fr. Al.* 23, 31
  'Parasitaster', *Ce.* 29 note
  'Scourge of Villanie', *Ce.* *3, 27, 29
  'What you Will', *Ce.* 77

Marvel, Andrew, *Ce.* 347
Massinger, Philip, *Ce.* 171, 185, 196
  'The Maid of Honour', *Ce.* 185; *Fr. Al.* 107
  'The Roman Actor', *Ce.* 171
  'Unnatural Combat', *Ce.* 428
Mathews, Sir Tobie, *Ce.* 40
*Matthew, Edmund, *Fr. Al.* 352
Mayne, Jasper, *Ce.* 212, 289
'Meeting of Gallants at an Ordinarie', *Ce.* 65
'Melancholy, Antidote against', *Ce.* 325
'Mercurius Britannicus', *Ce.* 252
Meres, Francis, *Ce.* 21, 24
'Merlin, Birth of', *Fr. Al.* 327, 330
'Merry Devil of Edmonton', *Fr. Al.* 316
Mervyn, James, *Ce.* 222
Meyricke, Sir Gelly, on Essex Rebellion, *Ce.* 35
Middleton, Thomas—
  'A Mad World', *Fr. Al.* 36, 56
  'Blurt, Master Constable', *Ce.* 51
  'Duke of Glocester', *Fr. Al.* 19
  'Family of Love', *Fr. Al.* 35
  'Father Hubburd's Tales', *Ce.* 60
  'Honest Whore', *Ce.* 51 note; *Fr. Al.* 35
  'The old Law', *Fr. Al.* 37
  'The Witch', *Ce.* 428
Mildmay, Sir H., *Fr. Al.* 121

Milton, John—
  Allusion to, *Fr. Al.* 315
  'Εἰκονοκλάστης', *Ce.* 274
  'Elegy to Charles Diodate', *Ce.* 460
  'Epitaph on Shakspere', *Ce.* 176
  Introduction to 'Samson Agonistes', *Ce.* 275
  'L'Allegro', *Ce.* 184
  'Prose Works', *Fr. Al.* 151, 164
Monmouth, Duke of, Ballad on, *Ce.* 387
Morhoff, D. G., *Ce.* 342
Motteux, Peter,* *Ce.* 367 note, 415
Mountfort, Wm., *Fr. Al.* 301, 302, 303
'Mournful Dittie', *Ce.* 56
*'Mucedorus', *Fr. Al.* 317
Mulgrave, *Ce.* 394. *See* Sheffield
Munday, A, &c., 'Sir John Oldcastle', *Fr. Al.* 15
Mynshul, Geffray, *Ce.* 456

N. (J.), *Fr. Al.* 333
Nabbes, Thomas, *Fr. Al.* 109
'Naps upon Parnassus', *Fr. Al.* 181
Nash, Thomas—
  * 'Anatomie of Absurditie', *Ce.* 421
  *Epistle prefixed to Greene's 'Menaphon', *Ce.* 421
  'Pierce Penniless', *Ce.* 5
* "Nest," the term, *Ce.* 61
'New Married Couple', *Fr. Al.* 251
'New Metamorphosis', *Ce.* 98, *440-48
'Newsletter', 1628, *Fr. Al.* 104
Niccholes, Alex., *Fr. Al.* 80
Nicholson, Samuel, *Ce.* 33; *Fr. Al.* 20
*" Noise" in music, the term, *Ce.* 304 note

*OLDCASTLE, Sir John, *Ce.* 65, 127, 164, 249, 266-69, 294; *Fr. Al.* 16, 29, 75, 76, 325

Oldham, John, *Fr. Al.* 257
*Oldys, J., Notes to Langbaine, *Fr. Al.* 319, 320, &c.
*Orrery, Lord, 'Henry V.', *Fr. Al.* 353 note
Otway, Thomas, *Ce.* 381; *Fr. Al.* 256, 271, 315, *354
Overbury, Sir Thomas, *Ce.* 114

PALMER, T., *Ce.* 272
Paman, Clement, *Fr. Al.* 185
Parker, Martine, *Ce.* 239
'Parnassus Biceps', *Fr. Al.* 180
Parsons, Father, *Fr. Al.* 30
Peele, George, *Ce.* 75
Pepys, Samuel, *Ce.* 316
Percy, Charles, *Ce.* 38
'Perfect Occurrences', *Ce.* 273
*Performances of Shakspere's plays, *Ce.* 79, 93, 97, 103, 157, 158, 169, 173, 316-324, 326, 342, 355, 415. See 'Downes', *Fr. Al.* 348-357
*Person of Honour, *Ce.* 386
Phillipps, Augustine, on 'Rich. II.', in Essex Rebellion, *Ce.* 36
Phillips, Edward—
  'Theatrum Poetarum', *Ce.* 359
  'Tractatulus de Carmine', etc., *Ce.* 344
"Phillis and Flora", *Ce.* 427; *Fr. Al.* 8
Pimlyco, or Runne Red-cap', *Ce.* 89
Pix, Mrs. Mary, *Fr. Al.* 248
*'Plaudite', at end of a play, *Ce.* 31, 156
*Players' vocation, *Ce.* 58, 277, 411
*Playhouses, London, *Fr. Al.* 349
'Poetical Revenge, A', *Fr. Al.* 185
'Poeta de Tristibus', *Fr. Al.* 277
Poole, Josua, *Ce.* 438
Porter, Henry, *Ce.* 427; *Fr. Al.* 9
Powell, G., *Fr. Al.* 299
Prince of Priggs Revels, *Ce.* 291
Prujean, Thomas, *Ce.* 255

Prynne, William, *Ce.* 195, 200
Pulleyn, Octavian, *Fr. Al.* 254
Puritaine, or Widdow of Watling Street,* *Ce.* 3, 78; *Fr. Al.* 326
QUARLES, J., *Fr. Al.* 173
*Quickly, Dame, *Fr. Al.* 185

RADCLIFFE, Alexander, *Ce.* 393
Ramesey, W., *Fr. Al.* 231
Ramsay, H., *Ce.* 215
Randolph, Thomas—
  'Cornelianum Dolium', *Ce.* 224
  'Hey for Honesty', *Ce.* 293; *Fr. Al.* 120
  'Jealous Lovers', *Ce.* 187
*'Rape of Lucrece', a play, *Fr. Al.* 101
'Ratsey's Ghost', *Ce.* xix, 67
Ravenscroft, Edward, *Ce.* 404; *Fr. Al.* 315, 328
Raynolds, John, *Ce.* 451
Raynsford, Sir George, *Ce.* 239
'Remuneration' in 'L. L. Lost', *Fr. Al.* 2
'Returne from Pernassus' II., *Ce.* 48, 68; I. *Fr. Al.* 12*
*Revells, Book of, spurious entries in, *Ce.* 426
Rich, Barnabe, *Fr. Al.* 79
*Richard III, King, traduced, *Ce.* 41, 402
Rivers, G., *Ce.* 428; *Fr. Al.* 139
Robinson, Thomas, *Ce.* 140
Rochester, Earl of, *Ce.* 364, 378
  " 'Valentian', Prolog to, *Ce.* 403
'Roscius Anglicanus', *Fr. Al.* 348-357
Rowe, Nicholas, *Fr. Al.* 259
Rowlands, Samuel—
  'The Night Raven', *Ce.* 454
  *'Tis Merry When Gossips', *Ce.* 423
  'Whole Crew of Kind Gossips, Meet', *Ce.* 85

Rowley, William, *Ce.* 197 note
Rump: Poems and Songs, *Ce.* 244
Ruskin, John, *Ce.* 247 note
Rymer, Thomas, *Ce.* 366, 367*; *Fr. Al.* 228

SAINT MARIE MAGDALEN'S Conversion, *Ce.* 57
S. (E.), Anthropophagus, *Ce.* 159
S. (I. M.), Lines prefixt to First Folio of Shakspere, *Ce.* 190
S. (J.), Prince of Priggs Revels, *Ce.* 291
S. (R.), Phillis and Flora, *Fr. Al.* 8
S. T. (gent.), *Fr. Al.* 202
S. (W.), The Puritaine, *Ce.* 78
Saltonstall, Wye, *Fr. Al.* 102
Sampson, Wm., *Fr. Al.* 124
Scoloker, Anthony, *Ce.* 64
'Daiphantus', *Fr. Al.* 33
Scrope, Sir Carr, *Ce.* 363
*Scudery, Georges de, *Ce.* 386
Sedley, Sir Charles, *Ce.* 418
'Serving-Men, Faith to the Gentlemanly Profession of', *Fr. Al.* 5
Settle, Elkanah, *Fr. Al.* 305
Shadwell, Thos., *Ce.* 365; *Fr. Al.* 304, 315, 328, 329, 355
*Shakspere's monument at Stratford, *Ce.* 298
Shakspere—
  *as Godfather to Jonson's child, *Ce.* 282
  *his Epitaph on Jonson, *Ce.* 277
  his name on a Bacon MS., *Fr. Al.* 1
  *his name 'Will,' *Ce.* 203
  *his native genius contrasted with art, *Ce.* 129, 314
  *his plays altered after the Restoration, *Ce.* 324, 356, 365, 369-70, 376, 380 note, 381, 389, 390, 391, 392. See 'Davenant, Tate,' &c.
  *his wealth, *Ce.* 67
  *Inscription on grave-stone, *Ce.* 121; *Fr. Al.* 331

I. GENERAL INDEX.

*Inscription on Tablet under Bust, *Ce.* 125
Lists of his Plays:
  Archer, 1656, *Fr. Al.* 176
  Goff, 1656, *Fr. Al.* 175
  Kirkman, 1661-71, *Fr. Al.* 190, 343
*Teacher of Lowen, *Fr. Al.* 353
*the play upon his name, *Ce.* 3, 227. 247, 300, 400
Verses prefixt to his Folio Works I, II, *Ce.* 141-156, 189, 190; *Fr. Al.* 340; III, *Fr. Al.* 335, 337, 340, 341; IV, 337, 338, 339, 340, 341, 342
Sharpe, Lewis, *Ce.* 230
Sharpe, Roger, *Fr. Al.* 69
Sharpham, Edward—
  'Cupid's Whirligig', *Fr. Al.* 50
  'The Fleire', *Fr. Al.* 50, 51
Sheffield, John, E. of Mulgrave, *Ce.* 394
Sheppard, Samuel—
  'Committee-man curried', *Fr. Al.* 159
  'Epigrams', *Ce.* 284, 285, 287
  'Times displayed', &c., *Ce.* 120, 261
Shirley, James, *Ce.* 186, 201
  Allusion to, *Fr. Al.* 237
  'Arcadia', *Fr. Al.* 144
  'Bird in a Cage', *Fr. Al.* 108
  'Captain Underwit', *Fr. Al.* 144*
  'Love-Tricks', Prolog to, *Ce.* 337
  'Schoole of Complement', *Fr. Al.* 106
  'The Sisters', *Ce.* 236; *Fr. Al.* 150
  'Triumph of Beauty', *Fr. Al.* 315
*Shylock, a comic character, *Fr. Al.* 356
'Sicilian Usurper' (N. Tate's), *Fr. Al.* 316
*Sidney, Sir Philip, *Ce.* 421
Smith, Sir Thomas, *Ce.* 453
*Smith, Wentworth, *Fr. Al.* 18
*" Sneak's noise," *Ce.* 304
Song of 17th Century, *Ce.* 419
Southampton, Countess of, *Ce.* 40

Southerne, Thomas, *Fr. Al.* 280
Southwell, Robert, *Ce.* 14
*Spedding on Bacon's MS., *Fr. Al.* 2
Speed, John, *Fr. Al.* 75
Speed, Samuel, *Ce.* 358
Spencer, John, *Ce.* 182
Spenser, Edmund—
  *'Teares of the Muses', *Ce.* 421
  *Spurious plays, *Ce.* 426
Stanhope, Lord Treasurer, *Ce.* 103
'State Trials', *Ce.* 296
'Stationers' Register', *Fr. Al.* 169
Stephens, John, *Ce.* 423
Stirling, Earl of, *Ce.* 423
*Stubbes's 'Anatomie of Abuses', *Ce.* 158 note
Suckling, Sir John—
  'Brennoralt', *Fr. Al.* 114
  'Fragmenta Aurea', *Ce.* 205, 208, 209, *218 note, *233 note; 'Aglaura', *Fr. Al.* 111-113
  'Goblins', *Ce.* 210; *Fr. Al.* 111-112
  Letters, *Ce.* 209
*" Swan of Avon," *Ce.* 150, 262, 265
Swan, John, *Ce.* 459
Swinhoe, Gilbert, *Fr. Al.* 183

TATE, Nahum—
  'Cuckold's-Haven', *Fr. Al.* 283
  'Ingratitude of a Commonwealth', *Ce.* 392; *Fr. Al.* 278, 316, 347
  'King Lear', *Ce.* 390, 391; Epilog to it, *Fr. Al.* 270
  'Loyal General', *Ce.* 379
  'Richard the Second', *Ce.* 380 note; *Fr. Al.* 326; Epilog to it, *Fr. Al.* 270
  'The Sicilian Usurper' (from 'Rich. II.'), *Fr. Al.* 267-9, 316
  'To Sir Fras. Fane', *Fr. Al.* 284
Tatham, Jo., *Ce.* 295
Tailor, Robert, *Ce.* 107
Taylor, John, the Water-poet—
  'Sir Gregory Nonsence', *Fr. Al.* 86

I. GENERAL INDEX. 369

'The praise of Hemp-seed', *Ce.* 133
'Three Weeks, three daies', &c., *Ce.* 126
'To Nobody', *Ce.* 179
'Travels to Prague', *Ce.* 178
Temple, Sir William, *Ce.* 382
Terrent, T., *Ce.* 218
Thorpe, Thomas, *Ce.* 86
Tofte, Robert, *Ce.* 25
Tourneur, Cyril, *Fr. Al.* 71
*Towers, W., *Ce.* 152
Trapp, John, M.A., *Ce.* 269 note
Travers, Elias, *Fr. Al.* 258
'Troilus and Cressida', Address prefixt to, *Ce.* 87
*Truepenny, old, *Fr. Al* 280
Trussell, John, *Fr. Al.* 125
Tubbe, Henry, *Fr. Al.* 161
'Two Noble Kinsmen',[1] *Fr. Al.* 210, 239, 314

*VAUGHAN, Henry, *Ce.* 424
Vaughan, *Fr. Al.* 224
Vendenheym, H. J. Wurmsser von, *Ce.* 93
Verstegan, R., *Ce.* 247 note
Villiers, George, 2d Duke of Buckingham, *Ce.* 346
'Vindex Anglicus', *Ce.* 256

WALKLEY, Thomas, *Fr. Al.* 87
Walsh, William, *Ce.* 412
'Wandering Jew', *Fr. Al.* 112
Ward, John, *Ce.* 327
Ward Richard, *Ce.* 429
*Warner, Wm., *Fr. Al.* 43
Warren, John, *Ce.* 235

[1] I now hold that none of this play is Shakspere's, not even the Miltonic prayer to Mars.

Watson, *Fr. Al.* 230
Webster, John -
 Appius and Virginia, *Fr. Al.* 29
 'Duchess of Malfi', *Fr. Al.* 27, 28
 *Induction to 'Malcontent', *Ce.* 66
 'Northward Hoe', *Fr. Al.* 12, 28
 'Sir Thomas Wyatt', *Fr. Al.* 25, 53
 'White Divel', *Ce.* 100; *Fr. Al.* 26
Weever, John—
 'Epigrammes', *Ce.* 16
 'Mirror of Martyrs', *Ce.* 42, 165
Weever's 'Ancient Funerall Monuments', *Fr. Al.* 105
West, Richard, *Ce.* 214
Whipping of the Satyre, *Ce.* 47
Whitlock, R., *Fr. Al.* 105
Wild, Robert, *Ce.* 340; *Fr. Al.* 158
Willobie, Henry, *Ce.* 7; verses prefixt to his 'Avisa', *Ce.* 6
Wilmot, John, E. of Rochester, *Ce.* 364, 378
'Wily Beguilde', *Ce.* 19
Winstanley, William, *Ce.* 400
Withers, George, *Ce.* 258
'Wits Labyrinth', *Fr. Al.* 160
'Wits Recreations', *Ce.* 228
'Wits, or Sport upon Sport', *Fr. Al.* 317
*Women Players, *Ce.* 195 note
Woodhouse, Peter, *Fr. Al.* 39
*" Works " and Plays, *Ce.* 233
Wright, Abraham, *Ce.* 219
Wright, James, *Ce.* 132
*' Wrong, king can do no," *Ce.* 174, 175
Wurmsser, Hans Jacob, *Ce.* 93
Wycherley, W., *Fr. Al.* 246

*' YORKSHIRE Tragedy', *Fr. Al.* 330

II. SHAKSPERE'S WORKS REFERD TO
IN THE EXTRACTS IN 'CENTURIE' AND 'FRESH ALLUSIONS.'[1]

(The line | between the figures denotes that the references on the *left* of it are between the dates 1591—1642. Those on the *right* are between 1642—1693.)

ALL'S Well, *Fr. Al.* 319
Antony and Cleopatra, *Ce.* 115, 188, | 333; *Fr. Al.* 104, | 259, 320
As you like it, *Fr. Al.* 48, 320
Comedy of Errors, *Ce.* 21, 45, 50, 74, 115, | 300 note; *Fr. Al.* 1, 12, 19, 35, 147, | 154, 165, 294, 320
Coriolanus, *Ce.* 439; *Fr. Al.* 23, 61, 150, | 316, 320
Cymbeline, *Ce.* 97, 118, 157; *Fr. Al.* 27, 28, | 233, 273 (Durfey), 313-314, 320
Falstaff, *Ce.* 2, 24, 40, 103, 114, 223, 233, | 254, 272, 280, 296, 299, 304, 309, 319, 329, 330, 333, 347, 378, 387, 388, 403, 412; *Fr. Al.* 9, 15, 69, 75, 76, 79, 104*, 112, 122, 125, 150, | 158, 159, 163, 181, 185, 201, 205, 206, 209, 219, 223, 226, 246, 252, 256, 261, 271, 279, 281, 291-2, 303, 321, 333, 357
    fat, *Ce.* 31, 47, 126, | 325, 398; *Fr. Al.* 15, 69, 79, 142, &c., &c.
    Oldcastle, *Ce.* 65, 127, 164, | 249, 266—269, 294; *Fr. Al.* 30, 75, 142, 325
Hamlet, *Ce.* 64, 66, 67, 70, 72, 73, 79, 117, 131, 135, 159, 160, 171, 185, 187, | 251, 316, 317, 322, 354, 373, 439; *Fr. Al.* 11, 12, 26, 27,
29, 31, 32, 33, 35, 36, 39, 41, 52, 53, 55, 61, 71, 80, 85, 98*, 99, 102, 105, 112, 113, 116, 120, 130 135, 151, | 161, 164, 201, 280, 297, 322, 332, 336, 337, 351, 357
Henry IV., Part I, *Ce.* 21, 24, 31, 117, 157, 201, 209, | 254, 316, 320, 322, 354, 387; *Fr. Al.* 25, 28, 36, 46*, 50, 53, 62, 126, | 160, 205, 281, 321, 349
Henry IV., Part II, *Ce.* 31, 38, 50, 61, 90, 223, | 387; *Fr. Al.* 15, 42, 74, 114, 144*, | 156, 160, 206
Henry V., *Ce.* 118, | 300, 319, 333, 439; *Fr. Al.* 19, 21, 36, 62, 73, 74, 118, 281, 318, 321
Henry VI., *Ce.* 2, 33, 118, 436; *Fr. Al.* 168, 262
2 Henry VI., *Fr. Al.* 23, 39, | 160, 266, 306, 321
3 Henry VI., *Fr. Al.* 36, 40, 53, | 160, 321
Henry VIII.,[2] *Ce.* 102, 169, | 318, 322, 346, 396-7; *Fr. Al.* 101, | 202, 203, 232, 287, 322, 352
Julius Cæsar, *Ce.* 42, 41, 53, 103, 157, 163, 174, 209, 232, | 333, 366, 367, 370, 374; *Fr. Al.* 23, | 201, 264, 297, 231*, 322, 334, 337, 350

[1] For the purpose of this Index, the character of Falstaff and his sayings are taken as a "work."   [2] A play so calld, not Shakspere's, *Fr. Al.* 101.

II. SHAKSPERE'S WORKS REFERRED TO IN *C.* AND *Fr. Al.*

King John, *Ce.* 21, 51, | 439 ; *Fr. Al.* 27, 62, 78, | 322

Lear, 131, | 380, 390, 391 ; *Fr. Al.* 111, 154, | 198, 258, 316, 323, 337, 338, 353, 354, 357

Love's Labours Lost, *Ce.* 14, 21, 25, 62, 71, 432, | 351, 438, 439 ; *Fr. Al.* 4, 29, 31, 35, 47, 135, | 172-3, 258, 323

Love labours wonne, *Ce.* 21, 23 note

Macbeth, *Ce.* 51, 78, 97, | 318, 319, 320, 321, 322, 351, 355, 439 ; *Fr. Al.* 43, 59, 79, 134, | 240, 244, 252, 254, 271, 297, 324, 336, 338, 354, 357

Measure for Measure, *Ce.* | 351, 408 ; *Fr. Al.* | 208, 307, 323

Merchant of Venice, *Ce.* 19, 21, 101, | 439 ; *Fr. Al.* 26, 47, 71, 108, | 197, 236, 272, 324, 356

Merry Wives of Windsor, *Ce.* | 316, 317, 320, 333, 371, 406, 415, 419 ; *Fr. Al.* 28, 47, 149, | 217, 291-2, 324, 350

Midsummer Night's Dream, *Ce.* 21, 71, 160, 179, 182, 232, | 317, 354, 439 ; *Fr. Al.* 10, 26, 49, 51, 86, 88*, 116, 124, | 163, 188, 199, 237, 283, 316, 325, 347, 355

Much Ado about Nothing, *Ce.* 103, 161, 233, | 408 ; *Fr. Al.* 48, 59, | 208, 256, 258, 307, 312, 323, 325

Othello, *Ce.* 93, 103, 131, 173, 219, 232, | 316, 319, 322, 330, 366, 374, 412, 415, 418, 439 ; *Fr. Al.* 28, 29, 98, 111, 116-18, 121, | 170, 224, 285, 288, 325, 337, 338, 349, 350, 355, 357

Passionate Pilgrim, *Ce.* 71, 99, 197 ; *Fr. Al.* 118

Pericles, *Ce.* 82, 89, 107, 113, 172, 173, 180, | 261, 295, 350, 398 ; *Fr. Al.* 83, (? 105), 120, 144, | 169, 326, 336, 350, 351, 357

Rape of Lucrece, *Ce.* 12, 13, 15, 16, 21, 26, 30, 32, 33, 44, 48, 57, 71, 106, 205, 430, | 261, 279, 344, 401 ; *Fr. Al.* 2, 31, 118, 139, | 174, 331

Richard II., *Ce.* 21, 35, 56, 79, 97, 173, 430, | 374, 380 ; *Fr. Al.* 2, 11, 12, | 160, 267, 326, 338

Richard III., *Ce.* 21, 29, 44, 45, 48, 57, 77, 109, 112, 157, 188, 430, | 274, 380, 411 note, 439 ; *Fr. Al.* 2, 14, 26, 45, 54, 62, 112, 128, | 160, 186, 316, 327, 357

Romeo and Juliet, *Ce.* 16, 19, 21, 27, 51, 52, 71, 95, 135, 154, 166, 167, 188, | 255, 317, 374, 430, 439, *Fr. Al.* 9, 14, 20, 22, 32, 33, 50, 59, 71, 106, 112, 131, | 172-3, 183, 184, 216, 224, 315, 327, 351

Sonnets, *Ce.* 21, 86, 116 ; *Fr. Al.* 70, 82, 114, 115

Taming of the Shrew, *Ce.* 85, 157, | 300 note, 307, 320 ; *Fr. Al.* 159, | 327, 356

Tempest, *Ce.* 103, 105, 118, | 321, 322, 346, 366, 372, 439 ; *Fr. Al.* 37, 119, 120, 132, 135, 151, | 222, 226, 249, 252, 267, 271, 278, 305, *311, 313, 314, 327, 354, 355

Timon of Athens, *Ce.* | 365 ; *Fr. Al.* 315, 329, 357

Titus Andronicus, *Ce.* 21, 60, 105, | 404 ; *Fr. Al.* 11, | 160, 315, 328, 338, 350

Troilus and Cressida, *Ce.* 57, | 369, 439 ; *Fr. Al.* 40*, | 291, 311, 313, 329, 355

Twelfth Night, *Ce.* 45, 233, | 316, 317, 322, 438 ; *Fr. Al.* 329, 352

Two Gentlemen of Verona, *Ce.* 21, 112, | 353 ; *Fr. Al.* 72, | 330

[Two Noble Kinsmen, *Fr. Al.* 210, 239, 314]

Venus and Adonis, *Ce.* 14, 16, 17, 21, 26, 30, 32, 33, 48, 71, 75, 80, 81, 87, 96, 106, 112, 140, 161, 186, 204, 224, 230, 238, 430, | 279, 341, 401 ; *Fr. Al.* 8, 10, 47, 56, 80, 85, 104, 127, | 167, 251, 253, 331

Winter's Tale, *Ce.* 97, 103, 118, 129, 157, 178, 214, | 331, 351, 408 ; *Fr. Al.* (? 102), 112, | 196, 330

II. ORDER OF POPULARITY OF SHAKSPERE'S WORKS.

THE following is the order of the most frequent mention of Shakspere's works (including the character of Falstaff as one) before, and after, the Civil War-time, in one or other of the four manners described in groups 2, 3, 4, 5 (see *Centurie*, p. xvii). The guage of popularity afforded by this summary is only approximate, because it cannot take into account the proportions of extracts in the anthologies (Appendix B), and repetitions in notices like those of Pepys, Cavendish, or Dryden.—L. T. Smith. (I made the list originally in totals, and Miss Smith split the totals into two.—F.)

	Before 1642.	After 1642.	
	Ce. F. Al.	Ce. F. Al.	Total.
Falstaff	13 + 7 = 20	22 + 22 = 44	64
Hamlet	15 + 30 = 45	7 + 11 = 18	63
Venus and Adonis	25 + 8 = 33	3 + 4 = 7	40
Romeo and Juliet	13 + 10 = 23	5 + 7 = 12	35
Othello	6 + 11 = 17	10 + 8 = 18	35
Tempest	3 + 5 = 8	6 + 15 = 21	29
Macbeth	3 + 6 = 9	8 + 11 = 19	28
Rape of Lucrece	16 + 4 = 20	4 + 2 = 6	26
Richard III	12 + 6 = 18	4 + 4 = 8	26
Henry IV—Part I	7 + 7 = 14	6 + 3 = 9	23
Julius Cæsar	9 + 1 = 10	5 + 8 = 13	23
Midsummer Night's Dream	6 + 7 = 13	3 + 7 = 10	23
Pericles	7 + 3 = 10	4 + 4 = 8	18
Love's Labours Lost	6 + 5 = 11	3 + 3 = 6	17
Comedy of Errors	5 + 5 = 10	1 + 4 = 5	15
Henry V	1 + 6 = 7	4 + 4 = 8	15
Henry VI	4 + 5 = 9	6 = 6	15
Much Ado about Nothing	3 + 4 = 7	1 + 7 = 8	15
Richard II	7 + 3 = 10	2 + 3 = 5	15
Henry IV—Part II	6 + 4 = 10	1 + 3 = 4	14
Titus Andronicus	3 + 1 = 4	1 + 9 = 10	14
Lear	1 + 1 = 2	3 + 9 = 12	14
Merchant of Venice	3 + 4 = 7	1 + 5 = 6	13
Merry Wives of Windsor	3 = 3	8 + 2 = 10	13
Winter's Tale	7 + 1 = 8	3 + 1 = 4	12
Henry VIII	2 + 2 = 4	4 + 4 = 8	12
Cymbeline	3 + 2 = 5	3 = 3	8
Coriolanus	3 + 2 = 5	2 = 2	7
King John	2 + 3 = 5	1 + 1 = 2	7
Sonnets	3 + 4 = 7		7
Taming of the Shrew	2 = 2	3 + 2 = 5	7
Twelfth Night	2 = 2	4 + 1 = 5	7
Anthony and Cleopatra	2 + 1 = 3	1 + 2 = 3	6
Troilus and Cressida	1 + 1 = 2	2 + 2 = 4	6
Two Gentlemen of Verona	2 + 1 = 3	1 + 1 = 2	5
Passionate Pilgrim	3 + 1 = 4		4
Measure for Measure		2 + 1 = 3	3
Timon of Athens		1 + 2 = 3	3
Love's Labour Won	2		2
All's Well		1 = 1	1
As you like it		1 = 1	1

www.ingramcontent.com/pod-product-compliance
Lightning Source LLC
Chambersburg PA
CBHW022134300426
44115CB00006B/174